ALEXANDER OF TUNIS
as Military Commander

ALEXANDER OF TUNIS

as Military Commander

W. G. F. Jackson

DODD, MEAD & COMPANY *New York*

First published in the United States of America 1972
ISBN 0-396-06474-4
Library of Congress Catalog Card Number 78-173197
Printed in Great Britain

Contents

Illustrations

With the exception of fig. 31 all the above illustrations are reproduced by courtesy of the Imperial War Museum, figs 1 and 2 coming from Miss Bloom's collection

ACKNOWLEDGEMENT

The Author and Publishers wish to thank the following for permission to quote from the books cited: Sir Arthur Bryant, *Turn of the Tide* (Wm. Collins Sons & Co. Ltd); Sir Winston S. Churchill, *The Second World War* (Cassell & Co. Ltd); Sir James Grigg, *Prejudice and Judgment* (Jonathan Cape Ltd), by courtesy of the Executors of the Estate of Sir P. J. Grigg; Rudyard Kipling, *Irish Guards in the Great War* (Macmillan & Co. Ltd), by permission of Mrs. George Bambridge; Harold Macmillan, *Blast of War* (Macmillan & Co. Ltd); Field Marshal the Viscount Montgomery of Alamein, *Memoirs* (Wm. Collins Sons & Co. Ltd); John North (ed.), *Memoirs of Field Marshal Earl Alexander of Tunis* (Cassell & Co. Ltd); Sir Stephen Talents, *Man and Boy* (Faber & Faber Ltd). Acknowledgement is also due to Her Majesty's Stationery Office for permission to quote from volumes of the Official *History of the Second World War* and from the *London Gazette*. Page references to these and to other works, from which short quotations have been made, are given in the text of this book.

PREFACE

The Trusted Commander

> At the same time, in Italy, Field Marshal Alexander's army of so many nations, the largest part of which was British or British Empire, struck their final blow and compelled more than a million enemy troops to surrender.
>
> Churchill's Victory Broadcast, 13 May 1945

Thus, Churchill summed up Alexander's final triumph, setting the seal on over 30 years of military achievement, not only in the service of Great Britain and the British Commonwealth and Empire, but also of their closest ally, the United States of America. In the Second World War the Western Allies were lucky to have at the heads of their armies a military generation with considerable experience of active service in the grim battles of the 1914–18 War and during the many minor campaigns of the troubled interwar period. This had rarely happened before in British or American history. More often a major war broke out so long after its predecessor that a new generation of soldiers found itself at the helm without any depth of practical experience. But in 1939 and 1941 there were men in command of the British and American forces, when each country declared war, who knew from bitter experience what to expect, what was practical and what was not. They were men who were determined not to repeat the mistakes of Haig's and Pershing's generation. The relative lightness of the army casualty lists in the Second World War are a tribute to the sound professional judgment of this generation of commanders, which included Harold Alexander—Field Marshal the Earl Alexander of Tunis.

The British, and to a lesser extent American, commanders, who rose to high command in the Second World War, went through the harsh selection system of war during their early careers and had already proved themselves as military leaders at regimental level. Those who eventually reached the very highest commands in the second war against Germany needed two further attributes: the ability to win, first, the confidence of their own nation and its armies; and, secondly, the respect of the political leaders, commanders and fighting men of its ally. The Allied 'selection board', in whose hands the ultimate choice of commanders lay, consisted of four men:

Churchill, with General Sir Alan Brooke as his military adviser, championing the British contenders; and Roosevelt and General George Marshall, looking after the interests of the American generals. Their choice fell upon two men who were, in the end, to have supreme command of the two Western European fronts: Eisenhower in North-West Europe and Alexander in Italy. Much has been written about the former as he commanded the main Allied effort and went on to be President of the United States. Less has been published about Alexander, although the sum of his actual military achievements is probably greater than that of his able American contemporary. The time has come to rectify this omission, which has been caused largely by his own reticence and his wish to let his successes speak for him.

It is in the field of operational experience that the greatest difference used to lie between the British and American Commanders. In the first half of this century the United States 'stayed in the pavilion', as Field Marshal Montgomery used to say, 'until the fifth wicket down in both first league matches'. In the second half of the century the position is being reversed, with the Americans accumulating operational experience while the British watch from the side lines. In 1942 the advantage of wide operational experience still lay with the British. Eisenhower's background was essentially that of a military planner and thinker who had trained himself in debate and policy making at the highest level. He was a strategist and a superb chairman of a council of war rather than a field commander. Alexander's background was very different, based as it was on active service experience as a platoon, company, battalion and brigade commander on the Western Front from 1914 to 1918, and then as a divisional, corps and army commander in the disastrous retreats to Dunkirk in 1940 and from Rangoon in 1942. His success as Commander-in-Chief of the British Forces in the Middle East in the direction of the El Alamein campaign and the subsequent advance to Tripoli made him the obvious and eminently suitable choice as Eisenhower's deputy and army group commander for the Battle for Tunis and the first half of the Italian Campaign. The two men had one important attribute in common: the ability to inspire men of the diverse nations to work together as a team. When their paths separated at Christmas-time 1943, Eisenhower returning to the United Kingdom to command the invasion of Normandy and Alexander staying in Italy to create the diversion of German strength southwards to make the cross-Channel operation practicable, the national contingents in both theatres felt that they were led by men of proven military judgment whom they could trust.

How did Alexander who was a modest, unassuming man come to inspire such trust in his own countrymen and among the officers and men of so many different nationalities? It was a trust common to all levels of command and to the political as well as the military worlds. At the lowest level it was reflected in the confidence which he inspired as a regimental officer in the Irish Guards throughout the four long years of World War I on the Western Front. At the opposite extreme, it was demonstrated at the highest level by the faith placed in him by Churchill and Brooke who entrusted to him the command of their favourite military enterprises in the Mediterranean from El Alamein onwards. This trust extended beyond the narrow confines of insular British emotion to officers and men of the many and varied allied contingents—Americans, Canadians, Australians, New Zealanders, Indians, Poles, Frenchmen, Germans, Latvians, Estonians and even Chinese, to mention but a few who fought at one time or another under his command. It also reached upwards to Roosevelt and Marshall who accepted Alexander as the commander of one of the largest bodies of American troops ever to serve under a British general.

The root of trust is confidence in a man's integrity and judgment. In Alexander, the former was so obvious to everyone who met him at any stage of his career that there is little need to dwell upon it. Brought up in the traditions of one of Ireland's great families, selfless service was his natural bent and duty service his instinctive desire. Development of sound and, in Alexander's case, outstanding military judgment is another matter. It is true that the starting point of such judgment is natural ability on which all else must be built; but the building depends on the man and to a lesser degree upon events which confront him during his early years in his chosen career. In few careers is first-hand practical experience more important to the development of sound judgment and yet more difficult to obtain than in the military profession. It is, after all, the task of the fighting services to deter war and hence to prevent themselves obtaining practical experience. How a soldier makes use of the active service that does come his way makes all the difference between his success or failure as a commander when he reaches the climax of his career. In other words, the creation of sound military judgment is the work of a lifetime, and depends upon an officer's own efforts.

Alexander not only made the best of his active service experience, he saw more fighting and survived more shot and shell than most of his contemporaries in either the British or American Armies. He knew how much men could endure, and conversely what was a reasonable military task. He had personally felt and seen the effects of fear—the crucial factor in all fighting. Hard-won experience in defeat taught him the unpredictability of events in battle and made him appreciate the need to close as many loopholes as possible to the random intervention of chance. This led him to prize forethought and carefully balanced dispositions from which it is possible to exploit success and stem misfortune. Through his apprenticeship in the Irish Guards at Mons, on the Marne, at Ypres, on the Somme, at Passchendaele, at Cambrai, and in the German offensive of March 1918, he learned how to organise, lead and inspire men through the harsh realities of war. Later, as a divisional commander in charge of the rearguard at Dunkirk in 1940 and as an army commander sent to retrieve years of British military neglect in Burma in 1942, he evolved his own unwritten principles of war which he used with success in the Mediterranean from El Alamein in 1942 to the German collapse in Italy in 1945. Thus, this book, which sets out to assess his military career, falls naturally into three parts:

PART I—Creation of a Leader: 1910 to 1939
PART II—Trial by Defeat: 1939 to 1942
PART III—Triumph of Experience: 1942 to 1945

It is a personal assessment of him as a commander by an officer of a later generation who did not join the British Army until Alexander was already the GOC of the 1st Division. It reflects also the story of the British Army in the first half of the twentieth century.

PART I

Creation of a Leader

It is undeniable the Colonel Alexander had the gift of handling the men on the lines, to which they most readily responded . . . his subordinates loved him, even when he fell upon them blisteringly for their shortcomings; and his men were all his own.

Rudyard Kipling, *The Irish Guards in the Great War*, 1923

I

Test of Fear

> The objects in view in developing a soldierly spirit are to help the soldier to bear fatigue, privation and danger cheerfully; to give him confidence in his superiors and comrades; to increase his powers of initiative and of self-restraint; to train him to obey orders, or to act in absences of orders for the advantage of his regiment under all conditions; *to produce such a high degree of courage and disregard of self*, that he will use his weapons in the stress of battle coolly and to the best advantage; and finally to teach him how to act in combination with his comrades in order to attain the desired end.
>
> The object of training as laid down by
> *Infantry Training 1911*

War can be defined as the conquest and application of fear. A soldier's impressions of his first action and first campaign are the most vivid and lasting. They stay with him all his life and ultimately make or mar him as a commander. If he has not experienced and resisted fear—the one essential element of war which cannot be simulated in training and which makes the difference between theory and practice in a military career—he is unlikely to be successful in high tactical command; conversely, if we are to understand the basis of a successful commander's career, we must look carefully at the impressions made upon him by his earliest military actions. The causes of success in these engagements tend to become his basic principles later; while those which led to failure are seen as mistakes to be avoided at all costs when he himself reaches high command. It is not only personal successes and failures in action which make a lasting impression. It is also the events of the epoch in which the future commander gains his early military experience that mould his judgment decisively. It is the failure of well-learned pre-war tactical dogma, of hallowed ideas of the senior officers of the day, and of mistaken national attitudes to stand up to the first shock of war, which make the deepest scars of all upon his mind and influence his thinking for the rest of his career.

The British Army, which 2nd Lieutenant Alexander joined from Sandhurst in 1911, was perhaps the most professional and highly trained army that the United Kingdom has ever owned in peace. It had three great assets, which were offset by an equal number of deficiencies that did not become obvious until revealed by the clash of war. The first was the Army's confidence in its own abilities, born of a hundred years' successful campaigning in every quarter of the globe. It had suffered set-backs like the early disasters in the Crimea and the Indian Mutiny, but, in the end, it had always triumphed. And backing this confidence was the equally strong self-assurance of the British nation at the height of its Imperial Era. The cynicism caused by the unrewarding sacrifices of two World Wars had not yet dampened national enthusiasm.

The British Army's second asset was the recent operational experience of most of its officers and senior NCOs who had seen service in South Africa, the Sudan or India. They knew how to look after themselves and live under active service conditions; they knew how to march long distances; they knew what it was like to be under fire; and, above all, they knew and acknowledged the value of strict discipline. They had reduced the complexities of soldiering around the world to a sound regimental folk-lore which it was not difficult for new officers and recruits to assimulate during the day-to-day activities of their regiment. It was not until 1905 that the first attempt was made to codify these principles in the first issue of *Infantry Training*. When Alexander joined the Irish Guards a much-improved version, *Infantry Training 1911*, had just appeared, but the unwritten code was still stronger than the new-fangled idea of tactical regulations which had a Germanic ring about them and seemed unbecoming to the amateur façade of the professional British Army.

The third asset was one which is essential to the success of any army in peace but is so rarely accorded to the British Army. The clear and undisguised German challenge to the United Kingdom's interests in Europe, at sea and in the colonial world was so obvious that the country was, for once, prepared to pay its defence insurance premiums. Alexander's arrival in his regiment coincided with a period of military expansion. Soldiering under such conditions is more rewarding than usual because the soldier knows that he is wanted by his countrymen and is playing an essential part in their affairs.

The hidden weaknesses of this long-service professional army, in which, unlike its European counterparts, all men were volunteers, tended to turn these assets into liabilities. Both its confidence and its experience were based on small wars outside Europe, or in what *Infantry Training 1905* aptly called 'savage warfare'. The Boer War had, it is true, increased the scale of British operations, giving senior officers more experience in handling larger formations. The forces they handled were still small compared with those deployed in the American Civil War or during von Moltke's triumphs of military planning and organisation in the Austro-Prussian and Franco-Prussian Wars. Serious British officers studied these campaigns in great detail and made a practice of visiting German and French manoeuvres each summer, being well aware of their lack of experience in continental warfare. Unfortunately they watched through the eyes of their own experience which, though more recent, was less relevant than that of their European colleagues. The Boers had taught them many sharp lessons, which they felt European Armies did not appreciate, and so they belittled German and French ideas, picking out those which accorded with British experience while discarding those which looked peculiarly European. Tragically this myopia prevented the War Office from making full use of the temporary open-handedness of the Treasury because senior British officers could not visualise the type nor the quantity of equipment which would be needed for a war between European powers. Thus it came about that the British Army, which Alexander joined in 1911, though highly professional as an Imperial Defence Force, was unsuited for its next and his first campaign.

Alexander left Harrow for Sandhurst in 1910. He had always wanted to be a soldier, and, being the third son of the fourth Lord Caledon in Northern Ireland, his early ambition was to join the Irish Guards. The regiment was then the most recently formed of the Household Brigade. It had been raised by Queen Victoria in 1900 ostensibly in recognition of the gallantry of her 'brave Irish soldiers' who had fallen fighting the Boers, but more prosaically as part of the expansion of the Army caused by the South African commitment and the growing threat of German aggression. At Harrow and Sandhurst Alexander proved himself an all-round athlete, an outstanding miler and a good cricketer. Academically his performance was creditable but no more. His only distinguishing mark in these early days was his clear determination to be a soldier and a complete master of his chosen profession. Unlike the majority of boys at that age, who find it difficult to make up their minds what they would like to do, Alexander had no doubts that he wanted to join the Irish Guards.

The period of Alexander's early peace-time apprenticeship in his chosen regiment was one of military enthusiasm and traumatic change. The pre-First World War British Army had not set foot in Western Europe for almost 100 years. A change of Government in 1906 brought a team of men into the War Office who were capable, as far as their imaginations would allow, of reorientating the Army's organisation, equipment and training towards European conditions. Haldane became Secretary of State for War with a brief to prepare the British Army to support the French in the coming struggle with Germany. His task was threefold: to raise and equip a British Expeditionary Force organised and trained for European warfare; to back this regular force with a territorial volunteer organisation to provide a basis for expansion if the war went on longer than the economists of the day and the British public at large judged practicable; and to provide a command and control structure capable of handling forces of the size envisaged. As regards the last of these tasks, the Esher Committee, which sat to consider what changes should be made in Britain's military structure as a result of the lessons learned in the Boer War, had already recommended the formation of a British General Staff—40 years after the creation of von Moltke's highly successful Great German General Staff in the 1860s.

The creation of what became the Imperial General Staff and the formation of a British Expeditionary Force at Aldershot, led, for the first time in British military history, to the formulation and promulgation of a British tactical doctrine. It is interesting now, some 60 years later, to read the first training manuals issued to Alexander when he joined his regiment. Most of the principles laid down in these small volumes—designed to fit easily into uniform pockets with specially rounded corners to prevent their catching as they were taken in and out—make sound sense even today, but it is easier to see in retrospect where the misappreciations lay which led to the disasters which overtook Alexander's generation in 1914. The best sections are those dealing with mobile, open warfare to which the authors were accustomed. The bulk of the regulations, which cover orthodox continental warfare, are culled secondhand from German and French sources and reveal the attempt to force European reasoning into the mould of British Imperial experience.

The new tactical doctrine taught at Sandhurst and in regiments of the BEF had an obvious French bias. Offensive action was considered the first and almost only ingredient of military success in a European setting. Defensive action was to be sustained only as a preliminary step to decisive offensive operations. *Field Service Regulations* laid down: 'Decisive success in battle can be gained only by a vigorous offensive' (Pt. 1, p. 107); '. . . a defensive attitude must be assumed only in order to await or create a favourable opportunity for decisive offensive action' (Pt. 1, p. 108).

But here the similarity with the French doctrine of 'L'attaque, toujours l'attaque' ended and the British lessons of the Boer War took over. In the British view, more realistic than the French, the key to success in both offensive and defensive fighting lay in winning the 'fire fight'. There were to be no massed infantry assaults in close column of companies as seen at Gettysburg, Sadowa or Sedan and later used by the Germans and French in 1914. The crucial paragraphs of *Infantry Training 1911* read:

> Normally, the action of infantry in attack may be considered to be, firstly, an advance to fire positions, which should be as close to the enemy as possible; secondly, a fire fight, with the object of gaining superiority of fire, during which, as the enemy's fire is gradually mastered, further progress is made up to a position from which it is possible to assault; thirdly, the assault, which is delivered when superiority of fire is gained. (p. 120)

Regulations for defence laid down the necessity of winning the fire fight in reverse. The Boers had taught the British Army the vital necessity of marksmanship, concealment and rudimentary protection. These lessons led to an emphasis on fire direction and fire control, an acknowledgment of the importance of concealment and of its tendency to conflict with the need for good fields of fire. There is relatively little about entrenchment except passing reference to the *Manual of Field Engineering*. British soldiers never enjoy digging and will only do so when necessity compels, but they have always taken pride in skill at arms. In the light of what was to happen in 1914 it is interesting to read the regulations given to Alexander for infantry subalterns in defence (p. 143):

> . . . section commanders are to see:
> (i) That every man can use his rifle effectively.
> (ii) That the cover is good.
> (iii) That the entrenchments constructed are concealed from the enemy.
> (iv) That ample ammunition and water is available.

The emphasis on ammunition supply, correct though it was, led to the first tactical misappreciation from which Alexander and his contemporaries were to suffer in their early actions. The British Army depended more upon its rifles, marksmanship and high rate of aimed fire than upon its artillery and machine guns.

Instead of appreciating that machine guns and artillery were likely to be the decisive weapons in European warfare, and, therefore, that their problems of ammunition supply must be solved as a matter of priority, the pre-1914 directors at the War Office limited the numbers of these vital weapons on unit establishments to match what they considered to be the practicable rate of ammunition supply. In this they underestimated European production and movement capabilities. In fairness to them, a great deal of thought was given to handling machine guns: *Infantry*

Training 1911 contains as many pages on their use as it allots to the principles of defence. Regrettably, artillery was given scant attention. There are only three short paragraphs on artillery cooperation in attack, and none to friendly artillery in the sections on defence. But there is a very revealing paragraph in the section on Fire Power advising infantry how to deal with artillery:

> Artillery coming into action, limbering up, or in movement is a very vulnerable target, against which rapid fire or even fire at long infantry ranges is justifiable. Infantry will experience difficulty in putting shielded artillery out of action by direct fire even at close ranges . . .

This picture of artillery and infantry engaging each other at close quarters was not to survive more than the first few weeks of the war.

The second misappreciation was the gross underestimate of the scale of European warfare. The regulations are couched in terms which assume fighting under at least numerical equality, if not superiority. Little thought is given to the possibility of fighting a numerically superior enemy. It was to take two long years of unrequited effort before the Irish Guards were to feel that they were being given adequate support. By then the old Regular Army, which Alexander joined in 1911, had perished at Ypres. The survivors, like Alexander himself, were commanding units of Kitchener's New Armies.

And herein lay the third and most serious misconception of all in the training of long-service British regular armies, which is as true today as it was in 1911. The standard of training laid down was only attainable by men who knew each other intimately; who lived together in the same company of the same regiment for a number of years; and who practised together for several training seasons. Basic training became so ingrained that it was possible to demand the flexibility of approach set out in this extract from *Infantry Training 1905* (p. 123):

> It is, therefore, strictly forbidden either to formulate or to practise a normal form of either attack or defence. To the training of troops in movements before the enemy, general principles and broad rules alone are applicable; and the practical knowledge of these principles and rules can only be instilled by intelligent instruction and constantly diversified exercises on broken ground.

As soon as the men of the Regular Army had given their lives in the disasters of 1914 and 1915, the professional system, which they had built up, died with them. Some simpler method of fighting, which could be learned in months or weeks rather than years, had to be devised for the rest of the nation as they donned uniform to take their place in the line. Alexander learned this lesson the hard way and became the leading exponent of the 'Battle School' techniques in both World Wars.

On 12 August 1914 Lieutenant Alexander embarked with No. 1 Company, 1st Battalion, Irish Guards, in the P & O SS *Novara* at Southampton as part of Sir John French's British Expeditionary Force, sailing to support the French after the declaration of war with Germany on 4 August. The battalion had mobilized at Wellington Barracks in London. Its regular reservists—men who had left the regiment within the last six years—had returned to the colours, bringing the battalion up to full war strength of 1,000 all ranks, compared with the 600 of today's battalions; mobilization equipment, war stores and ammunition had been issued; training stores, ceremonial clothing and other peace-time paraphernalia like officers' mess silver had been stored; the simple active service pay and accounting system had been inaugurated; and as these preparations had neared completion Field Marshal Earl Roberts and Lady Roberts arrived to bid the battalion farewell. It was a stirring moment for Alexander and the other young officers of the regiment as they marched through the streets of London to Nine Elms Station—the battalion marching out to war.

On mobilization, the Irish Guards became part of 4th (Guards) Brigade in the 2nd Division of Sir Douglas Haig's I Corps. The BEF consisted initially of Haig's Corps with 1st and 2nd Divisions; Sir James Grierson's and later Sir Horace Smith-Dorrien's II Corps, the change occurring on the sudden death of the former; and, as Army troops, Allenby's 1st Cavalry Division. The cross-Channel movement plan, which had been developed over several years in the greatest detail, worked with military precision. All the men were shipped through Southampton to Boulogne, Le Havre and Rouen. Guns, horses, wagons and heavy equipment went via Newhaven, Avonmouth and Liverpool. Men and materials met up again around Amiens, the first concentration area for the BEF before it commenced its march north-eastwards to join the extreme left flank of the French Army around Mons.

There are many historical parallels between the starting months of the two World Wars and just as many contradictions. In Alexander's case the parallels were predominant. As he looked over the rail of SS *Novara* while she embarked the Irish Guards, he could see other ships taking men of the 1st Division on board. Little did he realise that 25 years later the 1st Division would be embarking for France once more, this time under command of Major-General Alexander. Still less did he expect to fight as part of the rearguard in the Retreat from Mons in 1914 and then command the rearguard at Dunkirk in 1940. Apart from the level of his rank, there were two significant differences between the two periods. In 1914 no one could guess what lay ahead of the BEF. The British Army were strangers to Western Europe. In 1939 there were many officers and men still serving who knew what European warfare meant and who had no illusions about how long the Second World War would last.

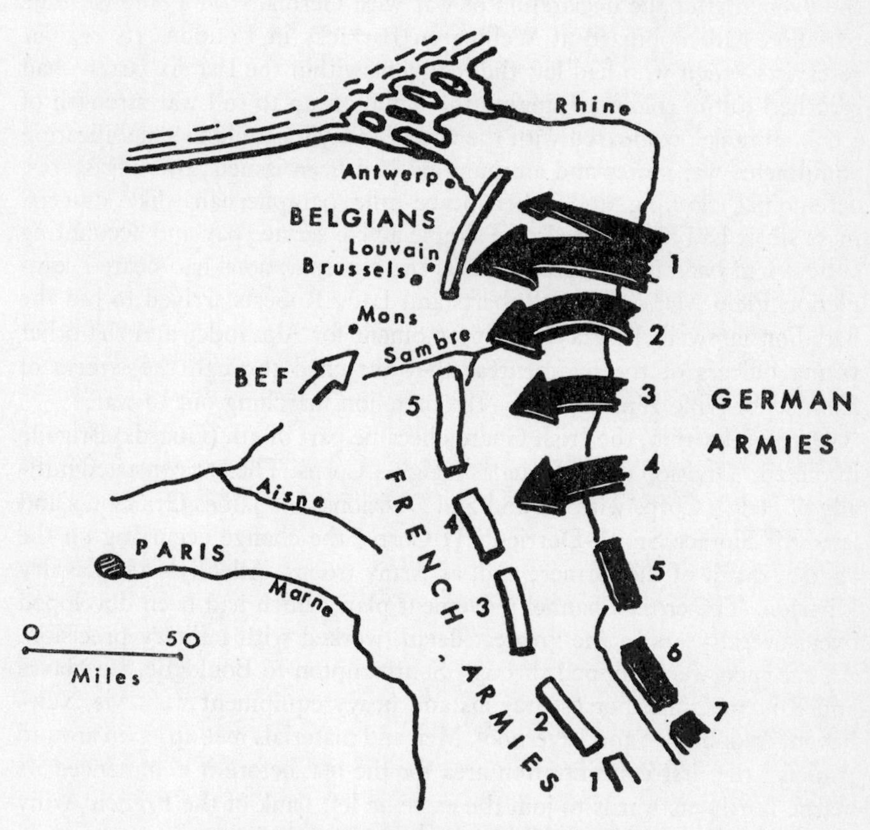

1 Situation in France before the Battle of Mons

The second difference lay in the absence of air power in 1914. All air forces were in their infancy. In 1914, their Lordships at the Admiralty deemed it safe, and were proved right, to ship the BEF direct to the French Channel ports. In 1939, the threat of German air attack made them insist on landing Lord Gort's BEF at the Atlantic ports for a first concentration at Le Mans instead of Amiens, although the second BEF came into the

Anglo-French line in much the same sector of the front as its predecessor. After the initial Allied débâcles, the first BEF extricated itself and reached the Marne intact; whereas the second BEF, faced with the greater speed, mobility and striking power of German armoured divisions and tactical air forces, was driven into the 'little ships' at Dunkirk. In both cases the British troops were inadequately trained and equipped for the type of war they were going to fight.

The errors, misappreciations and misconceptions of 1914 impressed themselves on those junior officers in Sir John French's BEF who were determined to take their profession seriously and who were to command Britain's forces in the Second World War. Most of the officers of the Irish Guards, Alexander among them, were worried that the war would be over before their battalion could reach the front. To them, the eight days which elapsed between the declaration of war and their embarkation seemed an age in itself; and, in spite of being one of the first units to embark, they felt that their chances of seeing active service were remote. The decisive clash between the French and German war machines would be over before the BEF could intervene, and the fate of Europe would be decided while it was still crossing the Channel. By the time the BEF arrived in the line the French would either be marching victoriously towards Berlin, reaping revenge for their humiliation in 1870; or the BEF's advance parties would be re-embarking for return to England in haste, a second Sedan having been fought and won by Germany.

Looking back on this period, one sees vividly Britain's capacity for self-deception. As an island power with strictly limited indigenous resources, but with potentially infinite commitments caused by worldwide trade, British policy-makers tend to fit resources to commitments rather than pursuing the more rational but more soul-searching approach of cutting commitments to match resources. If an Alliance requests Britain to plan the defence of some particular sector of a defensive front and she has at the most, say, four divisions available, the Whitehall machine—both the civil and military elements—will subconsciously create arguments to show that four divisions would be just about right for the task even though it is obvious from past experience that the resulting divisional frontages would be far too wide for successful defence and, in consequence, there would be inadequate reserves in support. Furthermore, if financial and economic considerations allow for, say, six months' stocks of ammunition and war reserves, then it is argued that six months is a balanced view of the likely duration of the conflict which the particular Alliance is designed to deter. This type of reasoning has been repeated so often that it emerges as one of

Britain's chronic psychological diseases. In 1914 she did not possess the troops or reserves to sustain a long war, and so the suggestion was that an anti-German war, if it ever came about, would be over by Christmas. The most strongly held view was that for economic reasons alone Europe could not sustain a long war.

None of these thoughts worried Alexander's generation at the time. All misgivings were set aside by the exhilaration of watching the troopships loading and seeing the grey hulls of the Royal Navy's escorts assembling in Southampton Water. As SS *Novara* set sail, HMS *Formidable*, lying off the Isle of Wight, made a signal wishing the Irish Guards 'plenty of fighting'. The might of Great Britain, which had ruled the world outside Europe for a century, was being displayed. There could be little doubt about the issue now that she had thrown in her lot with France—if only they could get there in time.

The Irish Guards reached Le Havre early in 13 August and, after an enthusiastic welcome, moved by rail to Wassigny some 40 miles south of Mons, arriving on the evening of 15 August. From there they marched to the brigade concentration area at Vadencourt where they went into French billets for the first time. For three days they stayed in Vadencourt while the rest of the brigade, its artillery, wagons and heavier equipment arrived from the different ports. Whatever the British staff lacked in operational imagination, they made up for with exact and practical administrative planning which was to prove invaluable to the BEF in the black days to come. The precision of the staff work gave everyone great confidence, although as Kipling points out in *The Irish Guards in the Great War* 'the battalion was not up to much' at Vadencourt because the doctors had taken the opportunity of the three days pause to inoculate the battalion against typhoid.

On 20 August the BEF started to advance towards Mons to come up on the seaward flank of General Lanrezac's Fifth French Army, which was already in action against the Germans on the Sambre, and to fill the gap between the French and the Belgian Armies, the latter fighting stubbornly to hold Brussels and Antwerp. Marching with his battalion, Alexander was naturally unaware of the tragedy developing in the higher levels of the Allied command, and which would repeat itself 25 years later when he would be entering much the same sector at the head of the 1st Division. Pre-judgment of the situation and subsequent self-deception were the undoing of the Allied General Staffs on both occasions.

Joffre, the French C-inC, was convinced that Lanrezac, supported by Sir John French, could outflank and destroy the German right wing—von

Kluck's First German Army—as it advanced southwards from Belgium. The truth about von Kluck's real strength lay hidden from GQG, the French Supreme Headquarters. Joffre believed that the failure of his offensive into Alsace against the German left wing, and the strength of the German forces attacking Brussels and Antwerp must imply a weakness in the German centre. Hence, he reasoned, the correct strategy should be to attack the weakened German centre with his 3rd and 4th Armies, while the 5th and the BEF assailed the German right flank. All intelligence, however much it pointed to other conclusions, was forced by the French staff to fit this thesis. The British staff were just as guilty of self-deception.

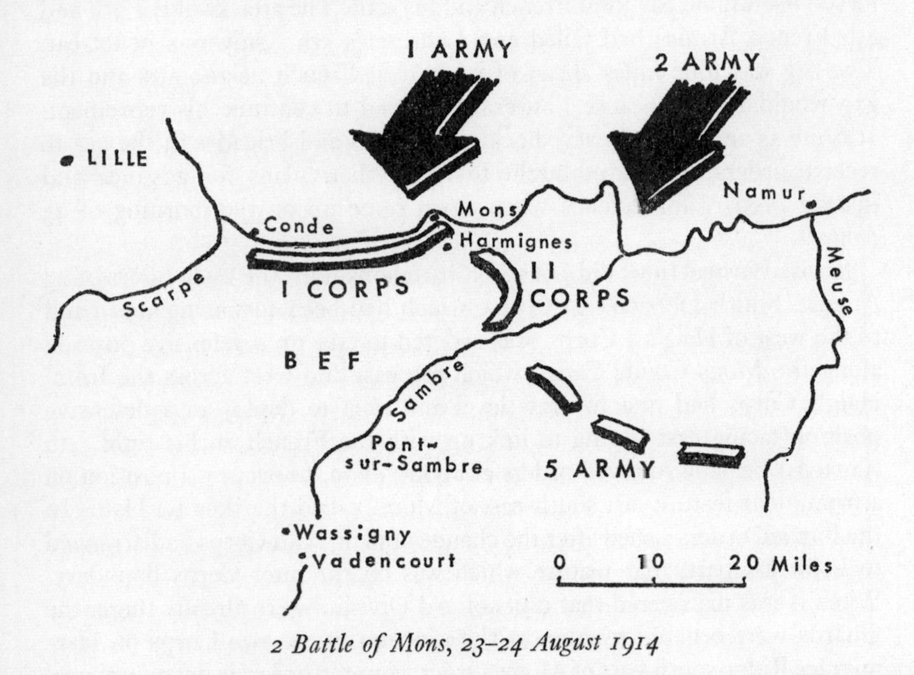

2 Battle of Mons, 23–24 August 1914

Their minds were set on offensive action which made them discount as exaggerations reports from Allenby's cavalry and the Royal Flying Corps of the movement of large German columns marching southwards from Louvain and Brussels on a collision course with the advance of the BEF. And so the march of the BEF continued with the staffs of both British Corps preparing to attack and destroy the German forces attacking Lanrezac's 5th French Army.

The march of 4th (Guards) Brigade towards the Belgian frontier took the Irish Guards along the valley of the Sambre, through Pont-sur-Sambre to the southern outskirts of Mons. There on the evening of 22 August they heard for the first time the rumble of artillery fire away to the east where Lanrezac's men were being heavily engaged by superior German forces. The weather was stiflingly hot. The reservists in the battalion were finding their fitness barely up to the strain of marching under the weight of field service marching order, and although there were commendably few stragglers, it would be some days before the battalion settled down to the rhythm of active service life.

That night the truth about the strength of the German right wing and about the potentially disastrous situation into which the BEF was marching, forced itself upon Sir John French and his staff. The attacks of the 3rd and 4th French Armies had failed and Lanrezac's 5th Army was in retreat. The BEF was nine miles ahead of its nearest French neighbours and the gap would widen because Lanrezac intended to continue his retirement. It came as an extraordinary shock to divisions and brigades in the BEF to receive orders around midnight to recast their plans for advance and instead prepare for defence when dawn came up on the morning of 23 August.

Revised instructions did not reach battalions until the early hours of 23 August. Smith-Dorrien's II Corps, which had been advancing ahead and to the west of Haig's I Corps, was ordered to take up a defensive position along the Mons-Conde Canal, which ran east and west across the front. Haig's Corps had first to draw level and then to deploy in a defensive position facing east, trying to link up with the French on his right. 4th (Guards) Brigade received orders at about 3 a.m. to occupy a position on a prominent feature just south-east of Mons, called the Bois La Haut. In the hurried orders issued after the change of plan, both Corps had arranged to hold this particular feature which was on the inter-Corps boundary. When it was discovered that units of 3rd Division were already there, the Guards were ordered to support the junction of the two Corps on Harmignies Ridge south-east of Mons. Order, counter-order, is not an unusual introduction to an encounter battle early in a war before the staffs have learned their jobs through practical experience; nevertheless it is always demoralising for troops to be committed to their first battle in this way. Thus, very early in his career Alexander experienced and was determined to avoid this type of mistake himself. He appreciated the need to give men the very greatest chance of success by what the soldiers call 'not b'ing them about'.

As far as Alexander was concerned the first day of the Battle of Mons wore on in much the same uncertain way. The main weight of the German attack fell upon Smith-Dorrien's Corps along the canal where British soldiers were astonished to see, for the first time, attacks by German regiments advancing en masse, almost shoulder to shoulder many ranks deep. Against such targets British training in marksmanship and fire control paid handsome dividends, but the British troops were equally surprised by the weight of German artillery fire which the Royal Artillery was not strong enough to subdue. It was not until late in the afternoon that German infiltration through Mons brought individual companies of the Irish Guards into action in support of the hard pressed Irish Rifles of II Corps. In this fight Alexander came under fire for the first time, and felt the exhilaration of action. Fear would come later in the company of its twin allies, physical and psychological fatigue.

Alexander's experiences in the next two months were to cover the four theoretical phases of war in the order in which they are usually taught at Staff Colleges—defence, withdrawal, advance and attack. As we have seen, Sir John French's force advanced; hoped to attack but was forestalled; defended momentarily and then withdrew in reasonable order it is true. Nevertheless it had to abandon all thought of offensive action. It was to be some seven disheartening weeks before it was able to complete the traditional cycle with an advance and attack in the Battles of the Marne and Aisne.

The withdrawal of Haig's Corps from Mons started at about 5.30 p.m. Alexander's battalion covered the retirement of 4th (Guards) Brigade, falling back themselves through positions held by 2nd and 3rd Coldstream Guards some three miles in rear. The whole brigade then acted as rearguard for 2nd Division for the first three days of the retreat, battalions leap-frogging through each other using the orthodox drill for a withdrawal action. They reached Landrecies, 30 miles south of Mons, in the early evening of 25 August. Little had been seen of the Germans who were trying to outflank the BEF to the west, and so were tending to engage Smith-Dorrien's II Corps, leaving Haig's I Corps free to withdraw unmolested. Unfortunately the withdrawal routes of the two Corps diverged south of Mons as they passed either side of the Forest of Mormal, the tracks through which ran from north-west to south-east in the diametrically opposite direction to the south-westerly withdrawal of the BEF. All would have been well had not von Kluck decided that the moment had come to turn eastwards to head off the BEF from any attempt it might be making to reach the Channel ports. He gave his orders slightly too late and in consequence his leading Corps cut across the front of Smith-Dorrien's rearguard and entered the Forest of Mormal unnoticed. Their advance down the tracks in the forest led them by chance to Landrecies at the south-east corner where Haig's headquarters were still established. Had it not been for the timely arrival of 4th (Guards) Brigade, the German advanced-guards would have arrived unheralded in HQ I Corps. As it was, a most unseemly panic ensued amongst the Corps staff which did no one

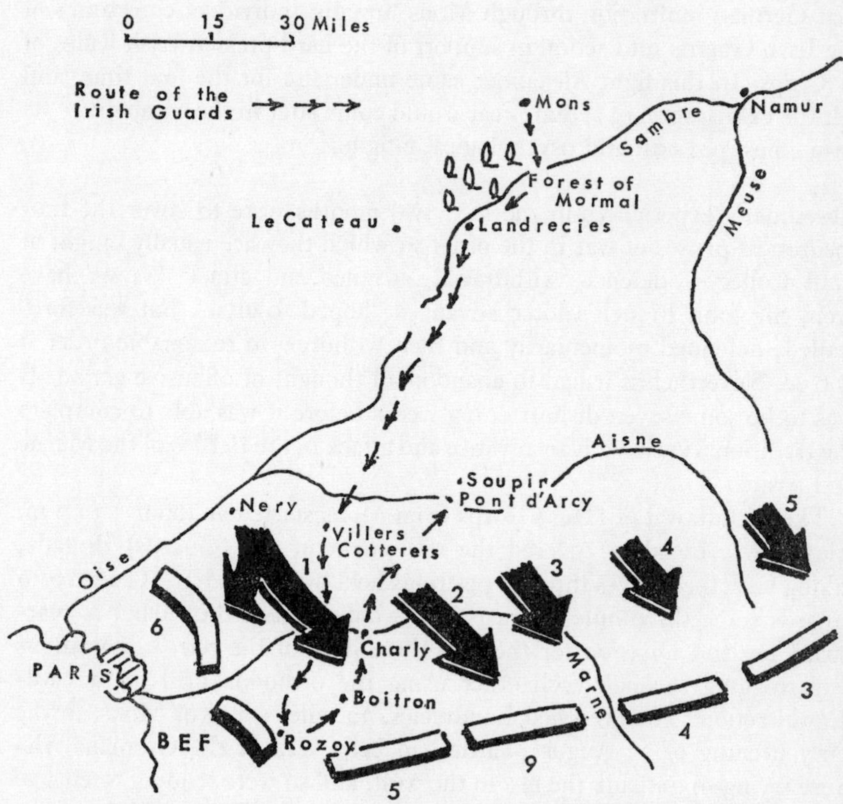

3 Retreat from Mons to the Marne and Advance to the Aisne, 25 August–2 September 1914

any credit. Fortunately 3rd Coldstream Guards met the German advance with their traditional steadiness, while the Irish Guards prepared the town itself for defence, covering the disorderly exit of Haig's staff. Alexander saw for the first time the effects of surprise on men who were not as yet inoculated against fear. Panic is never pleasant to witness. It is unnerving when soldiers see their higher headquarters losing self-control. Alexander was to remember Landrecies when his own General Headquarters was cut off by the Japanese in Rangoon in 1942.

By midnight 4th (Guards) Brigade had stabilised the situation sufficiently for an orderly withdrawal to start again. The Irish Guards provided the rearguard and for the next four days the retreat went on almost mechanically. Kipling describes the nightmare feeling:

> . . . the effect, doubtless, of that continued over-exertion which reduces men to the state of sleepwalkers. There was ten minutes halt in every hour, on which the whole Battalion dropped where it stood and slept. At night, some of them began to see lights, like those of comfortable billets by the roadside which, for some curious reason or other could never be reached. Others found themselves asleep, on their feet, and even when they lay down to snatch sleep, the march moved on, and wearied them in their dreams. (Kipling, I, p. 5)

The Irish Guards were not engaged again seriously with German advanced guards until 1 September when they were ordered with the 2nd Coldstream Guards to protect the rear of Haig's Corps in the closely wooded country around Villers-Cottérêts. It was to be a memorable but tragic day for Alexander's battalion. It was the first time they had fought together as a battalion instead of in detached companies. In the 'soldiers' battle' which ensued in the maze of forest tracks, they lost their CO and eight other officers. The battle was caused, like Landrecies, by von Kluck turning inwards again in a final attempt to crush the BEF once and for all. The blow struck the 1st Cavalry Brigade, covering Smith-Dorrien's withdrawal, and the composite Irish/Coldstream group, covering Haig's withdrawal. The clash with 1st Cavalry Brigade is famous for the action of 'L' Battery RHA at Nery in which the three surviving members of the battery won VCs, serving the last gun at point-blank range until ammunition ran out. The action fought by the Guards group was hardly less tenacious and was fought against superior numbers of German infantry in the deep, dank gloom of the beech woods. This was Alexander's first taste of the chaos and confusion of an encounter battle in which control can so easily be lost when officer casualties are high. Fighting in woods is an art, not to be undertaken for choice by the unskilled.

For two more days the withdrawal went mechanically on. In spite of the sound administrative arrangements made by Sir William Robertson, later to become CIGS, the BEF's logistic system finally broke down and the battalion was forced to eat its 'iron rations'. On 3 September it reached and crossed the Marne to relative security in which the quartermaster could requisition enough food to feed the men again. On the same day, Joffre realised that, at last, the riposte which he had always hoped to deliver from the seaward flank and for which the BEF had originally advanced to Mons, could become a reality. The direction of the German right wing, which had begun to change at the time of Nery and Villers-Cottérêts, was clearly aimed at driving the French and British forces away from Paris and ultimately to their destruction against the Swiss Alps. The German manoeuvre was based on the assumption that the French had too few reserves left in the Paris area to attack von Kluck's exposed right flank. Unfortunately for the Germans, Joffre had managed to build up a new French Army—General Maunoury's Sixth Army—around the capital. The stage was set for the 'Miracle of the Marne'.

For three more days the Irish Guards marched southwards to Rozoy, south-east of Paris, and on the afternoon of 6 September were again momentarily in contact with the German advanced guards. Alexander is mentioned by name for the first time (on p. 15) in Kipling's history, leading a platoon on reconnaissance to establish contact with this German force. His reconnaissance was significant as it was in a northerly direction; the tide, as far as the battalion was concerned, had changed.

Events were now flowing against the Germans. 4th (Guards) Brigade began its advance with the rest of the BEF back towards the Marne, driving into the flank of von Kluck's First Army. On 9 September, Alexander was involved in an advanced guard action at Boitron Wood in which the battalion captured a German machine gun company of three officers, 90 men and six guns—a lavish equipment by British standards. This was the first sizeable number of prisoners the battalion had taken, and the effect on its morale was out of all proportion to the size of the action. The enthusiasm of the British troops rose with the decline in fighting efficiency of the Germans who were leaving a growing trail of stragglers behind as they withdrew northwards under the combined pressure of Maunoury's Sixth Army and the BEF. The German soldiers in von Kluck's force had been as exhausted as the British by the time they reached the Marne, but had been buoyed up by the expectation of being first into Paris. Now that these hopes had faded, the adverse effect on their morale was all the greater. As a result the Guards Brigade saw no more fighting until it reached the Aisne. Five days hard marching—this time chasing instead of being chased—took them back across the Marne, over an intact bridge at Charly, which the Germans were said to have been too drunk to demolish; on north-eastwards to Pont d'Arcy, where they crossed the Aisne over a sapper pontoon bridge on 16 September. That afternoon the tactical picture altered as suddenly as it had done the week before at Rozoy. The Germans had decided to turn and fight on the Aisne. Although no one knew it at the time, they were to remain in possession of the high plateau overlooking the river for the next four years.

The whole character of the fighting in France changed in the middle of September. Until then the training, tactics and equipment of the BEF had stood up to the test of Continental warfare. Failure had come at the highest levels of command where self-deception had led to a radical misappreciation of German intentions. At Alexander's level there was no reason to be dissatisfied or doubt the professionalism of the British Army. It had come through the most demoralising and difficult of all operations of war—a withdrawal—with surprisingly little loss of morale. The officers and men had learned to live with the conditions which they found in France and the majority had passed the first test of war—the test of fear. They had learned to resist the unnerving crunch of artillery shell, the noise of the angry swarm of bees as machine-gun fire passes close overhead, and the characteristic rip of the rifle bullet, all of which were associated with sudden death or bodily harm. Eyes and ears had become accustomed to sensing danger. And from brigade commanders downwards officers had a more realistic idea of what was physically and psychologically possible. Deployment drills had become second nature, and orders were issued in time to give men a chance of a reasonable night's sleep without which even the best units fall apart. One thing, however, had not yet been revealed to Alexander and his contemporaries in its full starkness. They were soon to learn the meaning of German artillery superiority, first on the heights above the Aisne and then at Ypres.

4th (Guards) Brigade crossed the Aisne with 2nd Grenadiers in the lead. They cleared the village of Soupir in one of the re-entrants under the high wooded spurs on the north bank of the river. They then attacked what might have been another rearguard position around Coup de Soupir farm on the high ground above the village. Mist and heavy rain obscured observation, making it difficult to locate the German machine guns firing from the woods. Gradually all four battalions of the brigade were drawn into the fight. This was not another Boitron Wood. The Germans intended to stay.

That night Alexander bivouacked with his platoon in battle outpost formation on the edge of the wood which they had won at last light. No serious attempt was made to dig in as everyone expected the Germans to withdraw during the night. Next morning they were still in position about half a mile away and showing signs of concentrating for a deliberate counter-attack. The two forward companies of Irish Guards started to dig as the German gunners ranged their positions. Judged by later standards their efforts were little more than shallow furrows scraped out along the hedgerows. The counter-attack did not come in, but the German artillery, machine-gunners and snipers succeeded in creating a new and hostile environment quite unlike anything the British Army had experienced before. The original rough scrapes became deep fire trenches; tracks up to the forward positions became zigzagging communication trenches; and the first crude efforts were made to construct overhead cover for rudimentary dugouts. Nothing could disguise the inadequacy of the British artillery—outnumbered, outranged, out-gunned and lacking an adequate supply of ammunition. Two machine guns per British battalion was a mockery compared with the ample German quota. The only answer was to dig deeper and depend upon the alertness and skill at arms of the British professional soldier to make good these material deficiencies which could not be corrected for many months.

By the end of September the Irish Guards had established all the early elements of trench warfare. They had started to build wire entanglements, using plain agricultural wire gathered from nearby farms. Telephones had been established in front-line positions, and a system of reliefs had been organised. While half the battalion manned its sector, the other half rested close behind in the nearest farm buildings which had any slates left on their roofs. What surprised Alexander and his men most were the prodigious feats of digging which they themselves accomplished every night. The first clumsy efforts at trench warfare, which was to become their way of life for the next four years, and at which Alexander was to excel personally, had begun.

And so had the race to the sea. The BEF was to have one more momentary spell of open warfare before it was finally engulfed in the attritional struggle in the Flanders' mud. Since the crossing of the Aisne, Sir John French had wished to extricate the BEF from the centre of the French Line to move it back to the extreme left, closest to the Channel ports. His wishes did not conflict with Joffre's needs as the latter was already moving troops westwards to outflank the German front. The Germans were doing much the same thing and at much the same speed, causing a series of clashes as each new formation appeared on the open flank. The British II Corps moved first on 3 October; followed by the newly formed III Corps; and finally Haig's I Corps left the Aisne for Flanders in the middle of October. Sir John French and his GHQ Staff were once again full of confidence, sure that they could do serious damage to the German cause by a vigorous offensive. Two events were destined to nullify these plans. First, Antwerp fell

1 The young professionals: Lieutenant Alexander (*2nd from r.*) with other subalterns of the Irish Guards at Wellington Barracks in 1914

BEFORE THE FIRST WORLD WAR

2 The Irish Guards preparing to leave Wellington Barracks, 4 a.m., 12 August 1914

3 The German Infantry advancing 4 The German Artillery

THE OUTBREAK OF WAR, 1914

5 The start of trench warfare on the Aisne

releasing the large German beseiging force for operations elsewhere; and secondly, von Falkenhayn, who had superseded von Moltke as German Chief of General Staff, had managed to concentrate a new striking force composed of veteran troops moved from other sectors of the Western Front and four new Corps from Germany itself. When Haig's I Corps moved into the line east of Ypres with orders to attack towards Bruges, he found that French had misjudged the situation. Instead of attacking, he had to shore up the Allied line as it reeled under the attacks of von Falkenhayn's new striking force, reinforced by Antwerp's conquerors, in its attempt to break through to Calais.

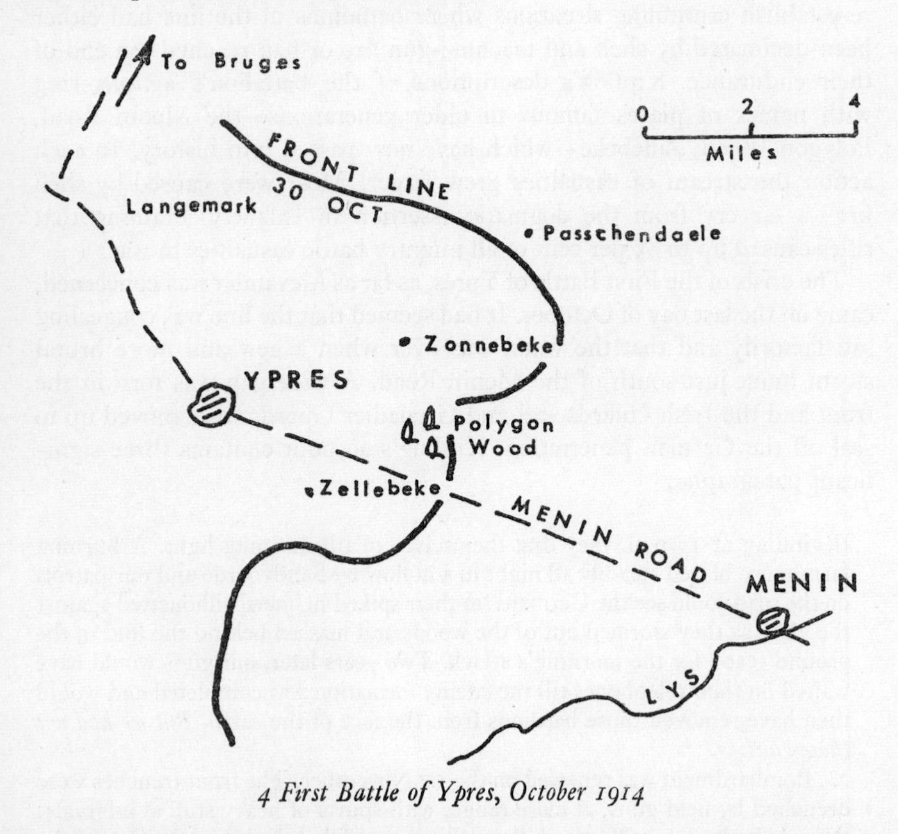

4 First Battle of Ypres, October 1914

The First Battle of Ypres lasted from 21 October until the end of November and has been aptly called 'The Death of an Army'.* Every unit and every man in Haig's Corps was needed in those grim six weeks in which the Germans delivered a series of massed infantry attacks supported

* The title of Farrar-Hockley's book on the First Battle of Ypres.

by the greatest weight of artillery experienced so far. The seige guns released from Antwerp contributed to the bombardments.

On the day that the first German attack started Alexander was waiting with the Irish Guards for their orders to advance and 'to drive back the enemy wherever met'. By evening all thought of advance had gone. The battalion was rushed forward to support the 7th Division struggling to hold Zonnebeke. Alexander had been promoted to the command of No. 1 Company and made his first successful counter-attack to clear the village and re-establish 7th Division's line in that sector. From then onwards, the battalion acted as a fire brigade, moving from breach to breach to re-establish crumbling situations where battalions in the line had either been decimated by shell and machine-gun fire or had reached the end of their endurance. Kipling's descriptions of the battalion's actions ring with names of places famous to older generations—the Menin Road, Polygon Wood, Zillebeke—which have now passed into history. In each action the stream of casualties grew larger. Most were caused by shell fire—a far cry from the dogmatic assertion in Infantry Training that rifles caused up to 85 per cent of all infantry battle casualties in war.

The crisis of the First Battle of Ypres, as far as Alexander was concerned, came on the last day of October. It had seemed that the line was congealing satisfactorily and that the worst was over when a new and more brutal storm burst just south of the Menin Road. A wide gap was torn in the front and the Irish Guards and 2nd Grenadier Guards were moved up to seal off the German penetration. Kipling's account contains three significant paragraphs:

> Beginning at 11 p.m. they dug themselves in till morning light. A burning farmhouse blazed steadily all night in a hollow by Sandvoorde and our patrols on the road could see the Germans 'in their spiked helmets' silhouetted against the glare as they stormed out of the woods and massed behind the fold in the ground ready for the morning's attack. Two years later, our guns would have waited on their telephones till the enemy formation was completed and would then have removed those battlions from the face of the earth. *But we had not those guns. . . .*
>
> . . . Bombardment was renewed on the 1st November. The front trenches were drenched by field guns, at close range, with spurts of heavy stuff at intervals; the rear by heavy artillery, while machine guns filled the intervals. One of the trenches of a platoon of No. 3 Company was completely blown in, and only a few men escaped. . . .
>
> . . . It was hopeless to send reinforcements; the machine gun fire would have wiped them out moving and our artillery was not strong enough to silence any one sector of the enemy's fire. . . . (Kipling, I, pp. 37–9)

The Irish Guards' losses in the 48 hours of this attack amounted to 350 all ranks, including Alexander himself, who was hit in the thigh and the hand and had to be evacuated back to hospital in England. These losses seemed catastrophic to a regular battalion whose officers and men had grown up together over the years and knew each other so well. The time was to come when this scale of loss would not be regarded as a heavy price to pay for a few hundred yards of shell-torn ground. Unfortunately the men who died at Ypres were the professionals—the seed corn from which new units could grow. By 1 November, the day Alexander was wounded, the strengths of the 84 British Infantry battalions engaged at Ypres were

18	under 100 strong	out of an establishment of 1,000 men each
31	between 100 and 200 strong	
26	„ 200 „ 300 „	
9	„ 300 „ 450 „	

(Figures from Farrar-Hockley, *The Death of an Army*, p. 169)

Alexander had survived his apprenticeship and had learned the meaning of fear. He had learned how much men can endure if properly led, and the consequences of poor leadership, which unhappily he had also witnessed at Ypres, where many units failed to withstand the unequal struggle between rifle and artillery fire. He had also learned at first hand how and how not to launch men into battle; the dangers of preconceived ideas of what is going to happen in war; and the need to think far enough ahead to be able to maintain an unruffled sense of the practicable however good or bad the situation may turn out to be.

Alexander had learned the basic essentials of his trade while Britain's old Imperial Army died fighting artillery and machine guns with rifles, discipline and comradeship. Years later he was to fight his own Ypres at Anzio in February 1944.

2

The Test of Command

> Some say that, whatever future war may bring forth, never again can men be brought to endure what armed mankind faced in the trenches in those years.
>
> Rudyard Kipling, *The Irish Guards in the Great War*

In the British Army success as a platoon, company and battalion commander is the fundamental criterion for promotion. There is no staff corps by which men can rise through organisational ability without having the essential qualities of leadership. Few commanders have been tested so thoroughly with troops as Alexander; and few have been so successful and survived so many major actions. After First Ypres his wounds kept him away from France until the Battle of Loos in the autumn of 1915. From then onwards he stayed with the Irish Guards, rising from company to brigade commander. Unlike his great contemporary, Montgomery, who was also badly wounded in 1914, he never served on the staff. Montgomery did not go back to regimental soldiering until after the war. He served instead, first as a brigade major, and then as a GSO I of a division. One of the major differences in the style and policies of the two men stems from this early divergence in level of operational experience. Montgomery sought success in careful planning and relatively inflexible modes of operation. He was the master of the set-piece battle. Alexander was just as careful in committing his troops, but the uncertainties of war led him to believe in greater flexibility and hence to his two-handed boxer style which we will see developing.

No two leaders are the same, nor would they necessarily have emerged in any generation or nation other than their own. They are the creatures of their time and are brought forward by the events of the day. They must possess the right basic clay of aptitude, but their characters are moulded by the interaction of events; are coloured by personal experiences; and, in the case of military leaders, glazed and hardened in the fire of responsibility in war. Whether they emerge as leaders depends on two further factors: the life which the man himself breathes into the figure created by events; and the acceptability of the finished work to superiors and subordinates alike. The latter—acceptability as a leader—rests upon the successful development of military judgment as well as personality. Before studying the building of Alexander's military judgment, let us look briefly at the former—the inner driving force behind the neat, unruffleable façade.

In Alexander's case it was particularly difficult to fathom his inner motives. Few observers could ever tell what lay below the surface. Sir James Grigg, who was Permanent Under Secretary at the War Office throughout the Second World War and who knew him well, expresses this feeling:

> I have thus known him longer than I have known any other soldier and I ought perhaps to know him better than I know any other soldier. In fact, I sometimes wonder whether I really know him at all. I know all the externals—his athletic prowess, his fighting career, his military achievements. I know his good looks, his courtesy and charm. *I know too his devotion to duty* and his scrupulous loyalty to colleagues or subordinates. But there is something inscrutable about him which gives me the feeling that there is another life beyond all this, a life of his own into which very few are allowed to enter. (*Prejudice and Judgement*, p. 426)

The words 'I know too his devotion to duty' hold the key to his character. Field Marshal Lord Harding, who was his Chief of Staff in Italy said, when talking to the author, 'One thing you must remember about Alex was that he was a *professional* soldier with the highest sense of *duty*.' This dedication was seen and interpreted in the same way by most people who worked with and for him during his long career. He seems to have been one of those men who gain greatest satisfaction in life from constructive service, but this is rarely the sole driving force in great men. Its high moral tone is often marred by the discordant notes of personal ambition and desire for public recognition; or by their inversions represented by the parade of self-denial practised by monastic orders. No man is entirely free from such influences, but Alexander seems to have been freer than most because his real satisfaction came from his deep sense of duty to his family, to his regiment, to the British Army, and to his country through the personality of the Sovereign. This sense of duty expressed itself in another way. Some great leaders rise to fame as reformers, but to be a successful reformer a man must have a radical streak. Alexander's policies were essentially conservative, building and improving on the past rather than sweeping clean. To him, the secret of success in the British Army lay in the attainment and steady improvement of professional standards in which nothing is amateur, nothing is slipshod, and in which every detail is attended to before relaxation is allowed. The imposition of such standards, particularly in war, demands moral courage and a deftness of touch on the part of British regimental officers. The standards of the martinet are required without his unreasoning methods. British soldiers must be led; they cannot be dragooned. Alexander had the ability to win willing acceptance of professional standards.

This picture of Alexander's character would be incomplete without the mention of another important facet peculiar to the British Army. The greatest happiness to him, and to innumerable British officers of his stamp, was the happiness of a regiment which knows that it is master of its trade; which has confidence in itself; and which has learned the real meaning of pride of regiment. Kipling expresses this satisfaction in his description of the 2nd Battalion, Irish Guards in 1916 when Alexander was its second-in-command:

> By this time they had discovered themselves to be a 'happy' battalion which they remained throughout. None can say precisely how any body of men arrives at this state. Discipline, effort, doctrine and unlimited care and expense on the part of the officers do not necessarily secure it. . . . It may be that the personal attributes of two or three leading spirits in the beginning set a note to which other young men, of generous mind respond. . . . (Kipling, II, p. 55)

Alexander was one of the leading spirits who formed the 2nd Battalion. In the British Army the professional happiness displayed by the battalion in spite of crippling losses at Loos, Ypres, the Somme, Cambrai and in the dispiriting days of the German breakthrough in 1918 cannot be built on the more rigid European or American techniques of the military leadership. Insistence on high professional standards has to be accompanied by humanity—humanity far in excess of anything needed in more peaceful walks of life. It could be said that Alexander was almost too humane for the harsh responsibilities of supreme command when these became his in the Second World War. The meticulous care for the feelings of others, which was so evident in his handling soldiers at regimental level, could turn into apparent weakness and indecisiveness above that level. As we shall see later, such accusations were levelled against him and might have proved his undoing if it had not been for a further saving grace. Long experience in war gave him a deep insight into other men's motives and an ability to discern how far each could be trusted and how each should be handled to draw the best from him. He developed, over the years, a style of command ideally suited to British and British Commonwealth Armies in which he preferred to use suggestion rather than direct orders. He could so identify himself with the problems of his subordinates that orders couched in the form of advice proved highly effective in the multi-national armies which he was to command at the height of his career, offsetting the obvious disadvantages of imprecision. Men worked with him rather than for him; and national susceptibilities were rarely bruised by his instructions.

In brief, then, we have a picture of a man in whom the highest sense of duty, demanding the strictest professional standards, is mellowed by sensitivity to the feelings of others.

Alexander spent two months in hospital in London, recovering from his Zillebeke wounds and was then sent on convalescent leave to his home at Caledon in County Tyrone when he was just able to walk. Like most young men of his ilk, he felt he was missing the excitement of active service, but what probably irked him most was the nagging thought that he was losing invaluable battle experience so essential to success in his chosen profession. There was still a feeling abroad—fanned by an overoptimistic press—that the war could not last much longer. As soon as British industry turned out enough guns and shells, and as soon as Kitchener's new armies were trained, the Germans would not stand a chance. He must get back before the decisive battles were fought in 1915.

Alexander's recipe for recovery was long walks over his native hills—a formula which he used throughout his life for keeping fit. Steadily increasing the distance each day, he proved himself finally to his own satisfaction with a two-day hike of 64 miles accompanied by the gamekeeper. The doctors needed more persuasion to pronounce him fit for active service. Instead of rejoining the 1st Battalion in France, he was posted to the new 2nd Battalion which was forming at Warley Barracks near Brentwood in Essex. The battalion was being formed around a nucleus of battle-experienced officers and NCO's, who, like Alexander, had recovered from wounds suffered in 1914, and others who had been sent back specially from the 1st Battalion to help train the new unit. Most of the soldiers had been recruited since the war began, although there were still a few older regular reservists available to help provide a leaven of experience. The majority of the officers were from the Special Reserve and hailed from all quarters of the British Commonwealth and Empire, and from almost every profession and age group from lawyers in their forties to school leavers in their teens. The guardsmen at this stage of the war were all Irish—the Micks, as they are called. The battalion itself had two aims in life; to live up to and, if possible, surpass the prowess of the 1st Battalion;

and to learn as much as possible of the practical business of soldiering handed on to it by battle-tried instructors.

On 16 August 1915, just a year after his first embarkation for France, Alexander marched out of Warley at the head of No. 1 Company, 2nd Irish Guards, to entrain at Brentwood Station for the journey to Southampton. That night the battalion crossed to Le Havre in the *Anglo-Canadian* and the *Viper*, escorted by destroyers. A fortnight later, on 1 September, it joined the 2nd Guards Brigade which was preparing for the Battle of Loos—a battle described by one of the senior officers in a talk to the battalion on its arrival as potentially 'the greatest battle in the history of the world'. The old 4th (Guards) Brigade had been disbanded earlier in the year as part of the expansion of the Army and the Guards Division had been formed in its place consisting of the 1st, 2nd and 3rd Guards Brigades. Alexander's old battalion, 1st Irish Guards, now belonged to 1st Guards Brigade.

While Alexander had been away from France, British tactical doctrine—indeed the tactical doctrine of all the nations taking part—had undergone radical revisions dictated by the realities of European warfare. Far from economic bankruptcy shortening hostilities, the increased resources available to industrial states gave each side an enhanced capacity to wage prolonged war, provided these resources were matched by moral determination. (It is perhaps worth reminding ourselves of this phenomenon today. If, as seems likely, the use of nuclear weapons will be tacitly barred because no conceivable political objective could warrant the resulting holocaust, then the short war theory may be found just as fallacious as it was in 1914–15.)

As a regimental officer, Alexander might not be expected to know much of events outside his battalion or possibly brigade sector of the Western Front, but he was intimately involved in the solution of the tactical problems which emerged as the struggle went on. After each operation, the reasons for success or failure—unfortunately more often the latter than the former—were analysed and debated by those who survived. The background was filled in by staff officers and special speakers sent round by GHQ to help units understand the overall situation beyond the narrow confines of their sectors. Newspapers added to officers' awareness of the larger picture, though these were often more an irritant than a help because they were written through rose-tinted spectacles for home consumption and rarely portrayed events with the starkness we have become accustomed to on television today. If we are to understand the principles upon which Alexander conducted his operations as a

Commander-in-Chief, we must look at the affairs of the Western Front on a wider canvas than the 2nd Guards Brigade sector.

The experiences of 1914 had affected both sides in three significantly different ways. The Germans' failure to win a decisive victory in the West compelled them to adopt a defensive policy in France until they could settle matters with Russia. The Allies, for their part, knew that they must drive the Germans from French soil before Russia collapsed and allowed the Germans to concentrate again in the West. This meant continuing the policy of offensive action in spite of clear indications that defence was currently superior to attack. The second factor was the differing views on fire power. Although the Germans had won their successes in 1914 by artillery superiority, the value of rifles and machine guns were impressed on their minds by the brutal losses suffered by the German infantry. The Allies, on the other hand, had suffered most from artillery fire and so became convinced that the panacea for success lay in more and heavier guns and unstinted supplies of shells. Thirdly, there was the superior tactical skill and willingness to dig displayed by the German soldier. Starting with a wider base upon which to expand their forces and a narrower, European (as opposed to world-wide) commitment for which to evolve their tactical doctrine, the Germans achieved a professional standard unequalled by the Allies until the last two years of the war. Together these three factors created the tactical impasse which lasted four years. The Germans held four outstanding cards; the machine gun manned by first class soldiers; skill with pick, shovel and barbed wire in protecting these weapons and their crews; time to create defences several lines deep; and an ability to move reserves rapidly to seal off any successful penetration of their defences. The Allies for their part held only three effective cards: an increasing supply of artillery with which to pulverise the German defences; a growing number of willing, but inadequately trained infantry with which to storm the resulting quagmire; and the prerogative of all attackers, the chance to achieve surprise. Unfortunately the last was negated by the first and the second. Allied dependence on artillery to smash the German defences robbed them of the crucial advantages of surprise and so churned the ground that their infantry could not maintain momentum.

One other factor affected the British alone. Starting with a small, regular but under-equipped army, the British required time to expand, train and arm their new armies up to continental standards. That time could not be vouchsafed to them. Constant political and military pressure from the French for immediate help could not be gainsaid. The British were always forced to attack before they had built up the necessary resources. In each succeeding act the British Army was drawn on by fleeting glimpses of success which shone through the dark clouds of successive failures. The principles of mobile warfare set out in *Field Service Regulations 1911* lay undisturbed in the recesses of British senior commanders' minds as the 'real war' towards which they should all be moving. Trench warfare was thought to be an unfortunate and unattractive cross-current in the main stream of the evolution of war. Before each battle the return to mobile warfare seemed to lie just over the skyline.

While Alexander had been training with the 2nd Battalion at Warley, Sir John French made the first tentative British efforts to help his French Allies with a series of attacks starting with Neuve Chappelle and ending with Loos. At Neuve Chappelle, Haig's First Army attacked a weak sector of the German line, achieving surprise, but failing to break through due to inadequate reserves and the problem—which was to beset all Allied operations for the next three years—of the loss of control once the initial impetus of the assault was spent. Shortage of artillery, which had restricted the initial bombardment to 40 minutes, did not seem to have an adverse effect on the battle. British spirits soared. It was clearly practicable to break the German line with their existing scale of guns and ammunition.

Two months later their hopes were dashed at Aubers Ridge and Festubert. At the former, the same 40-minute bombardment was tried, this time with disastrous results. The Germans had used the two months to so strengthen their defences that this meagre weight of shell only alerted the garrison and did not damage the wire and trenches. The German saying 'sweat saves blood' was proved true; and the British concluded that for the time being the Sapper had beaten the Gunner. In consequence, at Festubert the Gunners were given more time but could not, as yet, be given much more shell because British industry was still not geared to full war production. The preliminary bombardment lasted two to three days. The objectives were to be limited and progress methodical. Again Haig's First Army achieved a tantalizing partial success, confirming in British minds that the secret of success lay in building up their strength in artillery. This would need time but regrettably time was not on the Allies' side. The Russians had been heavily defeated in the battle of Gorlice-Tarnow. It would not be long before the Germans transferred their victorious divisions back to the Western Front. In spite of Sir John French's protests, Lord Kitchener, as Secretary of State for War, decided that the British must support their French ally in another major offensive before winter brought operations to a halt and before there had been any marked improvement in the British gun and ammunition supply. To make matters worse the sector chosen for this British effort was dictated by the need to attack alongside the French on ground which Sir Douglas Haig considered quite unsuitable, lying, as it did, among the slag heaps and pitheads of the mining district of Loos.

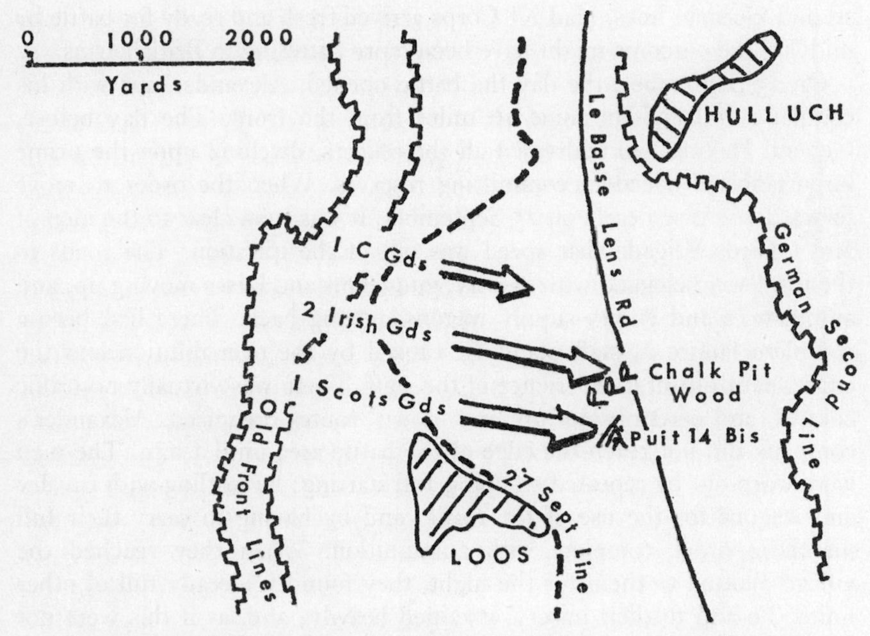

5 2nd (Guards) Brigade attack at the Battle of Loos, 27 September 1915

Three factors dictated Haig's plan for Loos. The lessons of Aubers Ridge and Festubert underlined the need for weight of bombardment, avoidance of too narrow a front upon which German retaliatory fire could be concentrated and the necessity of surprise. The British artillery was still weak and so Haig decided to employ gas on a large scale for the first time, emulating the German use of this hideous weapon five months earlier at Ypres. The frontage of attack was widened by Haig using all of his six divisions in the line. His only reserve was his cavalry division. He accepted this unsound deployment on the assurance that Sir John French's General Reserve would be moved up in his support as soon as the offensive started. The General Reserve was General Haking's XI Corps consisting of two new divisions—the 21st and 24th Divisions—and the Guards Division. The Guards were to be treated as the Corps d'Elite and committed last to achieve decisive results. Sir John French decided to hold his General Reserve well back so as not to prejudice surprise.

The story of Loos is too well known to need repeating here. Suffice it to say that five of the six divisions carried the German front line and in one sector penetrated the second, but by evening the attack had faltered for lack of reserves and had been fought to a standstill between the first and second German lines. Had XI Corps arrived fresh and ready for battle by midday, the outcome might have been more flattering to British arms.

On 25 September, the day the battle opened, Alexander was with his company at Lingham some 16 miles from the front. The day before, General Haking had addressed all the officers, dwelling upon the prime importance of speed in committing reserves. When the order to move forward was given early on 25 September, it was soon clear to the men of 2nd Guards Brigade that speed was out of the question. The roads to the front were clogged with cavalry, gun teams and buses moving up, and ambulances and empty supply wagons moving back. There had been a complete failure in staff planning, caused by the over-dilution and the consequent pitiful inexperience of the staff. There was virtually no traffic control, and certainly no 'up' and 'down' routes organised. Alexander's company did not reach the edge of the battle area until 1 a.m. The men were worn out by repeated stopping and starting; by jostling with cavalry and wagons for the use of the roads; and by having to carry their full marching order complete with ammunition. When they reached the village allotted to them for the night, they found it already full of other units. To add to their misery, it rained heavily; and, as if this were not enough, breakfasts had been ordered for 4.30 a.m. in case of a dawn move. In the event no orders arrived until midday. By then the men had been under arms for 36 hours with only three hours rest in a wet uncomfortable bivouac.

The move forward, when it came on 26 September, was worse than the previous day in that the battalion suffered long-range shelling and was meeting all the discouraging sights which appear in the rear of any great battle—demoralised men without equipment spreading rumours of disaster; dead men and horses lying in grotesque attitudes where some wagon lines or gun position had been; ambulances full of wounded and walking wounded making their way back to the relative safety of the rear areas; and over everything the all-pervading stench of cordite and unburied dead. Two company commanders—Alexander and Hubbard—were sent forward to reconnoitre routes into the position which the Irish Guards were to occupy preparatory to renewing the attack. The fog of war was dense. No one knew where the front line really lay. The 21st and 24th Divisions had been committed on the assumption that one more effort would tear the German second line apart. They, like the Guards, had arrived exhausted, having had no proper food or sleep for 48 hours and had advanced thinking that German resistance was on the point of collapse. Nothing could have been further from the truth. The German reserves, which were to bring so many British attacks to a halt over the next three years, were just arriving in strength. In spite of great individual gallantry these two new and inexperienced divisions had collapsed and the Guards had been ordered to fill the gap and to complete the task of breaking through the German second line.

It was about midnight when Alexander and Hubbard managed to shepherd their battalion into its allotted sector of the old German front line which was to be their assembly area. New orders then arrived telling the CO to push forward to another trench 500 yards further on to relieve any of the remnants of 21st Division who might be holding out. This took until dawn and they had not yet started preparations for their primary task of attacking the German second line.

The Irish Guards' objective in the coming attack was Chalk Pit Wood. On their right would be the Scots Guards, who were to take the mine workings called Puit 14 Bis. After a 90-minute bombardment both battalions went forward at 4 p.m. The leading companies of the Irish reached their objectives in the wood and the chalk pit itself, but the Scots ran into heavy machine-gun fire just short of Puit 14 Bis. Quite suddenly the Scots were seen to be retiring and with them went most of the Irish back to the start line. There was no panic. Myth has it that an English-speaking German shouted the order to retire which was handed on from section to section. It is more likely a spontaneous withdrawal took place. Men in action for the first time find it difficult to decide how much punishment it is reasonable to withstand and when withdrawal is acceptable because the odds are too great. If they see men going back on either flank, they jump to the conclusion that a withdrawal has been ordered and so pull back as well. A lone runner going back with a message can cause a spontaneous withdrawal of this type even among experienced troops. The mental processes of both officers and men had been slowed by nearly 60 hours without sleep, so it is hardly surprising that this débâcle occurred under the added stress of German artillery and machine gun fire. As the battalion rallied preparatory to renewing its attack, a runner arrived from the direction of Chalk Pit Wood. He carried a vitriolic message from Captain Alexander, demanding reinforcements for his company which had not been engulfed in the general disorder and was still holding the objective. Thanks to his forthright example, the battalion took new heart and reoccupied its lost positions, spending the night digging itself in securely in the unrewarding chalk which it was to come to know so well on the Somme the following year.

Alexander's actions and experiences at Chalk Pit Wood were to have two far-reaching results. First of all, they established his reputation as a fine soldier. His men trusted him because he organised them well and stood by them when everything was collapsing around them. His fellow-officers admired him and his seniors trusted him for his reliability under fire. He possessed both physical courage and tactical instincts which enabled him to judge what was practicable and what was merely foolhardy. Secondly, they contained the seeds from which his ideas germinated 28 years later in his victorious Battle of Tunis. Alexander's handling of his reserves at Tunis reflect all the lessons he learned by bitter experience at Loos. His reserve divisions were correctly positioned; their routes forward were carefully reconnoitred and clearly marked; and their subsequent action thoroughly thought through. The speed with which 6th and 7th Armoured Divisions swept through the partial breach made for them by the infantry divisions was in marked contrast to the actions of Haking's XI Corps at Loos. Nearly 250,000 experienced Axis troops were to fall into Alexander's hands. Loos was to be suitably avenged.

Within a month of the Battle of Loos Alexander, his tactical flair recognised, was given temporary command of the 1st Battalion. His short spell of command was marred by recurrent bouts of influenza during November and December. Towards the end of December a new CO arrived for the 1st Battalion and Alexander returned to the 2nd Battalion as second-in-command, helping in his light hearted way to enliven its Christmas festivities. Those who recall these early days of his career stress his essential lightness of touch and determination to make the best of every situation, however grim and disillusioning. He entered the dreary business of winter trench warfare with honest zest, believing that the only cure for boredom and acute discomfort was hard constructive work and a demand for the highest standards in the true tradition of the Brigade of Guards. Every sector occupied by the 2nd Battalion Irish Guards was improved out of all recognition by the time the battalion moved on. It was in Laventie in December and January; in Pont du Hem in February; and finally in Ypres salient for March and April. Two extracts from Kipling's account may serve to paint the picture of the winter of 1915–16:

LAVENTIE

In front, not a hundred yards off, a most efficient German trench with lavish machine guns sniped them continuously between breathing spaces of our shell fire. Our own big stuff bursting on or near that trench, shook and loosened the sides of our own. The entire area had been fought over for months, and was hampered with an incredible profusion, or so it struck the new hands (of the 2nd Battalion) at the time, of arms, clothing and equipment—from shreds, wisps and clods of sodden uniforms that twist and catch round the legs, to loaded rifles that go off when trodden on in the mud or prised up by the entrenching tools. The bottom and sides of cuts were studded with corpses whose limbs, and, what was worse, faces, stuck out of the mixed offal, and were hideously brought to light in clearing up. (Kipling, II, p. 29)

ENTERING YPRES

The impression on the new hands, that is, the majority of men and officers, struck in and stayed for years after. Some compared their entry to tiptoeing into the very Cathedral of Death itself; and declared that heads bowed a little and shoulders hunched, as in expectation of some stroke upon the instant. Also that, mingled with this emotion, was the intense curiosity to know what the place might look like by day. . . . I do not remember if 'twas moonlight or dark when we came in that first time. Dark it must have been though or we felt it was, and there was a lot of doings going on in that darkness, such as Military Police, and men whispering where we was to go, and stretchers, and parties carrying things in the dark, in and out where houses had fallen into lumps. And there was little blue lights showing here and there and around, and the whole stink of The Salient, blowing back and forth upon us, the way we'd get it up our noses for ever. (Kipling, II, p. 70)

As the fine spring weather returned to the Western Front, rumours began to circulate amongst the officers of the coming 'Spring Meeting'. Loos had shown what might be done when there were enough trained troops, a well enough trained staff, and enough guns and shell. Throughout 1915 the British had loyally supported their French Allies in spite of their unpreparedness. Now the fruits of British industrial expansion and of Kitchener's military training machine began to place in Sir Douglas Haig's hands the tools needed for success. He had superseded Sir John French after Loos and was keen to show what the British Army could do if properly led. Unfortunately, before he could elaborate his plans, von Falkenhayn seized the initiative by attacking at Verdun and in so doing set the Western Front ablaze for the whole of the summer and autumn of 1916 with the twin battles of deliberate attrition of Verdun and the Somme. When winter finally brought these nightmare battles to an end, the casualties had reached half a million each side.

The Guards Division was not involved in the opening phases of the Somme offensive when 61,000 British officers and men fell in the first few hours. The bombardment had lasted five days and nights, but had failed to destroy the German machine gun crews who had taken cover in the dug-outs tunnelled deep in the chalk of the Somme downs. As soon as the British barrage lifted, they emerged and manned their weapons with grim determination. Many had not been fed for days as no ration parties could reach them through the British barrage; much of their supporting artillery had been neutralized; and the wire entanglements in front of their trenches had been swept away by gun fire in many places. And yet

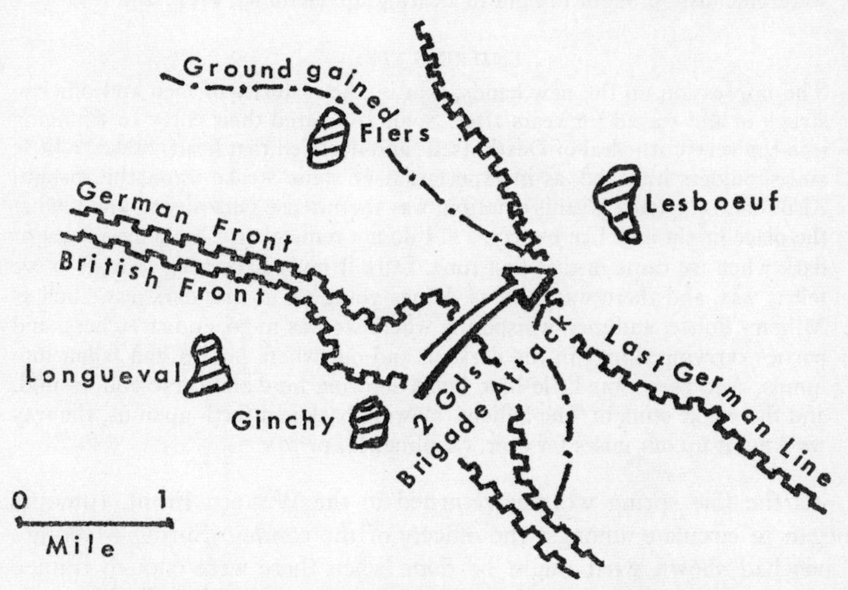

6 Guards' Division attack on the Somme, 15 September 1916

these men recovered, as their sons were to do later at Cassino, in time to bring the attacking British divisions to an unmistakable halt. The battle was not over. For the next four months Haig delivered a series of limited attacks with the aim of eroding the German positions while at the same time drawing German strength away from the hard pressed French troops, fighting to save Verdun. By the time the Guards Division was committed to the battle in September an advance of about five miles had been achieved on a 20-mile front, but there was no sign of a breakthrough or a German collapse. The French and German losses at Verdun were having a debilitating effect on both their armies, whereas British strength had not yet reached its peak. Haig felt that, having come so far at such cost, he could not give up. It was worth one more effort before winter made further progress impossible.

Alexander had arrived with the 2nd Irish Guards on the Somme battlefield in August and had spent the whole of that month holding various sectors without being involved in a major set-piece attack. On 9 September he caught his first glimpse of the tanks—some 30 of them, parked waiting to go into action on 15 September. The Irish Guards were to take part in the same attack but were not given the privilege of directly supporting these new, unwholesome-looking mechanical contraptions. 2nd Guards Brigade's objective was Lesboeuf which they were to attack from the existing front line near Ginchy.

In the planning of 2nd Guards Brigade attack, Alexander's tactical instincts again came to the fore. The regimental history records:

> Thanks, however, to the advice of Major Rooke and Captain Alexander as to the massing point, that blast (refers to German barrage which struck Ginchy) fell behind our men, who thus lived to progress into the well laid and unbroken machine gun fire that met them the instant they advanced. Their first objective (Green Line) was six hundred yards away through the mists of the morning and the dust and flying clods of the shells. A couple of hundred yards out, the 3rd Grenadiers and 1st Coldstream came upon a string of shell holes which might or might not have started life as a trench, filled with fighting Germans, insufficiently dealt with by our guns. This checked the waves a little and brought the Irish storming into the heels of the leading line, and as the trench lay obliquely across the advance, swung the whole of the 2nd Brigade towards the left. . . .
>
> The battalion (2nd Irish Guards), without landmarks to guide, did what they could. Under Captain Alexander and 2nd Lieutenant Greer, the Germans in the first unexpected trench were accounted for. . . . There had been instructions, in Brigade Orders, as to the co-operation of nine tanks that were to assist the Guards Division. . . . The infantry were warned, however, that their work 'would be carried out whether the tanks are held up or not'. It was. The tanks were not much more in evidence on that sector than the cavalry which, cantering gaily across shell holes, should have captured Bapaume! (Kipling, II, p. 101)

The first objective was eventually cleared and consolidated. The state of the brigade on this objective was Grenadiers 60, Scots 60, Irish 40 (including Alexander) and Coldstream 10. There was some discussion as to whether to wait for a new artillery bombardment before pushing on to the second objective but

> signs of German withdrawal across the bare down and the sight of some of

> their field guns trotting back suggested a sporting chance of pushing towards Lesboeuf, which Captain Ian Colquhoun of the Scots Guards and Captain Lyttelton of the Grenadiers thought worth taking. Their view was shared by Major Rooke, Captain Alexander and Lieutenant Mylne of the Battalion, so between them they amassed some hundred men and went out nearly half a mile to an unoccupied trench in a hollow, with standing crops in front. Here they halted and sent back demands for reinforcements. . . . (Kipling, II, p. 105)

Alexander had not only survived another major assault, but had gone farther than most of his battalion, seeing the sight that many soldiers dreamed about but never saw—the green fields beyond the swathe of devastation with the German gun teams limbering up and trotting off over the skyline as they withdrew. Once again he had demanded reinforcements as he had done at the Chalk Pit Wood only to find that disorganisation among the attacking units made further exploitation of success impossible. The next step in the evolution of war had, however, been taken. The success of one lone tank at Flers, to the north of the Irish attack, showed what might be accomplished by these machines when they and their tactics were more fully developed and there were more of them. Another year was to pass before Alexander gained his first real experience in armoured warfare at Cambrai in November 1917.

The second winter in the trenches brought greater misery to the battalion than the first had done, but for Alexander it also brought promotion and the increased responsibility of commanding a battalion in action. The misery of the winter took two forms. The voracious demands of a modern army for vast tonnages of ammunition and stores of all kinds led to demands for road, railway and depot construction which exceeded the engineer and civil labour effort available for such tasks. Deficiencies had to be made good by using infantry battalions when they were out of the line. Instead of training while in reserve, battalions were ordered to find working parties to help the Sappers, usually in the foulest weather. Taking a pride in the job was the Guardsman's answer to these backbreaking fatigues. Few battalions achieved a better record for high-speed rail laying than the Irish Guards.

The second cause of their misery was the mud of the Somme which they found worse than the flooded trenches of the Ypres salient during their first winter. 'The defences had been literally watered down to a string of isolated posts reached over the top across stinking swamp and the mounds and middens, called parapets, spread out dismally and collapsed as they tinkered at them.' The strain began to tell:

> The strongest cannot stand up beyond a certain point to exposure, broken rest, alarms all round the clock; laborious physical exertions, knee or mid-thigh deep in mud; sweating fatigues, followed by cooling off in icy blasts or a broth of snow and chalk-slime; and—more undermining than any bodily stress—the pressure that grows hourly of responsibility. (Kipling, II, p. 198)

The Somme was one overwhelming fatigue which impressed itself deeply on Alexander's mind. When urged by Churchill to continue the third battle of Cassino in the winter of 1944, he had no hesitation in calling the battle off and insisting upon the return of spring before attempting anything further. The following year he adopted the same policy when his autumn offensive in the Apennines was slowed by foul winter weather. He knew from his two winters at Ypres and on the Somme that there is a point beyond which it is profitless to struggle against the elements.

In the middle of December, while still engulfed in the glutinous mud of the Somme, Alexander was transferred again to the 1st Battalion to take command temporarily while its CO went on leave. On 3 March he was given command permanently when his predecessor was promoted to a brigade. He was just 26 years old; and was a substantive major with a DSO won at Lesboeuf and an MC won at the Chalk Pit Wood. He stayed commanding the 1st Battalion throughout the exciting weeks of the pursuit of the Germans when they withdrew to the Hindenburg Line in the spring of 1917. At last the slough of the Somme was left behind. It looked as if the corner had been turned and German resistance was on the decline. Events were to show that this was not so; nor was it to be the last the Irish Guards were to see of the desolation of the Somme.

The year 1917, which seemed to start so well, brought nothing but unrewarding effort to the British Army. Allied statesmen were misled by the glib arguments of General Nivelle, who promised to lead the French Army to decisive victory with a massive attack on the Aisne. Haig supported his French colleague with diversionary attacks at Arras and on the Ancre. Both battles were relatively successful and showed a marked improvement in British battle tactics. Any significance these British successes might have had was swept away in the disastrous defeat of Nivelle's offensive. The blow, which was to end the war in the West, almost did so—in the Germans' favour! The French Army had reached the end of its endurance. Shaken by its defeat, it could no longer withstand the feeling of pointlessness which welled up within its ranks. Open disobedience and mutiny occurred. From June onwards the British Army had to bear the brunt of the fighting to draw German attention away from the French sectors while Petain, who succeeded Nivelle, tried to restore the French Army's confidence in itself and in its leaders. Loyal British efforts to achieve these ends led to the battles of Messines, Third Ypres and Cambrai.

Alexander did not take part in the Battle of Messines because he was sent home to England on a senior officers' course at Aldershot. He had been in France without a break since August 1915 and deserved this well-earned three months' rest. When he returned in September he assumed command of the 2nd Battalion, whose CO had been killed a month earlier. He was just in time to plan the battalion's part in the last phase of the Third Battle of Ypres, better known as the costly Battle of Passchendaele.

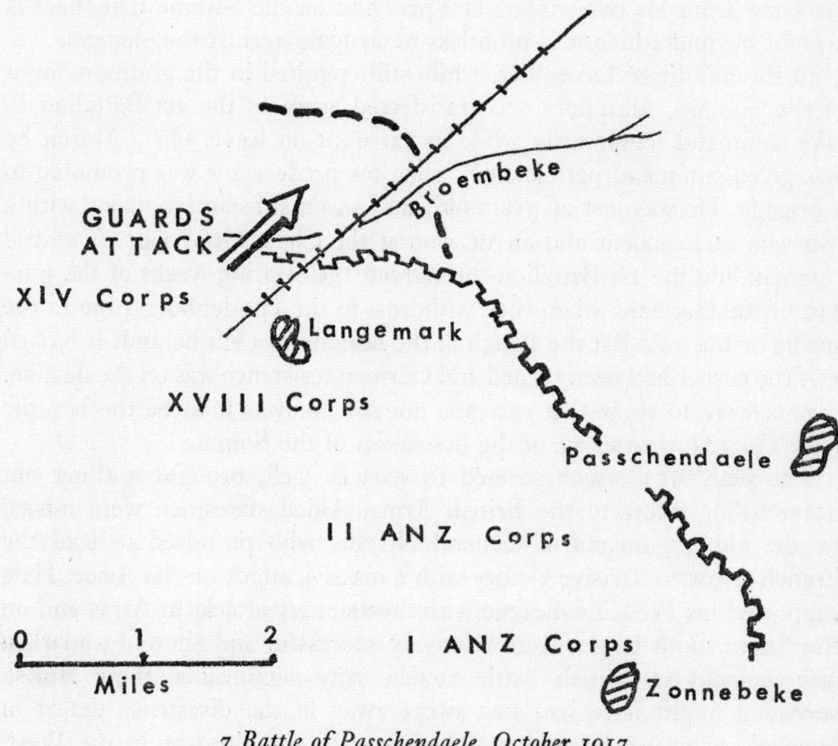

7 Battle of Passchendaele, October 1917

The Guards Division took over the extreme northern sector of the Ypres salient and was responsible for protecting the left flank of the main force attacking the Passchendaele ridge. This involved 2nd Irish Guards in a frontal assault across the Broembeke Stream which started on 9 October. It was an excellently organised attack, thought out by Alexander and his battalion staff in meticulous detail with artillery and infantry cooperation at its best. Nothing was left to chance. Every move was rehearsed step by step on 'mock ups' behind the lines, a system Alexander was to pursue later in Italy before his two great spring offensives in 1944 and 1945. Careful rehearsal then resulted in the same measure of success that he was to achieve at Broembeke.

The 2nd Battalion had come a long way since its first fumbling efforts at the Chalk Pit Wood. Working behind a carefully timed barrage the battalion took its three objectives in succession over a period of two days:

> Four barrages went on together—the creeping, a standing one, a back barrage of six-inch howitzers and 60-pounders and a distant barrage of the same metal, not to count the thrashing machine gun barrages. They moved and halted with the precision of stage machinery or, as a man said, like water hoses at a conflagration. The two leading companies crossed the river without a hitch, met some small check for a few moments in Ney Wood where a nest of machine guns had escaped the blasts of fire, and moved steadily on behind the death-drum of the barrage to the first objective a thousand yards from their start. There the barrage hung like a wall from the French flank. . . . The dreadful certainty of the job in itself masked all details. One saw and realised nothing outside of one's own immediate task, and the business of keeping distances between lines and supports became an absurd preoccupation. . . . (Kipling, II, p. 171)

The only tragedy in this professionally organised attack occurred when one of the French 75mm guns, supporting the attack, fired short, into the backs of the Irish. Had it not been for this, casualties would have been very light. Alexander could be justifiably pleased with his first major assault in command of a battalion. One officer and 20 men were killed and four officers and 89 men wounded. Alexander was among the wounded, but was able to stay at his post.

For the rest of the battle, the Guards battalions relieved each other in turn on the northern flank of the main assault on Passchendaele itself. The remains of the village fell on 6 November. Conditions had become worse than the previous winter on the Somme. Men drowned in mud if they slipped off the buck-boards which formed the tracks across the shell-torn morass. On 10 November Haig at last called off this ill-famed battle. By then Alexander was marching southwards with his battalion towards the old Somme battlefield. The Guards Division was assembling as part of the reserve for what Cyril Falls has aptly called 'The Great Experiment' —the Battle of Cambrai which was to revolutionize warfare.

Attacks so far on the Western Front had usually failed because prolonged bombardment needed to destroy the German wire, machine guns, artillery and mortars acted like an antibiotic, destroying the helpful as well as virulent bacteria. As has been pointed out already, it killed surprise, enabling the Germans to move up reserves; and it pulverised the ground over which the attackers' supports must advance to exploit successes won by the assault waves. At Cambrai the exponents of tank warfare tried to solve this tactical impasse by dispensing with the artillery bombardment

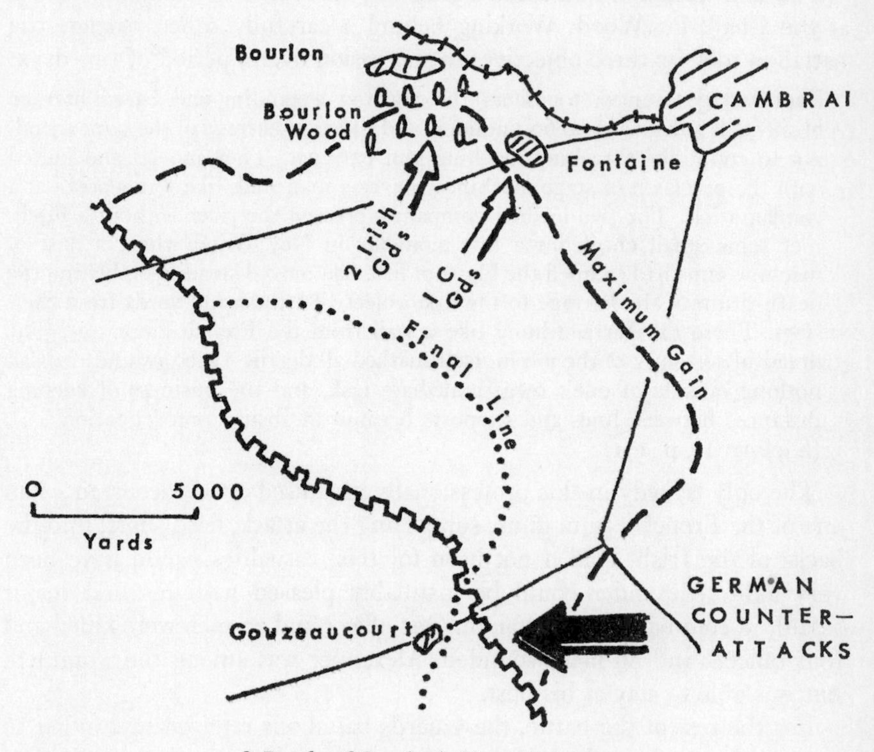

8 Battle of Cambrai, November 1917

altogether. The guns were not even allowed to carry out preliminary registration of their targets. Once the attack started the artillery would join in, and if a breach was made quickly enough, the British senior officers' dream would come true—the cavalry would advance through the gap to fan out in the German rear. Cambrai was planned with the idea of this cavalry climax.

The question of why the Cambrai experiment failed after a brilliant opening will remain a matter for debate. Its importance, as far as Alexander was concerned, lies in the effect it had on British military thinking between the wars and later at El Alamein and Tunis. Surprise was achieved at Cambrai in a startling fashion. A great gap was literally crushed through the Hindenburg defences, but then the twin ghosts of Loos appeared: the uncontrollability of the battle once the first planned phase was over; and the lack of properly constituted reserves ready to exploit success. Too much had been put in the 'shop window' and too little held in reserve. What reserves there were consisted, in the main, of cavalry divisions which were stopped with comparative ease by the German survivors struggling to seal the breach made by the tanks.

The Guards Division was not committed until the third day of the battle when it was ordered to seize the dominating Bourlon Wood ridge which overlooked the whole of the northern sector of the British breach. By this time German reserves, many of whom had just detrained quite fortuitously from the Eastern Front, had begun to arrive. 1st and 3rd Guards Brigades were committed first and failed to secure the great dark mass of Bourlon Wood. Three days later 2nd Guards Brigade's turn came with quite inadequate notice. The Brigade Commander was not warned until the afternoon of 26 November that he was to attack the wood at dawn the following morning. Alexander, whose battalion was to lead the attack, was away with his Assistant Adjutant, reconnoitring routes by which to take his battalion up to relieve another unit elsewhere on the battlefield. He received his orders to capture Bourlon Wood in the middle of a heavy hail-storm just as it was growing dark. The brigade plan was to move his battalion up on a compass bearing during the night and to despatch it into the wood at dawn behind a creeping barrage. No one in the battalion would see the ground in daylight and with the best will in the world Alexander could not issue his detailed orders before midnight. Speed was considered essential because further German reinforcements were known to be arriving. If the attack were delayed to give the Irish Guards more time, the German positions would solidify and might prove too strong to be rushed. While Alexander accepted these reasons for speed, he was under no illusions about the consequences. This could be no Broembeke attack with everything thought out and carefully rehearsed. He was being asked to undertake Villers-Cotterêts of 1914 in reverse with his guardsmen attacking rather than defending. Once in the wood control would be difficult and it would become a soldiers' battle. Success would depend initially upon surprise and then upon maintaining cohesion and direction. Kipling's description of the fight cannot be bettered:

> The Battalion spent the night of the 26th working its way up to the front line . . . bombs were issued, two per man . . . thence cross country through the

dark to the Bapaume-Cambrai road where they found the guides. . . . Just as they reached the south edge of Bourlon Wood, the enemy put down a barrage which cost forty casualties. Next it was necessary for the CO (Alexander) to explain the details of the coming attack to his Company Commanders, who re-explained it to their NCOs while the companies dressed in attack order, bombs were detonated and shovels issued. . . .

His account goes on:

Almost from the outset they met a line of enemy posts held in strength. . . . Here there was some quick killing and despatch of prisoners to the rear; but the Wood offered many chances of escape. . . . Meantime the Battalion took half a dozen machine guns and lost more men at each blind step. In some respects Bourlon was like Villers-Cottérêts on a large scale, with the added handicap of severe and well placed shelling. A man once down in the coppice, or bogged in a wood pool, was as good as lost, and the in-and-out work through the trees and stumpage broke up formations. . . . Not long after this they tried to dig in among the wet tree-roots, just beyond the Wood's northern edge. It seemed to them that the enemy had fallen back to the railway line which skirted it . . . officially, the objective was reached, but our attacking strength had been used up and there were no reserves. A barrage of big stuff, supplemented by field-guns, was steadily thrashing out the centre and north of the Wood, and somewhere to the rear of the Battalion, a nest of machine guns broke out viciously and unexpectedly. The whole fabric of the fight appeared to crumble, as, through one or other of the many gaps between the battalions, the enemy thrust in, and the 2nd Irish Guards, hanging on to their thin front-line, realised him suddenly at their backs. What remained of them split up into little fighting groups; sometimes taking prisoners, sometimes themselves being taken and again breaking away from their captors, dodging, turning and ducking in the dripping coppices and over the slipping soil, while the shells impartially smote both parties. Such as kept their sense of direction headed back by twos and threes to their original starting-point. . . . (Kipling, II, pp. 178–181)

When Alexander managed to reassemble his broken battalion that evening he could only muster 117 officers and men. It was finished as an effective fighting force until it could re-absorb its men left out of battle in the Divisional Reserve. In those days battalions sent back about a third of their strength before a major action so that they could be rebuilt with trained men as well as new drafts if disaster overtook them. Alexander was not allowed much time for rebuilding. The German reserve formations rushed by Ludendorff, von Falkenhayn's successor, to seal the Cambrai breach, were by now strong enough to launch a counter-offensive. This came as an ugly surprise to the British High Command when, on 30 November, their weak southern flank was suddenly assailed in great strength and driven in. At one moment it looked as if the Germans would regain all their lost ground, and inflict as serious a defeat on the British as they themselves had suffered ten days before. In spite of its losses on the Bourlon Ridge, the Guards Division was ordered to march south to stem the German tide. 2nd Guards Brigade advanced straight across country by the shortest route, marching in open artillery formation and taking up a blocking position at Gouzeaucourt in the path of the German advance amongst all the chaos and tell-tale signs of a major military disaster.

1 December was bitterly cold. The men were without greatcoats which they had left behind at the beginning of the forced march southwards. Alexander's battalion, reinforced up to 400 rifles, waited for the German attack to develop in hastily dug positions. None came. The Germans, like the British, were still unable to sustain the momentum of their attacks. The Battle of Cambrai died away in a blinding snow storm which brought the disappointing 1917 campaign to an abrupt and timely end.

The winter of 1917–18 was, physically, no less depressing than its predecessors. Psychologically it was worse. War weariness was taking its toll and a new sense of foreboding hung over the Western Front. Events in Russia and on the Eastern Front were moving fast. No one could foresee the outcome. Only one thing was certain: it was bound to be evil. It took no strategic insight to realise that the spring would bring a major German effort in the West, mounted by veteran divisions released from Poland. The French Army had not recovered fully from Nivelle's disastrous offensive and might suffer further moral illness through infection by the Red virus from the East. The British Army would be called upon again to bear the brunt of the fighting in the West.

For Alexander the winter of 1917–18 was important for two other reasons. He was to gain his first experience commanding a brigade; and secondly, he was to see a reorganisation of the British Army which was to last throughout his military service. Growing shortage of manpower compelled economy in the use of infantry and the greater dependence on material resources such as artillery, tanks and engineer devices. The number of infantry battalions in brigades was reduced from four to three, thus increasing the proportion of supporting arms to infantry. In this reorganisation his battalion, which was still very weak, was transferred from the Guards Division to the newly reconstituted 4th (Guards) Brigade* and became part of 31st Division. The change was not popular. This is

* 4th (Guards) Brigade, which was part of the original BEF, was disbanded in 1915 when the Guards Division was formed (see p. 32).

shown very clearly in the Irish Guards' history which avoids any mention of 31st Division. 4th (Guards) Brigade became the new focus of their life and loyalties, and it was as part of this brigade that 2nd Irish Guards were to fight their last and possibly greatest actions in the First World War, dying as a battalion in so doing.

Ludendorff's 1918 counter-offensive opened on 21 March against Byng's First and Gough's Fifth British Armies. Dense fog covered the initial advance of the German infantry. The defence was stout, but was smothered by a four to one superiority. News of the offensive reached Alexander at 1 a.m. on 22 March in the form of a warning order to be ready to move his battalion out of reserve near Arras to the front as soon as buses could be provided. During the journey all the ominous signs of disaster became apparent. Canteen stores were being burnt miles behind the lines: petrol dumps were billowing ugly black smoke; and Sappers were attempting the surprisingly difficult task of blowing up ammunition dumps. Rumours of all sorts were rife.

4th (Guards) Brigade came into the line due south of Arras near St Leger on the Arras-Bapaume road. Panic had broken out among some of the neighbouring formations but there was no general rout. From their disciplined ranks it seemed to Alexander's experienced 'Micks' that the spontaneous withdrawal, which they had suffered at the Chalk Pit and seen again so recently at Cambrai, was now spreading across the front. Their history records:

> But the situation was very curious. The enemy came up; our battered troops went away. That was all there was to it. Panic and confusion broke out occasionally, but the general effect on the beholder who was not retiring was that contageous 'rot' that overtakes defeated cricket or football teams. Effort ceased, but morale in some queer way persisted. (Kipling, II, p. 194)

For ten days Alexander fought his battalion back through a series of rearguard positions, leap-frogging with the other battalions of 4th (Guards) Brigade, until the momentum of the German offensive had spent itself. It was a repetition of the retreat from Mons on a much vaster scale. In the midst of the battle Lord Ardee, 4th (Guards) Brigade commander, was gassed. The command fell to Alexander who, at the age of 27, held the brigade together and fought it until a new brigadier was found. His own battalion had suffered further heavy losses, but a draft of 244 men arrived just in time to build up its strength for its last battle.

Ludendorff's first round had nearly brought him the decisive success that Germany needed to enable her to demand a negotiated peace. Like the other Allied and German offensives in the past three years, the problem of maintaining momentum was still unsolved and his attack stalled. He reopened his offensive but failed to make progress against the stout hearted defence of the old British regular 3rd and 4th Divisions and the new 15 (Scottish) and 56 (London) Divisions which were all to win fame in the Second World War under Alexander's command. A pause then ensued while Ludendorff assembled a fresh striking force for a last all-out effort, this time in the valley of the Lys. The final German attack again won an overwhelming initial superiority and tore a great hole in the Allied line, leaving the road to Hazebrouck and the Channel ports wide open. 4th (Guards) Brigade was ordered out of reserve during the night to plug the yawning gap.

> . . . buses thumped in out of the night, and their men stumbled forth, stiff legged, to join the shivering platoons. The night air to the east and southwards felt singularly open and unwholesome. Of the other two battalions of the Brigade there was no sign. The CO (Alexander) went off to see what he could discover. . . . (Kipling, II, p. 197)

By morning Alexander had established his battalion astride the Vieux Berquin road in dead flat country in touch with the 4th Grenadiers and 3rd Coldstream on his left and right. Confused fighting went on all that day (12 April) and the next, battalion headquarters having to move four times to avoid being overrun. The German attacks, which up until then, had been disjointed, turned into a concentrated assault designed to clear a way to the sea. Alexander was forced to improvise. Raking together every man he could find—cooks, clerks, storemen—and bringing up remnants of other battalions found nearby, he managed to shore up the line until darkness brought some respite to his exhausted men. Kipling records: 'That night, Saturday 13 April, the men, dead tired, dug in as they could where they lay and the enemy—their rush to Hazebrouck and the sea barred by the dead of the Guards Brigade—left them alone.' Haig in his despatches acknowledges his debt: 'and especially that of the 4th (Guards) Brigade on whose front of some 4,000 yards the heaviest attacks fell, is worthy of the highest praise.'

So severe were the 4th (Guards) Brigade losses that the Grenadiers and Coldstream were amalgamated to form one composite battalion. Alexander's Irish retained their identity, with companies reduced to 40 men each. It was the last battle the 2nd Irish Guards were to fight in the First World War. It dawned gradually on its officers and men that they were destined to become a training and reinforcement battalion in all but name. The summer slipped by while preparations were being made for the final Allied offensive of 8 August which was to end the war. Alexander commanded 4 (Guards) Brigade for a further short period while Lord Ardee was sick. And then, much to the consternation of his battalion, he was posted from them.

> On the 14th October, their small world was shaken out of all its talk by the really serious news that their CO . . . was to transfer to command the 10th Army School. He left on the 18th and the whole battalion turned out to bid him good-bye with an affection few Commanding Officers have ever awakened. (Kipling, II, p. 210)

One interesting commentary on Alexander's popularity as a CO is provided in the history of the Irish Guards. In all, the 1st and 2nd Battalions had 15 COs during the war. Only Alexander was given a separate eulogy. In 1923, long before Alexander started his rise to fame, Kipling wrote Vol. II, p. 215:

> It is undeniable that Colonel Alexander had the gift of handling the men on the lines to which they most readily responded; as many tales in this connection testify. At the worst crisis he was both inventive and cordial and, on such occasions as they all strove together in the Gates of Death, would somehow contrive to dress the affair as high comedy. Moreover when the blame for some incident of battle or fatigue was his, he confessed and took it upon his own shoulders in the presence of all. Consequently, his subordinates loved him, even when he fell upon them blisteringly for their shortcomings; and his men were all his own.

Alexander had passed the test of command.

3

Widening Horizons

We wanted to march on Riga . . . but in that case we should have had to knock Alexander on the head, and we liked him far too much, so we stayed quiet in our trenches and von der Goltz retreated.

A senior officer of the Baltic Landeswehr, 1920
(From Walter Duranty, *I write as I please*, p. 151)

I saw the hat at that peculiar 'Alex' angle like those of the white Russians we saw in Constantinople. It was 'Alex' who had faith in us and who brought us through without loss of prestige.

An Irish Guardsman on return from Constantinople, 1922
(*Journal of the Irish Guards Old Comrades*, 1922)

The end of a great war leaves a vacuum in the lives of those professional soldiers who have survived and proved themselves masters of their calling. Delighted though they may be that the waste of human life is over and that they are returning safely to their families, they fear the dull drabness of peace after the excitement of war. They know that, within a few months, demobilization will reduce the fighting services to a skeleton and with the flesh will go their hard-earned temporary promotion. They will revert to junior ranks more in keeping with their age than military prowess.

Behind these understandable emotions, professional British officers have deeper misgivings. Will their country be sensible this time? Will it learn its lesson? Or will it allow its defences to crumble and decay as it has done after all its previous wars? Instinctively they know that economic pressures, coupled with short memories and wishful thinking, will erode the services below the level of credible defence. They will be left to argue their case alone in an unreceptive and determinedly myopic forum. While peace lasts their efforts will, at best, be considered misguided; and, at worst, the machinations of the military to grab an unreasonable share of national resources. When the next war comes, they will be accused of preparing for the last, when, in truth, they have not been allowed to prepare for any war at all. Alexander was one of those men who, in spite of his concern for people, enjoyed the challenge and exhilaration of war. He was unmarried and ready to volunteer for any special mission for which his obvious military talents were suited. He did not have long to wait. Chance and his own initiative led him towards a widening horizon. It was to be five years before the tempo of his active regimental service slackened. By then his interests in higher defence policy was to be awakened by two years at the Staff College, Camberley.

The coincidence of events which set Alexander's course in the immediate post-war era began in 1914. At the time that he was leading his platoon northwards towards the crossings of the Aisne, Sir Stephen Talents, who was to become British political representative in Latvia, left his desk in the Board of Trade to join the Irish Guards. He fought with the 1st Battalion at Festubert where he was badly wounded in May 1915. Unfit for further active service, he returned to the Civil Service and, when the war ended, was sent to direct relief work in the shattered cities of Poland. Finding it difficult to work constructively in the bedlam of the Allied relief organisation without British assistants he wrote to his old regiment for volunteers. Alexander volunteered. Talents recalls:

> Of the two Irish Guards officers, Colonel Alexander and Captain Hamilton, 'Alex' was already known to me. We had last met practising grenade throwing with Michael O'Leary behind our Givenchy trenches in the winter of 1915. A gay, modest, gallant and athletic figure, Irish amateur mile champion in 1914, he had been wounded twice and had won many distinctions in the war. He began with my Mission in Poland the European career which he continued in the Baltic countries and Turkey. . . . (*Man and Boy*, p. 264)

Thus Alexander began a second apprenticeship, this time as an international regimental officer—an experience which was to stand him in good stead in the years to come and was to form the foundation of his intuitive handling of the many nations who were to make up his Allied Armies in Italy. In his first apprenticeship he had learned how to draw the best out of British troops. He had lived through one of the greatest wars in history, and, within the British Army, had established a reputation for imperturbability which was enhanced by his quiet confident manner and meticulous attention to dress—neat, correct, and yet, always original. Some of his closest rivals referred to him scathingly as 'little Alex'. The majority accepted him as a man of proven integrity, a natural soldier and a devotee of the highest professional standards. This might have been a forbidding catalogue of qualities had it not been for the element of fun that he imparted to serious affairs and without which professionalism is unacceptable to the British Army. But how would he fare when faced with men he did not know, in conditions he did not understand, and in an environment alien to his nature and upbringing?

Poland was not to be the principal scene of Alexander's second apprenticeship. It provided him with a useful initiation into politico-military problems of working in an Alliance, learning to appreciate other nations' points of view, disentangling the webs of political intrigue, and finding compromises that would make executive action possible. Early in 1919 Talents was sent to the Baltic States to report on the situation in the old Russian provinces which were to become the independent states of Estonia, Latvia and Lithuania. As the result of his report he was instructed

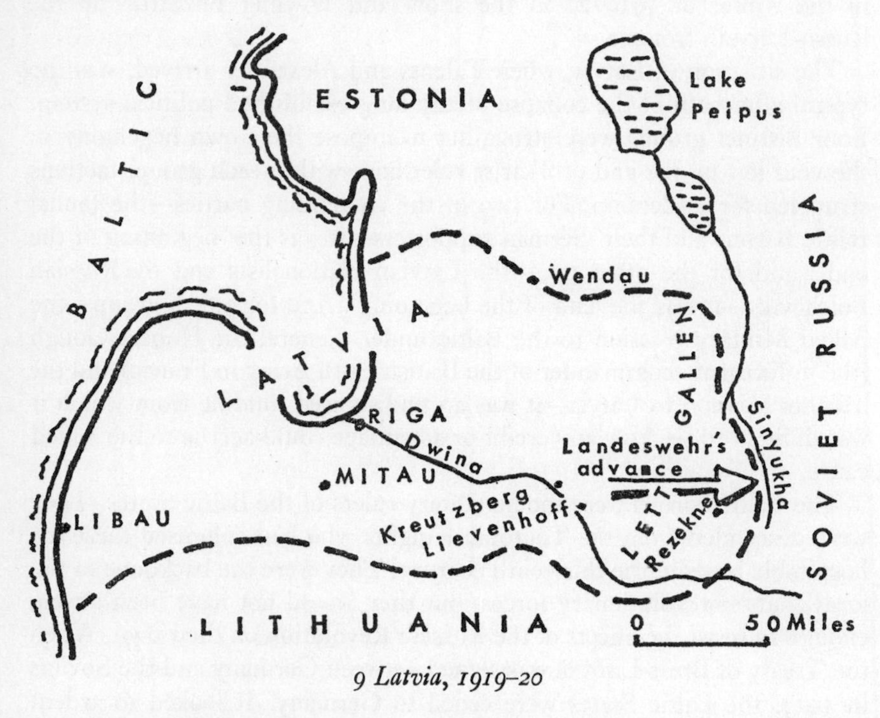

9 Latvia, 1919–20

to establish a British Mission in Latvia to which Alexander was transferred as 'Relief Adviser'. The Mission arrived at Libau at the end of May to find the situation in Latvia had deteriorated since Talents wrote his report. The instability reflected divided counsels in Versailles and London, placing the Talents Mission in an invidious position. Alexander was to learn at first hand how difficult it is to act with precision when directed, as must on occasion happen to military officers, by the political instead of the military departments in Whitehall. He was also to gain experience in handling the explosive mixture of nationalists, international revolutionaries, soldiers of fortune, self-styled politicians, placemen and adventurers of almost every

European nationality embroiled in the struggle for power at the periphery of the Russian Revolution. In doing so, he gained an enduring respect for the Germans and, in particular, for the German soldier. He had fought them for four years; now he was to command them in action. Field Marshal Lord Harding made this point talking to the author: 'There was only one thing on which Alex and I disagreed. He had a deep admiration for the German soldier. I am afraid I could not agree'. The Field Marshal, however, confessed that, unlike Alexander, he had not fought with them in the winter of 1919–20 in the snow and howling blizzards on the Russo-Latvian frontier.

The situation in Latvia, when Talents and Alexander arrived, was the typical aftermath of the collapse of any long-established political system. Four distinct groups were struggling to impose their own hegemony in the void left by the end of Tsarist rule; and, within each group, factions struggled for leadership. For two of the contending parties—the feudal Baltic Barons and their German supporters—it was the 'beginning of the end'; and for the other two—the Latvian Nationalists and the Russian Bolsheviks—it was the 'end of the beginning'. And for a fifth group—the Allied Military Mission to the Baltic under General Sir Hubert Gough (the unfortunate commander of the British Fifth Army in France) and the Talents Mission to Latvia—it was an undisguised muddle from which it was difficult to see how any credit or advantage could accrue to the Allied cause.

The Baltic Barons were the hereditary rulers of the Baltic States. They were descended from the Teutonic Knights who had colonised these inhospitable lands in the thirteenth century. They were the backbone of the local counter-revolutionary forces, but they would not have been strong enough to resist the effects of the Russian Revolution on their own. When the Treaty of Brest-Litovsk was signed between Germany and the Soviets in 1917, the Baltic States were ceded to Germany. It looked to ardent German geo-politicians as if their dream of the German '*drang nach osten*' was becoming a reality and that Germany would be able to re-establish the Teutonic Knights' Empire in the eastern Baltic as a stepping stone to German expansion in the underpopulated Slav Lands. A year later, the German Army's defeat on the Western Front and the German internal collapse ended these dreams as far as the German Government was concerned. The officers of the victorious German armies on the Eastern Front did not lose heart so easily. They set about salvaging as much of their national aspirations as they could by offering their services to the Allies to stem the Red surge from the East. Having no troops of their own avail-

6 The 'Road to Loos': the route by which the Irish Guards advanced

THE WESTERN FRONT, 1915–18

7 In the trenches after Loos: Captain Alexander with the 2nd Irish Guards

8 Major the Hon. H. R. L. Alexander, DSO, MC, The Irish Guards

ALEXANDER IN 1918

able for the task, the Allies reluctantly accepted this German help. Graf Rudiger von der Goltz, the German garrison commander, became *de facto* Allied military commander in the Baltic States and leader of the counter-revolutionary elements. His forces consisted of regular German troops, the local Baltic Landeswehr and the notorious German Frei Corps of free-booters from which the Nazi party and its storm-troopers sprang a few years later. The Baltic Landeswehr was a territorial force recruited exclusively from the Balts—the teutonic element of the Baltic population—and officered either by German expatriates or by hereditary Baltic barons. The Balts and the Germans were united in their aim of re-establishing Germanic rule as far east as possible at the expense of the Soviets.

At first von der Goltz made steady progress and came close to re-establishing German rule in Latvia and Lithuania. His success was his undoing. It opened the Allies' eyes to his real intentions. Some time before Talents and Alexander arrived, he had received orders from Marshal Foch, the Allied Supreme Commander, to withdraw all German troops back to Germany and to hand over control of the local forces resisting the Bolshevik invaders to the Allied sponsored native governments of Estonia, Latvia and Lithuania. One of the principal tasks of Gough's Allied Military Mission to the Baltic was to ensure compliance with these orders. Von der Goltz was in no hurry to obey.

Just before the Talents Mission arrived in Latvia, von der Goltz staged a *coup d'état* ousting the Lettish Government. Without the overt support of the German Government, he set in motion his personal plans to subjugate the Baltic States and, if it proved practicable, to march on St Petersburg 'to consolidate the Baltic Provinces', as he put it, 'on behalf of the allies'. He took Riga, using the Baltic Landeswehr to heighten the illusion that it was the Latvians themselves who were freeing their lands of Bolshevism. The Letts soon learned the meaning of 'liberation' at the hands of the Landeswehr and German Frei Corps. Three thousand men and women were shot in Riga and a further 500 in Mitau on the pretext that they were Russian collaborators. No distinction was made between Lettish Nationalists and Bolsheviks. Both were equally dangerous to Balt rule. One of Alexander's first tasks was to prevent any further executions being ordered by Major Fletcher, the Prussian commander of the Landeswehr, whom von der Goltz had appointed Governor of Riga.

Von der Goltz's next step was to invade Estonia in preparation for his advance on St Petersburg. Major Fletcher's Landeswehr was sharply checked at Wendau by the Estonians, and when von der Goltz reinforced him with the notorious 'Iron Division' of the German Frei Corps, it too was repulsed. Von der Goltz began to appreciate that his forces possessed neither the resources nor the cohesion to go it alone against the wishes of the Allies. His aim became to gain time while he transferred the bulk of his forces to a 'local' commander who would act as a 'front' for Germany in the Baltic until the Allied missions withdrew as they were bound to do one day. The man he chose was a White Russian romanticist, styling himself General Prince Awaloff-Bermondt, who dreamed of raising a great 'Russian Army of the West' to reconquer Bolshevik Russia. The Frei Corps commanders had little faith in Bermondt or in his fantastic schemes, but he served their purpose as von der Goltz pointed out in his memoirs:

> I was determined to hinder the withdrawal of German troops . . . obviously I wanted as slow a withdrawal as possible for in the meantime Bermondt could complete the recruitment of his corps . . . so much did I believe that the Bermondt Project was the last 'Heil' of Germany, that I was determined to do everything possible to see it through. (R. G. L. White, *The Vanguard of Nazism*, p. 124)

Alexander became embroiled in the military aspects of the negotiations which took place after von der Goltz's check at Wendau. He was instrumental in suggesting the compromises which led to the armistice of Wendau and von der Goltz's agreement to withdraw from Latvia. The problem then arose as to what should be done with the German officered Landeswehr. It could not remain under von der Goltz; nor could it be disbanded as it represented the only experienced local Latvian force with which the Lett Government could oppose the Soviet invaders when the Germans had gone. It had to be converted by some means or other into a part of the indigenous army of the new Latvian State. In a dispatch to the Foreign Office dated 13 July 1919, Talents reports the proposed solution to the Landeswehr problem:

> In the crisis through which we have been passing, I felt justified in agreeing with General Gough to the appointment of Lt Col Alexander as commander of the Landeswehr. This officer has exceptional qualifications of experience, intelligence and personality for this post. He is trusted by Balts and Letts alike, and if anyone can carry through the reorganisation of the Landeswehr, he will do it. (*Documents of Br. Foreign Policy, 1919–1939*, III, p. 18)

He expands this terse official account in his memoirs:

> The problem of the Baltic Landeswehr had also to be disentangled immediately. This force had stayed behind in Riga, when their German brothers-in-arms had left it, and it was for Gough, under our armistice, to choose a commander for them. They were restless and apprehensive about their future. Willing enough to fight against the Bolsheviks, they could not be expected to

fight in case of need with the Latvians against the Germans. Gough and I talked this question over and decided that Alex was the right, indeed the only, man for this particularly difficult command. He was already well liked and trusted by both Balts and Letts. Irish blood and Irish experience both helped him. (A year later I passed from the Baltic to work in Southern Ireland and was struck at once by the similarity of some of their problems, especially those due to racial differences between those who had owned and those who tilled the land.) So I agreed to spare Alex, and we arranged a meeting for him with the leaders of the Landeswehr. This was promising. Major Fletcher, I heard, behaved very well in the background at this point. He discouraged all suggestions of opposition and urged his men to accept the new regime with a good heart. So Alex, still in his twenties, took over command of some 2,000* Balts and led them off to the Bolshevik front up country in Latvia. (Talents, p. 345)

Von der Goltz protested vehemently about the transfer of the Landeswehr command to a British officer, and so it may seem surprising that Fletcher, a German officer, should acquiesce so easily. He had little choice. Von der Goltz wanted the Landeswehr to enter Bermondt's service, but Fletcher despised Bermondt as much as he admired Alexander with whom he had had many dealings during the past few months. He rated Bermondt's abilities and von der Goltz's chances of remaining in the Baltic States so low that he decided to throw in his lot with the Allies. He was an East Prussian by birth with greater sympathy for the Baltic people than other Germans. Thus, he countermanded von der Goltz's order to the Landeswehr to join Bermondt and notes in his own memoirs:

> The last favour that I could do for my beloved Balts was this: I did not lead the Baltic Landeswehr into the ranks of the so called Bermondt Army. . . . My successor, the English Lieutenant Colonel Alexander, was an English nobleman and a front fighter of the West . . . a true gentleman. (White, p. 121)

Walter Duranty, the New York Times Correspondent in the Baltic gives his impressions of Alexander at the time. In his book *I write as I please*, written in the mid 1930s, before Alexander emerged as an important military figure, he says:

> I found . . . a young British officer in khaki uniform with the insignia of a Colonel but wearing Russian high boots; beside him there was a grey astrakhan cap, of the type worn in the Cossack regiments. . . . Alex, as everyone called him, was the most charming and picturesque person I have ever met, and one of the two soldiers I have known who derived a strong, positive and permanent exhilaration from the worst of danger. (Duranty, p. 47)

* The figure was, in fact, 7,000 Balts.

Alexander's eventual success with the Landeswehr was not bought easily. He took over a force in which motives were dubious and often contradictory, and in which personal ambitions ran high and discipline was uncertain. His achievements are best judged by two yard-sticks: his troops' military success against the Bolshevik forces and its continued loyalty to the Latvian Government through himself as their commander. The former was not revealed until the turn of the year when the Landeswehr played a prominent part in the expulsion of the Red Army from Latvia; but the latter was tested almost at once.

Alexander's arrival to take over command was not auspicious. When the Guard of Honour, drawn up to receive him, was brought to attention, it smartly turned about in a studied insult to this interloping British officer. Alexander carried the day with a laugh and a good humoured remark about it hardly being a gentlemanly way to receive anyone, but that he understood how they felt.* Face was saved on both sides. The Baltic Barons recognised in him one of their own kith and kin from another land. He belonged to the hereditary establishment in which the code of the 'gentleman' was a potent factor. His Landeswehr Adjutant, Baron Joachim von Hahn, throws an interesting light on Alexander's political views in the early 1920s at the beginning of the social revolution which was set in train throughout the world by events in Russia. Hereditary class distinction was still unmistakably ingrained in the fabric of the British regular army at that time.

> Alexander was intelligent and understood quickly and instinctively, and thought things out with exceptional clarity and logic. His education had been typically English and, therefore, pragmatic. . . . For Germany he had sympathy and a high opinion of her army. . . . Politically Lt Colonel Alexander believed in democracy. I often discussed with him and he explained to me the system of democracy in Britain and North America. He stressed the need for us to reckon, in the circumstances in which we found ourselves, with this form of government, if we expected support from the West. . . . It was no good, he thought, to insist on ancient rights to property, to be guided by former political privilege and to live on the memories of past services rendered in the history of one's country. This way of thinking was out of date. (Nachrichtenblatt of the Baltic Gentries, Munich, December 1969)

Von der Goltz retired from Riga early in July. Much to the consternation of the Allies, he abruptly halted his withdrawal on a line about 15 miles south of the city ostensibly to be available to counter-attack any renewed Bolshevik offensive which might be launched in the wake of his

* Personal account of Colonel Lieven, son of Baron Lieven of the Landeswehr.

departure. By this time Alexander had marched at the head of the Landeswehr to oppose the Soviet forces at Kreutzberg on the Dwina River, 70 miles east of Riga. The Documents on British Foreign Policy contain an extract reporting this move:

> The Landeswehr are now in course of proceeding to the Bolshevik front. Colonel Alexander has had many difficulties with them, the latest being an objection on the part of the Landeswehr to go to the front, on the ground that the Lettish Command would probably place them in a position where they would be decimated by the Bolsheviks. This attitude was accentuated by a disinclination on the part of the People's Council to pass the amnesty, which was one of the points with which Mr. Ulmanis's Government undertook on their appointment to deal. There is some nervousness in Lettish circles lest the Landeswehr should combine with Colonel Bermondt if he reaches the front in their neighbourhood. On the whole, however, it appears probable that once they are engaged with the Bolsheviks, most of the difficulties hitherto experienced with this force will be forgotten. (III, p. 101)

Von der Goltz's halt south of Riga was designed to allow his German units to change their German colours to those of the Bermondt Army. One German officer remarked: 'We fastened the Russian cockades to our caps, though we cunningly allowed the German ones to show over the top of them. . . . We won the first battle for England. In the second we proposed to do the English out of what they had achieved by the first.'

All Talents' efforts to persuade von der Goltz to honour the Wendau armistice agreements and to continue his withdrawal to Germany failed. At the beginning of October Bermondt, with von der Goltz's backing, advanced on Riga to depose the Lett Government. Fortunately for Latvian independence, Bermondt proved as incompetent as Major Fletcher had forecast. His ill-assorted and ill-ordered forces met with resolute Latvian resistance and were repulsed in front of Riga by the newly raised Latvian Army, equipped by Gough with British weapons; and by the fire of ships of the Royal Navy in the Gulf of Riga and the lower reaches of the Dwina. During the battle, Talents tried to send orders to Alexander to leave the Landeswehr and to make for the nearest British Military Mission post because he felt certain that the Landeswehr would mutiny and rejoin von der Goltz. In the confusion prevailing in Riga, it proved impossible for the courier to reach Alexander in time. As Talents expected, the officers of the Landeswehr were sorely tempted to march on Riga to help the German forces, whom they felt were the most likely element in this untidy struggle for power to restore Balt supremacy. Walter Duranty explained why this did not happen:

Within a month of his taking command, the Landeswehr was devoted to Alexander, who combined the qualities of a first-class soldier with those virtues of aristocracy, courage, honour and 'noblesse oblige' which had reached a fine flower amongst the Baltic Barons. It was he, quite unconsciously, who prevented them marching on Riga to complete the von der Goltz-Bermondt plans that autumn. As one of them told me 'we wanted to march on Riga and perhaps we ought to have done it in our own interests, because these damned Letts have seized our estates and it is not likely that the British or French will do much for us to get them back, as the Germans would have done. But in that case we should have had to knock Alexander on the head, and we liked him far too much, so we stayed quiet in our trenches and von der Goltz retreated. (Duranty, p. 157)

Alexander had won the Landeswehr's loyalty with the same charm of manner, the same genuineness of purpose, and the same obvious professional military efficiency as he was to display a quarter of a century later when he first met the American and French forces in Tunisia. Claus Grimm, in his obituary to Alexander in the *Baltische Briefe*, writes:

Here on this god-forsaken front in the East, the foreign officer won the hearts and the loyalty of the Balt volunteers by his concern for them and by his character. Winter came early in 1919, and the poorly equipped troops suffered much from the fierce cold. Alexander asked his mother in Britain to organise a collection of winter clothing and to send this to the front. He contacted the Allied supply organs to improve the supplies of his troops and saw to it that this was done.

The military test of Alexander's leadership of the Landeswehr did not come until September when preparations were being made to drive the Bolsheviks out of Lettgallen, the most easterly province of Latvia. The Landeswehr held the centre of the anti-Bolshevik front around Kreutzberg (modern Krustpils) on the Dwina, with Polish forces to the south in Lithuania and the rest of the Latvian Army to his north. He followed the policy which he had learned from bitter experience with the Irish Guards of committing his new command carefully with very thorough preparation. Furthermore he decided to follow the British Army's traditional method of winning dominance by patrol action before launching a major assault. As a preliminary operation to build up the confidence of his command in himself and of the Latvian Government in the Landeswehr, he staged a limited offensive to seize the small town of Lievenhoff some ten kilometres to the east. The attack was successful, but the confidence which it should have engendered was marred by the discovery of clandestine communication between some of his officers and Bermondt's headquarters. This led to an awkward and unpleasant screening of all his subordinates to weed out the unreliable elements. His combination of tact and firmness kept the Landeswehr together and to its duty.

For the next three months Alexander continued to build up the morale and to improve the training of his force by a series of carefully rehearsed raids, designed to upset the motley collection of Soviet units opposing him, and to provide his Chief of Staff, Baron Rahden, with the intelligence of the enemy positions which he needed to plan the coming offensive. During this preparatory period Alexander moved constantly from detachment to detachment, carrying out personal reconnaissances on skis. One of these sorties nearly ended in disaster. He was fired on by mistake and slightly wounded by one of his own patrols. The incident was jokingly referred to thereafter by the Landeswehr as the 'Alexander Shoot'!

On 11 November and 20 December the Landeswehr carried out two substantial raids, taking 125 prisoners in the first and destroying a complete enemy artillery battery in the second. The Landeswehr was now ready for the offensive which the Latvian High Command ordered to begin on 3 January 1920.

The offensive lasted for the whole of January and was fought in the great snow covered wastelands of Lettgallen. The Landeswehr history is a prosaic record of advances made, villages captured, and so forth, but occasionally it gives a glimpse of the conditions (*Die Baltische Landeswehr*, pp. 28–38):

> . . . the advance was made in difficult conditions and required a great effort from the troops who moved forward for twelve hours over snow-bound roads, in blizzards and in a temperature of minus 27 degrees.
>
> . . . so far the Landeswehr had lost few killed, but it had undergone great hardship from the cold. There had been many cases of frostbite and conditions were made worse by a sudden outbreak of influenza. Meanwhile the enemy, who had withdrawn in depth, managed to regroup and reinforce with reserves, amongst whom were the International Communist Regiment. . . .
>
> . . . An enemy armoured train, carrying four guns and machine guns intervened in the action at close range. Despite stubborn Soviet defence the village was taken by assault. The armoured train withdrew still firing fiercely.
>
> . . . detachment was faced by 1 Soviet Regiment composed mainly of Chinese. The attack was made in difficult conditions with snow knee-deep, lack of any cover, and poor support from the Latvian troops on either flank . . . the Landeswehr reached all its objectives after heavy fighting. The enemy units broke up. 31, 23, 21 and 1 Soviet Regiments had had heavy losses and were withdrawing. . . .

The moral ascendancy achieved by the Landeswehr before Christmas resulted in the initial Soviet resistance being light and dispirited. As the advance went on, Soviet reserves were rushed up and fighting became more stubborn. Alexander made no attempt to interfere with the minor tactics of his subordinates. From Baron Hahn's account it seems that he used the style of command which he adopted later in the Mediterranean:

> In conference and briefings Alexander insisted on thorough presentation of the facts, asked some questions about the object of the course of action suggested and intended, and then gave his opinion. This opinion had to be respected and obeyed. When he made no comment to a suggestion it was a sign that it did not meet with his approval or that he considered the idea impracticable. (*Nachrichtenblatt*, December 1969)

Alexander rarely said 'no' openly, but it was quite clear when he approved or disapproved. Each subordinate drew his own conclusions, and, in so doing, felt that it was his own plan which he was implementing. If it went well, Alexander was never stinting in praise; if it went wrong, there were no recriminations, provided the officer concerned had done his best.

On 21 January the Landeswehr captured Rezekne, the capital of Lettgallen and by the end of the month had driven their opponents over the Sinyukha River which marked the traditional boundary of the Lett lands. In a month's fighting Alexander's men had advanced 160 kilometres under appalling conditions, engaging and routing six Soviet Regiments, taking 2,000 prisoners and suffering the surprisingly low loss of 29 killed themselves. The numbers of the wounded and frost-bite cases are not recorded. As a postscript to their campaign, they captured the entire staff of the 247 Bolshevik Regiment just before peace negotiations were started with the Soviets.

The Latvian Government were remarkably restrained in their victory. They did not attempt to annex more than their traditional lands. They signed an armistice with the Russians in March and a definitive peace treaty with them in August. Meanwhile the story of Alexander's Landeswehr moved towards a happy ending. Most of his officers and men decided to throw in their lot with the new Government of their native land. They accepted also the Government's proposals for the Landeswehr's absorption into the Latvian Army. On 31 March Alexander handed over command and in his farewell speech paid the Landeswehr a compliment which the surviving members prize to this day: 'You are gentlemen and sportsmen. I am proud to have commanded an Army composed entirely of gentlemen.'

General Ballod the Latvian C-in-C thanked him publicly the following day on behalf of the Government for his services to Latvia. On reaching England he returned to the Irish Guards, expecting to be engulfed in the peacetime routine of public duties in London and Windsor. He was mistaken. Peace had come to the Baltic, but not to the Eastern Mediterranean. The Irish Guards were not to stay in England much longer.

The Chanak crisis was the Suez of the 1920s. Things said and done by Lloyd George's Government in 1922–23 bear many similarities to those of the Eden administration in 1956. Mustapha Kemal played the Nasser of Turkey; Lloyd George and Churchill anticipated the roles of Eden and Selwyn Lloyd; and the Dardenelles stood in the place of the Suez Canal as the strategic issue at stake. The outcome might have been much the same had it not been for the personality of General Sir Charles Harington, the British C.-in-C. at Constantinople, and for the difference in the efficiency of the communication systems of the two eras. Had it not been for the political wisdom of Harington and for the inefficiency of the telegraph system between London and Constantinople, the ultimatum sent by Lloyd George's Cabinet to Harington for delivery to Mustapha Kemal might have led to Anglo-French military action in just as inauspicious circumstances as Eden's ultimatum to Egypt and Israel. In 1923 the fatal telegram arrived too late and stayed in Harington's pocket until the crisis was over.

The full story of the Chanak crisis does not belong to a book about Alexander because he and the 1st Battalion, The Irish Guards, whose command he assumed in 1922, formed part of the Constantinople garrison and were only indirectly involved. As a battalion commander Alexander was not closely associated with the formulation of Harrington's policies, but he did gain a ring-side view of the C-in-C's delicate balancing act amid the conflicting motives of Britain's war-time Allies. This view was important because it gave Alexander further experience in politico-military problems and in the pragmatism of British policy. There are echoes of Harington's patient firmness in Alexander's own style as an Allied C-in-C. The art lies in providing policies attractive to the Government of the day before the members of that Government have been able to define what it is they wish to do. It is rarely any use waiting for direction. Success lies in suggesting what the direction should be. Alexander was to exploit this technique to the full when acting as Churchill's champion in the Mediterranean in 1943–44.

There were five major parties in the Chanak crisis. The Turks, led by Mustapha Kemal, were determined to prevent further dismemberment of their country; the Greeks, first under Venizelos and then under King Constantine, were equally determined to grab as much of Turkey as they could, including Constantinople if the opportunity arose; Lloyd George's Government held the right of free passage through the Dardenelles as strategically and emotionally sacrosanct; the Allied Governments of France and Italy preferred to advance their own interests by covertly currying favour with Kemal while overtly supporting Great Britain in her self-imposed role of keeper of the sacred soil of Gallipoli; and finally the interfering Americans, represented by Admiral Bristol, were heartily disliked by all the other parties in the dispute.

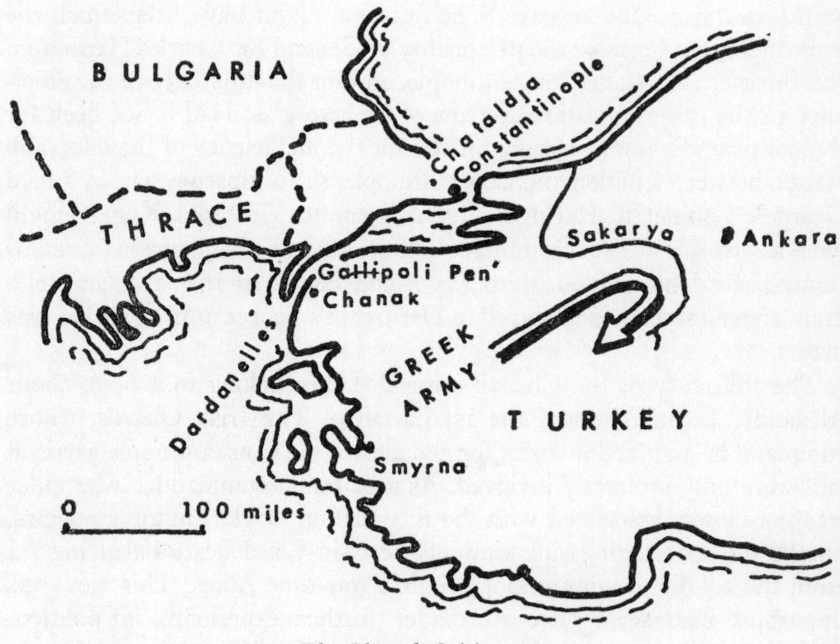

10 The Chanak Crisis, 1922–23

There was an important similarity between the Baltic and Chanak crisis. The British Government tried to use the Greek Army to impose the Allied will on the Turks in the same way that von der Goltz had acted as its agent against the Bolsheviks. The difference between the performance of the Greeks and Germans was soon painfully obvious. The Greek Army advanced on Kemal's capital at Ankara in July 1921. It was soundly beaten on the Sakarya River as much through its own ineptitude as by Kemal's brilliance. The resulting rise in Turkish morale and the clear danger to the Allied position in Constantinople and the Dardenelles, if Kemal decided to reassert Turkish sovereignty by force, led to Harington calling for reinforcements from England. Alexander's battalion was nominated by the War Office as part of these reinforcements.

For the third time in his career Alexander marched out of barracks at the head of his troops on his way to war—a platoon in 1914, a company in 1915 and this time as the peace-time commander of a battalion. The voyage to Alexandria and thence to Constantinople in the troopship *Derbyshire* took three weeks in cramped conditions. On disembarkation they marched to the old Turkish barracks at Tash Kishla, which was to be their home for the next 12 months. Alexander and his battalion had no experience of peace-keeping operations, but the techniques needed are so deeply ingrained in British military tradition that this proved no handicap. The battalion marched to Tash Kishla through the winding cobbled streets behind the pipes and drums with bayonets fixed, creating an impression of good humoured but disciplined power. There is something about British infantry battalions which give confidence to minorities without over-irritating a recalcitrant majority. The military appearance of the Irish Guards drew a personal note from the Commander-in-Chief: 'Just a line to thank you and to tell you I was very much struck with the appearance of your battalion yesterday. It was a treat to see them and I am sure everyone was very much impressed. . . .'

Three days later, on 15 May 1922, Alexander was gazetted a substantive lieutenant-colonel. He was just 31. The average age for such promotion in peace is 40–42. For the first time since 1914 his substantive rank coincided with that of his job. May in Constantinople marked another milestone in his career. So far he had never been faced for any length of time with the boredom of peace-time routine. In Constantinople boredom was the enemy. He had to find ways of alleviating the irksomeness of the numerous guards and pickets needed to keep the peace, and of providing counter-attractions to the brothels and cafés of the city. Instead of having to grapple with operational problems, he had to concentrate on the morale of his battalion, which, as always in such situations, depended on well-organised administration and an obvious fairness in the allocation of unpopular duties; and upon the British Army's panacea to all its woes—competitive games. Alexander had always been keen on physical fitness and set an example to the battalion, taking an immense pride in the selection and training of the company and regimental teams. If Kipling had recorded this period of the 1st Battalion's history, he would have repeated the phrase he used about the 2nd Battalion in 1915—'the battalion found itself a happy battalion'. It had a commander whom it trusted; in whom it had great confidence; and of whom it was justly proud.

In July the political and military situations worsened. The Greek Army in Anatolia had reached the end of its endurance. King Constantine and his advisers in Athens realised that a diversion was essential. The British Ambassador was curtly informed that the Greeks proposed to restore peace by occupying Constantinople. They had six divisions ready in Thrace. There was no time for detailed consultations with London. Harington had to act. Issuing a proclamation that any attack on Constantinople would be opposed by Allied forces whether it came from Greek or Turk, he set off with his staff and battalion commanders to inspect the Chataldja Lines covering the city from the west upon which the Turks had resisted the Bulgarians in the Balkan war of 1912. Alexander found himself briefing his company commanders on precautionary steps to be taken to oppose the Greeks if they carried out their threat.

In the initial deployment the Irish Guards were given the thankless task of preserving order in the city while the rest of the garrison took up defensive positions. A month later they relieved the Sherwood Foresters in Bunar Fort on the extreme right of the Chataldja Lines. The landscape could hardly have been more desolate. Little had been done to clear up the battlefield since the fighting in 1912. The ground was still littered with unexploded shell; old trenches were strewn with discarded ammunition boxes, cartridge cases and broken rusty bits of equipment; buildings were as roofless as they had been at the end of the battle; and many of the old Turkish guns stood forlornly dismantled in their emplacements. The days went by. The excitement of deploying for action waned. No Greek Army appeared. Harington's deterrent act of manning the city's defences succeeded. Disaster had befallen the Greeks elsewhere.

Constantine's threat to Constantinople led to the Turkish attack on the Greek Army on the Sakarya River. Kemal opened his offensive on 26 August. Greek morale snapped. Soldiers refused to obey their officers, and officers their generals. An indisciplined, frightened and vengeful mob, venting its fury on innocent Turkish villages in its path, cut its way back to the coast at Smyrna. News of the Turkish triumph and the Greek atrocities spread like a bush fire through Constantinople. Alexander was soon back with his Irish Guardsmen in the city ready to part Greek from Turk. The British battalions were ordered to show themselves and Alexander led his battalion on a series of marches through the narrow streets of the city. No incidents occurred, although the city remained sullen and tense for the next two months while the Chanak crisis itself flared up and then burnt itself out, thanks to the level-headedness of General Harington.*

It took a further two months for the Allied politicians to settle the affairs of Turkey at the Lausanne Conference. On 5 September Alexander embarked his battalion on ss *Egypt* and sailed with them for England.

An extract from the *Irish Guards Old Comrades Association Journal* sums up the battalion's tour in Constantinople and its impression of its commanding officer:

> I saw the square at Windsor when His Majesty King George V, accompanied by his sons, inspected the Battalion prior to their departure for Constantinople. I saw the *Derbyshire* steaming slowly through the blue Mediterranean Sea. I saw the landing at Constantinople where the Turkish dock labourers carried such an unbelievable load on their backs. I saw the march to Tash Kishla and the figure of General Sir Charles Harington as he took the salute.
>
> I saw the trenches we dug at Chataldja, the Trooping of the Colour at Constantinople in company with the French Spahis. I saw the 'armoury' where we held the guns from Kemal Pasha, the abdication of the Sultan when he sheltered in the guard room under the 'ever open eye' and the 'Blue, Red, Blue'. I saw the evacuation of Constantinople and the passage through the Straits of Messina when a sailor fell overboard. I saw the arrival at 'The Rock' and the race course at North Front, Buena Vista, and the St. Patrick's Day celebrations in pelting rain.
>
> I saw the return to Woking and then our London home at Wellington Barracks. But above all I saw the trim, slight, smiling figure which endeared itself to us all. I saw the hat at that peculiar 'Alex' angle like those of the White Russians we saw in Constantinople. It was 'Alex' who had faith in us and who brought us through without loss of prestige. (Millson, p. 52)

* The story of the Chanak Crisis is told in full in David Walder, *The Chanak Affair*.

4

Approach to High Command

> ... I, like all others who met him, was soon struck with his natural gift for leadership and his uncanny instinct for obtaining quickly and without apparent effort a solution to the many military problems given him to solve. The reason was that he is gifted with a mass of common sense, knows exactly how soldiers react in war, and is entirely practical in everything. He simply cannot be rattled.
>
> General Sir Robert Gordon-Finlayson,
> Instructor at the Staff College,
> Camberley 1926–27

There were two facets of British military life that Alexander, for all his active service experience, had not yet encountered: service on the staff and service in India. Both, in their different ways, were part of the orthodox road to high command in the British Army. Training at the Staff College—Camberley or Quetta—and a subsequent tour on the staff was one of the few ways of mastering the intricate organisational problems of a modern army. Service in India was complementary to staff training, providing practical experience in handling sizable formations of troops on active service. India was one of the few places in the world where Staff College theory could be practised in peace time. Units of the Indian Army were, unlike their counterparts in the United Kingdom, up to war strength; brigades and divisional sized forces took the field in earnest; and a live enemy gave military training a realism encountered nowhere else—tactical errors were penalised by the most ruthless military umpire, the tribesman's rifle.

It is significant that Alexander did not pass into the Staff College very high in 1926. His contemporaries in high command during the Second World War—Dill, Brooke, Montgomery and Slim—were all Staff College instructors between the wars. Montgomery was an instructor while Alexander was a student. It says a great deal for the Staff College system that a man of Alexander's practical aptitudes could do as well as he did in its theoretical atmosphere where skill in debate, both oral and on paper, takes the place of trial by action. General Sir Robert Gordon-Finlayson, summed up his impression of Alexander as a student:

> I . . . was soon struck by his natural gift for leadership and his uncanny instinct for obtaining quickly and without apparent effort a solution to the many military problems given him to solve. The reason was that he is gifted with a mass of common sense, knows exactly how soldiers react to war, and is entirely practical in everything. He simply cannot be rattled.

In 1928, when Alexander left the Staff College, the effects of war-time temporary promotions were still distorting officers' careers. In normal times, an officer entered the Staff College at about 30, well before he was due to command his regiment at about the age of 40. Alexander was then 35; too old for a junior staff appointment and yet too young to command a brigade. Reading between the lines of his record of service, it seems probable that the posting authorities found him difficult to place on the staff and welcomed a request by his regiment for him to return to them as Colonel of the Irish Guards Regimental District, an appointment which he held until January 1930 when he was selected to attend one of the first courses at the new Imperial Defence College.

In the British Army there are three levels of staff training: the Staff College (age 30) which turns regimental officers into 'all arms' officers capable of coordinating the actions of the different Arms which make up an Army; the Joint Services Staff College* (age 36) which teaches the coordination of sea, land and air forces; and finally the Imperial Defence College† (age 45) which deals with strategic problems, integrating foreign, economic, industrial and military policy. Alexander had entered the Staff College late, but he arrived at the IDC ahead of rather than behind his contemporaries, although he had still not held a staff appointment.

After his IDC Course, Alexander was given his first and only military staff appointment in Whitehall. He was appointed to the Directorate of Military Training at the War Office, a post for which he was eminently suited. If he could not be leading men in action, the next best thing was their training for action upon which all military success depends at tactical level. He had run successful training cadres in 2nd Irish Guards during 1915–17; then his battalion had become the Guards reinforcement training unit after their heavy losses in March 1918; and finally he had gone home to be an instructor at Aldershot in the latter half of 1918. His aptitude for training was to re-emerge in 1940–41. The surprising thing about his appointment was that he filled a General Staff Officer, 2nd

* Instituted after the Second World War, now renamed the National Defence College.
† Renamed the Royal College of Defence Studies in 1970.

Grade appointment, a post normally filled by a major, showing that the Military Secretary, who appoints officers on the Staff, was in some doubt about his abilities outside regimental affairs. These doubts did not last long. A year later, he was appointed General Staff Officer, 1st Grade, to Headquarters Northern Command at York, a post more appropriate to his rank of full colonel. He was not to return to Whitehall again until he became Minister of Defence in Churchill's last Conservative administration in 1952.

The change from 2nd to 1st grade appointment and the transition from London to York were accompanied by another change. He married Lady Margaret Bingham, younger daughter of the Earl of Lucan, direct descendant of Field Marshal the Earl of Lucan, who commanded the British Cavalry in the Crimean War. Two pleasant years followed in the north of England. Then his apprenticeship on the staff was brought to an abrupt end with a posting to India. He was to command the Nowshera Brigade on the North-West Frontier. He had commanded 4th (Guards) Brigade temporarily in 1918; the Nowshera Brigade was to be his first substantive brigade command and the first public acknowledgment by the British Army that he was to be one of its future commanders. The Nowshera Brigade was an operational force ready for immediate action. Instead of consisting of Guards battalions which he knew so well, its order of battle was:

2nd Battalion, The Duke of Wellington's Regiment
3rd Battalion, The 2nd Punjab Regiment
5th Battalion, The 12th Frontier Force Regiment
2nd Battalion, The 15th Punjab Regiment.

Looking to the days ahead it is worth noting how Alexander came to learn so much about the various national contingents which made up his Allied Armies in Italy. He had learned to respect his opponents, the Germans, fighting them in 1914–18 and commanding them in the Landeswehr in 1920. During the Talents Relief Mission he had lived with the Poles, who were to play such a heroic part in storming Cassino in 1944. Now he was to meet the Indian Army which was to provide no less than four divisions in the El Alamein and Italian campaigns. He was also to learn the rudiments of mountain warfare which were to stand him in good stead in the Italian fighting. He had ample experience of the rolling fields of Picardy, the water meadows of Flanders and the snow swept plains of Latvia. His knowledge of mountain warfare was confined to Staff College exercises and the hearsay of the large number of British officers who, for several generations, had toiled up Indian mountain sides.

In one respect, Alexander's arrival in Nowshera turned the clock back 20 years. It was like rejoining the Irish Guards in 1911. He re-entered the atmosphere of the old Imperial Army, which had died, as far as he was concerned, at Ypres in 1914. The organisation, training and thinking of the Indian Army had the feel of *Infantry Training 1905*. The First World War had been an unfortunate aberration. Real soldiering, as the Indian Army knew it, consisted of columns marching through inaccessible country, using pack transport, to deal with recalcitrant tribes by skill at arms rather than the weight of modern, expensive equipment. The parsimony of the Government of India and the predilections of the British officers of the Indian Army, ensured a return to the Kipling era.

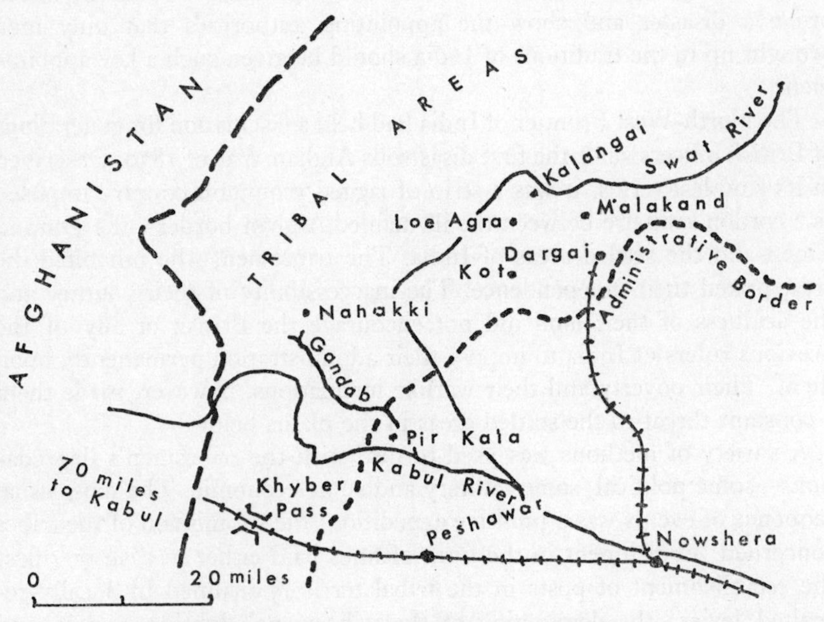

11 The North-West Frontier: Malakand and Mohmands, 1935

It is the dream of every brigade commander to see active service during his short tenure of command. In peace time this dream is rarely fulfilled. Alexander was lucky. In his three years in command of the Nowshera Brigade, he fought two frontier campaigns: the Loe Agra in early 1935 as the Force Commander; and the Mohmand in the latter half of the same year in which his brigade formed part of a much larger force. The Peshawar District, in which the Nowshera and Peshawar Brigades were stationed, lay astride the main route from India into Afghanistan through the famous Khyber Pass. Faint shadows of the future began to fall across Alexander's path. The commander of the Peshawar Brigade was Brigadier C. J. E. Auchinleck later to become C-in-C Middle East in 1941 in succession to Lord Wavell, and himself to be superseded—rightly or wrongly—on Churchill's instructions by Alexander in August 1942. The 'Auk' was a master of frontier warfare, trusted and beloved in the Indian Army as deeply as Alexander was to become in the British Army. It was the greatest help to Alexander in his first appointment in the Indian Army to have such a staunch and experienced guide so near at hand. Both men were devoted to their profession in a selfless way. Around them, there were many unkind critics, hoping that the appointment of this Guardsman, devoid of any experience of India, Indian troops and the Frontier, would prove a disaster and show the appointing authorities that only men brought up in the traditions of India should be given such a key appointment.

The North-West Frontier of India had held a fascination for generations of British officers since the first disastrous Afghan War of 1839. Described in its simplest terms, it was a strip of jagged mountain country imposed as a cordon sanitaire between the ill-defined Afghan border—the Durand Line—and the settled areas of India. The tribesmen, who inhabited the area, prized their independence. The inaccessibility of their country and the aridness of their land did not encourage the British or any of the previous rulers of India to impose their administration permanently upon them. Their poverty and their warlike inclinations, however, made them a constant threat to the settled areas in the plains below.

A variety of methods was used to deal with the tribesmen's depredations—some political, some military and some economic. The most usual sequence of events was a punitive expedition; the submission of the tribes concerned; punishment in the form of fines paid either in cash or rifles; the establishment of posts in the tribal territory manned by locally recruited levies; the destruction of the tribesmens' fighting towers and other fortifications; and, sometimes, the most obnoxious course of all as far as the tribesmen were concerned, the construction of a road into their mountains, thus weakening their independence. In later years, the most successful system was found to be the provision of financial subsidies in return for promises of good behaviour. Gradually over the years the tribes nearest the administrative border became 'protected' or subsidised tribes, while those farther away were left to their own devices.

The subsidy system worked well with one notable exception. It was not proof against the Moslem Mullahs, who, like the priests of other religious persuasions, tended to use their spiritual authority to further their temporal ambitions. The economic benefits of the subsidies were no defence against religious threats aimed at the superstitions of the tribesmen. An ambitious Mullah had little difficulty in misconstruing some minor action by a British political agent as a threat to Islam or to tribal independence. In 1934, an anti-Government Mullah of this type, the Faqir of Alingar, gained a degree of influence in the Mohmand country which made him a threat to the stability of the area. His immediate target was the Agra area which was at the western end of the British Protected Area of Malakand, lying in the great bend of the Swat River. A treaty had been made with the tribes in the Agra area in 1907, but the terms were never rigorously enforced. In spite of warnings by the British Political Agent not to do so, the Faqir crossed the Swat with a band of his followers on a tour of religious inspection. He persuaded the Agra 'Jirga', or tribal assembly, to vow obedience to him in future and to promise to have no further dealings with the Government of India. A party of Swat Levies sent to oppose him was attacked and forced to withdraw, suffering several losses.

The Government of India, after some delay, decided to meet the Faqir's challenge and authorised the despatch of a military column to enforce the terms of the 1907 Agreement. The directive issued by Army Headquarters, India, on 18 February 1935, makes interesting reading today. An extract runs:

1. The Government of India have decided to impose the following terms on certain tribesmen in the Malakand Agency:
a. The infliction of fines on the Jirgas of Khanori and Bura Tutai.
b. The reaffirmation of the 1907 agreement with the Agra Jirga, involving the practical absorption of the territory into the Malakand Protected Area.
c. The establishment of a Levy post in the neighbourhood of Loe Agra.
2. In order to enforce the above terms the Government of India have sanctioned the movement of a column in such strength and to such a point in the Malakand Agency as may be thought necessary by the Agent to the Governor General, North-West Frontier Province, in consultation with Headquarters Northern Command.
3. The date this column will move will be fixed by Headquarters Northern Command, in consultation with the Agent to the Governor General, North-West Frontier Province.
4. During the period of negotiations the column should be so disposed as to be immediately available for operations to enforce the above terms in case of a breakdown in negotiations, or to deal with incursions from across the Swat River, should such occur. . . .

8. Instructions are being issued to No. 1 (Indian) Group, Royal Air Force, to

comply with such requests for air co-operation as you may make in connection with operations. (*History of Operations on the North West Frontier of India, 1920–35*, III; p. 168)

The GOC-in-C, Northern Command nominated the Nowshera Brigade to form the Loe Agra column to support the Political Authority.

Successful commanders in frontier warfare need three things: first, a keen tactical sense with what soldiers aptly call an eye for country, or, in other words, that sixth sense which subconsciously reveals the tactical strength and dangers of a particular area; secondly, the organisational skill needed to handle the operational and logistic problems of a mixed force fighting in inhospitable mountains with only mules and men's backs for transport; and thirdly, the strength and yet mellowness of character to impose the willing acceptance of the strictest military discipline under conditions of great personal discomfort. The Indian loves to be, and feels himself to be, a good soldier, but he finds two things difficult: planning ahead and imposing standards. His British officers filled both needs, and a mutual confidence grew up between the two races over the 300 years of the Anglo-Indian partnership. Although an Indian Army column worked to a fixed drill known and practiced by all ranks, many officers and men in the Nowshera Brigade must have wondered how their new brigadier would fare in his first frontier operation. One thing they did know; he was immensely fit physically. They had seen him walking briskly over long distances across the Nowshera countryside—far longer hikes than they would have liked to have undertaken for pleasure. They knew also that he would do anything for their welfare. For years the Kabul River had flowed alongside the Nowshera Cantonment. No one had been able to persuade the Public Works Department to pump water from it to irrigate the camps. Alexander succeeded. The cantonment became infinitely more habitable during his tour of command.

The operational plan was for the Nowshera Brigade to march through the alienated tribal area from north to south, starting at Kalangai near the Swat River, passing through the village of Loe Agra itself, and emerging at Kot, a distance of 15 miles as the crow flies, but more like 30 on the ground. Sufficient pack animals were to be provided to give the column a four-day radius of action from the road-head. One battalion, with only one day's radius of action, was to start from the southern end to improve the track northwards and to act as a supply base for the column at the end of its march. The main column would have to cross several passes over 3,000 feet high and would have to piquet heights up to 5,000 feet to ensure that the column was not ambushed during its march. With any luck this show of force would bring the inhabitants of Loe Agra back to their allegiance to the Government. If not, the column would have to re-enter the area to impose the Government's terms.

Just four months after taking over command, Alexander led the Nowshera Brigade out of its cantonments in the Vale of Peshawar on 19 February 1935. He reached Dargai three days later and exchanged wheeled for pack transport. Pushing ahead of the column with his brigade major and the CO of the advanced-guard battalion, 5/12 Frontier Force Regiment,

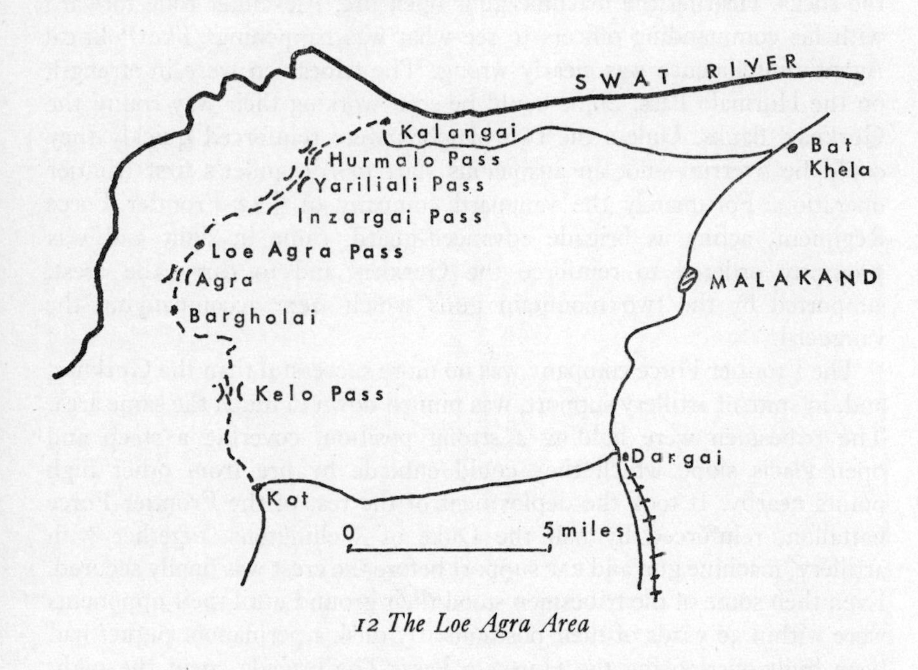

12 The Loe Agra Area

he met the Political Agent, Mr L.W.H.D. Best at Kalangai. He also met the CO of 1/4 Gurkha Rifles who had a detachment holding the area as a base for the operation. Alexander intended to march from Kalangai to Loe Agra with his column in one day. The Political Agent reported that, as far as he could tell, the nearest hostile tribesmen were on the Swat River, west of Loe Agra. Reports suggested that they were afraid to advance any further, and so it appeared that the column was not likely to be opposed during its march. The first place at which opposition might occur was on the Hurmalo Pass which could be seen from Kalangai. Alexander decided, prudently as it transpired, to piquet the Pass; and to save time ordered the CO of the Gurkhas to establish two platoons on the heights overlooking the Pass early next morning before the brigade reached Kalangai.

23 February saw a typical frontier action develop. The two Gurkha platoons set off early and were half way up the mountain side when tribesmen were seen moving along the sky-line to intercept their advance. Machine guns covering the Gurkhas opened fire and the tribesmen disappeared behind the crest. Shortly afterwards the platoons came under fire, while still well short of the crest, from tribesmen concealed amongst the rocks. Hearing the machine guns open fire, Alexander rode forward with his commanding officers to see what was happening. The Political Agent's intelligence was clearly wrong. The tribesmen were in strength on the Hurmalo Pass. Some could be seen working their way round the Gurkhas' flanks. Unless the two platoons were reinforced quickly they could be overrun—not an auspicious start to Alexander's first frontier operation. Fortunately the vanguard company of 5/12 Frontier Force Regiment, acting as brigade advanced-guard, came in sight and was promptly ordered to reinforce the Gurkhas and to carry the crest, supported by the two mountain guns which were accompanying the vanguard.

The Frontier Force company was no more successful than the Gurkhas, and, in spite of artillery support, was pinned down in much the same area. The tribesmen were holding a strong position, covering a steep and open glacis slope which they could enfilade by fire from other high points nearby. It took the deployment of the rest of the Frontier Force battalion, reinforced by half the Duke of Wellingtons, together with artillery, machine gun and RAF support before the crest was finally secured. Even then some of the tribesmen stood their ground until their opponents were within 30 yards of their positions. By dusk a permanent piquet had been built overlooking the Hurmalo Pass. The brigade spent the night being sniped in a defended camp at Kalangai. Casualties had been typical of such an action—one killed and two wounded in the Frontier Force. Three tribesmen were reported killed and 17 wounded.

Next day Alexander decided upon a reconnaissance in force, taking every precaution against further surprises, before committing the column to its march on Loe Agra. The brigade advanced in three sub-columns, one either side of the track and one up the track itself. No opposition was met on the Hurmalo Pass and so he advanced to the next pass, the Yariliali, where further piquets were established ready for the main advance to Loe Agra next day. The Sappers and Miners, helped by the infantry, set about improving the very bad track up the Hurmalo Pass so that it could be negotiated by pack animals. As dusk approached the brigade withdrew back into its camp at Kalangai for the night.

The final advance on Loe Agra was something of an anti-climax. Determined not to be forced to establish another brigade camp between Kalangai and Loe Agra, Alexander decided to use the tactic of an early start which he was to repeat on many occasions, and which broke the Indian Army's rule of not leaving a defenced camp before daylight. The brigade left camp while it was still dark and had relieved its piquets on the two passes before the sun came up. Any possible attempt by the tribesmen to oppose the advance was forestalled and the brigade found itself checked only by the physical difficulties of the country. The track was so narrow and steep that the column had to march in single file; any movement of machine guns or even commanders along the column being impossible. The country was so big that piquetting became impracticable in the time available and so risks had to be taken. Great outcrops of rock made the pack animals' task difficult, some 30 of the mules losing their footing and rolling down the mountain side with their loads. As many infantry as could be spared worked with pick and shovel alongside the Sappers and Miners to widen the track which became worse when rain began to fall later in the day. It was a tired brigade which camped that night at its objective, Loe Agra. The village was deserted and it took the Political Agent some time to re-establish contact with the inhabitants of the area, who, when they did reappear, proved to be friendly.

The brigade stayed a day in Loe Agra, reconnoitring and improving the route southwards, while the Political Agent persuaded the local Jirga to accept the Government's terms. A levy post was established and manned by Swat Levies before the brigade set off for Kot. Three days later it was back in its cantonments in Nowshera. No one believed that this was the end of the affair. The pack animals were, therefore, left at Dargai, ready for a return match with the Faqir of Alingar.

The second round started on 5 March. Intelligence arrived that the Faqir had crossed the Swat with a large lashkar (a tribal force varying in size from about 200 to 2,000 men) and was heading for Loe Agra to re-establish his authority. That night the levy post was evacuated in the face of the advancing lashkar and the Nowshera Brigade was ordered to return immediately. Anticipating just such an order, Alexander had organised a small mobile force, ready to move at short notice, called 'Flycol', consisting of the 3/2 Punjab Regiment with a mountain and a medium artillery battery, a Sapper and Miner section, a rifle company and machine gun section of Gurkhas, and the usual signals and logistic detachments. This time Alexander decided to enter the Agra area from the south and to use Bargholai as an advanced base for operations in the Loe Agra area.

'Flycol' moved fast and established itself at Bargholai four days ahead of the rest of the Brigade. Its first night was quiet; the second was disturbed by snipers; and on the third, the commander of 3/2 Punjab Regiment, Major H. P. Radley, laid a classic ambush to intercept the snipers as they moved into their sniping positions near the camp. Five tribesmen were hit, three of whom died. Next day the brigade arrived, and the day after Alexander was back in a deserted Loe Agra. The levy post was reestablished and the Faqir withdrew across the Swat. The operation had

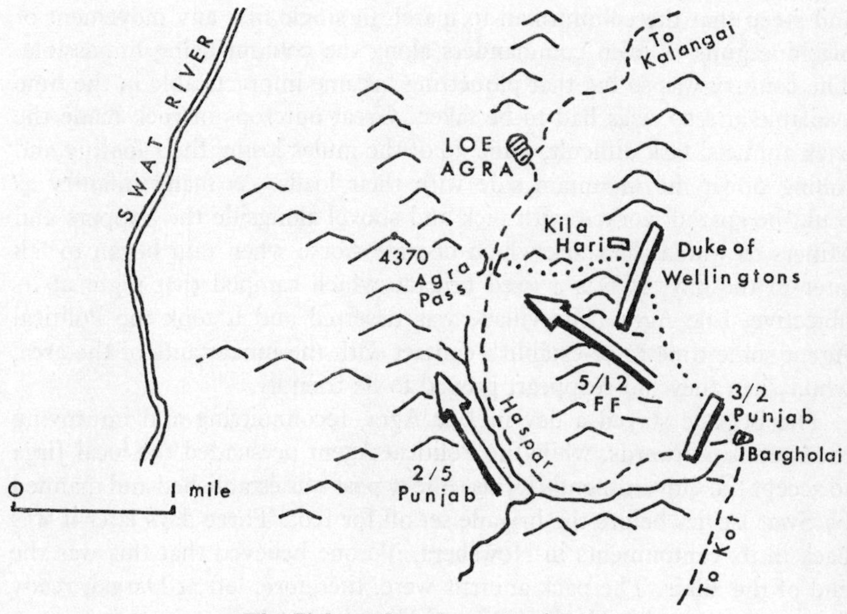

13 The Fight at Loe Agra, April 1935

been quick, neat and successful, but the Faqir had not been discredited by battle. Alexander decided to lay the ground work for an even quicker return next time. Before withdrawing he improved the tracks into the area from the south, and stationed the Duke of Wellingtons with a mountain battery at Bargholai with 'Flycol' in support at Kot. He was ready for the third and final round.

Within ten days reports arrived of the Faqir crossing the Swat once more, this time opposed by the local inhabitants and the Swat and local levies. Alexander issued orders that Loe Agra was to be denied to him by fire and that positions were to be taken up for this purpose during the night. 'Flycol' occupied the highest points on the ridge overlooking Loe Agra from the south-east and established a fortified post there to hold an infantry company and machine gun platoon, which became known as the Kila Hari piquet. Nothing happened. The battalion withdrew to Bargholai, leaving the piquet garrison to watch events.

Alarms and excursions: conflicting intelligence reports; RAF reconnaissance flights which revealed little; sniping of camps by night; relief of piquets by day; work on tracks; and all the other daily chores of frontier life went on for a week without positive evidence of the Faqir's movements. On 5 April several hostile groups were seen and engaged at long range, but no attempt seemed to be being made to enter Loe Agra. All troops, apart from the Kila Hari piquet, withdrew as usual to Bargholai camp by last light. Not long after dark, the sound of tribal drums was heard below the Kila Hari piquet, and shortly afterwards a series of attempts were made to rush one of the platoon posts. The attack then became general and lasted all night. Groups of yelling swordsmen tried to burst into the posts, but were repelled by close sustained rifle, Lewis Gun, and machine-gun fire. On occasions some of the swordsmen managed to get under the lee of the rough stone walls of the posts and either tried to leap over or to grab the garrison's weapons, only to be beaten off with revolvers and bayonets. As the attacks developed the company commander was able to identify the areas in which the lashkar was forming up its assault groups, and to bring down artillery fire upon them from the mountain batteries at Bargholai. Towards dawn a series of light signals were seen in the valley. The attacks stopped. The tribesmen withdrew while it was still dark, dragging with them the bodies of 28 killed and an unknown number wounded. In the piquet, losses were not as high as might have been feared. One Viceroy's commissioned officer died of his wounds; one Indian other rank was killed and seven were wounded. A dead tribesman was later found under the wall of a machine gun post still gripping his sword.

There was now no doubt that the Faqir's lashkar was in Loe Agra and the surrounding area bent upon a trial of strength with Alexander's column. Alexander was ready to meet the challenge, but, as was the political custom on the frontier, adequate warning in the form of an ultimatum demanding the dispersal of the lashkar had to be issued before the gloves were taken off. The Faqir, as expected, ignored the warning.

The test of success or failure in operations of this type was how little fighting occurs and not how much. The aim was to discredit the rebel leaders. If the operation was well planned, the tribesmen soon appreciated that the odds of success were too slender. They were justified, in their own minds, in deserting the cause because the mullah had been misguided enough to lead them into an impossible situation. This did not mean that the tribesmen were easily discouraged; nor that they had no stomach for a fight. On the contrary: if the odds were slightly against them, they would fight in the hopes that some tactical mistake by the Indian Army would give them the advantage. They would spot such an error and penalise it quicker than any other race. Nothing could be left to chance.

Alexander's plan was simple but effective (see fig. 13, p. 80). The RAF would interdict all movement in the Swat Valley while the medium artillery, deployed at Kalangai, would harass any bands of tribesmen who tried to escape northwards. The Nowshera Brigade itself would advance from Bargholai in a north-westerly direction on Loe Agra driving the tribesmen into the RAF and medium artillery interdiction line. The brigade would use the Haspar Valley as its axis of advance, taking and clearing the Agra Pass before descending into Loe Agra itself. The Duke of Wellington's held a firm base on the Kila Hari Ridge, while 5/12 Frontier Force and 2/5 Punjab Regiment cleared the high points on the eastern and western sides of the valley, joining hands at Point 4370 to the west of the Agra Pass. The reserve battalion, 3/2 Punjab Regiment, would exploit in any direction in which the lashkar withdrew. The operation would start with a noisy 20 minutes of artillery fire on suspected hostile positions to make sure that the Faqir was in no doubt that Alexander meant business.

The plan had just sufficient over-insurance to make the tribesmen doubt the mullah's wisdom. The attacking battalions scaled the ridges against half-hearted opposition and all objectives were overrun without loss of men or time. Exploitation proved less easy because it could not be planned or rehearsed in such detail. When the Swat Levies re-entered Loe Agra with Mr Best, the Political Agent, they were ambushed. In the subsequent clearing operation, Best was shot dead by tribesmen concealed in some standing crops near the village. By nightfall all opposition had died away and the brigade camped for the last time in Loe Agra, ready to continue its operations north-westwards towards the Swat.

The next day, 12 April, proved to be the last day of the Loe Agra campaign. Alexander's advance towards Kalangai was sporadically opposed as the Faqir made despairing attempts to hold his lashkar's loyalty. His men started to melt away to their homes, leaving him to issue empty threats of an imminent return with another and larger lashkar.

These threats were never carried out in Agra itself, but Alexander was to meet the Faqir's minions five months later in the much larger Mohmand campaign.

The Nowshera Brigade left troops in the Agra area until the one thing that the Faqir did not want was achieved. A road was built from Kot to Loe Agra and a permanent levy post was established at the roadhead. By 12 June the brigade was back in Nowshera. The conclusion of the official report reads:

> The objects of the operations had been achieved, hostiles had been ejected from the area and political control had been re-established. . . . Battle casualties had been three killed and sixteen wounded. . . . That the casualties had been so small could be attributed to the very effective use of available fire power, which demoralised the enemy and affected his shooting, also to the high state of training of Brigadier Alexander's brigade. (*Operations on the North-West Frontier*, III, p. 188)

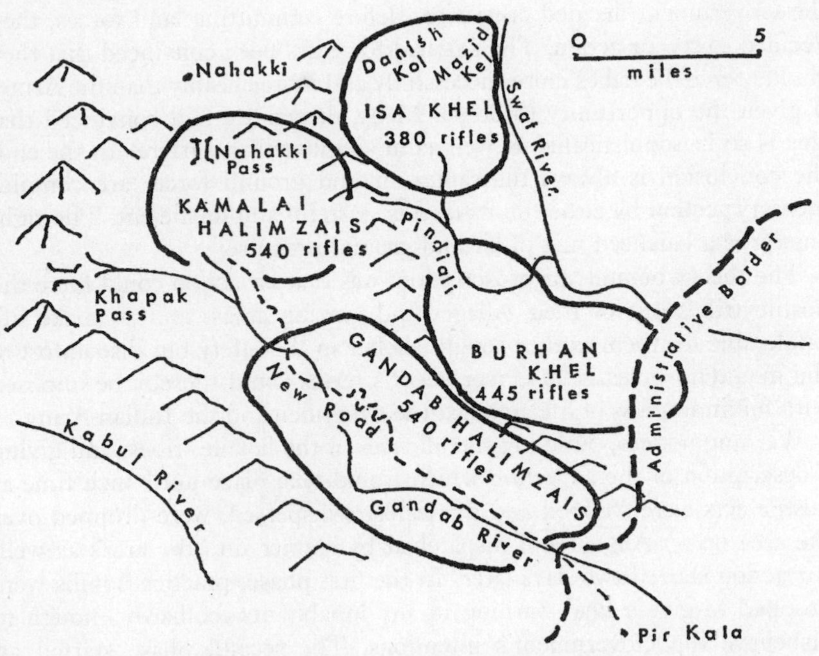

14 The Mohmand Area, Showing Tribal Strengths

As Alexander was not the principal commander in the 1935 Mohmand campaign, and as conditions were similar to the Loe Agra operations, there is no need to trace events in detail. The Government of India's opponents this time were the Haji of Turanzai and his three sons, Badshah Gul I, II and III, who were in league with Alexander's old opponent, the Faqir of Alingar. In 1933 the Haji had led a lashkar into the Lower Mohmand to punish the clans for their loyalty to the Indian Government. His defeat resulted in the construction of a road up the Gandab Valley. This road became his primary target in his continued struggle with the British Raj.

In the middle of August 1935, Badshah Gul I attacked the road with a lashkar of 1,400 men. The Peshawar Brigade was duty brigade, but its commander, the 'Auk', was on leave, and so Alexander took over temporary command of both brigades. He moved the Peshawar Brigade to Pir Kala near the Administrative Boundary at the mouth of the Gandab Valley. At Pir Kala Alexander could either intercept Badshah Gul if he tried to raid into India or he could advance up the valley to reopen the road if the Government of India authorised him to do so. On this occasion the Government decided otherwise. Before committing land forces, they decided to try air action. The RAF had for years been convinced that they could coerce the tribes more successfully and more cheaply than the Army, if given the opportunity to do so. Many airmen are still convinced that this is so in sophisticated as well as in simple tribal warfare. In the end, the conclusion is always the same: air and ground forces are complementary; action by either on its own is wasteful and inefficient. The right answer is a balanced mix of air and ground pressure.

The theory behind 'air proscription' was that air action could force the hostile tribes out of their villages and grazing areas, and so make life intolerable for them as they sought shelter in the safety but discomfort of the mountain caves. The Government's terms could thereby be imposed with minimum loss of life amongst the tribesmen and the Indian Army.

Warning notices, outlining the offences of the hostile tribes, and giving a description of the air action which would take place until such time as hostile acts were stopped and the lashkars dispersed, were dropped over the area on 17 August and dispatched by runner into the areas as well. Air action started two days later. In the first phase, practice bombs were dropped to give a final warning to any inhabitants foolhardy enough to disbelieve the Government's intentions. The second phase started an hour and a half later, in which any movement seen was attacked, not to cause casualties, but to keep the inhabitants in their caves and away from their homes and fields. In the third phase, slightly later, the villages and, in some cases, the actual houses and fighting towers of known ringleaders were destroyed by deliberate bombing.

After four days of air action, reconnaissance showed that the proscribed areas had been evacuated, but there was no sign of any submission on the part of the disaffected tribes. Complementary land action would be needed. The Nowshera Brigade was ordered to join the Peshawar Brigade at Pir Kala, together with additional force troops which would be needed for artillery support and logistic purposes. For a few days Alexander was in command of a divisional sized force, given the title 'the Mohmand Force'—'Mohforce' for short. Auchinleck arrived back from leave before operations started and assumed command of the Force, while Alexander reverted to his own brigade. Years later in Italy, he was reminded of the Mohmand air proscription when the Allied Air Forces made similar extravagant claims about Anzio and Cassino. His sarcastic remarks (see p. 277) about General Maitland Wilson's air plans probably had their origin in this period of his career.

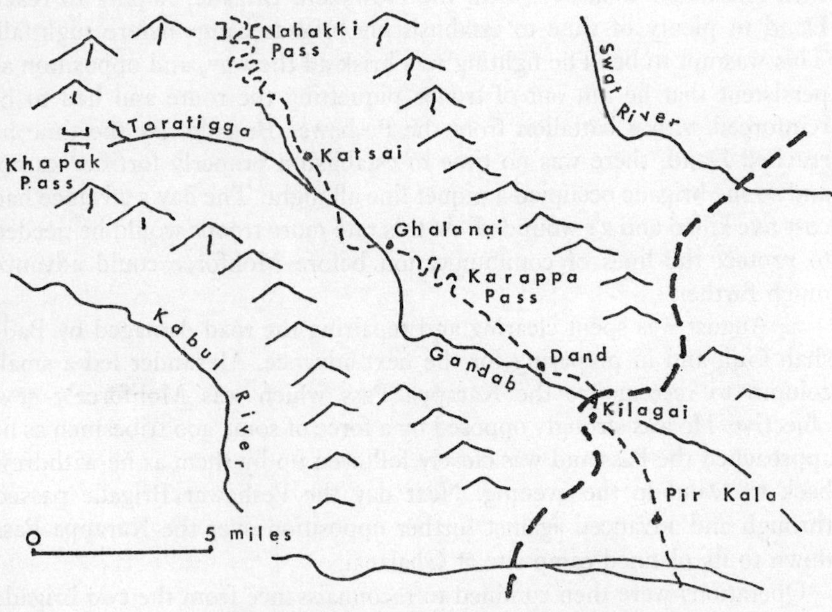

15 Mohmand Operations, August–September 1935

On 23 August the Governor of the North-West Frontier Province warned the tribes formally by proclamation that the Government intended to reopen the Gandab Road. The Government's subsequent action would depend on the attitude of the tribes. It did not take much eloquence on the part of the Haji of Turanzai to persuade the tribesmen that the next step by the Government would be the extension of the road deeper into their territory and over the Nahakki Pass. Resistance was worthwhile.

Auchinleck's plan was to advance up the road, leap-frogging his two brigades. One would piquet while the other advanced. It was some 30 miles to the head of the road which stopped at the bottom of the Nahakki Pass. For most of the way, the road ran up the Gandab Valley. There were tactically significant areas where trouble was likely: at Dand, seven miles from Pir Kala, where the road crossed a low col; at the Karappa Pass, five miles further on; at Ghalanai where it crossed the Gandab River bed; and at Katsai where the Toratigga Valley leads up to the Khapak Pass. Thereafter, the road turned into a track as it climbed the 3,000 ft Nahakki Pass which became the natural objective of 'Mohforce'.

The first day's advance was heavily opposed by Badshal Gul's lashkar. The Peshawar Brigade led up to the Administrative Border at Kilagai and then Alexander took over with the Nowshera Brigade, hoping to reach Dand in plenty of time to establish his brigade camp before nightfall. This was not to be. The fighting was brisk all the way, and opposition so persistent that he ran out of troops piquetting the route and had to be reinforced with a battalion from the Peshawar Brigade. By the time he reached Dand, there was no time to establish a properly fortified camp, and so the brigade occupied a piquet line all night. The day's advance had cost five killed and 21 wounded. At this rate more troops would be needed to protect the lines of communication before Mohforce could advance much further.

24 August was spent clearing and repairing the road damaged by Badshah Gul, and in preparing for the next advance. Alexander led a small column to reconnoitre the Karappa Pass which was Mohforce's next objective. He was strongly opposed by a force of some 400 tribesmen as he approached the Pass and was closely followed up by them as he withdrew back to Dand in the evening. Next day the Peshawar Brigade passed through and advanced against further opposition over the Karappa Pass down to its planned camp site at Ghalanai.

Operations were then confined to reconnaissance from the two brigade camps, Dand and Ghalanai, until extra troops could be brought up to guard the Lines of Communication and to allow more time for air proscription to take effect. In the meantime, Auchinleck made the Nowshera Brigade responsible for Lines of Communication while the Peshawar Brigade reconnoitred towards Katsai and the Toratigga Valley. Protecting some 13 miles of mountain road was no easy task and could only be accomplished by establishing piquets on dominant features and using vigorous patrolling between them. It says much for Alexander's dispositions and energetic handling of his brigade that no vehicles or mule columns were ambushed while his brigade held the Lines of Communication.

The losses suffered by the lashkar opposing the initial advance to Ghalanai weakened rebel determination. The elders of the tribes were disposed to negotiate, but the younger hot-heads would not give in. Two tribes did submit and others made attempts to do so. The Faqir of Alinjar joined the Haji and his sons. Their combined efforts put new life into the rebellion. A new build-up of hostile tribesmen was reported at the Nahakki and Khapak Passes. The results of air action were still falling short of the hopes of the RAF. The 2nd and 3rd Indian Brigades joined 'Mohforce' enabling the Peshawar and Nowshera Brigades to advance to disrupt this new threat. As a first step the Peshawar Brigade reconnoitred Katsai in force on 27 August. Two days later it advanced to cover a personal reconnaissance by Alexander up the Toratigga Valley toward the Khapak Pass. Preparations went ahead for the final thrust to the Nahakki and Khapak Passes, but before it could begin Alexander went down with malaria, which he had originally contracted in Constantinople. He had to be evacuated to hospital and was not present when his brigade fought its severest action trying to take the Khapak Pass. An error in tactical judgment led to two platoons of 5/12 Frontier Force being overrun and heavy casualties being incurred in four other platoons of the regiment. The adjutant of the battalion, Captain G. Meynell, was awarded a posthumous VC for his efforts to save the two platoons. This was but small consolation for the loss of 31 killed, 41 wounded and 38 injured by falling down precipitous crags on the mountain side. The action proved to be the last of the campaign. The Nowshera Brigade had lost heavily, but they had inflicted worse punishment on the enemy. On 1 October the Mohmand tribes decided to submit, and on 15 October the Governor of the North-West Frontier Province imposed the Government's terms. As the Haji foretold, the road was extended to Nahakki. The war with the Mohmands, which had started over 85 years before, was finally brought to a close as the rearguard of the Nowshera Brigade left the Gandab Valley at the beginning of November.

Alexander's part in the Loe Agra and Mohmand campaigns was deservedly rewarded with two mentions in despatches and his appointment as a Commander in the Order of the Star of India.

The rest of Alexander's stay in India was less eventful. In 1936 he was appointed ADC to King George V. What perhaps pleased him most was a request by the 2nd Punjab Regiment to become their Colonel. His links with India and her Army were secure. He renewed his acquaintance with Montgomery, who was an instructor at the Staff College, Quetta. Montgomery brought over a number of his students to study at first hand the methods and tactics of Alexander's Nowshera Brigade—a compliment indeed from this master of war. Alexander had shown during his two campaigns a mastery of tactics under what were to him new and strange conditions. He had also shown himself to be an able organiser of a force of all arms who could draw the best out of Gunners, Sappers, and logistic Services—British or Indian—just as easily as he could from his own arm, the Infantry. He won acceptance without pandering to popularity or relaxing the high standards of his upbringing in the Brigade of Guards. He had become 'Alex' to both the British and Indian Armies.

Meanwhile events in Europe were moving towards a climax. Hitler had reoccupied the Rhineland, giving the Western Powers full warning of the shape of things to come. The main change, as far as the British Army was concerned, was the appointment of Hore-Belisha as Secretary of State for War with a surgeon's mandate to rejuvenate the Service. In his determination to kill the 'Buggins' turn next' system of promotion in the Army he replaced Sir Cyril Deverell, the 63-year-old CIGS with Lord Gort, who was 53; and, in choosing the next generation of divisional commanders, he dipped down the Army List, making two far-reaching selections: Alexander was appointed to command the 1st Division and Montgomery the 3rd Division. Both divisions were designated part of the British Expeditionary Force.

In January 1938, Alexander and his family bade farewell to India. The first cycle of his career was over. Within 18 months he would be setting sail for France at the head of a division instead of a platoon. The leader had been created; could he withstand the pressures of high command in war?

9 The phoney war: Alexander showing Mr Attlee and Lord Gort round 1st Division's positions at Bachy, January 1940

10 Coast watching: Alexander about to introduce officers to Churchill near Grimsby, August 1940

11 Close Links with Brooke: Alexander talking to Sir Alan Brooke and Brigadier Morgan – later his Chief of Staff in 1945 when he became Supreme Commander, Mediterranean

EXPEDITIONARY FORCE COMMANDER (DESIGNATE)

12 Battle schooling: Alexander and Montgomery watching a Battle School demonstration, March 1941

PART II

Trial by Defeat

In this his first experience of independent command, though it ended in stark defeat, he showed all those qualities of military skill, imperturbability and wise judgement that brought him later into the first rank of Allied war leaders.

Churchill, *The Hinge of Fate*

D

5

Defeat in Flanders

> The responsibility for the Defence of Dunkirk rests with the French Admiral Commanding-in-Chief, the Naval Forces of the North; you will act under his orders; but should any orders which he may issue to you be likely, in your opinion, to imperil the safety of the Force under your command, you should make an immediate appeal to His Majesty's Government. . . .
>
> From Lord Gort's final directive to Alexander before handing over at Dunkirk, 31 May 1940 (*The War in France and Flanders* p. 234)

It has often been said that no general is worthy of his steel until he has suffered and surmounted the cruel disappointments of defeat. Alexander had experienced lost battles at regimental level; he had now to do so in higher command. Dunkirk was to mirror the Retreat from Mons; and the evacuation of Burma, the disasters of March 1918. Dunkirk and Burma were sour experiences. He makes no secret of this in his own memoirs: 'I have told my story of victory in North Africa. Now I must chronicle two defeats—Dunkirk and Burma. . . .' Summing up on Dunkirk, he says: 'It should be apparent that I recall the whole affair of Dunkirk with extreme distaste; and there still lay ahead the bitter pill of Burma. . . .' And of Burma: 'The evacuation of Burma was a complete military defeat—and we had been beaten in a straightforward fight by an enemy who was not greatly superior in numbers but whose troops had been trained and equipped for jungle warfare. Our troops were not.'

In assessing this period of Alexander's career we cannot judge his prowess in terms of success. We can only consider how much worse the situation might have been if his steadying hand had not been on the tiller. It is the British people and their short-sighted policies which stand to be judged, rather than the abilities of their military commanders in the years of endurance from 1939 to 1942. The cover provided by an insurance policy is directly proportional to the premium paid. Not only did the British fail to take out adequate defence insurance policies in the years between the wars; they tended to insure against the wrong risks. Because they lived in a moated island, they used the small amounts of money, which they were prepared to spend on defence, to equip their naval and air forces, neglecting the Army. In 1938 the British Government concluded after a long strategic debate, which had begun in 1936, that 'in a war with Germany the British contribution to Allied strength should consist mainly of naval and air forces. We should avoid sending a large army to the Continent: the role of the army would be limited to home defence and the defence of British territories overseas.'

The 1938 decision to concentrate on sea and air, taken in April, was reversed by the autumn as the ripples of the Münich crisis spread through Britain's body-politic. Without deep thought and without a plan, a land commitment was accepted. From then on Alexander's generation of British generals bought the time needed to enlist, equip and train a continental army, losing four armies in the process—in France, in Greece, in Malaya and in Burma.

One of the maxims of British military life is never to be in the 1st Team at the outbreak of war. The men, who eventually lead the British to victory, belong to the 2nd Team. They can make their names by saving the day at the lower levels of command, while their seniors are dismissed for the débâcles caused by their country's mistaken peace-time policies. It is interesting to speculate who the British military heroes would have been if the Second World War had begun three years earlier or three years later. If earlier, men like Gort, Ironside and Paget might be remembered as the victors; if later, Brooke, Alexander and Montgomery might have suffered eclipse in the early disasters of unpreparedness. Alexander would probably have suffered most because he was always too ready to shoulder responsibility and to take the blame; always too willing to give superiors and subordinates the benefit of the doubt; and always too selfless in his concept of duty. He would never excuse himself, preferring to let events speak for him. Events at the beginning of British wars are seldom reliable witnesses; and political leaders, in defeat, are rarely generous. Alexander would have been an ideal scapegoat.

The 1939 mobilization plan worked as smoothly as its counterpart in 1914. Organising skill and mental ability are the keys to such plans. Lack of financial resources are no constraint, and so the War Office could achieve a standard in mobilization planning which it could not match in the equipment field. The British Expeditionary Force left for France under-equipped in tanks, artillery, anti-aircraft and anti-tank weapons, and in signal equipment. Its only new weapons were the Bren light machine gun, a Czech weapon, manufactured under licence and its light armoured carrier—the Bren carrier—which became the maid-of-all-work of the infantry battalions throughout the war. Little else had changed since 1918, except motor vehicles had just replaced horse transport and the 25-pounder gun was replacing the old 18-pounder.

It will be recalled that the BEF, which Lord Gort took to France in 1939, consisted of two Corps: I Corps under Sir John Dill, with the 1st and 2nd Divisions; and II Corps under Sir Alan Brooke with 3rd and 4th Divisions. Alexander commanded 1st Division and Montgomery 3rd Division. During the next nine months of the 'phoney war' the BEF grew to a strength of five regular divisions, four territorial divisions, and three partially equipped divisions used for labour on the lines of communications and in construction of defences. III Corps was formed under General Sir Ronald Adam, and General Michael Barker took over I Corps when Sir John Dill was recalled to the War Office to become Vice-Chief of Imperial General Staff.

There was one important difference, already pointed out in Chapter 1, between the BEFs of 1914 and 1939. In 1914 no one in the British Army knew what continental warfare would be like. In 1939 most lieutenant colonels and above wore First World War medal ribbons. As they returned to France, memories came surging back. They knew it could not be exactly the same: the horses had gone and aircraft had developed a potency unthought of in 1918; but no one expected the nine months' stagnation which followed.

The impression left by Alexander on officers serving in his division during the long dreary winter of 1939 was one of quiet determination to have 1st Division at a peak of efficiency whenever the German offensive might begin. His trim, dapper figure was seen everywhere in the divisional area. He demanded high standards, but, as at Nowshera, he ensured that the administration of the Division was as near perfect as the available resources would allow. A fit man himself, he insisted on his division being just as fit. Visiting units, he was unfailingly polite, drawing the views of officers and men with a genuine interest in their ideas. Good suggestions and reasonable complaints were always acted upon. He had a happy knack of being able to talk to soldiers, but officers found him more difficult to chat to informally. They could never read his thoughts clearly enough to feel completely at ease with him. When he spoke at conferences or study periods they were surprised by his quiet, shy manner. What he said was always sound and to the point, but it lacked the colourful phraseology of Montgomery or the clipped clarity of Brooke. Nevertheless, few officers in the division were not glad that they were part of 1st Division. They had complete confidence in their commander. As one officer put it: 'This was the 1st Division of the British Army and its standards were a 1st Division's standards. Everything worked. There were no flaps.'

It is unfortunate that the 1st Division has never published a history of its activities in 1940. Alexander only devotes nine uninformative pages in his memoirs to this period. The account, which follows, of his handling of 1st Division during the Dunkirk campaign has been culled from the histories of seven of his nine battalions, from the diaries of such men as Brooke, from the official history and Lord Gort's despatches, and from discussions with officers who served in 1st Division at the time.

The story of May 1940 has been told so often that this account will be confined to three aspects: those which influenced Alexander's tactics and strategy later in the war; those which reflected the handling of his division in action; and, finally, those which impinged on his controversial actions as the rearguard commander at Dunkirk. For the first, we must look at the larger strategic picture because the German development and handling of the Blitzkrieg were to have a marked influence on his own strategy at El Alamein, Tunis and Rome. For the second, we must trace briefly the fate of 1st Division during the campaign. And for the third, we must delve into the British and French political as well as military accounts of the last four days of the campaign to balance the divergent national views on Dunkirk and on Alexander's part in bringing about some of the bitterest French criticism of British action in 1940.

In 1914 Alexander had withdrawn with his battalion from Mons, marching south for 14 days and forming part of the rearguard every three to four days as regiments took it in turn to cover the retreat. Discipline had been maintained and the Allied riposte had come on the Marne in the first week of September. The initial defeat of the BEF at Mons had been due to a French misappreciation of German war plans. Von Kluck's mistake of wheeling inwards too soon was superficially responsible for the Allied recovery on the Marne. The real reason, however, was that Joffre possessed the necessary character and determination to control the French Armies in defeat. In 1940, the French repeated their misreading of German intentions; and the Germans made a number of strategic errors which could have been exploited; but the French military leaders proved to be men of straw. The Germans not only won strategic surprise; they unhinged and deranged the whole of the French command structure. No second Battle of the Marne was fought because control was lost by the French Supreme Command. The Battle of Tunis, with which Alexander was to avenge Dunkirk, and the Battle of Rome, which gave him his

Field Marshal's baton, were based on achieving similar surprise. The Germans never lost control of their troops like the French, but they were defeated by being surprised and thrown off balance at the very start of these battles.

The German success in the West taught him something else. Winning strategic surprise is one thing; the ability to exploit surprise is another. He had already learned from bitter experience that in war events only go according to plan in the glossy accounts of the press releases. The random coincidence of events, the interaction of the two sides, and such unpredictable factors as the weather, all highlight the dangers of being over-dogmatic and the need for flexibility in exploiting initial success or failure.

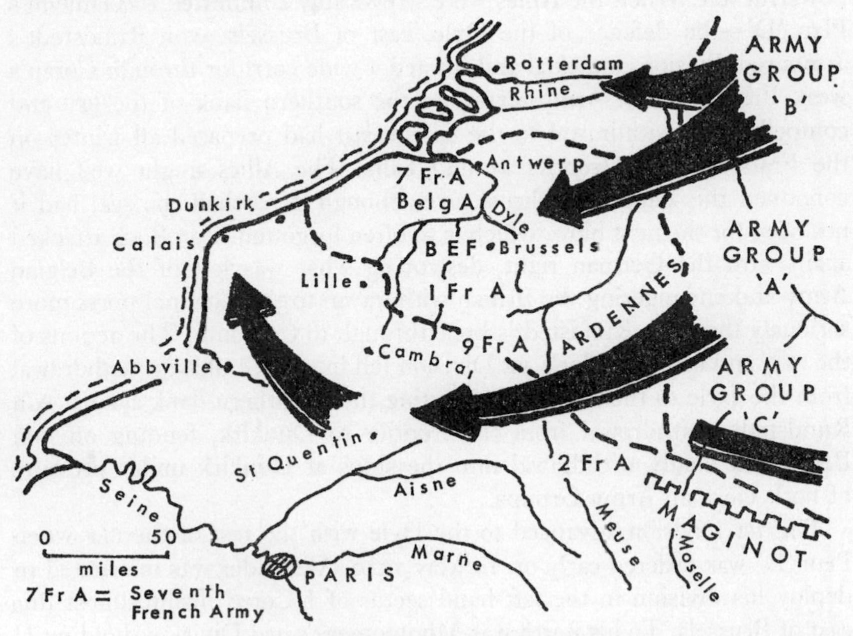

16 German Blitzkrieg in the West, June 1940

Alexander had always been attracted by the analogy of the boxer using his right and left hands intelligently to defeat his opponent—feint with one, hit with the other; two feints with one then hit with the other; sometimes feint with the left and sometimes with the right; sometimes at the body and sometimes at the head—a wide variety of options to match the permutations of chance in battle. In the German Blitzkrieg of 1940 in France he saw and experienced the effects of the two-handed punching. In his own major offensives this concept lay at the root of his planning.

It is commonly supposed that the German success in 1940 was the result of a single concentrated punch by their panzer divisions through the difficult Ardennes country to the sea at Abbeville, encircling the BEF and forcing its evacuation from Dunkirk. This is only part of the story. There were two German fists in action: von Bock's Army Group B opposite Holland and Belgium was the German right hand; and von Rundstedt's Army Group A opposite the Ardennes was the German left. Von Leeb's Army Group C was not part of the striking force and was positioned to keep the defenders of the Maginot Line quiet. The Germans struck first with their right, drawing the Allies forward to the assistance of the Dutch and the Belgians, while concealing the strength and direction of their powerful left. When the Allies were irrevocably committed to Gamelin's Plan 'D'—the defence of the Dyle, east of Brussels—von Rundstedt's armoured divisions attacked and blasted a wide corridor through Corap's weak French Ninth Army, exposing the southern flank of the BEF and compelling its withdrawal to the defences it had prepared all winter on the Franco-Belgian frontier around Lille. The Allies might well have contained this dangerous thrust, even though it reached the sea, had it not been for the next blow, which is so often forgotten. Von Bock attacked again with the German right, destroying what was left of the Belgian Army and endangering the British withdrawal to the Channel ports more seriously than von Rundstedt's breakthrough to the south. The actions of the BEF, and of Alexander's 1st Division fell into three phases: withdrawal from the Dyle to the frontier, protecting their southern flank against von Rundstedt; withdrawal from the frontier to Dunkirk, fending off von Bock; and finally withdrawal into the ships at Dunkirk under pressure of both German Army Groups.

The 1st Division advanced to the Dyle with the rest of the BEF when Plan 'D' was ordered early on 10 May 1940. Alexander was instructed to deploy his division in the left hand sector of I Corps' front almost due east of Brussels. To his north was Montgomery's 3rd Division, holding II Corps' front around Louvain; and to his south lay 2nd Division. He decided to hold his sector with 2nd and 3rd Brigades up on the river itself and 1st (Guards) Brigade in reserve. 12 and 13 May passed relatively uneventfully as his battalions dug in and the rest of the division organised itself for a major defensive battle. 14 May brought the first piece of depressing news: the Dutch Army had surrendered to von Bock. The appearance of many of the Belgian troops withdrawing through the divisional sector did not inspire confidence. Air activity began to increase and on 15 May contact was made with the leading German reconnaissance units. The only sustained attack fell on the Louvain sector and was repulsed by Montgomery's 3rd Division. 16 May was more active but no serious pressure developed; and so it was with some bewilderment that the brigades of 1st Division received the order to withdraw that night. 2nd Brigade were to act as rearguard while 1st (Guards) and 3rd Brigade fell back to the River Senne. The German breakthrough in the Ardennes had compelled General Billotte, commanding the Allies' northern armies, to order a general withdrawal through a series of delaying positions: to the Senne on the night 16–17 May; to the Dendre 17–18 May; and to the Escaut 18–19 May.

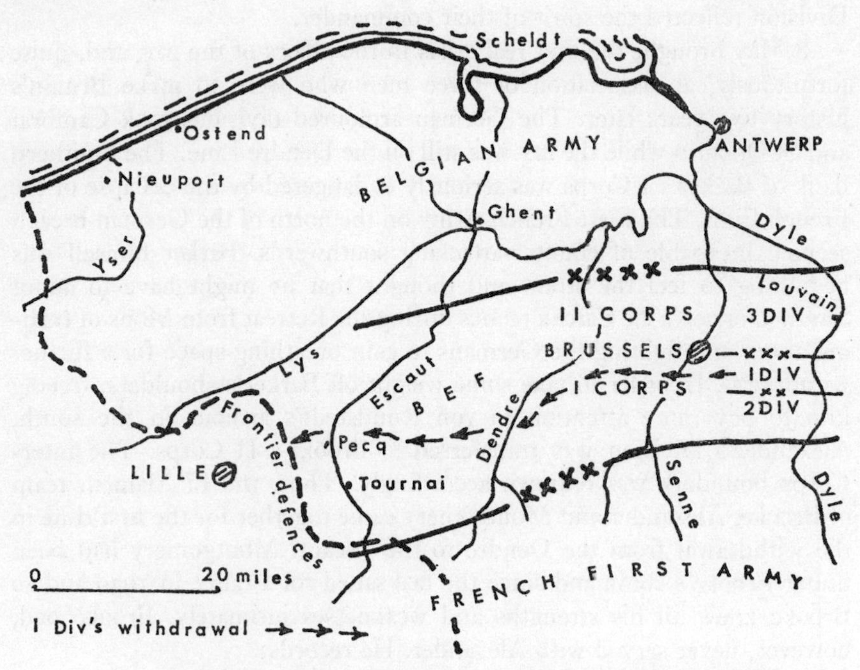

17 British Withdrawal from the Dyle to the Franco-Belgian Frontier, 11–22 May 1940

The pattern of withdrawal in Alexander's division would have done justice to any Staff College instructor. David Divine in his book on Dunkirk rightly refers to Alexander's impeccable handling of his division which held the centre of the British line throughout the withdrawal. Brigades took it in turn to provide the rearguard, and battalions within brigades thinned out in succession like any withdrawal exercise. But however good the commander and his staff, and however well disciplined the units, a long retreat takes a cumulative toll of men's physical and mental stamina. Fear plays a greater part in withdrawal than in any other phase of war. As men get tired, through carrying out forced marches by night and fighting by day, rumours grow and fear of being cut off stalks men's minds. Even the staunchest troops find it difficult to resist the infection of panic which spreads from the civil population to the less well-disciplined administrative units and thence to the fighting troops. The discipline of 1st Division did not falter. After a fortnight's withdrawal over 150 miles, fighting seven rearguard actions, the battalions embarked at Dunkirk with all their personal weapons and their spirit unbroken. The units of the 1st Division reflected the spirit of their commander.

18 May brought the first real crisis in the affairs of the BEF, and, quite fortuitously, an association of three men who were to make Britain's history two years later. The German armoured divisions took Cambrai and St Quentin while the BEF was still on the Dendre Line. The Southern flank of Barker's I Corps was seriously endangered by the collapse of the French front. The First French Army on the north of the German breach seemed incapable of counter-attacking southwards. Barker himself was beginning to feel the strain and thought that he might have to adopt Smith-Dorrien's Le Cateau tactics during the Retreat from Mons of turning about and fighting the Germans to gain breathing space for a further withdrawal. In order to take some weight off Barker's shoulders, freeing him to pay more attention to von Rundstedt's armour in the south, Alexander's Division was transferred to Brooke's II Corps. The inter-Corps boundary was redrawn accordingly. Thus, the El Alamein team of Brooke, Alexander and Montgomery came together for the first time in the withdrawal from the Dendre to the Escaut. Montgomery had been under Brooke's command since the BEF sailed for France in 1939 and so Brooke knew all his strengths and weaknesses intimately. Brooke had, however, never served with Alexander. He records:

> In taking over the 1st Division I was for the first time having the experience of having Alexander working under me. It was a great opportunity . . . to see what he was made of, and what an admirable commander he was when in a tight place. It was intensely interesting watching him and Monty during those trying days, both of them completely imperturbable and efficiency itself, and yet two totally different characters. Monty with his quick brain for appreciating military situations was well aware of the very critical situation he was in, and the very dangers and difficulties that faced us acted as a stimulus on him; they thrilled him and put the sharpest of edges on his military ability. Alex, on the other hand, gave me the impression of never fully realising all the very unpleasant potentialities of our predicament. He remained entirely unaffected

by it, completely composed and appeared never to have the slightest doubt that all would come right in the end. It was in those critical days that the appreciation I made of those two commanders remained rooted in my mind and resulted in the future selection of the two men to work together in the triumphal advance from Alamein to Tunis. (Bryant, *The Turn of the Tide*, pp. 107–8)

In the crisis on the BEF's southern flank, the staff work of Headquarters I Corps lost some of its precison. Coordination of withdrawal timings with Brooke's II Corps went wrong and Alexander found his southern flank exposed by the premature withdrawal of I Corps units. Alexander realised what had happened and on his own initiative ordered the I Corps reconnaissance regiment to cover his flank. His quick action saved his 3rd Brigade, which was acting as rearguard, from being encircled. It was a close run thing. The bridge at Tournai was blown too soon, cutting off the rearguard armoured carriers of the Duke of Wellington's Regiment. These had to be abandoned, the crews swimming the river to safety.

1st Division held its positions on the Escaut for the next four days. On 21 May they were heavily attacked at Pecq bridge where German storm troopers managed to establish a small lodgement across the river between 2nd Coldstream and 3rd Grenadier Guards. In the subsequent fighting L/Cpl H. Nicholls won the VC. 3rd Grenadiers lost eight officers and 180 other ranks in their successful fight to restore the situation. Next night the Division fell back with the rest of II Corps to the defences on the Belgian frontier on which they had worked for nine months although in a different sector. So many troops had been withdrawn to protect the long exposed southern flank of the BEF, that the two Corps were not strong enough to man these defences properly. Most of the historians among the officers felt that this was the equivalent of crossing the Marne in 1914. They expected the retreat to stop and the counter-attacks to begin. They were, of course, right, but did not know that the public image of the French High Command had no substance. The over-publicised Weygand plan for a combined offensive from north and south of the German armoured penetration evaporated during the next four days while the BEF stood on the Franco-Belgian frontier. The Germans never looked like losing the initiative. On 20 May their tanks reached the sea at Abbeville and by 22 May were beginning their attack on Calais and Boulogne.

Part of the Weygand plan had depended upon the British providing two divisions to attack southwards alongside two French divisions. In the regrouping which took place to release these divisions, Alexander's 1st Division went back to I Corps' control. Brooke's diary notes: 'I was sorry to lose Alex and had formed a very high opinion of his ability during the short time that I had him under my command.' Brooke was to see a great deal of him during the second phase of the BEF's withdrawal which was about to begin.

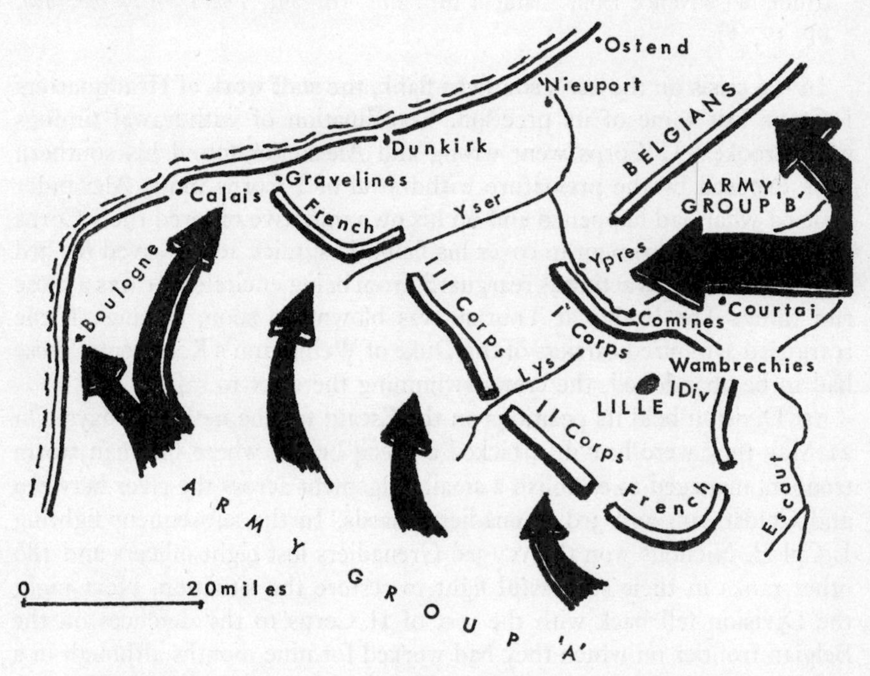

18 Withdrawal from the Frontier to Dunkirk, 23–29 May 1940

While the French High Command was prevaricating about the nebulous Weygand Plan, the Germans settled matters by punching again with their right. Von Bock attacked the junction of the British and Belgian Armies near Courtai. Von Rundstedt, with the German left, had reached his planned objectives—Plan Yellow—and had halted to regroup and replenish his armoured divisions for the next stage of the campaign—the advance on Paris, called Plan Red. There have been many arguments as to why the German left was halted so near to Dunkirk. Many suggestions have been made: that Hitler did not want to destroy the British; that his armour might get stuck in the Flanders mud; that Göring wanted to finish the job with the Luftwaffe; and so on. The plain fact is that von Rundstedt was following the original German concept of the two-handed punch and saw no reason to alter it. Hitler confirmed his proposals. While von Rundstedt regrouped, von Bock took up the running by striking the right of the

Belgian Army with a concentrated punch by seven divisions. Four years later Alexander was to remember the timing of this secondary attack when he launched General Truscott's VI (US) Corps from Anzio against the flank of the retreating German Tenth Army south of Rome. The effect of von Bock's renewed offensive was decisive as far as the British were concerned. The Belgian Army had reached the point of collapse. Its defeat meant the envelopment of the BEF's northern flank. There could be no southward counter-attack. The two divisions which were to have taken part in the Weygand Plan marched north to help Brooke fill the yawning gap which was appearing near Courtai. Next day (25 May) the British Government authorised the BEF's withdrawal to the coast. The threat from the north was now more serious than that from the south. Brooke's II Corps with the help of several of Alexander's battalions was to save the day.

As the BEF unfolded from its salient around Lille, the front line was shortened, enabling some troops to be sent back to Dunkirk to start manning the perimeter of the proposed bridgehead. Alexander's Division was squeezed out from the centre of the line and ordered to fall back by bounds direct to Dunkirk. The reaction of his troops to the news is recorded in the History of the Coldstream Guards:

> We sat down on chairs making a circle round the room and waited. The Commanding Officer looked up, and, after a pause, said: 'We are to march 55 miles back to the coast'—he paused again and looked around at us. Our hearts sank. Fifty-five miles seemed a bit too much. Then he went on—'and embark for England!' Immediate sensation. No one had expected this. We had had vague ideas of falling back as the armies of 1914 had fallen back until, somehow, some time, we too should stand and fight our victorious battle of the Marne. But this! There was a sudden loosening of the tension we had been living under so long. We felt a surge of contentment beneath our anxiety about the war news in general and our own immediate prospects in particular. Then we thought again of the 55 miles and wondered. (Howard and Sparrow, p. 48)

In thinning out from the frontier each brigade sent back one battalion in its first wave. The three battalions were 3rd Grenadiers, 2nd North Staffords and 2nd Foresters. Being first out proved a misfortune to these battalions. Alan Brooke says why:

> As I had heard that the 1st Division had already started withdrawing three battalions from the line and that these battalions were somewhere west of Ploegsteert Wood. I decided to endeavour to secure their assistance. After some hunting I found I Corps HQ in one of the old Lille forts, and I obtained Michael Barker's agreement. I therefore proceeded again to Wambrechies to see Alexander to request him to issue orders to these battalions to come under

orders of 5th Division and to move forward at once. Alexander, as I expected, co-operated at once, and these three battalions played a great part in restoring the situation on the right of the 5th Division front. (Bryant, *The Turn of the Tide*, pp. 136–7)

The German attacks on the northern flank had penetrated 5th Division's newly formed front and were threatening the rear of II Corps near Ypres. The three 1st Division battalions lost heavily in their efforts to stem disaster on the Ypres-Comines Canal. 3rd Grenadiers alone lost 9 officers and 270 men by the time they were able to disengage to withdraw to the bridgehead. Alexander's willingness and ability to help in this crisis created a further bond between him and Brooke.

The withdrawal of the rest of 1st Division was impeded only by roads cluttered with the debris from bombing, by pathetic trails of refugees and by units of other divisions using wrong routes. Brooke notes in his diary

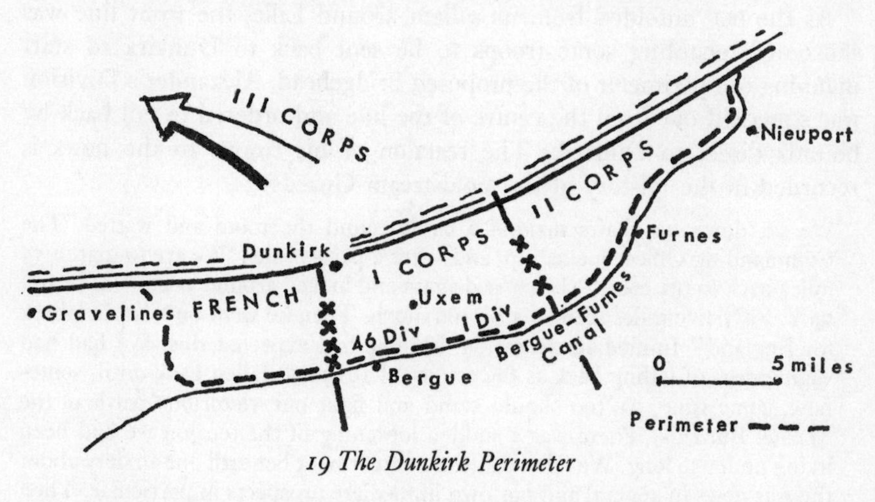

19 The Dunkirk Perimeter

that he had some trouble with 1st Division itself poaching his Corps' routes, but this was quickly settled by a visit to Alexander's headquarters. It rained most of the two days in which 1st Division was withdrawing. Though uncomfortable for the tiring men, low cloud reduced the attacks from the air, which were relatively few. When the troops approached the perimeter congestion grew, as units destroyed unwanted transport and equipment before moving into their alloted sectors or to embarkation points. The blockage became so great that Alexander himself records:

I myself reached the beaches on a pushbike after abandoning my car some miles back, because the roads were hopelessly blocked by French, Belgian and British soldiers. The car was set alight in order that the Germans should not have the enjoyment of my personal belongings or the use of the vehicle itself. Thus my sole remaining possessions for the remainder of the battle were my revolver, my field glasses, and my brief case. (*Memoirs*, pp. 77–8)

Sir Ronald Adam had laid out the British half of the bridgehead in three Corps sectors. His own III Corps, which had the shortest distance to march from the southern flank, was nearest Dunkirk; then came I Corps; and finally II Corps was to hold the extreme easterly sector beyond the Franco-Belgian frontier towards Nieuport. The evacuation plan was based on clearing as many specialist and administrative troops as possible before the fighting troops arrived, and then to evacuate III Corps, probably followed by II Corps, and finally I Corps, which was to provide the rear-guard. The exact order would depend on the circumstances at the time.

By now the people of Great Britain had begun to realise that the chances of saving their army were slender indeed. The War Office started to turn its attention to rebuilding a new army. GHQ had already been ordered to send back experienced officers and men from all units to provide the cadres from which new divisions could be raised. Brooke himself received an order to hand over his Corps as soon as its retirement to the bridgehead was complete and to return to England for another unspecified appointment. He had no hesitation in selecting Montgomery as his successor. On 31 May, Lord Gort, the C-in-C, received a direct order from Anthony Eden, Secretary of State for War, to hand over his command and return home as soon as his force was reduced to a size appropriate to a Corps Commander. This summons was initiated by Churchill who appreciated that Gort would never leave his Army in its distress. The crucial passage in the message ran:

You should now nominate this commander. If communications are broken you are to hand over and return when your effective fighting force does not exceed the equivalent of three divisions. This is in accordance with correct military procedure, and no personal discretion is left you in the matter. On political grounds, it would be a needless triumph to the enemy to capture you when only a small force remained under your orders. The Corps Commander chosen by you should be ordered to carry on the defence in conjunction with the French and evacuation whether from Dunkirk or the beaches, but when in his judgement no further organised evacuation is possible and no further proportionate damage can be inflicted on the enemy he is authorised in consultation with the senior French Commander to capitulate formally to avoid useless slaughter. (*The War in France and Flanders*, p. 230)

Montgomery now takes up the story in his memoirs and gives the background to Gort's decision to appoint Alexander as the commander of the rearguard (p. 64):

> It is commonly supposed that at this final conference Gort 'nominated' Major-General H. R. L. G. Alexander to command after he himself had left. This is not so; moreover, Alexander himself was not even present at the conference. I will describe what actually happened.
>
> The two Corps Commanders at the conference were Lieut.-General M. G. H. Barker, 1st Corps, and myself, who had just taken over command of 2nd Corps.
>
> Gort's plan was based on the War Office telegram and he ordered that I was to withdraw 2nd Corps the next night, 31st May/1st June, and that the 1st Corps would then be left in final command. He informed Barker that as a last resort he would surrender himself, and what remained of his corps, to the Germans. The conference then broke up. I stayed behind when the others had left and asked Gort if I could have a word with him in private. I then said it was my view that Barker was in an unfit state to be left in final command; what was needed was a calm and clear brain, and that given reasonable luck such a man might well get 1st Corps away, with no need for anyone to surrender. He had such a man in Alexander, who was commanding the 1st Division in Barker's corps. He should send Barker back to England at once, and put Alexander in command of the 1st Corps. I knew Gort very well; so I spoke plainly and insisted that this was the right course to take.
>
> Gort acted promptly . . . Alexander took over the 1st Corps. The two corps were now commanded by two major-generals and we met the next day in La Panne to discuss the situation; we were both confident that all would be well in the end. And it was; 'Alex' got everyone away in his own calm and confident manner.

To the British, who flocked to their churches on that grim Sunday, 31 May 1940, to pray for the safe return of their Army, the 'Deliverance of Dunkirk', as Churchill called it, was a direct answer to their prayers. To the French, it added one more example of the perfidiousness of the British. At the root of French disquiet lay the name of Alexander. To the British, he was the gallant rearguard commander, who, by his steadiness in adversity, saved the last three divisions of the BEF. To the French, he was the man who went back on Churchill's promise to ensure that British and French soldiers would be embarked in equal numbers and that the British rearguard would fight it out shoulder to shoulder with the French. How did this misunderstanding arise?

The facts of the case are relatively simple to discover, but the national interpretations of the facts are as different as the mental make-up of the two nations. In British eyes neither Gort nor Alexander had any other option but to withdraw the last British troops on the night 1–2 June. In continental eyes, there was no need for the BEF to embark at all. Many an isolated fortress, garrisoned by determined men, had held out long enough to change the whole course of a war. The quick answer 'but not against modern air power' fails in the face of the subsequent British and Australian success in the first siege of Tobruk, and of the German garrisoned western Channel and Atlantic ports which held out long after the Allies had broken out from the Normandy beach-head in 1944.

There had been misunderstandings between the British and French Governments and their high commands ever since the Germans unnerved the French command structure with the strategic surprise in the Ardennes. The specific misunderstanding over Dunkirk sprang from a basic difference in national outlook. General Spears, who was Churchill's military liaison officer with the French Government, puts the situation in a nutshell:

> I suddenly realised with a clarity that had never before been vouchsafed to me in all the long years I had worked with the French Army, that to them the sea was much the same thing as an abyss of boiling pitch and brimstone, an insurmountable obstacle no Army could venture over unless they were specially organised colonial expeditions endowed with incomprehensible powers. . . .
>
> To fall back to Dunkirk represented retiring into a fortress, which might be supplied by sea, but from which there was no retreat. (*Assignment to Catastrophe*, I, p. 192)

The French visualised the line of the River Lys as the outer perimeter of the future Dunkirk fortress; and the line, which Sir Ronald Adam had laid out, as the inner keep. They intended to emulate Marshal Bazaine, who threw his army into the Fortress of Metz during the Franco-Prussian War of 1870—with disastrous results, it may be added! The British, for their part, looked upon the Lys line as the final delaying position to be held just long enough to cover the occupation of Adam's Dunkirk perimeter, which, in its turn, would be progressively shortened and finally abandoned when all troops had been embarked.

Before Gort handed over to Alexander, he had been instructed by the British Government to share embarkation facilities with the French. It had not been possible to evacuate equal numbers so far because Admiral Abrial, the French Naval C-in-C responsible for the defence of Dunkirk, was not authorised to evacuate any French troops until late on 29 May. Thereafter a loyal attempt to do so was made by the British embarkation staff. Gort went to see Abrial before he left for England to make sure everything was now working smoothly. Abrial assured him that he was satisfied. Gort then told him that Alexander, as Commander I Corps, would operate under the Admiral's overall command, a gesture of doubtful validity because Gort's written instructions to Alexander included the traditional break-clause given to British commanders placed under Allied command:

'You will act under his [Abrial's] orders; but should any orders which he may issue to you be likely, in your opinion, to imperil the safety of the Force under your command, you should make an immediate appeal to His Majesty's Government. . . .'

Meanwhile Churchill had arrived in Paris for a Supreme War Council Meeting. He found that the French in Paris knew as little of the situation around Dunkirk as the British did about French action south of the German breach along the Somme. He reported the evacuation of 165,000 men including 15,000 French. An altercation with Weygand followed. Weygand pointed to the meagre 15,000 French, forgetting that Abrial had only just been authorised to evacuate any Frenchmen at all. The first draft communiqué composed by Admiral Darlan as an instruction to Admiral Abrial read:

1. A bridgehead should be held round Dunkirk.
2. As soon as you are convinced that no more troops outside the bridgehead can make their way to points of embarkation the troops holding the bridgehead shall withdraw, the British embarking first. . . .

Churchill intervened and insisted on the last phrase reading '. . . the British forces acting as rearguard as long as possible'. This was accepted gratefully by the French. The two remaining clauses read:

3. Once Dunkirk has been completely evacuated of land and naval units, the harbour will be blocked. The British Admiralty shall be responsible for this action. . . .
4. The evacuation of Dunkirk will be carried out under your orders. (Benoist-Mechin, *Sixty Days that Shook the West*, p. 208)

Unfortunately these orders do not seem to have been relayed to Alexander nor to the War Office which was directing him. No mention is made of this agreement in the Official History, but it is confirmed by Churchill in in Vol. II of his history of the Second World War, *Their Finest Hour* (p. 98).

Alexander was faced with a situation known all too well by many generations of British commanders—conflicting political and military direction. On assuming command, he reviewed the situation in the British sector and concluded that he was unlikely to be able to hold the reduced perimeter, which excluded the empty II Corps area, for more than another 36 hours; that is the nights 31 May–1 June and 1–2 June. If the perimeter were further reduced, German artillery would be able to interfere with embarkation, even by night. Moreover, the intensity of German air attacks and artillery bombardment would increase proportionately with the decrease of perimeter since fewer targets would be available to the same number of aircraft, and more guns would come within range.

Having taken this decision, he went to see Admiral Abrial and General Fagalde, the French garrison commander, during the afternoon of 31 May. Abrial proposed the reduction of the perimeter to an intermediate line running diagonally from Bergue, through Uxem to the sea. Alexander objected, saying that in his view this was impractical because it would bring German artillery within range of the Dunkirk Mole from which the bulk of the troops were being evacuated. In his view the existing perimeter could not be held beyond 1–2 June and he proposed, therefore, to withdraw his force that night. Benoist-Mechin describes the scene from the French point of view:

> 'But Lord Gort placed you under my orders!' replied Fagalde.
>
> 'Lord Gort is now at sea,' said Alexander. 'I alone am responsible for British troops still in France. If we remain here another twenty-four hours we shall be taken prisoner. Consequently I have decided to re-embark without delay.'

This statement is said to have stunned the French. Abrial and Fagalde strove to get Alexander to go back on his decision, but in vain. 'All I can do', he said, 'is to delay my embarkation until tomorrow, 1st June. But I can go no further.' At their insistence Alexander agreed to telephone London.

He returned a few hours later. In the meantime Admiral Abrial had received a telegram from Paris informing him that in the meeting of the Supreme War Council it had finally been decided:

1. That the British and French embarkation should be carried out pari-passu;
2. That the British should form the final rearguard.

Admiral Abrial showed his despatch to Alexander.

> 'Had my Prime Minister been here instead of in Paris [declared Alexander], he would never have subscribed to these conditions. And I have been in touch with Mr. Anthony Eden. He has ordered me to co-operate with the French forces in the fullest measure compatible with the security of the British troops. I consider their existence seriously threatened and I am sticking to my decision to embark tomorrow, 1st June.' (Benoist-Mechin, p. 201)

This account may be over-dramatised, but it is substantiated in its essentials by the Official History, Alexander's own Memoirs and his Appendix to Gort's despatch. A true ally would have stayed, but British commanders reflect their country's view and will always place the safety of their troops above considerations of an alliance. Mistrust of foreigners runs deep and invariably comes to the surface in times of crisis. In this case, communication between the two sides was breaking down long before this final breach. Alexander's estimate of how long the perimeter could be held was proved wrong by events, because he had no idea how many French troops were still available in the bridgehead. Had he known that there were three divisions worth of disorganised French troops in the British sector alone, he might have made a different appreciation. It is difficult to understand quite how out of touch with each other's dispositions the two sides were. The psychological strain of defeat, it seems, had benumbed men's minds, making inter-allied cooperation, which is difficult enough under normal circumstances, impossible at Dunkirk.

During 1 June, the Germans attacked all along the southern face of the bridgeheads. 1st Loyals were eventually driven out of Bergue, but managed to stabilize their line north of the canal. The 1st East Lancashires and the 1st Duke of Wellington's had to give ground but allowed no breach to occur. Captain Ervine-Andrews of the East Lancashires won his VC during this nerve-wracking day which seemed never-ending to the men holding the perimeter. They knew that if they could survive until dark, they would be away to the ships. The keynote was patient determination to sit out the hours of daylight. Richard Collier describes Alexander at this time.

> None set the tone more than General Alexander himself—sometimes surveying the battle from a deck chair on the Mole, sometimes moving amongst the troops, munching an apple. . . . The fate of the thousands still trapped at Dunkirk rested in his hands—yet his calm immaculate bearing showed nothing of this. . . .
>
> Only when Captain William Tennant opined that if things got much worse they would have to capitulate, did a glint of steel show through. As Tennant asked, 'How did one capitulate?' Alexander answered grimly, 'I have never had to capitulate'. (*The Sands of Dunkirk*, pp. 218–20)

At dusk Alexander gave the final order to thin out and embark as planned. The remnants of this three divisions pulled back through Fagalde's Frenchmen on the Uxem Line. Most got away that night, but dawn came before the last 4,000 could be embarked. Alexander and this small remnant of the once proud BEF stayed hidden in the dunes until the following night, covered by the French still holding out on the line which he had said could not be held.

After another long day, dusk fell and the last soldiers of the BEF embarked. Something went wrong with the French embarkation control, because far too few Frenchmen could be found to fill the available ships. In the early hours of 3 June, Alexander and Captain Tennant, who had been Senior Naval Officer, Dunkirk, thoughout the evacuation toured the beaches and when they were satisfied that all British troops had left, they themselves set course for Dover.

The French fought on for a further 24 hours which enabled one more night's evacuation to take place. The perimeter was so reduced that Abrial was forced to accept that 3–4 June must be the last night. He and Fagalde left for England with the last ship. Next morning some 40,000 Frenchmen still in the perimeter surrendered to the Germans.

The question remains, if Alexander had placed the Allied cause before the safety of British troops, could the whole Anglo-French force trapped in Dunkirk have been saved to fight another day? The French certainly think so; and what actually happened seems to support their view, but it is only tenable if the French troops in the perimeter were under disciplined control. Few were. The majority had given up the struggle several days earlier and were waiting for the end to come without further harm to themselves. It will not be the last time that a British commander is faced with a similar dilemma. Alexander's firmness ensured the achievement of his primary aim—the safety of his own troops. General Sir Miles Dempsey, then a Brigadier, was listening while Alexander phoned the War Office after his clash with Abrial. He heard Alexander say, 'I just don't propose to hold beyond Sunday night—after that we're all coming home'. As the phone went down Dempsey thought: 'Thank God—there's a man who is in control.'

Anthony Eden, then Secretary of State for War, records the same incident from a different angle:

> The last message I received from the BEF was from him [Alexander]. He told me of the extreme danger which threatened his force. I agreed to immediate evacuation, but asked him to give the French troops equal facilities with his own to get away. His work done, Alexander came to report to me in my room at the War Office as soon as he reached England. After he had given me an account of what had passed, I congratulated him and he replied, with engaging modesty, 'We were not pressed, you know'. (*The Reckoning*, p. 112)

Whatever the French may think of Alexander's actions at Dunkirk, three things had occurred which were to enable him to make more of British history: he was known to and trusted by Brooke, the future CIGS; he was known to Churchill and had become part of Churchill's legendary world; and his name was becoming known to the British public. A week after landing at Dover, he was appointed Commander I Corps in succession to Michael Barker with the rank of Lieutenant-General and with the task of refitting, retraining and preparing I Corps to repel the German invasion of England if the RAF ever allowed it to set sail from the ports which the BEF had just left.

6

Defeat in Burma

> No troops in our control could reach Burma in time to save it. But if we could not send an army we could at any rate send a man . . . it was resolved to send General Alexander by air to the doomed capital.
>
> Churchill, *The Hinge of Fate*, p. 146

The Norwegian Expeditionary Force, with which we have not been concerned because Alexander took no part in its affairs, and the BEF arrived back in England about the same time with little more than their personal arms. Despite their loss of heavy equipment, they had gained something more valuable than tanks and guns. These could be reprovided, in due course, by Britain's expanding war industries; and, later, from the United States through the generosity of American lend-lease. The priceless asset which they gained from the military disasters in Norway and France, was battle experience. The British Army contained men of all ranks, from generals down to privates, who had met the German Blitzkrieg and had the measure of its challenge. There was, it is true, an understandable bitterness against the War Office for its failure to provide the right weapons to match the German Panzer Divisions; and against the Royal Air Force, unfair though this was, for its inability to win for the Army a tolerable air environment in which to fight. It is also true that some men had regrettably lost the will to fight, but the great majority were quite simply determined to do better next time. There was a refreshing sense of originality within the ranks of the young veterans from France and Norway. They knew what war was like. They were sure that given the proper equipment they could master the German challenge. Once their units were reformed and provided with a minimum scale of weapons, they would eliminate the deficiencies in their performance by training with a realism never seen before. But, first, the immediate threat of German invasion had to be met with whatever lay to hand.

Within a week of landing back in England, Alexander received a posting order confirming him in command of I Corps. His Headquarters and Corps Troops were reassembling in northern England and had been made responsible for the defence of Lincolnshire and the East Riding of Yorkshire, areas he knew well from his days in Headquarters Northern Command before the war. The detailed layout of his corps and his defensive measures are of little significance today because they were never tested. What is important about this period is that Alexander was compelled by force of circumstances to make a detailed study of the problems of repelling a seaborne invasion. He was never to face an amphibious landing himself, but in 1943 he was to plan and execute the invasion of Sicily and then the landings at Salerno and Anzio. His experience in planning the Lincolnshire and Yorkshire coastal defences gave him a clear insight into the problems of his future opponent—Field Marshal Kesselring, the defender of Sicily and Italy.

Brooke took over from Ironside as C-in-C Home Forces soon after Alexander arrived in the north. Anti-invasion measures taken so far had a 'Maginot-mindedness' about them which appalled the senior officers of the BEF when they took over their sectors. Thousands of small hexagonal pill-boxes were being spawned over the countryside; artificial anti-tank ditches and rows of concrete anti-tank blocks wound their way across hill and dale; and road blocks of various ingenious and often impractical designs were appearing at the entrances and exits of every town and village. England was making the French mistake of putting her trust in concrete—which later demolition exercises incidentally proved to be very inferior concrete! Local building contractors made a handsome profit. Alexander's views coincided with those of Brooke:

> I had suffered too much from these blocks in France not to realise their crippling effect on mobility. Our security must depend on the mobility of our reserves, and we were taking the very best steps to reduce this mobility . . . I stopped any further construction and instructed existing ones to be removed where possible. (Bryant, *The Turn of the Tide*, p. 198)

Alexander learned in Yorkshire that coast defences can, at best, be no more than a deterrent façade. The sea with its unpredictable currents, tides and storms is the real obstacle. Most of the troops locked in beach defences are troops lost when the invasion starts because only those in the sector attacked can bring fire to bear. The rest must wait, looking at an empty sea, for subsidiary landings. The most dangerous form of defence from the attacker's point of view is the observation screen with limited delaying potential, supported by mobile reserves held well back in the hands of the higher levels of command. In assessing Kesselring's Sicilian defences three years later, Alexander did so with an experienced eye.

The summer and autumn of 1940 dragged slowly and anxiously by. The Battle of Britain was fought and won, and, as the equinoctial gales made the United Kingdom more secure, so the British High Command turned away from anti-invasion work and started to look to the future. On 2 December Alexander received a new posting order. He was to succeed Auchinleck as Commander-in-Chief Southern Command, when the latter became Commander-in-Chief India. Brooke, who, as Commander-in-Chief Home Forces, played a leading role in selecting senior officers in Home Commands, was placing the men he trusted in the key appointments to supervise the rebirth of the British Army.

Alexander was in his element in this training phase of the British Army's history. His great contribution was the Battle School system. Good ideas usually spring up in many different minds at the same time, and so it is often difficult to apportion credit. Brigadier (later Major-General) J. F. Utterson-Kelso was one of the principal pioneers of the battle school technique, but Alexander was the man who seized upon the idea and gave it the support needed for success. He realised that, if the Army was to beat the Germans, three things had to be done: first, men must have a simple drill to which they would react automatically in times of stress—battle drill; secondly, some way must be found to reduce the effects of fear caused by the noise of dive-bombing, shelling, mortaring and machine gunning, which had an effect on untried troops out of all proportion to the actual damage done—battle inoculation; and thirdly, physical fitness without which men cannot stand the stress of battle—battle fitness. These three ingredients were welded together into the syllabus of the battle schools which were set up under Alexander's guidance throughout Southern Command, and, eventually, throughout the Army. Those who went through these schools will never forget them. The simple themes of the battle drills such as 'down, crawl, observe, fire'; the firing of live artillery barrages and machine guns over troops to inoculate them; and the hideous rigours of the battle obstacle courses; all had a decisive effect on British troops entering battle from 1941 onwards.

It was not only the Army's commanders whose minds had swung towards future offensives overseas. Churchill was already inundating the planning staffs in Whitehall with wild, often impossible, schemes. Hitler's invasion of Russia in June 1941 gave new urgency to his ideas. In July an embryo expeditionary force called 'Force 110' was assembled in Scotland to prepare for some of the more practical of Churchill's brain-children. Alexander was appointed Force Commander (designate). He continued to command Southern Command, but had to spend much of his time giving the Force Commander's assessments of the various plans which emanated from Whitehall. Force 110 was officially established to plan and execute the invasion of the Canary Islands, but Alexander was already aware that Churchill was looking upon him as the next British Expeditionary Force Commander.

Nothing came of Force 110's planning during the summer of 1941. The highlight of the season's training was Brooke's anti-invasion exercise 'Bumper' in which four armoured and nine infantry divisions manoeuvred through a wide swathe of southern England, stretching from the Wash to Southampton Water in an arc around north-west London. Alexander commanded the defending forces, and Montgomery was chief umpire. The success of the exercise was a measure of the new found confidence and competence of the Army, which, by then, was better equipped than it ever had been before, although it still lacked key equipment like its full establishment of tanks. These were drained away to the Western Desert quicker than they could be manufactured. Brooke, in his summing up of the exercise, complimented the Army on the strides it had made in 12 months, but criticised Alexander's handling of his armoured divisions. Many officers present wondered why Alexander did not reply to what they believed was an unfair assessment. Alexander explains why:

> I felt moved to get up in the conference and defend my action—and then I remembered a story that had impressed itself on my mind many years before. When I was General Sir Francis Gathorne-Hardy's Chief of Staff, he told me that, when he was a young captain in the Grenadiers, he went to the Kaiser's grand manoeuvres, where he was attached to a certain high-ranking German general. At the close of the manoeuvres his general was unfairly criticised . . . Gathorne-Hardy . . . said to him, 'But, General, why didn't you get up and point to the error in the director's criticism?' The General looked at Gathorne-Hardy severely and said: 'Young man, to criticise the Commander-in-Chief before the Army would be a death blow to the whole of German military discipline!'
>
> There is sound reason for this acceptance of criticism in the conduct of exercises. The director will have designed his manoeuvres to bring out certain lessons—lessons of great value to all those taking part, and it would be a poor act of one individual, in defence of his own dignity, to destroy the value of the main lesson. That is why I have never expressed any resentment at being quite unfairly criticized during 'Bumper'. (Memoirs, p. 81)

October brought a series of new Churchill projects for Alexander to consider. Plan 'Whipcord' was an invasion of Sicily, which might be undertaken if Italy showed signs of collapse or if she sought Allied aid to withdraw from the Axis partnership while Hitler was embroiled with

Russia. Little did Alexander know that he was criticising one of the plans which he would be asked to execute two years later.

After 'Whipcord' came 'Gymnast', which was a plan for the invasion of French North Africa, if the French there gave any indication of wishing to break with Vichy. 'Gymnast' in its original form came to nothing because the Japanese attack on Pearl Harbour brought America into the war, inspiring a new upsurge of Churchillian plans set in an Anglo-American context. A joint descent on French North Africa figured prominently in these plans. 'Gymnast' was resurrected under the codename 'Super Gymnast', in which Alexander was to command a British Task Force of one armoured and two infantry divisions alongside General Joseph W. Stilwell, commanding an equivalent American Force. The Japanese successes in the Far East and British failures in the Western Desert destroyed these optimistic plans. 'Super Gymnast' returned to its pigeonhole. By the time it was taken out again and converted into Eisenhower's 'Torch' operation in November 1942, Alexander and Stilwell had jointly fought one more Allied withdrawal campaign in Burma, and Alexander and Montgomery had won the decisive Battle of El Alamein.

The fall of Singapore in February 1942 changed the course of Alexander's career. Among Churchill's many other worries, there arrived a cable from the Viceroy of India, suggesting that the failure of Indian troops to fight as well as expected in Burma was due to lack of drive and leadership at the top. Churchill repeated the signal to Wavell, adding 'the CIGS wants to know what you think. If you concur with the Viceroy, he will send Alexander out at once.' Wavell did not support Linlithgow's proposal immediately, because General Hutton had been his Chief of Staff and he had selected him personally for command in Burma. Then Wavell received an operational appreciation from Hutton, followed by an urgent signal, giving what Wavell considered to be an unduly alarmist view of the situation in Burma. Losing confidence in Hutton, he cabled Churchill requesting Alexander's immediate dispatch. Churchill sums up the reasons for sending Alexander out: 'No troops in our control could reach Rangoon in time to save it. But if we could not send an army we could at any rate send a man . . . it was resolved to send General Alexander by air to the doomed capital. . . .' (*The Hinge of Fate*, p. 146).

Alexander was briefed in London by Brooke, who had succeeded Dill as CIGS, just one week after his appointment as 'Commander of an Expeditionary Force' for 'Super Gymnast'. John Kennedy, who was Director of Military Operations in the War Office, was present when Alexander said good-bye to Brooke. On being wished the best of luck, Alexander smiled and said 'I will do my duty. You must help me all you can.'

There is no need to dwell for long on the painful circumstances which brought Alexander from the heady atmosphere of planning the first Allied counter-offensive against Nazi Germany with well-equipped armoured and infantry divisions to the military poverty and disillusion of Burma.

The unpreparedness of Burma was due to her low priority on the list of British defence commitments. Americans, like those who accompanied Stilwell to Burma in 1942, found it difficult to appreciate how it was that the British, who built a world empire, could lose it so easily. The answer is simple: the Empire was founded on mutual self-interest. The British needed stable trading conditions; the people welcomed external protection and, for those days, advanced standards of internal administration. A small locally enlisted army under British officers was quite sufficient to back the internal administration, while external defence lay in the capable hands of the Royal Navy. The rise of Germany and Japan, bent on aggrandizement, coupled with the development of air power, destroyed the basis of British Imperial Defence. The fall of France in 1940 enabled the Japanese to enter French Indo-China and from there to occupy Thailand, almost completing their blockade of China. Had it not been for the existence of the Burma Road into China, over which American lend-lease supplies could still reach Chungking, Burma might not have become a Japanese target until much later in the war.

The first Japanese attack on Burma came from the air. Rangoon was bombed on 23 and 25 December 1941, resulting in civilian panic. Most of the dock labour force fled and the civil administration was overwhelmed in the mass exodus from the city. When the Japanese invasion started on 19 January there were two weak and partially trained divisions available in the country: the 1st Burma Division under Major-General J. Bruce Scott and Major-General Sir John Smyth's 17 (Indian) Division. Bruce Scott's division had two Burmese brigades, made up of locally enlisted Burma Rifle battalions, and one Indian brigade from the Indian Army. Smyth's division had been training in India for desert warfare in the Middle East when it was sent to Burma. It had three Indian Army brigades. There were only two British battalions in Burma at that time, and although this number rose to six later, the whole force will be referred to as Imperial rather than British to make the point that this was, in the main, an Indo-Burmese force officered and supported by the British. Bruce Scott's Burma Division started the war deployed in the Shan

States, covering the possible Japanese invasion routes from Thailand via Chiengmai and Chiengrai. When Smyth's division arrived just before the invasion, it took over responsibility for the Tenassarim coast guarding the string of RAF staging airfields running down the Kra Isthmus to Malaya.

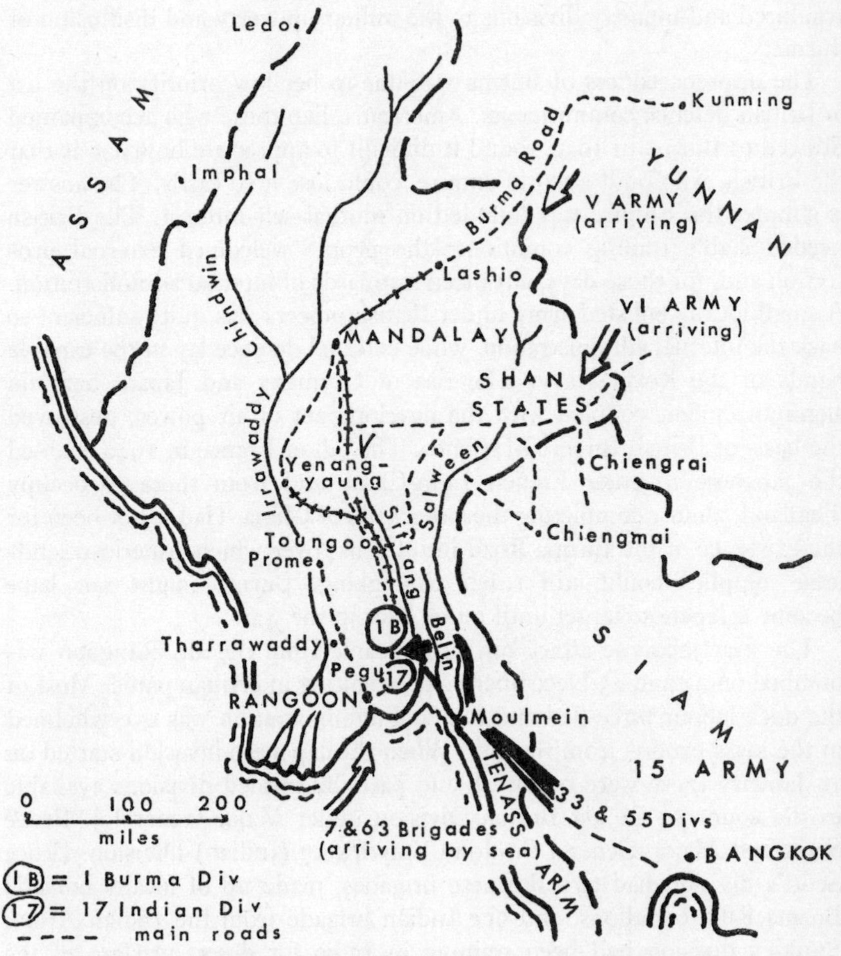

20 Situation in Burma when Alexander assumed command, 5 March 1942

The British Command misappreciated the Japanese intentions. They expected them to advance from Chiengmai and Chiengrai into the Shan States to sever the Burma Road and to isolate Rangoon. Instead General Iida, commanding the 15th Japanese Army based on Bangkok, advanced into Burma via Moulmein, encountering Smyth's newly arrived units before they had time to become accustomed to their new surroundings. The Japanese 33 and 55 Divisions had earned their battle experience in the long Sino-Japanese War and were fully trained and equipped for jungle warfare. Smyth's men were not. After some unfortunate disasters early in the campaign, 17 Division settled down to fight a series of delaying actions. Moulmein was abandoned at the end of January; the lower Salween River line in the middle of February and the Belin River line towards the end of February. Nothing went right in Smyth's withdrawal from the Belin to the Sittang River, the last major defensive position covering Rangoon. Due to one of his units issuing orders in clear over the radio, the Japanese anticipated his withdrawal and reached the great Sittang Bridge before the bulk of the division were across. Smyth's withdrawal had also been delayed by the exhaustion of his troops and by an unfortunate attack upon them by Allied aircraft. He was forced to order the demolition of the bridge with two brigades still engaged with the Japanese on the far bank. The men cut off had to abandon their equipment and swim the 700-yard river. When the division mustered at Pegu on 24 February it had barely 3,500 infantry left of whom only 1,400 were still armed. Had it not been for the timely arrival of Brigadier Anstice's 7 Armoured Brigade from the Middle East and 63 Indian Brigade from India, and for the physical difficulties of crossing the now bridgeless Sittang, the Japanese could have marched into Rangoon almost unopposed. Such was the situation when Alexander reached Calcutta to be briefed by Wavell before setting out for Rangoon. He had been faced with many unpleasant situations before, but none as depressing as this.

Wavell briefed Alexander in Calcutta on 3 March, stressing the importance of holding Rangoon. If the port was lost, there would be no way of reinforcing or supplying Alexander's Burma Army until a road could be built over the mountains of Assam from India into Burma. Although construction had started, it would take many months to complete. Wavell also told him that he had replaced Smyth, who was a sick man, with Major-General D. T. Cowan. Cowan and Bruce Scott were both 6th Gurkhas. Before long a third member of that great regiment was to arrive —General William Slim.

Alexander arrived in Rangoon by air on 5 March and went forward to 17 Division's Headquarters that afternoon where he met Hutton and Cowan. As the Official History remarks, 'a very unpromising situation confronted the new commander'. The Japanese were across the Sittang in force and were pushing their way between Cowan's and Bruce Scott's Divisions. The latter had been able to move south from the Shan States on the arrival of the Chinese VI Army, sent by Chiang Kai-shek to help defend the Burma Road. Cowan's 17 Division had been reinforced by 7 Armoured Brigade, but 63 Indian Brigade had not yet completed its disembarkation in Rangoon. Alexander saw at once that he had two options: close the gap between the two Imperial divisions thereby cutting off any Japanese who were already west of the breach; or abandon Rangoon. As his primary mission was to save Rangoon he had to try the former before he would contemplate the latter. His first action, on assuming command, was to countermand Hutton's order for a further withdrawal and to substitute orders for an attack by 17 Division in a north-easterly direction towards the Sittang, while 1 Burma Division attacked southwards. Like Weygand's plan in May 1940, Alexander's counter-offensive was doomed from the start. It was just as abortive and even shorter lived. Cowan had some local successes during 6 March, but by evening it was Cowan rather than the Japanese who was in danger of being cut off. Reports reached Alexander of a Japanese amphibious force approaching the mouth of the Rangoon River, while a much larger force was marching on a route which would enable it to cut Rangoon's road and rail links with the north. If he delayed ordering the destruction of the oil refinery and the port facilities and stocks, there might not be enough time to complete the demolition plans before the Japanese broke through. Once the port had been destroyed there would be little further purpose in fighting for Rangoon. It could not serve as a reception port for reinforcements for the Burma Army nor for lend-lease supplies for China. In the late afternoon of 6 March, just 24 hours after assuming command, he gave the order for the final evacuation of the city, the implementation of the demolition plan, and the withdrawal of 17 Division and the Rangoon Garrison up the road to Prome on the Irrawaddy River.

The advanced guard of 17 Division left at once for Tharrawaddy, its next concentration area, on the Rangoon-Prome road and met no Japanese. A little later Alexander set out with his headquarters escorted by the Rangoon Garrison, the 1st Battalion the Gloucestershire Regiment, to follow the same route, only to hear that the road had been cut by the Japanese behind the advanced-guard and that they were holding a block on the road covered by infantry and anti-tank guns. Not only was the new GOC Burma, his headquarters and the Rangoon Garrison cut off, but so was the rest of 17 Division withdrawing from its abortive counter-attack towards the Sittang. Several attempts were made to clear the Japanese off the block without success, so Alexander decided to mount a properly coordinated attack at first light next morning. Preparations were put in hand and battalions moved into their attacking positions during darkness.

The night 6–7 March was full of surprises. The first came when a detachment of the advanced-guard, which had come back to find out what had happened, sighted a Japanese column crossing the road north of the block. It took three hours to cross the road, but the advanced-guard detachment were unable to contact 17 Division by radio and so no one south of the block heard about this Japanese force. In the early hours of the morning a report reached 17 Division that a large body of Japanese were moving southwards on the west side of the Rangoon-Prome Road. This report was treated with some scepticism. Then just before the attack on the block was due to start, a patrol from 7th Hussars found the block deserted. Alexander and his trapped force made good their escape to Tharrawaddy.

What had happened? 33 Japanese Division had been ordered to advance round the north of Rangoon to attack the city from the least likely approach —the north-west. In order to ensure complete secrecy, Colonel Sakuma, the Japanese commander of the outflanking force, had removed his road block as soon as his force was safely across the road. Sakuma achieved surprise, but not in the way he had expected. When he reached the city he found no garrison. Turning about, he pursued the retreating Imperial rearguard for some 30 miles and then gave up for lack of supplies. For the moment, General Iida contented himself with the consolidation of Rangoon and Lower Burma while his troops were rested and reorganised. Alexander records in the early paragraphs (14, 15) of his Despatch:

> A period of comparative quiet followed the withdrawal from Rangoon. Apparently at this time the enemy was resting and refitting in the Rangoon area whilst his propaganda machine exploited to the full the fall of the city. This period of quiet was most welcome as my forces were badly in need of rest and reorganisation.
>
> Having failed in my primary task of holding Rangoon, I now had to consider my secondary task which was the retention of Upper Burma. . . .

In his Memoirs he confesses (p. 93):

> Looking back over the years with the knowledge I now have of the situation that existed when I took over command early in March 1942, I realise that I ought to have ordered an earlier evacuation of Burma. But at the time I was not prepared to admit defeat before I had done everything possible. This delay resulted in the whole of our forces in the south of Burma being encircled and gave the Japanese the chance to destroy them as organised formations—they missed their chance!

The Burma Road had been rendered useless to China for lend-lease supplies, but Burma herself had much to offer. She was one of the world's biggest producers of rice which China badly needed; and her oilfields at Yenangyaung could not be ignored. And there were other strategic reasons for attempting to hold Central and Upper Burma. First of all, India needed all the time she could buy to build up the defences of her eastern frontier which had never been threatened before. Secondly, from the higher

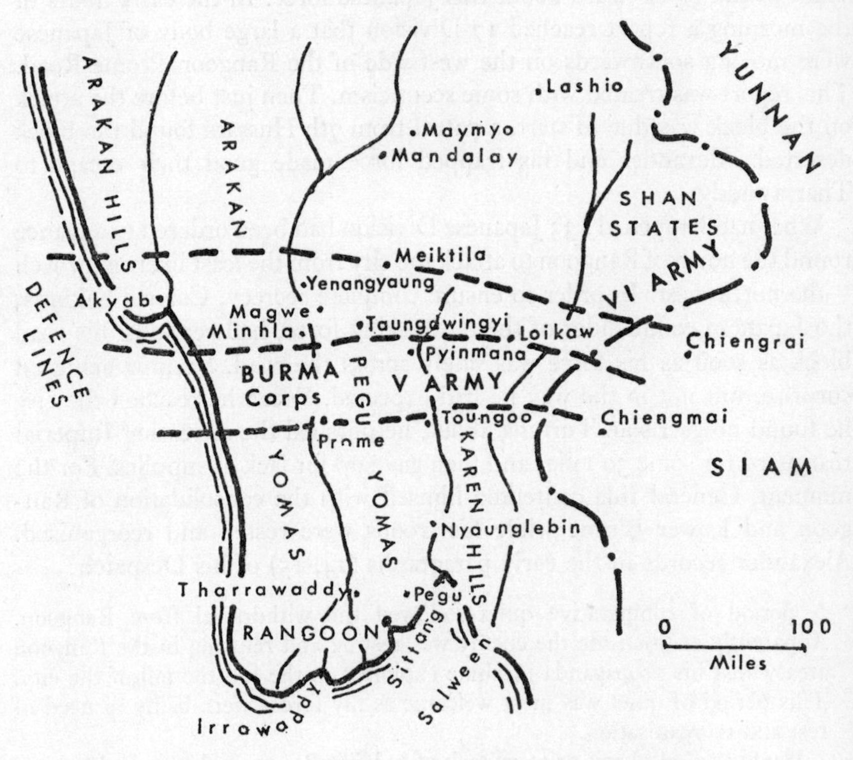

21 Alexander's Plans for the Defence of Central Burma

political point of view, it was desirable to keep touch with China, thereby lending moral support if nothing else, in keeping her in the war against Japan which she had been fighting for five long years already. And thirdly, even in this hour of failure, thoughts were already turning to the eventual counter-offensive when Allied strength had been rebuilt in the Far East. A hold on any part of Burma would be useful as a spring-board when that time came.

Alexander's aim in the second half of the First Burma Campaign

13 Chinese allies: Wavell and Alexander talking to two Chinese Generals

BURMA, 1942

14 The Burma team: Alexander, Wavell and Slim

15 Alexander, GOC-in-C Middle East, August 1942

CAIRO, AUGUST 1942

16 New Directives are issued: Alexander, Churchill, Montgomery and Brooke in Cairo, August 1942

became to delay the Japanese northward advance as long as possible to give India time to build up her defences and to keep touch with the Chinese. To recapitulate briefly, the forces at his disposal were Cowan's badly shaken and under-strength 17 Indian Division; the intact, but partially trained and equipped, 1 Burma Division under Bruce Scott; the 7 Armoured Brigade under Brigadier Anstice; and two Chinese armies, the V Army under General Tu and the VI Army under General Kan, each not much stronger than an Imperial division.

The ground over which Alexander was to fight his delaying action was like a hand pointing downwards from the Himalayas towards Rangoon. The little and third fingers represented the Arakan Hills and Arakan Yomas; the middle finger, the Pegu Yomas, dividing the valleys of the Irrawaddy and the Sittang; the first finger, the Karen Hills, dividing the Sittang from the Salween; and the thumb, the frontier mountains of China proper bordering the Shan States. The Japanese advance, when it was renewed, would probably use the road, railway and river communications in the Irrawaddy and Sittang valleys which were the main arteries of trade between Upper and Lower Burma. Once they secured Toungoo in the Sittang Valley, they could branch eastwards into the Shan States, using the Salween River Valley without having to force the passes above Chiengmai and Chiengrai. A route from Toungoo could lead them through the Shan States to Lashio, the terminal of the Burma Road. Chiang Kai-shek, when offering his troops for the defence of Burma, had insisted on their being given a self-contained sector. His VI Army under General Kan, an officer who turned out to be as inferior as his army, was already in the Shan States. General Tu's very much better V Army was advancing by slow stages southwards to Toungoo. Thus the Chinese conveniently occupied a suitable sector with routes leading back to China, leaving the wide Irrawaddy Valley for the Imperial troops to hold, equally conveniently covering the route back to India, primitive though it was. Neither the tracks into India nor the roads into China were of any real significance from the supply point of view because those into India were inadequate for the purpose and those into China were redundant because the British had agreed to feed and administer the Chinese armies while they were in Burma. Never had the Chinese armies 'had it so good'. They were in no hurry to return to China. They were keener on hoarding rice given them by the British than fighting on their behalf.

While the sectors of responsibility dictated themselves, the complexity of the command structure rivalled the Allied problems in the Baltic and at Constantinople. Churchill and Roosevelt had offered Chiang Kai-shek the Supreme Command of the China War Theatre to balance the American supremacy in the Pacific and the British supremacy in the Indian Ocean. In return the Generalissimo had accepted General Joseph Stilwell as his Deputy Supreme Allied Commander. He had gone further. He had made Stilwell titular head of the Chinese Expeditionary Force to Burma. Stilwell had reached Chungking about the same time that Alexander had arrived in Rangoon. Chiang and Madame Chiang had shown themselves candidly anti-British in their talks with Stilwell. Although the British were administering their troops in Burma, they said they preferred to place them under Stilwell's operational command. They did not trust the intentions or abilities of the British after their poor showing in Malaya and so far in Burma. Furthermore, they hoped that Stilwell would be given command of the British and Chinese forces, a proposition that Stilwell knew would not be acceptable to Churchill or Roosevelt.

Stilwell was one of the more controversial American commanders. He is aptly described in the British Official History in the following terms:

> Stilwell, who knew the Chinese well and spoke their language, was an unconventional man of fifty-eight, but with the mental and physical toughness of a much younger man. He was outspoken to the point of rudeness, his criticisms were often unjustified and he could be utterly uncompromising. These traits made him many enemies and earned for him from his compatriots the nickname 'Vinegar Joe', but those who knew him in action testified to his great courage and determination and his powers of leadership in the field. (*The War against Japan*, II, p. 154)

Alexander's own description of Stilwell runs:

> I don't think that Stilwell had much of an opinion of us British, but personally he and I got on well together. I always felt that he disliked his position with the Chinese: he was a very senior American general and probably had the feeling that he ought to have been playing a greater part in the war, instead of being relegated to a backwater.
>
> I am aware that most British accounts are unsympathetic to 'Vinegar Joe'—if only for his practice of 'cussing' the British troops under his command beyond the point of endurance; but—to quote an anonymous commentator—Stilwell knew well (none better after his experience with the American Marauders and his sometimes impossible Chinese) that disaster overtook any army whenever it passed a strange and possibly moveable psychological breaking point where hard-pressed Allied troops suddenly sat down and felt sick and hard-pressed Japs sat down and actually died.
>
> Certainly, in those dark days he was no defeatist: on the contrary, he showed great courage and fight. When the campaign collapsed he found his way back

> to India through the jungle on foot, having done all he could for his Chinese forces. (Memoirs, p. 95)

Stilwell's remarks about Alexander were never complimentary, but nor were they about anyone other than a very few of his trusted personal staff. Other British commanders would have treated Stilwell as *persona non grata*. Alexander had learned over the years how to handle difficult personalities. He tolerated Stilwell, making allowances for his idiosyncracies. The fact that the two never fell out is to Alexander's credit rather than Stilwell's. The latter may well have contributed to the unfavourable impression of the American Army which built up in Alexander's mind in the early days of the Tunisian Campaign. Had it not been for Stilwell's constant bragging about American military prowess, Alexander might not have been so uncharitable about American failures in the Kassarine battles.

The two men met for the first time on 14 March at Maymyo, in the hills east of Mandalay, where Alexander had established his headquarters alongside the Government of Burma which had withdrawn there after the fall of Rangoon. Stilwell describes this first meeting in his diary (p. 78):

> *Friday 13th:* Alexander arrived. Very cautious. Long sharp nose. Rather brusque and standoffish. . . . Astonished to find me—mere me—a goddam American in command of Chinese troops. 'Extraordinary!' (*sic*) Looked me over as if I had crawled out from under a rock.

Stilwell announced his assumption of command of the Chinese V and VI Armies on the orders of the Generalissimo, and, in this capacity, proposed to concert his plans with Alexander as his co-equal commander of the Imperial Forces in Burma. Alexander accepted what Stilwell said, but noted that he had neither the staff nor communications for the purpose. Ten days later Alexander flew to Chungking to pay his respects to Chiang Kai-shek and to confirm that his administrative arrangements for the Chinese armies were satisfactory to the Chinese Government. He was warmly received by Chiang and his wife, who seem to have been impressed as much by Alexander's worth as a soldier as by his arguments for a simple command structure. Alexander was surprised when Chiang changed his mind about his original objections to Chinese troops coming under British command and asked him to assume overall command of the Chinese as well as the Imperial forces in Burma. Had Alexander known how fickle Chiang's mind was, he would have discounted much of the apparent advance he had made in Chinese favour.

On return to Maymyo, Alexander told Stilwell of Chiang's change of heart. Stilwell, who by then seems to have accepted Alexander as a man he could trust—though with many reservations—agreed to serve under his overall command. Thus both sides won what they wanted: Alexander controlled operations in Burma, but did not have the worries and frustrations of dealing direct with the Chinese who remained, in name, under Stilwell's command; and Stilwell retained command of the Chinese troops, whom he loved so much, and was able to go on being sarcastic about the British.

The British command structure also presented difficulties. Alexander was in the position of a theatre commander responsible for the wider strategic and political issues of the campaign. He could not command the Imperial troops in the field as well. Accordingly he repeated a request, made by Hutton as early as mid-February, for a Corps headquarters to command 1 Burma and 17 Indian Divisions. He would then have two principal field commanders under him: Stilwell commanding the Chinese in the Sittang Valley and in the Shan States; and a British corps commander directing the Imperial troops on the Irrawaddy. On the advice of his staff, he asked for General Slim by name. He could not have made a better choice. Slim arrived by air with a skeleton headquarters, called Burma Corps, and assumed command of Bruce Scott's, Cowan's and Anstice's troops on 19 March.

While the command structure and responsibilities of the two tactical commanders were being argued out, Alexander was assessing his tactical plan. He knew that the length of time he could delay the Japanese advance and the line on which the Japanese would eventually be halted depended on the speed with which their high command reinforced Iida. With the Port of Rangoon in their hands, and their campaigns in Malaya and Indonesia successfully concluded, they were not short of fresh troops and aircraft. Alexander was not prepared to surrender any more of Burma than he was forced to; yet he was equally conscious of his lack of troops and supplies for a prolonged defensive battle on any particular line. Time could only be bought by trading space. He would have to conduct a well-judged withdrawal, standing on a given line just long enough to inflict the greatest damage on the Japanese without allowing any part of his force to be encircled by superior numbers. He would have liked to have met the renewed Japanese advance on the line Tharrawaddy-Nyaunglebin (see fig. 21, p. 120) to which Cowan and Bruce Scott had retired after the fall of Rangoon. The Generalissimo, suspicious of British intentions and abilities, had refused to allow Tu's V Army to deploy south of Toungoo. This meant that Alexander's first line of defence had to lie between Prome on the Irrawaddy and Toungoo on the Sittang and thence to the Shan-Thai border if he was to occupy the shortest line to conserve troops.

At this stage he did not publish his subsequent lines of resistance. His tentative plans were to fall back to the line Minhla on the Irrawaddy—Taungdwingyi on central railway—Pyinmana on the Sittang—Loikaw in the Shan States, to cover the oilfields at Yenangyaung. When this line had to be abandoned, he would retire to a line running east and west through Meiktila, 70 miles south of Mandalay. He was determined not to be forced into the trap of having to fight with his back to the unbridged Irrawaddy. When the Meiktila line became untenable, he would withdraw to the north bank of the river, abandoning Mandalay if need be.

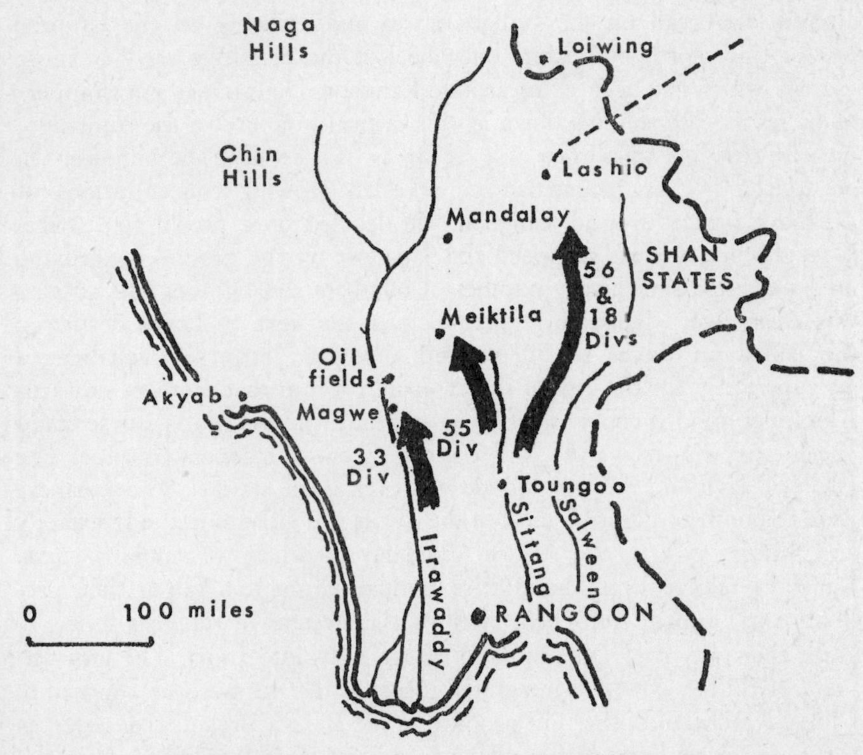

22 General Iida's plans for the occupation of Upper Burma

General Iida decided not to wait for reinforcements before advancing north. In his planning, he took into account the expected arrival of two new divisions, the 18th from Singapore and the 56th from Japan. He decided to drive northward, as Alexander expected, using his 33 Division up the Irrawaddy with its objective the oilfields, and his 55 Division up the Sittang aiming for Meiktila to cover the forward concentration of his two new divisions. These he proposed to use in a wide encircling movement through the Shan States to prevent the Chinese Armies escaping back to China, and to cut the Burma Road. 55 Division had the special task of capturing Toungoo airfield undamaged by *coup de main* for use by Japanese aircraft supporting Iida's strong right hook.

Besides doubling their army, the Japanese doubled their air force in Burma, sending bombers and fighters from Malaya and Indonesia. The Royal Air Force and the American Volunteer Group* had held their own up to this point in the campaign. Hindsight suggests that the Air Officer Commanding in Burma would have been prudent to have withdrawn his aircraft to Akyab on the Indian Ocean and Loiwing on the Chinese border, just north of Lashio, once he lost the primitive early warning system, which had been set up around Rangoon. Determined not to appear to be letting the soldiers down at this critical juncture in the campaign, he withdrew his squadrons only as far as Magwe near the oilfields. On 20 March his air reconnaissance revealed growing concentrations of Japanese aircraft around Rangoon. He decided on a preemptive strike. Next day his aircraft surprised the Japanese on the ground, destroying or damaging a satisfactory number of bombers and fighters. His success was short lived. Japanese retaliation over the next 36 hours destroyed the Allied air forces in Burma and gave the Japanese unchallenged air superiority for the rest of the campaign. From that moment onwards Alexander and his commanders fought blind, whereas the Japanese could check every Imperial and Chinese move by close air reconnaissance. The effect on civil and military morale was even more serious. The Japanese were to bomb and destroy most of the towns and villages in the Irrawaddy and Sittang valleys, and reduce Mandalay to a heap of smoking ruins. Railways, telegraph, public utilities gradually came to a halt as their predominantly Indian staffs fled, swelling the streams of refugees trying to make their way over the Chin and Nagga Hills into India. The Government of Burma slowly disintegrated. Most of the Burmese, as opposed to Chins, Karens and other hill peoples, in the Burma Brigades, deserted as the weeks went by to return home to protect their families. And in the steadier British, Indian and Chinese units, the effect of constant air surveillance, followed by air attack, had a cumulative effect on morale as it had done in the BEF in France. The feeling that further resistance is point-

* Chenault's Group of American Volunteer airmen formed to help China in her struggle with the Japanese before the US entered the war.

less, which is one of the by-products of loss of air cover, reduced the fighting efficiency of the Burma Army more than any other factor.

The first probing attacks, heralding the renewed Japanese offensive, started on 15 March. 17 Division withdrew from Tharrawaddy to the Prome area, and 1 Burma Division fell back through the leading division of the Chinese V Army at Toungoo. It was then lifted by train to the Irrawaddy Valley where it started to assemble at Allanmyo as Slim arrived with his Burma Corps HQ. Slim was far from ready to meet the new Japanese advance and hoped for another ten days or so in which to sort out and regroup his new command to his own satisfaction.

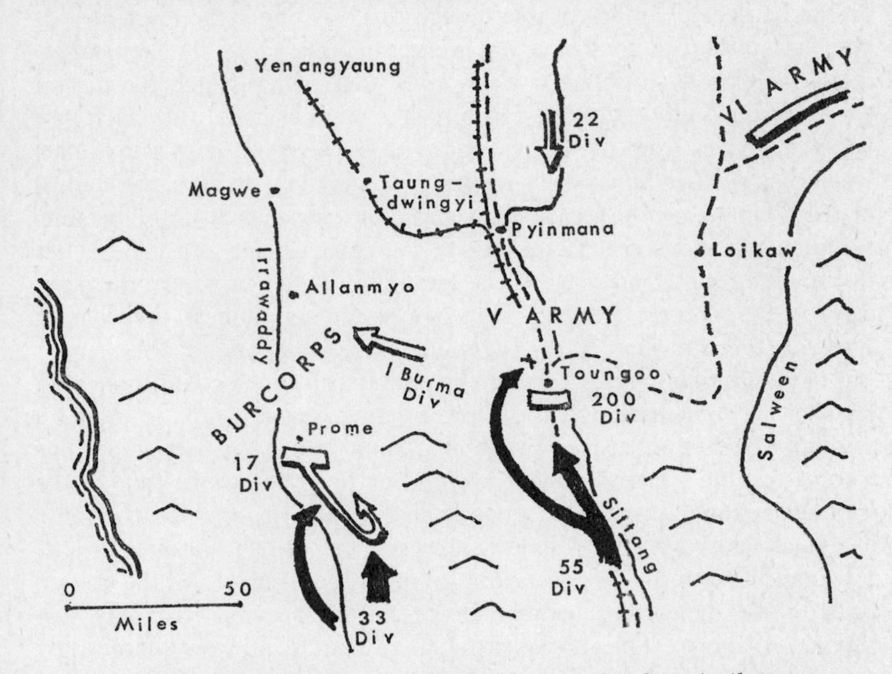

23 Operations on the Prome–Toungoo Line, 15 March–3 April 1942

The first major Japanese attack struck Tu's Army at Toungoo. On 24 March a Japanese force, evading detection, slipped round the Chinese defenders of Toungoo and seized the airfield to the north of the town. The 200 Chinese Division fought a creditable action in the defence of Toungoo itself for over a week after the loss of the airfield in their rear. Stilwell reacted by ordering the concentration of the two nearest Chinese divisions intending to counter-attack. Much to his chagrin nothing happened. Neither division moved. 200 Division fought its way out of the Japanese encirclement and retired northwards on 30 March. Stilwell's authority over the Chinese armies proved to be a politely engineered façade with no substance. No Chinese army or divisional commander would execute an order from Stilwell without first referring it to Chiang Kai-shek in Chungking, 1,000 miles away. This was not an auspicious start.

Alexander was in Chungking when the Toungoo battle was at its height. The Generalissimo, as he and Stilwell were soon to discover, fought every Chinese battle personally from his capital, ordering or authorising divisional deployments from day to day as if he were present on the battlefield. Impracticable though this was under the most favourable circumstances, confusion was worse confounded by the Generalissimo's inability to maintain a clear, consistent policy which his distant subordinates could anticipate. His bird-like mind changed with each new set of telegrams from the front, and, as these were two days out of date when they reached him and his replies took a further two days, the control of the Chinese armies was hesitant and their movements unpredictable.

Hearing of 200 Division's troubles in Toungoo, Chiang asked Alexander to launch a counter-offensive in the Irrawaddy Valley to relieve the pressure on the Chinese although only one of the six Chinese divisions in Burma had fired a shot. At the beginning of his joint command Alexander was in no position to refuse, though he doubted any good could come of it. He sent an immediate signal to Slim ordering Burma Corps to mount a suitable relieving offensive. The timing could not have been more unfortunate. Slim's Corps needed every hour to get ready to receive the coming Japanese attack. Slim himself, like Alexander, doubted the value of this attack. Unlike the Chinese, however, the British did obey orders. Slim gave Cowan the task of making an offensive sweep down the eastern bank of the Irrawaddy because Bruce Scott's division had only just reached Allanmyo. The attack started on 29 March and went surprisingly well during the first day. Slim, without air reconnaissance, did not know that the Japanese had themselves launched their offensive northwards on both banks of the river. Cowan had stopped the easterly thrust, but the Japanese force on the west bank crossed the river behind him and established road blocks on his withdrawal routes. These were eventually cleared at a cost of ten tanks and 300 men whom Cowan could ill afford to lose. The attack had no effect on the Japanese operations at Toungoo, whereas it did further damage to the confidence of 17 Division which Slim and Cowan were doing their best to restore.

Wavell visited Burma on 1 April and accompanied Alexander to see

Slim. Their joint conclusion was that the loss of Toungoo made it unwise to go on holding Prome as Slim's eastern flank was now exposed due to the Chinese withdrawal. Moreover, the next line through Taungdwingyi, covering the oilfields, was in Burma's dry belt where the country was more open and suitable for tanks. With Wavell's concurrence Alexander authorised the withdrawal of Slim's Corps and Stilwell's Chinese to the Taungdwingyi line.

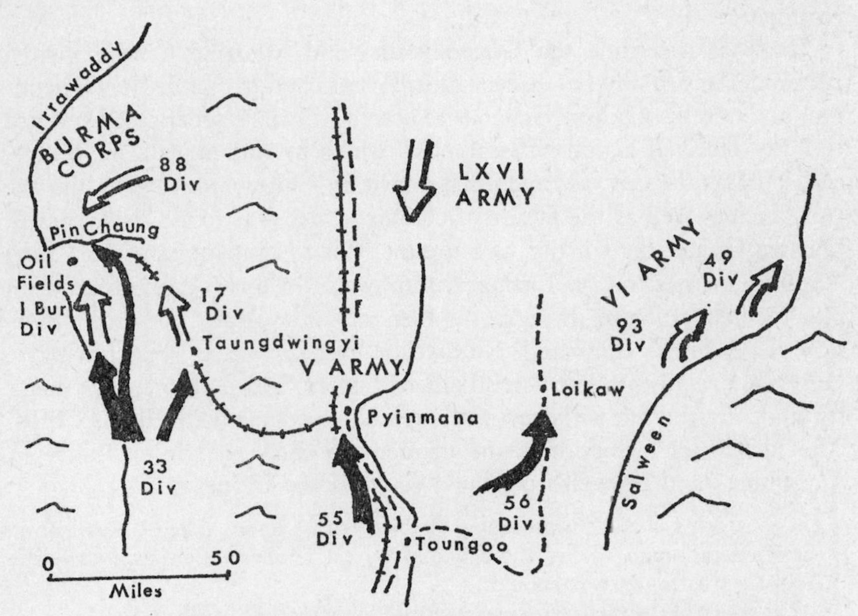

24 Operations on the Taungdwingyi Line, 8–22 April 1942

The Taungdwingyi Line, though more suitable for tanks and artillery than positions further south, had one major weakness. Burma Corps' sector was wider than it could be reasonably expected to hold with the troops available. On the Prome Line, the river, road and railway had been close together, making their defence relatively easy. Burma Corps' sector of the new line stretched from the Irrawaddy over 40 miles eastward to Taungdwingyi, which had to be held strongly because it lay on the oilfield spur of the Rangoon-Mandalay railway. Slim pointed out this weakness in an appreciation of the future conduct of his Corps' operations which he had sent to Alexander on 3 April. More troops were obviously needed. The problem was how to find them and at whose expense. Alexander decided to call on the Chinese to help defend Taungdwingyi so that Slim could concentrate more of his Corps in the Irrawaddy Valley and build up a corps reserve. Alexander felt himself justified in making this request because any failure at Taungdwingyi would expose Tu's V Army flank at Pyinmana. Moreover, troops of the Chinese LXVI Army were beginning to arrive in the Mandalay area from Lashio. Stilwell made his usual carping remarks about having to do the Imperial troops job for them, but Tu agreed to send, first, a battalion and then increased this to a regiment.

At about this time the Generalissimo and Madame Chiang visited Alexander at Maymyo to discuss future plans; and to enable the Generalissimo to tell his Chinese Generals to accept Stilwell's orders. Stilwell had recently received his official seals with which to authenticate his orders, and, perhaps naively, assumed that a visit by Chiang would give him the substance as well as the façade of command. He was to be disillusioned. During the meeting Chiang, as Supreme Allied Commander of the China Theatre, insisted on no further withdrawals. In answer to Alexander's plea for help at Taungdwingyi, the Generalissimo agreed to place a division under Slim's command. No division ever arrived at Taungdwingyi; nor even a regiment. The British official history, in a footnote, says that a battalion arrived but withdrew without making contact with Slim's Corps. The US official history uses the incident to show the impossibility of Alexander's and Stilwell's positions vis-à-vis the Chinese:

> On the 10th Lo and Tu presented Stilwell with a letter, dated 9 April, fr om the Generalissimo saying there would be no Chinese division to aid the British; a battalion was enough. . . .
>
> On 10 April the Generalissimo reversed his stand of the 9th and wrote:
>
> '. . . According to our original plans a strong division must be speedily sent to support the British forces in meeting the northward advance of the enemy along the Irrawaddy. This is a strategic move which can by no means be neglected. . . .'
>
> On the 12th he again ordered the reinforcement of two key points within the British sector. On the 15th the Generalissimo wrote:
>
> '. . . The British forces moreover are now in a hopeless position and to reinforce them by a division will not avail to maintain their lines. They will not wait . . . but will voluntarily abandon their positions . . . our forces must quickly frame new plans for independent action without reference to the British. . . .'
>
> . . . On 20 April the Generalissimo reversed himself once again and ordered Stilwell to rescue the British. As a result of these reversals and the physical impossibility of moving divisions about at that rate, when the British did take their stand on the line Minhla-Taungdwingyi on the right flank of the

Chinese, there were no Chinese to help them in their attempt to hold a forty mile front with 10,000 men and thirty-six guns. (*Stilwell's Mission to China*, p. 124)

The failure of the Generalissimo to make good his promise of a Chinese division to hold Taungdwingyi was to be one of two events which led to Alexander abandoning the Taungdwingyi line. Slim in his *Defeat into Victory* heads his chapter dealing with this period 'A Chapter of Accidents'. Every operation Burma Corps mounted at this time seemed to go wrong. The reasons were not hard to find: too few units for the front; all units under strength with no hope of reinforcement; officers and men tired and over-strained; an increasingly hostile local population; enemy air superiority; and enemy superiority in jungle tactics to mention but a few.

The battle fought to cover the oilfields lasted for over a week and was fought principally by Bruce Scott's 1 Burma Division, which was forced to give way and fall back slowly on Yenangyaung. On 14 April Slim decided he could no longer save the oilfields and ordered the demolition of the installations which was completed successfully by the following evening. In the absence of Chiang Kai-shek's promised division, Slim had been forced to leave the bulk of Cowan's division at Taungdwingyi, holding the Japanese advance up the railway. Cowan was not hard pressed, but was too far away to help Bruce Scott effectively. Disaster struck when the Japanese penetrated the wide gap between the two Imperial divisions and established a strongly held block on the only passable ford over the Pin Chaung—a tributary of the Irrawaddy—just north of the oilfields and across Bruce Scott's line of withdrawal. Slim had no reserve with which to counter-attack the Japanese block from the north and had to appeal to Alexander for help.

Alexander's only recourse was to ask Stilwell again for Chinese help. The 88 Division of the Chinese LXVI Army had just reached Mandalay. Stilwell agreed that it should be diverted to help Slim rescue Bruce Scott. There could hardly have been a happier decision. General Sun, commanding 88 Division, proved himself a great ally and undid much of the damage done by the Chinese failure to help hold Taungdwingyi. Sun was one of the best Chinese divisional commanders. He had been educated at the Virginia Military Academy and spoke English well. Sun did not hesitate or wait for authority from Chungking. He agreed to cooperate straight away and was as good as his word. He mounted a series of attacks to free 1 Burma Division, and with his help Bruce Scott managed to break out to the north-east, losing much of his heavy equipment and transport, it is true, but saving his division to fight again. Slim and Sun worked admirably together. Had it been possible, Sun would have liked to have withdrawn with Slim into India when the time came to leave Burma.

The arrival of Sun's division put new life into Burma Corps, and enabled Slim to contemplate a counter-offensive against the exposed eastern flank of 33 Japanese Division when it advanced north from the oilfields. Alexander and Stilwell agreed and a plan for a counter-offensive starting on 22 April was drawn up by Slim and Tu, the V Army Commander, using three Chinese divisions and 17 Division. There seemed a fair chance of being able, at last, to seize the initiative from the Japanese now that enough Chinese troops had arrived to enable Alexander to create a central reserve. These hopes were soon dashed as the second event, which caused Alexander to abandon the Taungdwingyi line, revealed its true significance on 20 April.

The loss of Toungoo three weeks earlier had uncovered the road from the Sittang Valley into the Shan States (see fig. 24, p. 129) theoretically held by Kan's VI Army. His 55 Chinese Division, of known inferior quality, held this road while his better divisions, 49 and 93, guarded the Chiengmai and Chiengrai passes from Thailand through which it was still expected another Japanese force would emerge.* As early as 9 April 55 Division had been attacked and had given ground to what was thought to be a very small Japanese force. Stilwell visited VI Army on 11 April and was thoroughly dissatisfied with Kan's performance. He appreciated the danger of a major Japanese offensive into the Shan States, but was pinning his hopes on a counter-offensive which he had agreed with Chiang Kai-shek should be launched from around Pyinmana and for which he was concentrating as many troops as possible. He did not wish to become involved in the Shan States any earlier than necessary, but events were to over-take him. The two new Japanese divisions, 56 and 18, had already reached the front, the former being directed on Lashio, supported by the latter. On 18 April, Kan's 55 Chinese Division was overrun and all communication with it was lost. Kan made a half-hearted attempt to move his 93 Division to support 55 Division. Discretion became the better part of valour, and he withdrew his two surviving divisions back into China taking as much British rice with him as his divisions could carry. The road to Lashio was wide open. Any idea of a master stroke at Pyinmana or Yenangyaung died as Alexander, Stilwell and Slim grappled with this new situation. It looked as if the time had come to consider leaving Burma.

Alexander's staff had been working for some weeks on a series of contin-

* Japanese records show that no such force existed in Thailand.

gency plans in case a situation of this type made the retention of Upper Burma impracticable. Alexander had discussed the various possibilities with Wavell during his visit early in April. On 18 April, just before the collapse of Kan's front, he had received a directive from Wavell telling him that his objectives were to be: to keep touch with the Chinese; to cover the Kalewa-Tamu track back into Assam, the eastern province of India; and to keep his force in being with as many 'cards for re-entry' as possible for the eventual reconquest of Burma. In view of the weakness of India's eastern frontier, Wavell was relying on as much help as possible

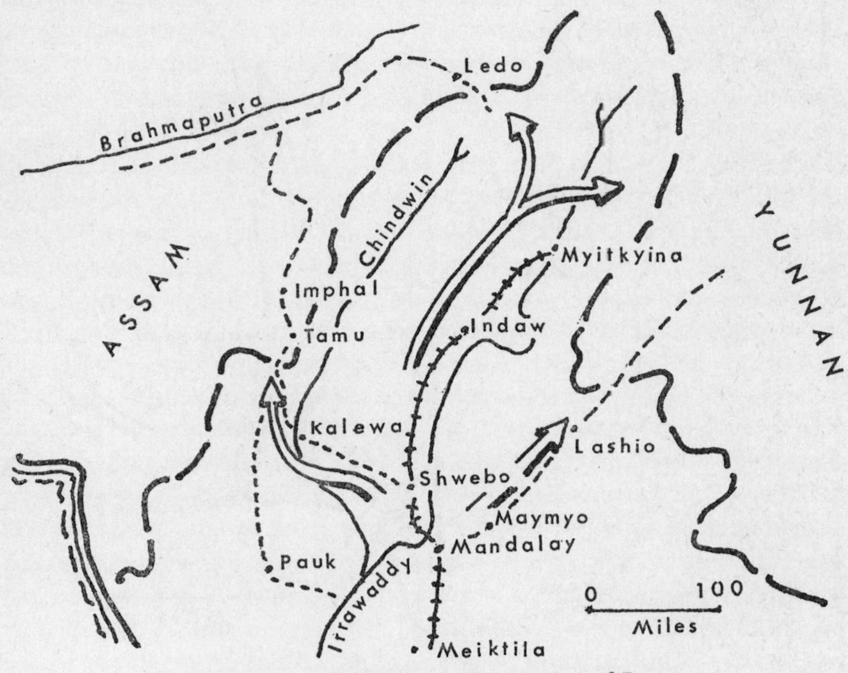

25 Contingency Plans for the Evacuation of Burma

from the Burma Army, but Alexander's prime concern was to keep touch with the Chinese.

Alexander's first ideas for carrying out this directive were for Bruce Scott's division to cover Kalewa; Cowan's to retire northwards to cover the construction of a road from Ledo into Northern Burma; and Anstice's armoured brigade, supported by one of Cowan's infantry brigades, to act as the rearguard for the Chinese withdrawing up the Burma Road into China. An administrative plan had been drawn up to effect these decisions when it was found that a severe famine in Yunnan would mean starvation if the Chinese withdrew north-eastwards. Alexander, therefore, proposed that they should all retire northwards, possibly into India via Ledo. The collapse in the Shan States made it certain that the Burma Road would not be available.

On 21 April Alexander conferred with the Generalissimo's liaison officer at Maymyo. They concluded that it would be a mistake for any

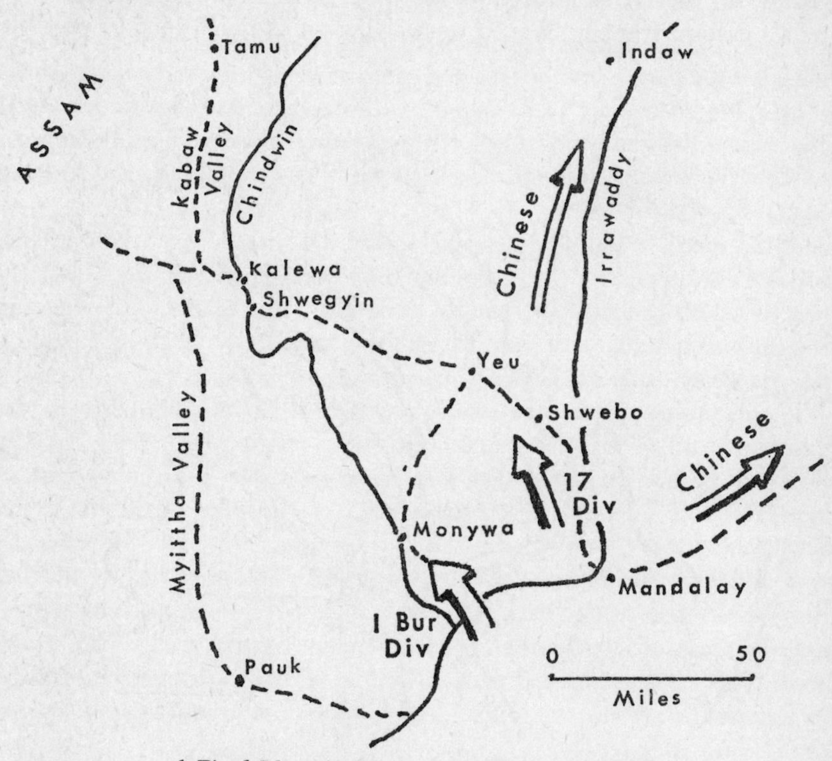

26 Final Phase in Burma, 23 April–20 May 1942

Imperial forces to retire into China and it would be preferable for 7 Armoured Brigade to cover a Chinese withdrawal through Shwebo into Northern Burma. Slim's Corps should be kept together and withdraw to India via Kalewa. To ensure that this would prove practicable when the time came, Alexander gave instructions for ferries and rafts to be prepared on the Irrawaddy west of Mandalay for the use of Burma Corps. He had no intention of repeating the Sittang affair. There was only one bridge over the Irrawaddy—the long Ava railway bridge near Mandalay.

Alexander had long foreseen the danger of being outflanked in the east and forced to fight with his back to the wide Irrawaddy. He was also aware that the Monsoon would break on about 15 May. Once this happened the rough track from Kalewa to Tamu would become impassable. If he could not defend Northern Burma and the Burma Road until the monsoon brought Japanese military operations to a standstill, then he must get out before the rains came. The news from the Shan States grew steadily worse. Stilwell worked harder than anyone to goad his Chinese generals into attacking the advancing Japanese columns. Confusion on the railways; refusals by Chinese authorities in Lashio to send back lend-lease trucks to lift Chinese troops;* and shameless disobedience of orders destroyed any chance Stilwell ever had of retrieving the situation. The collapse of the Chinese Armies made it clear that the time really had come to leave Burma for the time being.

On 25 April, Alexander gave orders for the withdrawal over the Irrawaddy to begin and for the final evacuation of supplies from the Mandalay base to stock the withdrawal routes back into India. He had only one aim now: to reach India with as much of the Burma Army as possible before the monsoon made the Kalewa-Tamu track impassable.

There was but one route which the Burma Army could take for its withdrawal into Assam. A rough cart-track, which Alexander's Sappers did their best to improve, ran for 107 miles from Yeu, north-west of Mandalay to Kalewa on the Chindwin River. 30 miles of this track ran through waterless country, and the last few miles were so obstructed by rock outcrops that it was useless for vehicles. The only way of moving guns, tanks and trucks back into India was by ferry from Shwegyin to Kalewa. From Kalewa to Tamu on the Indian frontier there was a rough hewn track up the malarial Kabaw Valley, which could just be used by vehicles in the dry season. A metalled road then ran from Tamu to Imphal and on into India.

As soon as Alexander gave his order to start the withdrawal, his administrative staff did their best to stock this precarious route with supplies from what was left in the Mandalay depots and Wavell's GHQ India did the same from Imphal working in the opposite direction, hoping time would allow the whole route to be stocked. A minimum of a week was needed to dump the supplies on the route. Could Alexander buy that week?

There were three places at which the Japanese could intercept his withdrawal as soon as their air reconnaissance showed them that the Burma Army was intent on escape to India. A Japanese column could make its

* Stilwell asked for 150 out of the 850 lend-lease trucks in Lashio but only 22 were sent.

way via Pauk, west of the Irrawaddy, to the Myittha Valley and hence to Kalewa. Slim ordered the 2nd Burma Brigade to withdraw by this route to cover his flank. Or the Japanese might ferry troops up the Chindwin, cutting the withdrawal route at Shwegyin. Precautions were taken to guard this river route by placing a boom across the Chindwin south of the Shwegyin ferry berth. Somehow a third point of danger was overlooked, possibly because, on the map, there seemed to be a number of alternative routes available in the area. This was the landing stage and small town of Monywa.

The withdrawal over the Irrawaddy was carried out with commendable skill. Slim used Cowan's 17 Division and Anstice's 7 Armoured Brigade to cover the withdrawal. Both had their tails well up and were fighting better than they had done so far. Slim's Corps had settled down under his firm leadership and gave its best. He fought a series of well-conducted rearguard actions while the Chinese V Army withdrew north towards Shewbo, covered by Sun's 88 Chinese Division. At midnight on 30 May, when Slim was satisfied that as many Imperial and Chinese troops were over the river as were ever likely to reach it, he ordered the demolition of the Ava Bridge. The Battle of Mandalay was over; the withdrawal to Imphal had begun.

Once over the Irrawaddy, Alexander decided to delay his withdrawal as long as possible to clear his wounded and to give the streams of Indian refugees as much time as possible to reach India before the fighting units started to fall back. He has been accused of paying too little attention to the plight of the civil population, but this is unfair. His administrative staff did all they could to assist the civil government. His pause on the north bank of the Irrawaddy after the Ava Bridge was blown almost lost him the race with both the Japanese and the monsoon. The first sign of trouble came when Bruce Scott's 1 Burma Division approached Monywa after crossing the Irrawaddy by ferry. A Japanese force had reached the town first and was established across his withdrawal route. It took two days fighting to clear a way round the block. The chances were that other Japanese would be making their way up the Chindwin to Shwegyin.

Alexander met Stilwell for the last time during the campaign late on 1 May at Yeu, and agreed that the Irrawaddy line should be abandoned in view of the situation at Monywa. Stilwell agreed to release 7 Armoured Brigade which had been supporting Sun's 88 Chinese Division on the river opposite Mandalay. Stilwell intended to withdraw with Tu's V Army to North Burma and then to cross either into India or China. He found that he could no longer influence his Chinese and so gave up the unequal struggle, taking his American staff, including the Burmese nurses belonging to the Seagrave Medical Mission, on foot back to Imphal by a route to the north of Alexander's withdrawal. Stilwell's personal courage and strength of character brought his party through the rigours of that march. Sun's 88 Division eventually made its way to Imphal as well. Some Chinese units reached Ledo. The majority escaped to China.

Covering the retreat of the Burma Army was now in Slim's capable hands. There was little more that Alexander could do as Army Commander. The Japanese made their attempts to cut the rearguard off at Shwegyin and succeeded in stopping the ferry to Kalewa earlier than was hoped. The last action of the campaign was fought around the small sandy bay which served as the ferry embarkation point at Shwegyin. The action lasted throughout 10 May. In the evening the 17 Division's rearguard fired off what was left of its gun and mortar ammunition, destroyed its last guns and vehicles, and slipped away over the rough narrow track to Kalewa.

On 12 May the rains started while 17 Division was still on the Kalewa-Tamu track. All Alexander's worst fears about this route were proved right. Many men, already exhausted by three and a half month's fighting without relief, could not withstand this last blow. Fortunately the rain stopped any attempt by the Japanese to pursue the dazed survivors of the First Burma Campaign. The last unit reached Tamu on 19 May.

The British Official History sums up:

> During the campaign the Army in Burma, without once losing its cohesion, had retreated nearly one thousand miles in some three and a half months—the longest retreat ever carried out by a British Army—and for the last seven hundred miles had virtually carried its base with it. (*The War against Japan*, II, p. 210)

On 20 May Alexander handed over command of the Burma Army units to IV (Indian) Corps which Wavell had charged with the defence of Assam. His first major operational command had come to a bitter and disappointing end. Wavell in his report to Churchill said 'he had performed a fine feat in bringing back the army'.

Was it a fine feat? The many journalists' accounts and junior officers' books published on the campaign leave no doubt that all the horrors, destruction and uncontrolled panic of defeat and withdrawal were experienced on the Allied side. Imperial unpreparedness and Japanese air superiority ensured that this would be so. Many tactical mistakes were made, and sometimes undeserved disasters occurred. In spite of all this, Alexander's force never slipped uncontrollably in rout as it might so easily have done. No part of the Burma Army failed to break out from the many encirclements. By the end of the campaign the Imperial units were fighting better than they had done at the beginning.

How had cohesion been maintained? Primarily by common sense forward planning, carried out in Alexander's own inimitable way. As Alan Brooke had realised when he was comparing Alexander with Montgomery, 'Alex' carried on without appearing to appreciate the full dangers of his position. This apparent calmness was infectious and is reflected in many unit accounts of the campaign which refer to the extraordinary effect his presence had on the soldiers. 'It's OK lads, Alex is here.' To Hutton, his predecessor, and Winterton, his Chief of Staff, must go the credit for the logistic foresight which ensured the Burma Army and the Chinese Expeditionary Force never starved. Alexander pays them a well-deserved tribute in his despatches and memoirs. But no Chief of Staff, however good, can do his detailed work unless his commander provides the inspiration and follows a consistent operational policy. Without them, decisions cannot be taken in time and confusion follows. Alexander gave clear direction, basing his operational estimates on judgment rather than fine calculation. His hunches were usually right and, as a result, he rarely asked his soldiers to hold on for too long or leave their positions unnecessarily early. The only obvious tactical error that he made was ordering Slim, from distant Chungking, to take the offensive south of Prome before he was ready.

What of his handling of Stilwell and the Chinese? He had never served with Americans or their Chinese Allies before. It is doubtful whether 'Vinegar Joe' and Alexander ever liked each other. The two men were opposites: Alexander always immaculate, even under the worst conditions, charming on all occasions and militarily calm. Stilwell usually dressed in slovenly GI style, irascible, thoughtless of the feelings of others, and militarily excitable. Stilwell accepted Alexander's overlordship though it irked him; in return, Alexander did his best to help ease Stilwell's problems with the Generalissimo and his Chinese generals. The two men's personal relationships settled at a level which did no harm to the Allied cause in Burma. As far as the Chinese were concerned, Alexander realised that they needed very special handling. Given the support of Imperial artillery and tanks, their men fought excellently as infantry. If treated fairly, as Slim treated Sun, they gave their best. At the higher levels they behaved in much the same way as the British. They cooperated fully when it was in their interests to do so, but they, like the British, had a mental, if not a written, break clause in all their agreements. They would withdraw from an operation with little or no warning if the safety of their troops, in their opinion, was in jeopardy. Paul Renaud's remark, when he heard that Alexander was determined to withdraw I Corps from Dunkirk on 1–2 June 1940, 'I note that the decision to have a united command only lasted 24 hours' might have been uttered by Alexander after the loss of Toungoo and on many subsequent occasions. Cooperation between Alexander and the Chinese improved markedly as the campaign progressed. If the Stilwell-Slim counter-offensive had been launched successfully on 22 April, inter-allied cooperation might have blossomed as confidence was established. As it was, the two sides fell apart in the withdrawal past Mandalay and the campaign was over.

But what of Alexander's generalship? Slim, in *Defeat into Victory* (p. 118) is critical, feeling that the aim of the campaign was not clearly enough defined. As a result he felt it became a patchwork of improvisation with objectives changing with the weeks. This is certainly true. There were never less than about three aims, but these were given to Alexander by Churchill and Wavell. A military genius of Napoleonic brilliance might have used the hills between the two Japanese axes of advance up the Sittang and Irrawaddy as a means of defeating each Japanese force in detail. He would probably have placed a light covering force in each valley and concentrated the rest of his army as a mobile striking force to hit first one Japanese column and then the other. This would have been the classic manoeuvre. Was it possible in Burma in 1941? It is doubtful for three good reasons: first, the Chinese armies could not be manoeuvred in this way; secondly, the Imperial troops were not well enough trained; and thirdly, Napoleon did not operate under an adverse air situation, as Alexander did. Nevertheless, there are grounds for feeling that a more inspired operational concept might have been possible. This suspicion tends to grow as Alexander's subsequent campaigns unfold. Burma gives the first inkling that it was his soundness rather than his inspiration which carried him to the forefront of the Allied military commanders. In Burma the Japanese never achieved numerical superiority, but General Iida held the initiative throughout. Alexander himself confesses that 'the evacuation of Burma was a complete military defeat. . . .'

And what of his personal reactions? He was sent out to save Rangoon. He failed, but everyone accepts that his mission was hopeless from the start. Then he tried to hold Central and Northern Burma, failing again after two and a half months fighting. He saw the Burma oilfields destroyed; Mandalay reduced to rubble; the British administration of the country collapse; and hundreds of thousands of Indian refugees streaming hopelessly away from the Japanese advance and from the vengeance of the local Burmese. His own Army had escaped without its heavy equipment, and his Chinese allies had been driven back into China. He was a defeated general. As Slim comments in his conclusion to his story of the First Burma Campaign (p. 121); 'Defeat is bitter to the common soldier, but trebly bitter to his general. . . . "I have failed them" he would say to himself, "and failed my country".' These thoughts are sure to have passed through Alexander's mind as well though he never expressed them. As far as he was concerned, he had done his duty.

Alfred Wagg, the US War Correspondent, writing immediately after the campaign, before he knew of Alexander's future successes, describes meeting him the day he reached Tamu:

> That was a day of days! General Alexander was just as calm, as quiet, as he had been the last time I had seen him in Maymyo. Every time the car stopped, he'd get out and talk to his men who were 'going home'. . . . Everyone called him just 'Alex'. 'Alex' is probably the combination of all good things a general can possess. Gentle but strong, kind but determined, and one of the few great men whose vanity doesn't need the boost of being told so. Like America's Generals Marshall and Stilwell, he is what he is—you can take it or leave it. (*A Million Died*, p. 110)

Churchill's summing up of Alexander's performance showed that he had not lost confidence in him:

> In this his first experience of independent command, though it ended in stark defeat, he showed all those qualities of military skill, imperturbability and wise judgement that brought him later into the first rank of Allied war leaders. The road to India was barred.

It may be argued that this was Churchill consciously building an 'Alexander' legend. Brooke, a much harder and more professional judge of soldiers, did not lose faith in him. On the contrary, he noted in his diary on 25 July:

> Was then sent for by PM who wanted to hear results of our morning meeting with Marshal and King. I told him we had fixed up question of command of North Africa. US, to find Supreme Commander, with British Deputy. Under him two Task Force Commanders, one US for Casablanca front and one British for Oran front. I wanted Alexander for Task Force Commander. He wanted him to be both Deputy Supreme Commander and Task Force Commander. . . . (Churchill, *The Turn of the Tide*, p. 429)

The next phase of Alexander's career was already being shaped for him in London and Washington.

7

Defeat Redeemed

> Strangely, as I studied the directive, I remembered the exhilaration I had had when I was ordered to the Middle East, a premonition that at last our fortunes were about to change.
>
> Alexander in his Memoirs, p. 12

The turning points of the Second World War—the Battle of Midway to the Americans, the Battle of Stalingrad to the Russians, and the Second Battle of El Alamein to the British—were not discernible as such in 1942. They were like the momentary improvements which occur during a stock-market slide. No one knew whether these successes portrayed an upward trend in Allied fortunes or a pause before the index plunged again on its downward course. 1942 had been a disastrous year. Only the most perceptive speculators would have started buying Allied stock when Alexander arrived in Cairo in August 1942 to assume command in the Middle East. The Japanese were still extending their conquests in Asia; the Germans were marching across the Southern Ukraine and were approaching the Caucasus Mountains; and the British Eighth Army stood unsurely at El Alamein, a bare 200 miles from Cairo, contemplating the possibility of further withdrawal and the loss of the British position in the Middle as well as the Far East.

It looked as if the vast envelopment dreamed about by Axis geopoliticians might be coming to pass: Rommel's Africa Corps advancing from the west; von List's Army Group A descending through the Caucasus from the north; and the Japanese Fleets of Admiral Kondo and Admiral Nagumo sweeping across the undefended Indian Ocean from the east to a strategic junction of Axis forces near Suez. In retrospect, we know that this was unlikely to happen, but in 1942 Allied defeats had been so persistent that each new setback, however small, seemed to spell the approach of further disaster. In looking critically at the events of the autumn of 1942, it is easy to overlook the psychological conditions which prevailed at the time. The British were upon the verge of losing faith in themselves. It was a period for strong nerves, singleness of purpose and intuitive conviction that success could still be wrested from failure. Many writers who belittle the actions of the victors of the second Battle of El Alamein, forget the agonies and uncertainties of 1942.

While Alexander was withdrawing the remnants of his Burma Army into Assam in the first week of May, Churchill felt the first pangs of doubt about Auchinleck as Commander-in-Chief Middle East. Malta was being heavily bombed by Axis aircraft and could not be revictualled unless the British reoccupied the Martuba airfields in Cyrenaica from which supply convoys could be given fighter cover. Churchill anxiously awaited Auchinleck's proposal for an offensive westwards from the Gazala Line, just west of Tobruk, when he received a cable from him suggesting the adoption of a defensive policy in the desert so that more reinforcements could be sent from the Middle East to help Wavell in the defence of India. Arthur Bryant records Churchill's fury:

> It was only with the utmost difficulty that Brooke was able to persuade him not to demand Auchinleck's immediate recall and his supersession by Alexander, then in the last stages of his race against the Japanese and the rains through the jungle defiles of the Indian frontier. (*The Turn of the Tide*, p. 380)

Alexander's defeat in Burma was not being held against him in Whitehall. On the contrary, command of two successful rearguards at Dunkirk and in Burma, endeared him to Churchill's romantic mind, turning him into a British Marshal Ney. Churchill was beginning to place a blind faith in Alexander without any concrete evidence of his real abilities in high command. The Neys of this world are apt to find themselves lost when commanding-in-chief. The problems confronting men in supreme command are rarely as clear cut nor are the options as few as those of a tactical commander. There were dangers in Churchill's fixation on the name of Alexander. He needed a St George to win back all that had been lost in 1942. Wavell had failed him in 1941; Auchinleck in 1942; Alexander, untried except in defeat, seemed to be his last hope of finding a victorious British General before it was too late. Brooke supported Churchill in his confidence in Alexander, but he could not allow him to relieve Auchinleck without substantial cause. Furthermore, he had other plans for Alexander.

By the time Alexander arrived back in England, the planners in London and Washington had started to look into the old 'Super Gymnast' pigeon-holes and to dust off the plans for an invasion of French North Africa. The Americans had begun to appreciate that their British Allies were determined not to rush back into Europe until Nazi Germany had been weakened more seriously than was likely to be the case in 1942 or even 1943. Roosevelt and Marshall were equally certain that American troops must be brought into the war against Germany at the earliest opportunity otherwise American political and military pressure would grow for their despatch to the Pacific instead. An invasion of French North Africa was welcome to both sides: to the British since it would threaten the Axis position in the Western Desert; while to the American it would meet their desire to blood their army as soon as possible against the Germans. Thus it happened that Alexander was reappointed British Task Force Commander for the invasion of French North Africa. General George Patton took Stilwell's place as American Task Force Commander. General Eisenhower was given overall command of the operation, which was renamed 'Torch'. His deputy commander was to be General Mark Wayne Clark with whom Alexander was to become very closely associated in the years ahead.

Alexander's first meeting with Eisenhower is interesting because he seems to have created the same favourable impression that he made on Chiang Kai-shek. Eisenhower's Naval Aide, Captain Harry Butcher, noted in his diary:

> Ike had General Sir Harold R. L. G. Alexander to lunch at the appartment alone. . . . This was an important luncheon, for with Ike junior to General Alexander in rank, with no actual battle experience . . . there was a touchy question of how acceptable Ike might be to Alexander. I was in Ike's office . . . when Ike returned from lunch. His first comment was: 'That guy's good! He ought to be Commander-in-Chief instead of me!'
>
> This evening I asked how he felt they could click. 'Fine', he said, 'The last thing Alexander said as we were going out of the door after lunch was: 'You're off to a good start.'
>
> Ike construed this as approval of him which is important. (*Three Years with Eisenhower*, p. 37)

He was not to have the opportunity to 'click' with Ike for another nine months. Churchill's loss of confidence in Auchinleck grew with Ritchie's defeat at Gazala, with the fall of Tobruk and with the long retreat to El Alamein. Auchinleck's success in defeating Rommel in the First Battle of El Alamein could not expunge his earlier failures. Churchill needed a victory—and quickly—if he himself was to stay in power after all the set-backs of 1942. He set off for Cairo with Brooke to see for himself. Visiting the commanders in the desert, talking to men like General Smuts, who had come up to Cairo from Cape Town especially to meet him, and in long debates with Brooke, Churchill decided to replace Auchinleck with his current favourite, Alexander. The Eighth Army was to have been commanded by General Gott, but he was shot down in an aircraft bringing him back to Cairo. His untimely death resulted in Montgomery's selection as the Eighth Army Commander, bringing together the team that had held the centre of the British line in France in 1940—Brooke in London as CIGS, Alexander in Cairo as Commander-in-Chief Middle East, and Montgomery in the desert commanding the Eighth Army, facing Rommel's Panzer Army Africa. The three men knew and respected each other. Moreover, their characters interlocked with an unusual nicety. Their names alone gave the British in Egypt the one thing they lacked most of all—confidence.

The history of war contains many examples of the perfect matching of leaders and chiefs of staff—Napoleon and Berthier, Hindenburg and Ludendorff, Churchill and Brooke, Roosevelt and Marshall, to quote but a few. There are far fewer examples of successful matching of two commanders in a one-over-one situation. Clashes of personality, rival ambitions and barren recrimination when things go wrong, all tend to upset such relationships; but, on 15 August 1942, a two-man command team was formed in Cairo which was to prove the exception to the rule. Each man was ideally suited to his specific task and level of responsibility, and avoided stepping into the other's sphere. Alexander, gifted with great charm, with unrivalled military experience, and with proven military judgment, commanding by suggestion rather than order, was the best possible overlord for the rasping military genius of Montgomery—strong willed, opinionated and egocentric, but with that indefinable quality of original inspiration which Alexander seemed to lack. Montgomery was a man whom subordinates either worshipped or detested. The pro-Monty school claim the victory of the Second Battle of El Alamein totally for their Messiah: his denigrators give Alexander more credit than is his due. Neither school is correct. El Alamein was Montgomery's tactical victory; the El Alamein campaign was Alexander's strategic success. Alexander was the chairman of the board of directors; Montgomery was the managing director. In the light of the heavy responsibility that Alexander carried of ensuring success for his political and military patrons, Churchill and Brooke, he showed immense courage and self-restraint in not over-supervising his managing director—a man who, at that time, be it remembered, was unproven. The second battle of El Alamein had yet to be fought.

Sir Ian Jacob, who was Lord Ismay's assistant in the Chiefs of Staff Secretariat at the time, working closely with Churchill, throws an interesting light on Alexander's selection. The Prime Minister was not a good judge of military commanders; nor had he a clear idea of how the command system of a twentieth-century army worked. He assumed that as soon as the campaign began Alexander would move forward from Cairo and take personal charge of the battle as Marlborough would have done in the seventeenth century. He was quite upset when Brooke explained that this would not be so. Montgomery, the Eighth Army Commander, would fight the battle and not Alexander. Brooke had judged the personalities of the two men with precision. Montgomery was the man to put new life into Eighth Army and drive it in battle; Alexander would create the atmosphere in which Montgomery's genius could flourish. It looked and was a balanced team.

Alexander reached Cairo on 9 August. Next day he received his directive from Churchill, written in his own hand upon a sheet of British Embassy paper:

1. Your prime and main duty will be to take or destroy at the earliest opportunity the German-Italian Army commanded by Field-Marshal Rommel together with all its supplies and establishments in Egypt and Libya.
2. You will discharge or cause to be discharged such other duties as pertain to your Command without prejudice to the task described in paragraph I which must be considered paramount in His Majesty's interests. (British Official History: *The Mediterranean and the Middle East*, IV, p. 369)

In order to ease Alexander's task, Persia and Iraq were detached from the Middle East Command and formed into a separate command under General Sir Henry Maitland Wilson. Alexander was still left with a very large area of responsibility covering Palestine, Syria, Trans-Jordan, Arabia, and North-East and Central Africa. His day to day business was carried out, on the one hand, in the Middle East Commander-in-Chief's Committee at which he dealt with the overall strategic problems of the Theatre in conjunction with Air Chief Marshal Tedder, C-in-C Middle East Air Forces, and Admiral Harwood, C-in-C Mediterranean; and, on the other, in his own General Headquarters, which directed and administered all the land forces and base installations in the Middle East, amounting to perhaps three times the strength of the Eighth Army. The change, which eased his burden most, although it was not fully appreciated at the time, was the appointment of Montgomery as Eighth Army Commander. Since General Sir Richard O'Connor, Wavell's victorious commander in the Western Desert, had been captured by the Germans in February 1941, there had been no successful commander of the Eighth Army.

Auchinleck had been forced to relieve Cunningham and then Ritchie during battles with Rommel; and, in the end, had taken over command himself. It was not possible, as Brooke frequently pointed out to Churchill, to command a theatre and a subordinate army at the same time. Alexander was never forced to combine both roles—Montgomery saw to that.

Brooke had thought, at one time, of placing Montgomery in charge of Eighth Army under Auchinleck, but, 'I felt some very serious doubts as to whether an Auk-Monty combination would work. I felt that the Auk would interfere too much with Monty; would ride him on too tight a rein.' The Alex-Monty combination had seemed a sounder team; and so it proved. Alexander knew how to stand back from his subordinates and let them develop their own skills. He avoided falling into the worst fault a Commander-in-Chief can commit of thinking and meddling at platoon level—a weakness to which many brave fighting commanders are prone when they reach high command, and one which Brooke found in Lord Gort in 1940. Standing back when great issues are in the balance is not an easy thing to do; the success of the Alex-Monty combination lay in Alexander's ability to do so.

Montgomery arrived in Cairo three days after Alexander. He had thought out his future policy on the way out and was ready to assume command almost before the wheels of his aircraft touched down at Cairo. Fortunately the background and military training of the two men was sufficiently close for them to take a very similar view of the situation which they found in Egypt. They were at one in their assessment of the military needs of the situation: restoration of the Eighth Army's confidence in itself; the proper professional planning and execution of the coming campaign; and the thorough training and rehearsal of the troops who were to take part. These three requirements were closely inter-connected and their solution formed the basis of the plan for the Second and final battle of El Alamein.

On morale, Alexander noted (Memoirs, p. 12):

> There were many troops in the Cairo area: too many, I should have thought. The great majority of them had been in the desert, and they looked tough and fit enough, but it struck me that they lacked something of the cheerfulness and confidence which one usually associates with our soldiers. They were, in fact, not in good spirits. From my talks with various officers and men I formed the impression that something had gone wrong which they couldn't understand —they were bewildered, frustrated, fed up. I know that Winston has observed that, after a visit to the front three days before my own arrival, he found 'the troops were very cheerful'. But who wouldn't cheer up at the sight of Winston and his cigar?

He also noted other things: the tacit assumption at all levels of command that there would be another withdrawal next time Rommel attacked; the myth that had grown up of Rommel's invincibility; the unhealthy divorce between troops in the desert and GHQ in Cairo; and the absence of saluting, the sure sign of lack of confidence in any army. Rightly he decided to leave the correction of the last until he and Montgomery had proved themselves worthy of those salutes. Saluting becomes easy when pride is high; its absence shows disillusion and lack of confidence in the commanders. That confidence had to be restored before the symbols of its existence could be reinstated.

The first and most important step in the restoration of confidence was taken when Alexander issued firm instructions that no further withdrawals were to be contemplated. The Eighth Army would fight where it stood. Exaggerated steps had to be taken to impress the no-withdrawal policy on the cynical minds of officers and men who had heard such protestations of intent before on other defensive lines in the desert. They had not prevented withdrawals in the past: why should they in the future? By the time Alexander and Montgomery had finished their first whirlwind tours of units in the desert and the Nile Delta, few doubted that the new team meant what they said. The effect was electric because it was what the troops wanted to hear but never believed would be possible. A new sense of purpose sprang up in Cairo and at El Alamein like the desert flowers opening after a shower of rain. The spirit was there; the battle experience was there; the only thing missing was confidence in the higher command. The new team gave the majority of officers and men renewed hope of success; the less charitable waited for time and the Germans to prove their competence.

The myth of Rommel's invincibility was not so easy to destroy and could only be achieved by his defeat in battle. The defeat was being arranged, but preparations took time and success would depend, in some measure, on a counter-myth being created. Montgomery needed no prompting and took it upon himself to create a Montgomery myth. The Australian felt hat covered with regimental badges, the two-badged black Tank Corps beret, the carefully contrived informality of dress, the hand-outs of cigarettes and the clear colourful talks which he gave, were all aimed at building up the image of Rommel's rival. Alexander appreciated Montgomery's flair for flamboyant leadership and accepted his extrovert style because it met the psychological needs of Eighth Army at that critical moment.

Another facet of the fight to lay the Rommel legend was Montgomery's demand for a *Corps de Chasse* to counter the fame of Rommel's Africa

Corps. Before going out to the desert Montgomery had persuaded Alexander that this was the first thing which must be organised. Alexander had little difficulty in agreeing. Memories of the failure of Haking's XI Corps at Loos and his unfortunate experiences with the Guards Division at Cambrai made him well aware of the importance of a properly constituted reserve, ready and able to intervene decisively when a battle nears its climax. Montgomery knew it was not worth consulting Auchinleck's Chief of Staff about this, so he turned to the Deputy Chief of Staff, General John Harding, and asked what could be done. By the time he returned from his first visit to Eighth Army, Harding was able to report that a *Corps de Chasse* could be provided. The Headquarters X Corps was responsible for the defence of the Nile Delta and could be released to command three of the four armoured divisions which would be available in time for the offensive.

The physical separation of GHQ from the troops in the desert was easily overcome. Alexander ordered his operational and key administrative staffs to move out of Cairo to a desert site at Mena near the Pyramids at the start of the road leading into the Western Desert. A large part of GHQ could not leave Cairo because it controlled the vast sprawl of base installations, which had grown up around Cairo and in the Canal Zone, but Alexander achieved his psychological aim. In his Memoirs he points out (p. 14):

> I remember very clearly from the First World War, when I was a front-line soldier in the Irish Guards, that our superior commanders and their staffs lived in the great chateaux of France and Belgium, with little opportunity of knowing the immediate conditions in which their troops were fighting. The commander should ensure that his troops shall see him and feel that he has their interests at heart; but throughout my service as a regimental soldier from 1914 to 1918, no commander above brigade commander ever visited my front line sector. I realise, of course, that other junior commanders may have been more fortunate.

Determined that no gulf should exist between himself and the troops under his command Alexander went further. He established a small personal operational headquarters with communications, messing and sleeping accommodation in caravans and a few tents just to the rear of the headquarters of Eighth Army and the Desert Air Force. This enabled him to visit the forward area without imposing upon Montgomery or Air Marshal Coningham, the commander of the Desert Air Force. He called his camp 'Caledon Camp' after his home in Northern Ireland. From El Alamein onwards it followed him wherever he went and was always to be found hidden away unobtrusively in a secluded spot close to the main headquarters commanding the tactical battle at the time.

These measures, designed as a direct attack on the problem of morale, could not bear fruit unless the planning and execution of the next offensive showed that the new team was better than the old. Both men were as agreed in their diagnosis of the operational faults of the Desert Army as they were about its psychological weaknesses. Lack of professionalism lay at the root of most of its troubles. Its amateur performance, while good enough against the Italians, was useless against the Germans. Alexander and Montgomery were professionals in different ways; Alexander by inclination, by training as a guardsman, and as part of his concept of duty to his sovereign; and Montgomery as a deliberate act of policy in becoming the master of his profession. Both were agreed that failure in the earlier desert campaigns was due to lack of control which resulted in fighting actions piecemeal instead of to a master plan. They had both experienced the disasters of mobile warfare in France in 1914 and 1940, and they knew that mobile warfare, which is the aim of every good soldier, required experienced commanders and well-trained troops. The Eighth Army, in spite of all its experience in the desert, possessed too few of either. If success was to be achieved in the short time available, the plan had to be simple and within the capabilities of the troops. The spirit of the 'Jock Column', laudable though it was for all its fine Prince Rupert or Sheridan-like qualities of speed, mobility and initiative, had to be stilled. Divisions must be fought as divisions under control of corps commanders who, in turn, would work implicitly to the concept laid down by the army commander. No undue risks were to be taken. Rommel was never to be allowed to catch the Eighth Army unbalanced as he had done so often in the past. This time there would be a master plan, to which every subordinate commander would conform.

Some of the older desert hands felt pangs of doubt when they heard what the new policy was to be. It had a ring of the Somme about it and seemed to put the clock back 26 years rather than giving the Eighth Army a new battle-winning tactic. The similarity between the Somme and the El Alamein battlefields was not all that far-fetched, but fortunately Alexander was not a Nivelle. He had neither the intention nor the originality to produce a military panacea which is so attractive to politicians and so fatal to armies. The front, which Panzer Army Africa was holding at El Alamein, like the Somme, had no open flanks. In all the other desert battles the southern flank of both armies had been wide open, offering scope for manoeuvre. This time the front stretched for 45 miles between the Mediterranean in the north and the militarily impassable Qattara Depression in the south. Minefields laid in great depth and areas of soft sand took the place of the deep belts of wire and the mud of the Somme. There was no way round. The front had to be breached if the Italo-German Panzer Army was to be driven out of Africa. Experience of Flanders in the First World War had its part to play in Rommel's defeat.

Alexander and Montgomery were captives of their own past when thinking out the problems which confronted them. Alexander had fought in Flanders as a regimental officer; Montgomery, on the other hand, had served on divisional staffs after he was severely wounded in 1914. Their experience was thus complementary. Alexander could feel the reactions of the soldiers in a massive breaching operation, whereas Montgomery understood the organisational problems involved. Alexander remembered the failures to move up the reserves in time at Loos and his isolation in the Chalk Pit; the day he had reached the 'green fields beyond' the Somme mire; his own carefully planned and rehearsed attack with his 2nd Irish Guards at Passchendaele which reached its objectives with little loss; and the terrible scramble of the ill-planned assault on Bourlon Wood during Cambrai which decimated his battalion. Montgomery had similar memories of the shoddily planned attacks of the earlier years; failure of information to reach divisional headquarters in time for counter-action to be taken; and the success of the meticulously thought out attacks of August 1918. In planning their own great offensive, the new team had to mount a second battle of Cambrai in which the right type of reserves would arrive in time and in which there would be no Bourlon Wood.

There was one aspect of the preparatory phase on which the two men were not united. Alexander's sympathetic style of command prevented him from hurting anybody unnecessarily or from dismissing an officer without careful thought. This is not to say that he accepted inefficiency or would not get rid of unsuitable subordinates. The men he chose and the way he handled them ensured that few fell by the wayside. Montgomery took a harsher view. Either an officer was up to his standards or he was not; and, if he was not, he must go. He preferred to work with men whom he knew already and could trust. He could see little good in the old desert team which he was inheriting and, if Alexander had allowed him to do so, he would have replaced most of the men in key appointments with his own nominees from England. In short, he demanded proven talent; Alexander made talent. Alexander took as his Chief of Staff, General Richard McCreery, who had been his GSO 1 in his 1 Division in France in 1939–40. McCreery had disagreed with Auchinleck and was about to leave for

England. He had opposed a further extension of the 'Jock Column' system and had fallen from favour. Alexander was delighted to reprieve his old friend and never regretted it. Montgomery knew the Brigadier General Staff of Eighth Army, Brigadier de Guingand, and had little hesitation in keeping him on as Chief of Staff. The selection of Corps Commanders presented problems. Gott of XIII Corps had been killed and was replaced by General Horrocks from Montgomery's old command in England. Ramsden of XXX Corps disagreed with the new Army Commander and was replaced by General Leese from the Guards Armoured Division in England. And then there was Lumsden in command of X Corps which was to be the *Corps de Chasse*. Montgomery would have preferred another nominee of his own, but Alexander was not prepared to let him replace a man of Lumsden's ability and experience of desert and armoured warfare without adequate reason. Lumsden stayed with his Corps, but his relationship with his Army Commander was never happy. He left after the fall of Benghazi and his Corps was taken over by Horrocks, who in turn was replaced by General Dempsey, another of Montgomery's protégés sent out from England. All three—Horrocks, Leese and Dempsey—proved their worth and Montgomery's confidence in them.

There was another obvious difference between the two men. Montgomery was a showman, a sparkling and lucid speaker with a mischievous turn of wit, who could hold an audience by the very originality of his presentation. Alexander had none of these attributes. He was a disappointing speaker, unable to conjure up apt verbal images, nor able to achieve the relaxed informality either in manner or, for that matter, in dress. Wisely he left the drum beating to Montgomery who enjoyed it and would have done it anyway. There could not be two 'town cryers'. Alexander remarks in his Memoirs (p. 19):

> There is no doubt at all that Montgomery, during his address, gave brilliant emphasis *to the agreed policy*. He informed his audience that he had ordered all withdrawal plans to be burnt, that the defence of the Delta meant nothing to him, that all resources earmarked to that end were to be used to strengthen the Eighth Army. When, as his next move, he ordered back the transport that had been laid on for a possible withdrawal—the story at the time was that every man had reserved a seat!—the soldiers were left in no shadow of a doubt that the new command meant business.

The words in author's italics are interesting: 'to the agreed policy' not to Montgomery's policy. Although Montgomery was 'managing director' of the desert front and Alexander the 'chairman' of the Middle East Theatre, the desert claimed Alexander's first attention because this was the key strategic area in his command. His directive from Churchill had made it abundantly clear that this was where his first duty lay. Before he issued a directive to Montgomery and then gave him a free hand, he carried out his own extensive reconnaissances of the El Alamein position and discussed its problems with the principle commanders and staffs, making up his own mind how he thought the coming battles should be fought. The first requirement was to ensure that the front did not falter, and that he was not to be forced to repudiate his words about no withdrawal. It was known that Rommel was building up his forces and might decide on a gambler's throw to break through to the Nile Delta before Eighth Army grew too strong. The next suitable date for an offensive was around 26 August when the moon would be full. A full moon was needed by whichever side attacked to enable its sappers to clear lanes through the minefields with just enough light to see what they were doing and yet not enough to disclose their work. Alexander accepted Montgomery's immediate proposals for strengthening the front and authorised the despatch of 44 Division from the Delta to reinforce the important Alam Halfa Ridge. He issued the following directive to his Army Commander on 19 August, just a week before the dangerous date of 26 August and a mere four day after taking over command:

1. Your prime and immediate task is to prepare for offensive action against the German-Italian forces with a view to destroying them at the earliest possible moment.
2. Whilst preparing this attack you must hold your present positions and on no account allow the enemy to penetrate east of them. (Despatches, p. 844)

Montgomery's first problem was to make sure he could carry out para. 2, before setting planning in train for para. 1.

The story of the Battle of Alam Halfa has been overtold with some writers pointing to Montgomery's handling of the battle as the first signs of genius, while others belittle his efforts and claim that he used a plan devised by his predecessor. Alexander is quite clear on this point:

> I cannot conceive that Montgomery is likely to have been in the least interested in other people's ideas on how to run the desert war; and in my own conversations with Auchinleck, before taking over command, there was certainly no hint of a defensive plan that at all resembled the pattern of the battle of Alam Halfa as it was actually fought. (Memoirs, p. 22)

What Montgomery did take over, and which he could do relatively little about in a week, was the front as it stood with its maze of minefields, its strong points dug into the slight rises in the desert and its dumps of ammunition and supplies. He could only adjust his dispositions within these fixed constraints to meet his own ideas of how the defensive battle should be fought. The front had been divided into two equal sectors with XXX Corps in the north and XIII Corps in the south. XXX Corps sector ran from the coast to inclusive Ruweisat Ridge and was the most strongly held because it covered the main road to Cairo. The northern half of XIII Corps sector was strongly held also as far south as Bare Ridge. The southern half, however, was blocked by minefields, and only covered by the light

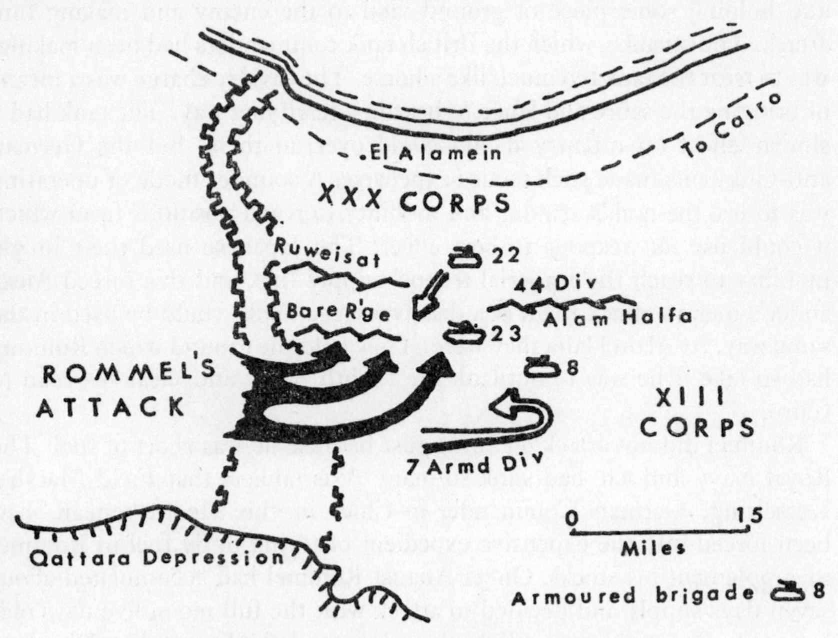

27 Battle of Alam Halfa, 31 August–1 September 1942

armoured forces of 7 Armoured Division. Almost due east from Bare Ridge lay the Alam Halfa Ridge which Auchinleck had prepared as a defended locality, but had not garrisoned it strongly. If Rommel attacked as usual around the southern flank, Alam Halfa would serve as a firm base from which the British armour could operate to block this approach. Montgomery made two important changes. He garrisoned the Alam Halfa Ridge with 44 Division and changed the tactics to be used by the armoured brigades. There was to be no 'loosing' the armour in the traditional cavalry style at the supposed crucial moment of the battle. Two armoured brigades were to hold 'hull down' positions in the likely path of Rommel's panzer divisions to the south and south-west of Alam Halfa. The remaining available armoured brigade would be held behind the main front, but would rehearse moves down to similar counter-penetration positions between Bare Ridge and Alam Halfa. Montgomery issued strict instructions to Horrocks not to allow Rommel to maul the British armour. The German tanks were to be destroyed moving in the open while the British tanks remained concealed as long as possible.

Alexander endorsed this plan wholeheartedly. His experience of the Japanese road-block technique had highlighted the advantages of seizing and holding some piece of ground vital to the enemy and making him attack. The mistake, which the British tank commanders had been making, was to treat the tank too much like a horse. The cavalry charge was a means of bringing the sabre and lance to bear in a terrifying way. The tank had a similar effect on infantry if you could overrun them, but the German anti-tank guns made such tactics expensive. A sounder mode of operating was to use the tank's armour and mobility to reach positions from which it could use its weapons to best effect. The Japanese used their jungle mobility to reach the Imperial troops' supply line, and this forced Alexander's men to attack them at a disadvantage. Tanks could be used in the same way. At Alam Halfa they were. They held the ground which Rommel had to take if he was to outflank the Eighth Army and clear his road to Cairo.

Rommel did not attack on 26 August because he was short of fuel. The Royal Navy and RAF had sunk so many Axis tankers that Field Marshal Kesselring, German Commander-in-Chief in the Mediterranean, had been forced into the expensive expedient of trying to fly fuel to Rommel to supplement his stocks. On 31 August Rommel had accumulated about seven days supply and decided to attack with the full moon five days old, leaving his troops less moonlight than they needed. His attacking divisions were detected forming up opposite the southern sector, very much where the British expected to find them, and were heavily bombed by the RAF during the afternoon. When his troops advanced against 7 Armoured Division's lightly held sector after darkness fell on 30 September they took much longer than Rommel had hoped in forcing their way through the minefields. 7 Armoured Division fell back as planned. When daylight came the RAF resumed its attacks and delayed the German operation still further. Rommel then decided to turn north sooner than he had planned, possibly to conserve fuel, possibly due to false information deliberately fed to him on a 'doctored' map showing soft sand in his path further east, but most likely because his timing had been upset. For two days he pressed his attacks on the British tanks and infantry holding the Bare Ridge-Alam

Halfa Ridge positions while the RAF pounded him from the air. His losses were severe. As he pulled back in a deliberate withdrawal on 2 September he heard that another ship carrying fuel had been sunk by the RAF. Horrocks made two counter-attacks: one by 8 Armoured Brigade from the east of Alam Halfa against Rommel's exposed flank ran into an anti-tank gun screen and was not pressed; and the other by the New Zealanders southwards from Bare Ridge also met stiff opposition. With Alexander's full support, Montgomery stuck to his master plan of not committing Eighth Army to a major attack before it was trained and ready. He called off any further attempt to interfere with Rommel's withdrawal. The new team maintained its determination not to be caught by an ill-considered move, however tempting it might seem.

By winning the Battle of Alam Halfa, Montgomery had achieved three things in a remarkably short time since taking over: he had restored Eighth Army's confidence; he had shown the doubters that he knew what he was about; and he had confirmed to Alexander's and his own satisfaction that their policies were on the right lines. The RAF's magnificent support during the battle had improved Army-Air Force relations and had created a bond between Montgomery and Coningham. The second paragraph in Alexander's directive to Montgomery (see p. 152) had been rendered superfluous; preparations to achieve the aim set out in the first paragraph could go ahead unhindered.

Montgomery's single-mindedness had stopped Eighth Army rushing into a premature offensive. Alexander now had to display similar mental toughness in repelling attacks of a different type from a very different quarter. Churchill had asked him in the middle of August for an estimate of when he could mount his offensive in the desert so that it could be synchronised with Eisenhower's landings in North Africa. Alexander had tentatively suggested the end of September. When Churchill and Brooke visited Montgomery's headquarters on their way back from Tehran, they received a masterly presentation of his future plans in which he gave two important timings which stuck in Churchill's mind and caused trouble later. When asked how long it would take him to get ready, Montgomery had been more cautious than Alexander and insisted that the first week of October was the earliest date by which he could open his offensive. In describing the actual battle, as he had planned it so far, he was at pains to stress that success would not come quickly or easily: 'It would mean hard fighting and would take him *some seven days* to break through, and he would then launch his Armoured Corps. . . .'

The 'first week in October' and 'seven days' became key dates in

Churchill's strategic thinking, illustrating how dangerous it is to give politicians figures which they can grasp easily and remember. By the very nature of their calling, they are forced to generalise, and in so doing disregard all the qualifying clauses, giving the broadest estimate an exactitude which the original author never intended. Detailed planning for 'Lightfoot', the El Alamein offensive, soon revealed that Montgomery's estimate of the first week of October was not soundly based. The next full moon was on 24 September which was too early for the completion of training and logistic preparations. The following moon (23 October) was just about right from Montgomery's point of view. And as far as Alexander could tell it also matched the strategic requirement of a victory in the desert before Eisenhower landed in North Africa in the first half of November. He knew it was important to beat Rommel just before the landings so as to encourage the French in North Africa to slide off the fence onto the Allied side, and to discourage the Spaniards from jumping down onto the Axis side. A fortnight's fighting would decide the issue one way or the other. If the British had not crushed Rommel by then, they would have exhausted themselves and their supplies of shell and equipment. The case for 23 October as D-Day for 'Lightfoot' seemed reasonable. Much to his surprise, his signal to London recommending this date caused a Churchillian explosion which it took Brooke all his persuasive powers to dowse. In the months to come Alexander was to experience many similar crises with Whitehall. He soon learned, as Brooke had done, that there was only one solution; deploy logical and valid arguments and then stand your ground. Alexander put the arguments to the Middle East Commanders-in-Chief Committee who endorsed his stand. Churchill gave way:

Prime Minister to Commander-in-Chief Middle East

23 Sep 42

We are in your hands, and of course a victorious battle makes amends for much delay. Whatever happens we shall back you up and see you through.

What Alexander did not tell Churchill was that Montgomery had insisted that if Whitehall wanted an earlier offensive then a new Eighth Army Commander must be found. Puckishly Montgomery had added, 'My stock was rather high after Alam Halfa!' Montgomery's second figure —the seven-day battle—was to have its impact on events later.

The story of Montgomery's Battle of El Alamein will be told as often as Nelson's Trafalgar and Wellington's Waterloo. This account will sketch only the outline and highlight the occasions on which the Commander-in-Chief was personally involved. Rommel had left his Panzer Army after Alam Halfa and gone back to Germany on sick leave. His place had been taken by General Stumme from the Russian front. Stumme had laid out his defences rather differently from Rommel. The main line of Axis resistance consisted of deep minefields protecting fortified infantry posts. The minefields nearest the British were covered by an outpost line. The main defensive posts lay towards the rear of the minefields. The Axis

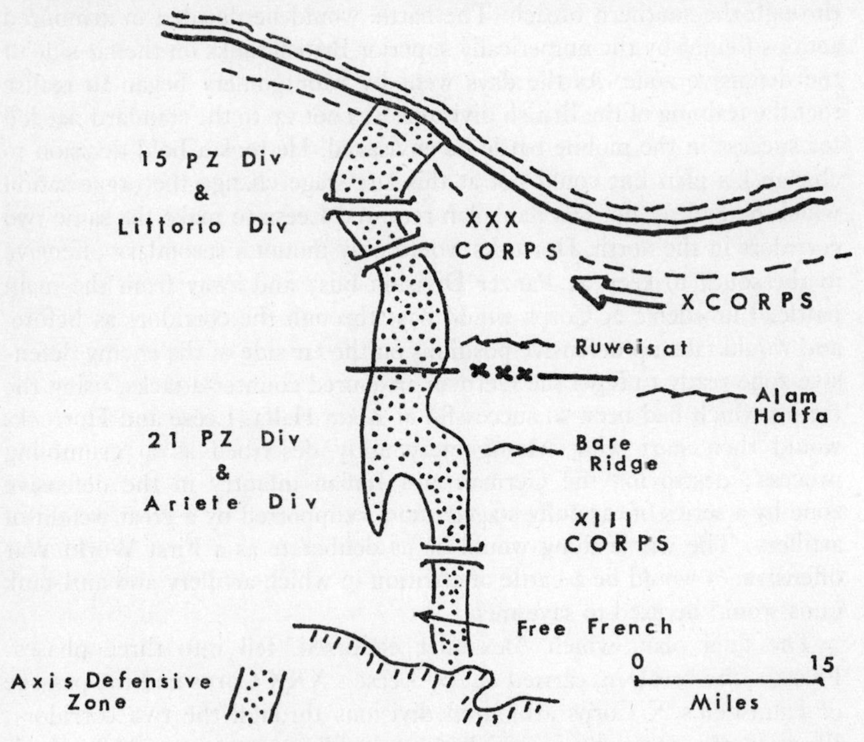

28 First Phase of the Battle of El Alamein, 23 October–1 November 1942

defensive zone was, on average, about three miles deep. Behind this zone Stumme deployed mixed groups of Italian and German tank units ready to counter-attack any penetrations. Lack of fuel probably prevented the Germans from concentrating the Africa Corps as they had normally done in the past. 21 Panzer Division covered the southern sector with Italian Ariete Armoured Division, and 15 Panzer Division covered the north with the Littorio Armoured Division. The same pairing was used amongst the infantry in the defensive zone, where Germany infantry and parachute units 'corsetted' the Italians. Only the German 90 Light Division and the

Italian Trieste divisions were out of the line guarding the coast in the German rear.

Montgomery's first plan envisaged a two-handed punch of the type that Alexander favoured. Leese's XXX Corps would drive two corridors through the Axis' northern sector, while Horrocks' XIII Corps blasted one through the southern sector. Lumsden's X Corps would pass through Leese's breaches, while Horrocks passed his 7 Armoured Division through the southern breach. The battle would be decided in armoured actions fought by the numerically superior British tanks on the far side of the defensive zone. As the days went by Montgomery began to realise that the training of the British divisions was not up to the standard needed for success in the mobile battle he envisaged. He took a bold decision to change his plan but could not at this late stage change the organisation which he had set up. His new plan required Leese to make the same two corridors in the north. Horrocks would only mount a secondary offensive in the south to keep 21 Panzer Division busy and away from the main battle. Lumsden's X Corps would pass through the corridors as before, and would take up defensive positions on the far side of the enemy defensive zone ready to repel the German armoured counter-attacks, using the tactics which had been so successful at Alam Halfa. Leese and Horrocks would then start what Montgomery aptly described as a 'crumbling process', destroying the German and Italian infantry in the defensive zone by a series of carefully staged attacks supported by a great weight of artillery. The whole thing would be as deliberate as a First World War offensive. It would be a battle of attrition in which artillery and anti-tank guns would be used to save men.

The final plan, which Alexander endorsed, fell into three phases: Phase I, the break-in, carried out by Leese's XXX Corps and the passage of Lumsden's X Corps armoured divisions through the two corridors; Phase II, the dog-fight, in which the crumbling process would be used; and Phase III, the routing of Rommel's Army when collapse became imminent. Phase I was to be completed during the hours of darkness of the first night. Phase II might take anything up to 10–12 days. The key paragraph in Montgomery's note for his final address to his officers before the battle ran:

9. *Operate from firm bases.*

Quick re-organisation on objectives Keep balanced Maintain offensive eagerness Keep up pressure	} If we do all this victory is certain

Two important aspects of the coming offensive lay outside the sphere of the Eighth Army Commander—the Naval and Air Plans. These were the responsibility of the Middle East Commanders-in-Chief Committee which set the stage for the principal actor's performance. The Royal Navy and Royal Air Force had for months been drawing the naval and air blockade tighter and tighter around the axis supply lines. The pressure was to be intensified. The RAF had three further tasks before turning their attention to supporting the Army during the battle: subduing the Axis air forces; providing fighter cover for both the Army and Navy; and providing and preventing air reconnaissance. The new team went out of its way to improve Army-Air cooperation; Alexander and Tedder at Theatre level and Montgomery and Coningham at Eighth Army-Desert Air Force level. It is interesting to note in Tedder's book *With Prejudice* that he is rarely critical of Alexander, but there was little love lost between him and other Army commanders. From October 1942 onwards the Eighth Army rarely had reason to complain about lack of air support. The bad days were over.

One unfortunate series of operations was launched during the preparatory phase before 'Lightfoot'. There were in existence a number of plans for raids on Rommel's lines of communications. Alexander reviewed these with his fellow Cs-in-C and authorised two; an attack from sea and land on Tobruk, and one from the land on Benghazi. Admiral Harwood was keen on the Tobruk attack because it would give the Navy a more obvious part in the coming operations. Tedder was opposed to both because the targets were beyond the range of fighter cover. Alexander cast his vote in their favour because, although the risks were high, the forces were small and their effect might be far greater than the effort involved. Even if both failed the Germans would be forced to guard their lines of communications more seriously and hence weaken their forward troops. Both operations did fail. Two destroyers were lost off Tobruk. Tedder made his point in an expensive way, but it was a valuable lesson which Alexander did not forget when he came to plan the invasion of Sicily and the landing at Salerno.

At 9.40 p.m. on 23 October the artillery opened at El Alamein with a 15-minute intense bombardment of the enemy artillery positions. It then moved for five minutes to the forward defences and afterwards onto a pre-arranged programme of timed-concentrations and barrages when the infantry and minefield breaching parties moved forward at ten o'clock. Over 1,000 guns were in action. Never had the British Army received such support since 1918. Professionals were stage-managing its battle at last. The enemy outpost line in the forward edge of the minefields was overrun without much difficulty. Fortunes varied as the attacking brigades worked their way deeper into the Axis defensive zone. Some brigades reached their objectives on the far side; others fell short. Close on their heels came the corridor mine-clearance parties of Lumsden's X Corps. Neither corridor was completely cleared by dawn and the leading armoured brigades were still in the minefield when daylight came. The crumbling process had to start at once to help the tanks onto their objectives, and it went on for seven long hard fought days. The battle was living up to its billing as a battle of attrition which the British were bound to win in the end because their losses could be replaced whereas the Panzer Army's could not. The difference between El Alamein and the Somme lay in the casualties. In the first week at El Alamein the British lost about 10,000 men; on the Somme they lost 61,000 on the first day.

Half way through this process of attrition Rommel arrived back to take command. General Stumme had died of a heart attack on the first day of the battle and so the Axis command was not at its best. Moreover, Rommel was still a sick man. On 27 October he managed to concentrate his two panzer divisions and launched one of his old style counter-attacks out of the setting sun, which had so often won him the battle in the past. This time the British, equipped with the more powerful American Grant and Sherman tanks and the new 6-pounder anti-tank gun, repulsed each German effort. The turning point had come, but, as so often happens in a great battle, it was not obvious at the time. The people of the British Empire and the United States held their breath, willing the Eighth Army success, and yet fearing one more failure. Ominously British communiqués started to use a phrase barely less damaging than 'strategic withdrawal'. Montgomery was said to be regrouping. Hearts sank. Alarm spread in Whitehall and Cairo. The premonition grew of another Rommel victory; of another team of unsuccessful British generals; and of another reverse for British arms. Churchill, whose political future hung on victory, was justifiably nervous as he read in the situation reports that Montgomery was withdrawing divisions from the line. Montgomery had told Churchill that there would be a seven-day dog-fight. The seven days were up and he was relaxing the pressure. Something must be wrong. Brooke, more nervous than he cared to admit in public, found himself unconvincing as he tried to explain to Churchill that Montgomery was doing what all good commanders should do at this stage of a battle—recreating reserves for the final decisive thrust. He had an equally difficult time persuading the Cabinet Defence Committee, which met that afternoon, that all was well; and preventing Churchill from sending ill-advised signals to the Commanders in Cairo. The signal that went off on 29 October only stressed the Defence Committee's view that Alexander should not relax the pressure whatever the risks:

The Defence Committee of the War Cabinet congratulate you on the resolute and successful manner in which the decisive battle which is now proceeding has been launched by you and General Montgomery. The Defence Committee feel that the general situation justifies all the risks and sacrifices involved in the relentless prosecution of this battle, and we assure you that whatever the cost you will be supported in all the measures which you take to shake the life out of Rommel's army and to make this a fight to the finish. (Churchill, *Hinge of Fate*, p. 535)

The Defence Committee need not have revealed its lack of confidence. Alexander with his Chief of Staff, General McCreery, and Mr Casey, Churchill's political representative in Cairo, visited Montgomery at his headquarters that same day. Montgomery, as Brooke surmised, was busy regrouping to provide Lumsden's X Corps with the necessary forces for a decisive breakthrough which he code-named 'Supercharge'. The only point for debate was the most profitable axis upon which to launch 'Supercharge'. Montgomery favoured the north where the Australians were making useful progress in their crumbling operations towards the coast. McCreery thought a more southerly axis would do more damage. Alexander thought so too, but did not intervene as he was perhaps tempted to do. This was Montgomery's battle fought within Alexander's broad directive. The Army Commander was responsible for tactics, and not the C-in-C. There is no hard and fast dividing line to guide a senior commander in such circumstances. Each situation is different and must be judged on its merits at the time. The balance is often very fine. The loss of the battle would have been Alexander's responsibility; and yet to have insisted on the southern axis might have destroyed the working relationship between the two men at a crucial juncture. Alexander stood back, giving Montgomery no hint of lack of confidence. Montgomery continued to plan the use of the northern axis for a few more hours.

From the political point of view, the most important outcome of the visit was that Alexander and Casey were able to answer the Cabinet Defence Committee's cable in an encouraging way when they received it later that day:

Montgomery and I are fully agreed utmost pressure of our offensive must be maintained. Enemy minefields and anti-tank guns have caused a lot of trouble and delay. We are now however about to put in a large-scale attack with infantry and tanks to break a way through for X Corps. If this is successful it will have far reaching results. (Churchill, *Hinge of Fate*, p. 535)

Alexander left Montgomery still working on plans for the northern axis. Intelligence reports soon revealed that the bulk of Rommel's reserves had moved north to stem the Australian successes. Montgomery wisely changed the axis of 'Supercharge' to the area originally favoured by

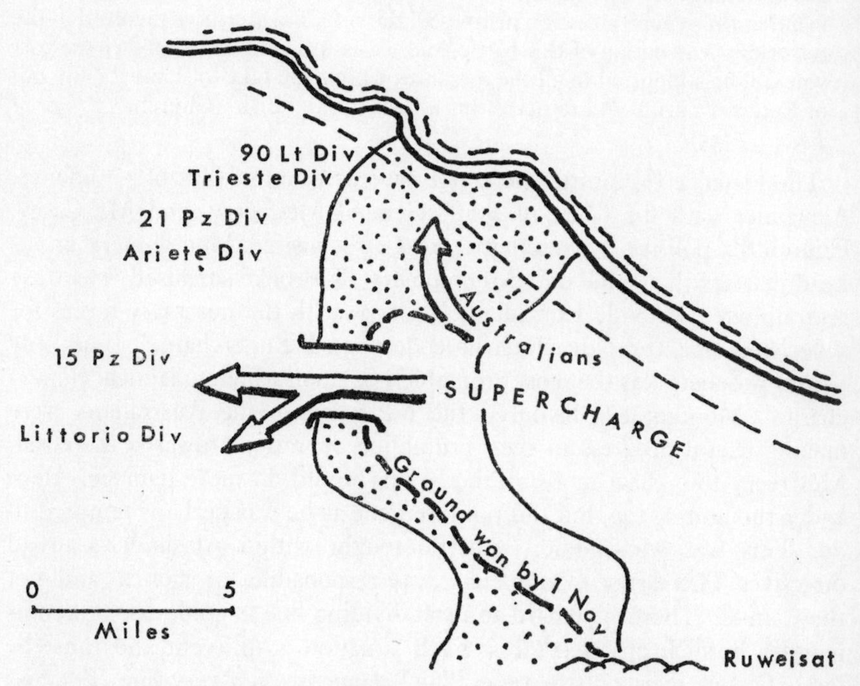

29 Final Phase of the Battle of El Alamein, 1–3 November 1942

McCreery. It looked as if the new attack would fall on Italian rather than German troops. Alexander, recording this incident, says:

> There is no doubt at all in my mind that this was the key decision of the Alamein battle, nor have I any doubt that Monty was suitably grateful to my Chief of Staff. He himself records: 'The change of thrust line for 'Supercharge' proved most fortunate', though, of course, being Monty he afterwards informed Eisenhower that never again would he take anybody's advice in the running of a battle! (Memoirs, p. 28)

Montgomery had hoped that regrouping could be completed by the night 31 October–1 November. This proved too optimistic. The plan for

'Supercharge' was very similar to the original 'break-in' battle, carried out on one instead of two axes. Again little was left to chance. The attack was methodical and covered by an artillery programme which might have been fired for one of the 1918 attacks on the Hindenburg Line. The corridor was cleared of mines successfully and the armour debouched before daylight. This was the beginning of the end, but the battle had still to be fought without loss of intensity for another 48 hours, thanks to the gratuitous intervention of Hitler and Mussolini. Early on 2 November, Rommel appreciated that the time had come to begin a methodical withdrawal if he was to save his Panzer Army from annihilation. He reported his intentions to the German Supreme Command and was aghast when he received orders to stand fast. It took 24 hours to persuade the two dictators that their orders were impracticable. By then it was too late to save the non-mechanised troops—mostly Italian—of the Panzer Army. The British detected the signs of withdrawal and stepped up their attacks. Their air effort reached a peak on 4 November. Renewed attacks on land that night met with failing resistance. The Second Battle of El Alamein had been won; the pursuit of the beaten Panzer Army was about to begin. There were unfortunately few fresh troops left to complete Rommel's discomfiture and gather in the bulk of the Italian component of his Army which he was forced to abandon. Alexander reported to Churchill:

General Alexander to Prime Minister : 4 Nov 42
After twelve days of heavy and violent fighting the Eighth Army has inflicted a severe defeat on the German and Italian forces under Rommel's command. The enemy front has broken, and British armoured formations in strength have passed through and are operating in the enemy's rear areas. Such portions of the enemy's forces as can get away are in full retreat, and are being harassed by our armoured and mobile forces and by our air forces. Other enemy divisions are still in position, endeavouring to stave off defeat, and these are likely to be surrounded and cut off.

The RAF have throughout given superb support to the land battle and are bombing the enemy's retreating columns incessantly.

Fighting continues. (Churchill, *Hinge of Fate*, p. 537)

and on 6 November he followed this cable with:

General Alexander to Prime Minister: 6 Nov 42
Ring out the bells! Prisoners estimated now 20,000, tanks 350, guns 400, MT several thousand. Our advanced mobile forces are south of Mersa Matruh. Eighth Army is advancing.

The bells were not, in the event, rung until Churchill was sure that Eisenhower's forces were securely ashore in French North Africa.

The Second Battle of El Alamein was Montgomery's battle in every sense of the word. Alexander laid no claim to the credit for its tactical handling. All he was prepared to claim was that his strategic timing had been exact. Two days before Eisenhower landed the world knew that the Rommel myth had been laid. Eighteen months later he was to repeat this feat of strategic timing when his armies entered Rome two days before Eisenhower crossed the English Channel.

But, although there is no doubt that Montgomery deserved the accolade of the Victor of El Alamein, there is another side to the coin. If he had failed, Alexander would have carried the blame as well as his Army Commander. His stewardship would have been called into question as Wavell's and Auchinleck's had been challenged after previous failures in the desert. Another Army Commander would have been appointed and a new C.-in-C. would have arrived. Alexander has every justification for one of the few critical remarks he ever made about his great subordinate.

> . . . yet he [Montgomery] is unwise, I think, to take all the credit for his great success as a commander entirely to himself; his prestige, which is very high, could be higher still if he had given a little credit to those who made his victories possible, and there are those besides his own fighting men to whom he owes something. (*Memoirs*, p. 16)

Alexander had played his own part as it should have been played. He gave Montgomery the free rein which his personality demanded; inspired him and the rest of the senior officers of the Middle East to give their best; and protected them from the worries and ill-considered demands from above. Had he not known how to handle such a wide variety of men, particularly those of the Montgomery stamp, events could have taken a different course. The battle was not fought as he would have fought it. The single-handed punching did not appeal to him. The difficulties, which Montgomery faced at El Alamein through over-rigidity in planning, encouraged Alexander to put his own ideas of the two-handed punch into practice later. His own summing up of El Alamein was:

> Some may argue that Monty's master-plan for the battle collapsed because the armour failed to break through the two 'fore-ordained' corridors, which were sealed by powerful anti-tank screens. But nothing in battle can ever be regarded as fore-ordained. I would agree that too great a task was imposed on the armour on the first day of the battle and that there ought to have been two bites at the cherry—a double bombardment. Nevertheless, the essence of the plan was to blow a hole—preferably two holes—in the enemy front. One such hole was blown, at what point makes no matter. The plan worked.
>
> An attrition battle hardly lends itself to master planning. I would say that

El Alamein was a soldiers' battle, and was fought, though with modern weapons, very much in the style of the battles in France in the First War. . . . (*Memoirs*, p. 28)

The pursuit of Rommel's beaten forces went on with varying success and with some justifiable grounds for criticism until the remnants of the Africa Corps withdrew over the Tunisian border. Rommel stood momentarily at Fuka on 6 November; at El Agheila on 12 November; Buerat on 7 January; and surrendered Tripoli on 23 January. Alexander could then send Churchill his famous signal:

General Alexander to Prime Minister

Sir,
The orders you gave me on August 10, 1942, have been fulfilled. His Majesty's enemies, together with their impediments, have been completely eliminated from Egypt, Cyrenaica, Libya and Tripolitania.
I now await your further instructions.
(Churchill, *The Hinge of Fate*, p. 646)

Alexander had redeemed his defeat in Burma. He was now a proven Commander-in-Chief, capable of rising above tactical detail and handling the politico-military problems of supreme command. His next appointment had already been decided. The Casablanca Conference of Allied leaders had just been concluded.

8

Victory out of Chaos

> *17 Feb 1943*
> You are appointed Deputy Commander-in-Chief of the Allied Forces in French North Africa. Further you are appointed Commander of the Group of Armies operating in Tunisia.
> Eisenhower's directive to Alexander (*Despatches*, p. 885)

> *13 May 1943*
> Sir, it is my duty to report that the Tunisian campaign is over. All enemy resistance has ceased. We are masters of the North African shores.
> Alexander to Churchill (*Despatches*, p. 884)

The El Alamein campaign was a combined operation. The reporting of the International Press highlighted Montgomery's part, which, in consequence, drew the world's applause, but one group of important men appreciated Alexander's worth. Churchill, Roosevelt and the Combined British and American Chiefs of Staff met at Casablanca in January 1943 to decide the next step in the war against the Axis. Their long, hard-fought debate led to two specific agreements: first, Sicily was to be the next Anglo-American target in Europe with D-Day set for the 'July moon'; and secondly, Eisenhower was again to be in overall command with three British officers holding the executive posts of commanders of the naval, land and air forces engaged—Admiral Cunningham at sea, Alexander on land, and Tedder in the air. It was then but a short and logical step to deciding that these three men should assume their commands for the final stages of the Tunisian campaign. Alexander was to take command of all land forces in Tunisia as soon as Eighth Army crossed the Libyan frontier west of Tripoli and came within supporting distance of the Allied forces fighting in the French North African Mountains. His headquarters was appropriately named 18 Army Group as he would be coordinating the actions of Anderson's First Army in Tunisia with Montgomery's Eighth Army advancing from Tripoli.

Alexander and Tedder were summoned to Casablanca by Churchill to report on the desert war. Both men gave masterful presentations of the situation on Eighth Army's front. Alexander was never a rhetorical speaker. He developed his theme with a straightforwardness and honesty of purpose which left no one in any doubt about his intentions or ability to carry them out. He looked and sounded the part of a highly professional C-in-C who needed no flamboyance to make his mark. Arthur Bryant paints the picture: 'Alexander, who had flown in from Cairo to Casablanca for consultation and was charming everyone at the Conference by what Churchill called his "easy smiling grace" and contagious confidence. . . .' Churchill confirms this impression:

> A day or two later Alexander came in, and reported to me and the President about the progress of the Eighth Army. He made a favourable impression upon the President, who was greatly attracted by him, and also by his news which was that the Eighth Army would take Tripoli in the near future. . . . His unspoken confidence was contagious. (*Hinge of Fate*, p. 605)

The possibility of substituting Alexander for Eisenhower passed through many minds, particularly in the International Press. Robert Sherwood (p. 674) comments:

> For a time there was some doubt whether Eisenhower would remain in Supreme Command of 'Husky' (code-name for the invasion of Sicily). General Alexander who outranked him . . . was tough, professional competition for Eisenhower at a moment when his own position was most insecure.

Axis commentators, attempting mischief, broadcast similar divisive ideas. Commander Butcher (p. 215) recorded ruefully: 'The Berlin radio predicts that Ike will be transferred back to London and Alexander will take charge in North Africa. It comes at a time when the critics in Britain and at home are needling Ike and hinting that he should be replaced. . . .'

Eisenhower's position was never seriously in doubt. Churchill admired his tactful handling of his Allied team and knew that the Supreme Commander had to be an American to ensure that the US war effort remained focused on Europe instead of the Pacific. He was content with the Casablanca arrangement because command of the troops was in the hands of the man whom he had picked and built up to be a British champion since the disastrous days of Dunkirk. Alexander had never let him down. He had high hopes of him in Tunisia which must be cleared of all Axis troops by May if the invasion of Sicily was to be practicable in 1943. The Americans had reluctantly agreed that operations in the Mediterranean should continue after the fall of Tunis only as a means of keeping their troops in action against Germany until the invasion of North-West Europe could be mounted in the spring of 1944. They were not attracted by Churchill's advocacy of an approach to the 'soft underbelly' of Europe; and they were insistent that all troops, shipping and aircraft needed for Normandy should leave the Mediterranean in the autumn. Churchill was equally determined to prove his Mediterranean strategy before the Allies were irrevocably committed to a cross-Channel assault in 1944. He expected Alexander not only to clear the Axis from North Africa but to do so in time to allow him to develop his assault on Southern Europe before the intervention of winter weather and American opposition put a stop to further operations.

Alexander arrived in Algeria on 18 February. He brought General Dick McCreery with him as his Chief of Staff, and a party of hand-picked British officers from Cairo to create the nucleus of his 18 Army Group Headquarters which was to be organised on British lines. Eisenhower's Allied Force Headquarters in Algiers, though manned co-equally by British and American officers, was run on the American staff system. Alexander spent his first night in Algiers re-opening the relationship with Eisenhower which had been so abruptly broken off almost a year before. Commander Butcher (p. 228) records the gist of the talks that evening:

> General Alexander said he had been disappointed when his first assignment under Ike for TORCH had been cancelled only twenty-four hours after he had received it, that he had wanted to work under Ike, that this was an American sphere, and he fully recognised it was not only necessary but a privilege to come under the American C-in-C.
>
> Ike made it clear to him his great satisfaction at the job done in chasing Rommel as Alex and Monty had done so splendidly and that he realised that with the succession of victories under their belts, many would have expected Alex to be the boss. But Alex was thoroughly content, and anxious to get to the front to see for himself 'the lay of the land'.
>
> Alex ventured the firm opinion that the Hun in the present drive, which has been tough and has cost the Americans at least eighty tanks to date, was headed for Tebessa. . . . Alex was afraid our units had been dispersed too much, and that the Hun would gobble them up one by one, about what is happening.
>
> Said he thought it would be best to give Anderson one sector, as the front is too much for one man to handle, give Fredendall a part, and then there would be Montgomery coming along from Tripoli.

The Allied position in Tunisia had deteriorated sadly since the Casablanca conference. The Axis Powers had reinforced their troops more quickly across the short sea-air bridge from Italy via Sicily to Tunis and Bizerta than the Allies had managed to do over the long sea-haul from England and America. Rommel's Panzer Army had abandoned Tripoli after destroying the port facilities and blocking the harbour, and had fallen back into Tunisia to join hands with von Arnim's Fifth Panzer Army holding Central and Northern Tunisia. Montgomery would be unable to follow until the Port of Tripoli was working again and he had been able to build up sufficient supplies for a further advance. By the middle of February the Axis High Command had achieved a dangerous numerical superiority in Tunisia which they were bent on exploiting with a series of offensive operations which began just before Alexander arrived to take command. Fortunately there was as much confusion and indecision in the Axis camp as Alexander found on the Allied side.

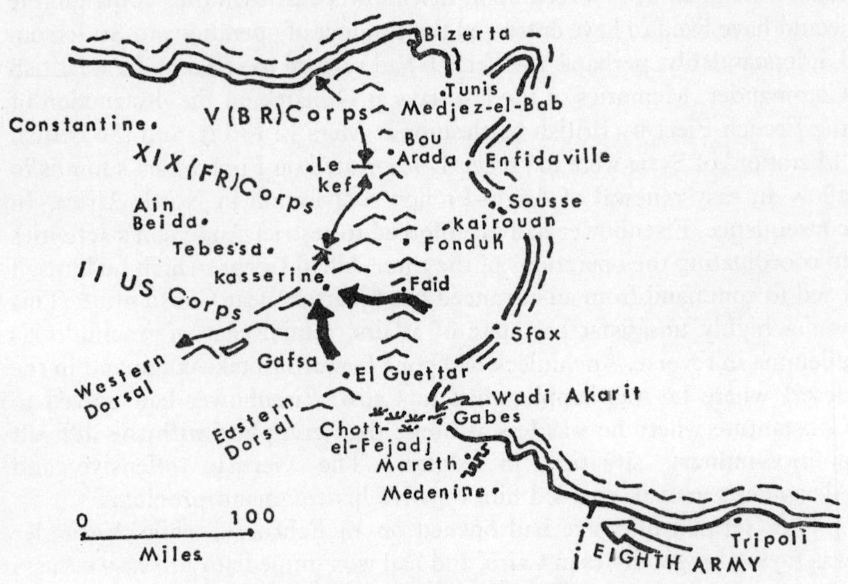

30 Situation in Tunisia, 18 February 1943

Eisenhower had been forced by circumstances to act as impressario and conductor of the motley Allied orchestra in Tunisia. In the north, Anderson's weak First British Army had been halted by von Arnim's troops in the great arc of mountains around Tunis and Bizerta. Anderson had only one Corps: Allfrey's V (British) Corps with one armoured and two infantry divisions and a parachute brigade.* Beyond Anderson's southern flank, which rested on the hills south of the Bou Arada Valley, the Allied line

* V (Br) Corps consisted of
46 Inf Division
78 Inf Division
6 Armoured Division
1 Parachute Brigade.

ran southwards along the hills of the Eastern Dorsal. General Koeltz's XIX (French North African) Corps held the northern half, while General Fredendall's II (US) Corps held the southern end. Fredendall's force was even weaker than Anderson's. He had part of the 1 (US) Armoured Division and one French North African Division under command to hold a sector stretching 100 miles southward to El Guettar in the southern Tunisian desert. The rest of the US troops in Tunisia were deployed in support of the French and British Corps, which were less lavishly equipped, particularly with tanks and long range artillery.*

These untidy arrangements had grown out of the desperate improvisations which had been forced upon Eisenhower earlier in the campaign. He would have liked to have entrusted the conduct of operations to Anderson. Understandably, perhaps, the French had refused to serve under a British Commander. Memories of the last days at Dunkirk, of the destruction of the French Fleet by British battleships at Mers El Kebir, and the British 'liberation' of Syria were too recently imprinted on Frenchmen's minds to allow an easy renewal of Anglo-French cooperation in North Africa. In consequence, Eisenhower had been forced to restrict Anderson's activities to coordinating the operations of the three Allied Corps, which he himself tried to command from an advanced headquarters near Constantine. This was a highly unsatisfactory state of affairs, reminiscent of Auchinleck's dilemma in reverse. Auchinleck had gone forward to take command in the desert where he was happier than in Cairo; Eisenhower had moved to Constantine where he was less at home than grappling with the difficult politico-military situation in Algiers. The German offensive and Alexander's arrival, enabled him to solve his command problems.

The German offensive had opened on 14 February, while Alexander was saying his goodbyes in Cairo, and had won immediate and easy success over the American and French troops holding the southern end of the Eastern Dorsal. Von Arnim with two panzer divisions had broken through Fredendall's defences of the Faid Pass, and Rommel with the Africa Corps' assault group had overrun El Guettar and Gafsa. The shattered remnants of Fredendall's Corps streamed back to the Western Dorsal—the next potential defensive position blocking the roads to the supply bases of Tebessa and Le Kef deep in the Allied rear. It was at this inauspicious moment with a strong whiff of panic permeating the Allied

* XIX (French) Corps was supported by 1 (US) Infantry Division
34 (US) Infantry Division
One Combat Command of 1 (US) Armoured Division.
V (Br) Corps was supported by one Regimental Combat Team of 1 (US) Infantry Division.

lines that Alexander made his first tour of the Tunisian front preparatory to taking over command on 20 February. Memories of March 1918 in Flanders, of June 1940 at Dunkirk, and of March 1942 in Rangoon, flooded back as he set out to visit Anderson whom Eisenhower had now placed in overall tactical command of the Tunisian Front, overriding French susceptibilities.

The situation which Alexander found as he drove from headquarters to headquarters with McCreery was far from encouraging. Although Anderson had done his best in his dour, determined way, there could be no disguising the fact that things were in a mess. The command structure was confused; nationalities were hopelessly intermingled; units were split up and fighting in *ad hoc* groups; and a general air of disorganisation prevailed. Loss of confidence, particularly among the Americans, was obvious. Alexander had seen too many defeated formations in his long career not to understand what was happening. The Americans, though magnificently equipped, were just beginning to realise the difference between the heroics of the strip cartoon and the effect of live shell. On the night 19–20 February Rommel drove them off the Kasserine Pass in the Western Dorsal opening the way to Tebessa or Le Kef. Hastily assembled British reinforcements arrived in time to help stem the tide, but they too were far from experienced and certainly well below the standard of battle-worthiness set by Montgomery's Eighth Army. The French, for their part, were so ill-equipped that no amount of courage could offset their glaring deficiencies. Alexander had to devise and impose a coherent plan which would restore confidence and enable the many, varied personalities to pull together in the common cause in spite of their deep-seated prejudices and narrow national outlooks.

Alexander decided to take charge of 18 Army Group on 19 February, a day earlier than intended, because the situation north of Kasserine would not wait upon the niceties of a military assumption of command. It would be unfair to Anderson and Fredendall to suggest that Alexander's new team played much part in stopping Rommel's advance. Useful though the German success had been, Rommel appreciated that he had neither the resources nor time to press his offensive much further. He could not afford to leave Montgomery building up his supplies on the southern Tunisian frontier undisturbed. On 22 February, he ordered his troops to disengage and drew them back to the passes of the Eastern Dorsal which he intended to hold while he dealt with Eighth Army.

Alexander's first letter to Brooke, written after assuming command, summarises his impressions:

> The general situation is far from satisfactory. British, American and French units are all mixed up on the front, especially in the south. Formations have been split up. There is no policy and no plan of campaign. The air is much the same. This is the result of no firm direction or centralised control from above. ... We have quite definitely lost the initiative.... (*The Mediterranean and the Middle East*, IV, p. 204)

Three days later, when unbeknown to Allied intelligence, Rommel was already withdrawing, he cabled: 'Situation on battle front is critical and the next day or two should decide issue. ... My main anxiety is the poor fighting quality of Americans. ...'

After a few more days experience in his new command he unburdened himself to Churchill and Brooke:

> ... I am frankly shocked at whole situation as I found it. Although Anderson should have been quicker to realise true state of affairs and to have started what I am now doing he was only put in command of whole front on 24th January (*sic*).* Real fault has been lack of direction from above from the very beginning resulting in no policy and no plan. Am doubtful if Anderson is big enough for job although he has some good qualities. ... Hate to disappoint you but final victory in North Africa is not just round the corner. A very great deal requires to be done both on land and in the air. General Eisenhower could not be more helpful.... (*The Mediterranean and the Middle East*, IV, p. 304)

Two themes ran through Alexander's thoughts and public utterances in the last days of February: first, the lack of an intelligible plan, and, secondly, the disappointing performance of the American troops. It was in his power to remedy the former; he was far from sanguine about the latter. How much his earlier dealings with the carping Stilwell influenced his views on American prowess, is hard to tell. The fact remains that his unfortunate experiences with his American colleague in Burma, coupled with his first meeting with the ill-trained and self-opinionated members of Fredendall's II (US) Corps staff during the Kasserine affair, made a deeply adverse impression upon his mind. He knew that the Americans would have to be carefully handled for a time, but he misappreciated how quickly Americans recover and learn from their mistakes. There is justice in the American Official History view that: 'General Alexander's unfavourable estimate was destined to linger, encouraging him to depend more heavily upon British units than later circumstances warranted.'

Whatever plan Alexander devised would have to take into account the very wide spectrum of training, experience and battle proficiency dis-

* The actual date was 3 February.

played by the various components of his international Army Group. Amateur strategists, looking through Napoleonic spectacles from their deep armchairs in London and Washington clubs, could see many splendid strategic opportunities which Alexander seemed to neglect in the coming months. The most obvious was the possibility of concentrating a striking force, say, in the Fonduk area and bursting through the Eastern Dorsal to Kairouan and thence to the sea at Sousse; or from Faid to Sfax, cutting communications between the two German armies and then defeating each in detail. Such an operation had been in Eisenhower's mind since December and had been planned by II (US) Corps under the code-name 'Satin'. Eisenhower had discussed 'Satin' with Alexander at Casablanca when the latter was nominated as the Allied land force commander. Alexander had little hesitation in advising against the concept even though he did not know at that time how brittle Fredendall's Corps was to prove itself to be. The Allies were dealing with a battle-experienced adversary who would react as viciously as a trapped tiger to a threat of this type. The Germans would probably welcome such an American advance as a means of snatching a quick, cheap victory. Fredendall's force would be caught in the open plain between the two experienced Panzer Armies and would be destroyed before Eighth Army could intervene. Eisenhower had no need to take such risks before his troops were thoroughly battle inoculated and able to match the tactical skill of the Germans. El Alamein had been won on a 'no risk' basis. The same policy would have to be pursued in dealing with the combined forces of Rommel and von Arnim.

Alexander was no Napoleon. He relied on sound commonsense and the fruits of experience. In making his master plan, four factors stood out from among the tangled complexities of the situation. The first was the simple fact that the Axis forces were growing stronger both on land and in the air, and would continue to do so unless the short sea-air bridge to Sicily could be severed. The key to doing this was the establishment of Allied air superiority over the Sicilian Channel; which, in turn, depended upon the seizure of enough airfields within effective fighter range of the sea approaches to the Tunisian ports. The majority of the Axis airfields lay in the Central Tunisian plain between Gabes in the south and Enfidaville in the north. Their capture would have the welcome subsidiary effect of clearing the Luftwaffe from the skies above the Allied forces in Tunisia. While the Desert Air Force had won clear skies for Montgomery, the Allied North-West African Tactical Air Forces—the British 242 Group and the American XII Air Support Command—were far from achieving a comparable immunity for Anderson, Koeltz and Fredendall. Once air superiority had been won, it would be possible to draw a tight noose round the Axis North African bridgehead and compel its capitulation without excessive loss of Allied life.

Secondly, there was the respect with which the two Panzer Armies had to be treated. They were far from beaten. On the contrary, Hitler was known to have ordered their reinforcement to keep the Allies at arm's length from the shores of Southern Europe. Since Kasserine the Axis command structure had undergone a reorganisation which parallelled the changes on the Allied side. A new headquarters, called Army Group Africa, had been set up under Rommel to coordinate the actions of Panzer Army Africa in Southern Tunisia with those of von Arnim's Fifth Panzer Army in the north. The Italian General Messe took over Rommel's Panzer Army Africa, which was renamed the First Italian Army. It still contained a strong German element under command of the German Africa Corps Headquarters, but the three panzer divisions in Tunisia—10, 15 and 21—were treated as a mobile reserve under Rommel's hand. Alexander's plans had to take into account this formidable armoured force which Rommel was so expert in using.

The third consideration was the capability of his own Army Group. He had taken over the role of conductor of the Allied orchestra from Eisenhower before it had gained any corporate feeling or cohesion. Anderson's First Army in the north was achieving a creditable level of efficiency and was growing stronger with the arrival of General John Crocker's IX (British) Corps Headquarters and two fresh infantry divisions* from England. Koeltz's XIX (French) Corps was experienced in hill warfare but was poorly equipped, and difficult to handle due to national sensitivity. Fredendall's II (US) Corps, on the other hand, was over-equipped and under-trained, but full of latent enthusiasm, possessing a bitter-sweet mixture of keenness to learn from others compounded with determination to operate in its own American way. And away to the south lay Montgomery's Eighth Army with a professional standard unmatched by the other elements of the Army Group. Thus, Alexander's most pressing need was to raise the standard of the Allied forces in Tunisia to something approaching Eighth Army's efficiency in time to clear Tunisia of Axis forces by May. He decided that three things were needed: first, the front must be reorganised into national sectors so that as far as practicable troops would be fighting under their own commanders; secondly, the El Alamein formula of divisions fighting as divisions instead of *ad hoc* groups

* 1st and 4th (British) Divisions.

must be instituted in Tunisia; and thirdly, divisions must be given tasks within their capabilities so as to build up their battle confidence.

The fourth and last factor was topography. The Axis Army Group Africa lay in a vast corral with the sea to the north and the east, and the mountains of the Eastern Dorsal and of Northern Tunisia to the west. The southern end was covered by the salt marshes of the Chott-El-Fejad, which stretched from the southern end of the Eastern Dorsal to Gabes on the Mediterranean coast. There were only two ways round this obstacle: a long detour through the desert around the western end, or an advance along the coast road through the narrow Gabes Gap between the marshes and the sea. The former was impractical for a major force, and the latter was obstructed by the naturally strong defences of the Wadi Akarit, and covered in depth by the old French fortifications of the Mareth Line some thirty miles further south. It would be foolish to try conclusions with Army Group Africa until Eighth Army was through the Gabes Gap.

These four factors dictated Alexander's strategy, which he sums up with characteristic clarity:

> The campaign would be divided into two phases. In the first the main object would be to get Eighth Army north of the Gabes Gap where it would gain contact with First Army and gain freedom of manoeuvre to develop its superiority in mobility and fire power. . . . In the second phase the efforts of both Armies would be directed towards securing airfields which would enable us to develop the ever-growing strength of our Anglo-American air forces. When we had achieved that we should be able to co-ordinate to the full the striking power of all three services in drawing a tight net round the enemy's position. (Despatches, p. 870)

His tactical policy was equally clear. His operational directive issued on 14 March lays down:

1. *Object*—To destroy the Axis Forces in Tunisia as early as possible.
2. *Grouping*—Eighteenth Army Group will directly control:
   Eighth Army
   A US Corps
   First Army with French troops (XIX Corps) under command.
3. *Sectors*—British, French and American troops will be allotted separate sectors as far as possible under their own commanders.
4. *Organisation*—Divisions will live, train and fight as divisions and will not be split up into small groups or combat teams.
5. *Specialist Troops*—such as parachute troops and Commandos will be withdrawn for rest, refitting and training as early as possible.

6. *Eighteenth Army Group Reserve*

6 Armoured Division One British Infantry Division 9 Corps troops 1 Parachute Brigade 1 and 6 Commandos	IX Corps

IX Corps will carry out intensive training for offensive operations under Commander IX Corps.

7. *Local Reserves*—Corps sectors must aim at having the equivalent of one infantry division or one armoured division in Corps reserve.

8. *Armour*—Tanks will be withdrawn from the front line and grouped as local reserves for the counter-attack role.

9. *Firm Bases*—Key positions will be prepared and held strongly as firm bases, and pivots, well supported by artillery and tanks. Areas between these bases will be carefully patrolled and watched. Enemy penetration into these gaps in small numbers will be dealt with by local reserves. Enemy penetration in strength will be dealt with by Corps reserves.

10. The front will at present be held defensively but in an offensive spirit with active patrolling and minor operations undertaken to improve positions, train units and keep the initiative over the enemy. . . . (Despatches, p. 886)

Thus Alexander adopted the tactical formula which had proved so successful before El Alamein, though on the larger scale of an Army Group. Divisions were to fight as divisions operating from firm bases; intensive training was to be carried out; and a *Corps de Chasse* was again created.

In one respect he did not follow the El Alamein formula. Only one senior commander lost his job and that was at Eisenhower's and not Alexander's instigation. Eisenhower visited Fredendall's II (US) Corps after the Kasserine battle and realised that a change must be made as the Corps had lost confidence in its commander. He summoned General George Patton from Morocco where he had started planning the American share of the invasion of Sicily for which he had been appointed US Task Force Commander. Patton was a true American, convinced that he and his troops could and would excel all others. The challenge of disproving the verdict of Kasserine appealed to him. He was determined to win laurels for II (US) Corps in a far shorter time than anyone, and most certainly Alexander, considered possible. Alexander devotes a section of his memoirs to 'Two American Generals'—Eisenhower and Patton. He admired both and showed that he understood both. It is doubtful whether Patton ever understood Alexander. The two met for the first time when

Patton visited Tripoli in January. Alexander appreciated his worth as a colourful leader, commenting 'Patton should have lived during the Napoleonic Wars—he would have been a splendid Marshal under Napoleon.' But he also realised that, while Patton might restore II (US) Corps' confidence overnight, he could just as easily destroy his new command by some rash offensive move before his men were ready for another clash with Axis troops. Alexander had learned this lesson as long ago as the advance to the Aisne in 1914 and was determined not to let others repeat the same mistakes. Until men know what war is about they should be committed with the greatest care. This was not Patton's idea of war, but Patton—good soldier that he was—obeyed.

Alexander's Tunisian symphony had a prelude and two distinct movements with an interlude between them. We will examine each in turn.

The Prelude

> Before these plans could be put into effect or any thorough reorganisation undertaken I found myself faced once more by a new enemy initiative.
>
> Alexander, Despatches (p. 871)

Army Group Africa came into being under Rommel's command on 23 February. The Axis High Command instructed him to mount an offensive against Eighth Army at the beginning of March. Accordingly, Rommel ordered 10 and 21 Panzer Divisions into reserve to refit while Headquarters Africa Corps returned to the Mareth front with 15 Panzer Division. Von Arnim was not content to sit idly by while the Italian General Messe was operating in the south. He flew back to Rome without reference to Rommel, and persuaded Field Marshal Kesselring to allow him to mount an offensive of his own against Anderson's First Army on the grounds that the Allies must have denuded their northern sector during the Kasserine crisis. Rommel seems to have acquiesced and agreed to von Arnim attacking on 26 February, followed by Messe in the first week of March.

Although Rommel's Army Group contained the equivalent of 17 divisions, it is easiest to follow the sequence of events on the Axis side by watching the moves of the three panzer divisions because they reflected the priority accorded to the various actions. Von Arnim's attack was mounted with infantry divisions only and met with some success against the British in the extreme north and around Medjez-El-Bab and Bou Arada. The fighting was scrappy and badly coordinated by von Arnim. In consequence, it died away, leaving Anderson free to carry out Alexander's instructions to reorganise and train First Army.

Messe's attack on Eighth Army at Medenine, just south of Mareth, met with unredeemed disaster. The three panzer divisions together with 90 Light Division ran onto and were defeated by the anti-tank guns of XXX British Corps. The Axis lost some 50 tanks, while the British lost none.

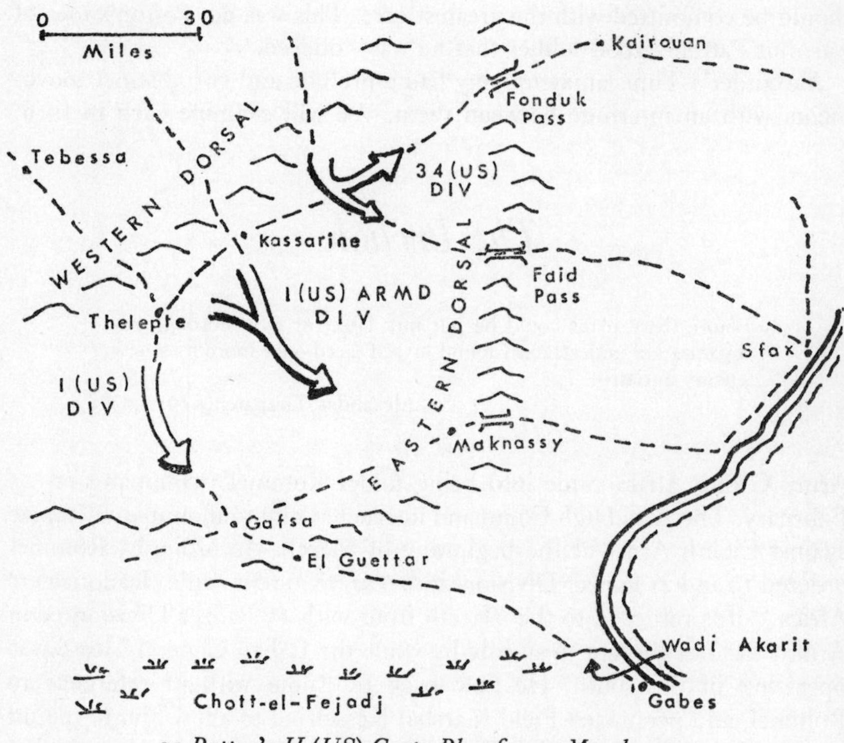

31 Patton's II (US) Corps Plan for 17 March 1943

The Battle of Medenine was the Alam Halfa of the coming battle of Mareth. The Axis had failed to regain the initiative. Alexander was able to turn his full attention to the problems of passing Eighth Army through the Gabes Gap.

On 14 March Alexander moved his Army Group Headquarters forward from the old location of Eisenhower's tactical headquarters near Constantine to Ein Beida (see fig. 30, p. 169) on the road to Tebessa where he would be centrally placed and able to keep in closer touch with Montgomery, Patton and Anderson. Each of these commanders was given a clear and unambiguous task. Montgomery was to mount one of his deliberate set-piece attacks to breach and destroy the Mareth Line. Patton was to support Montgomery by drawing enemy reserves away from Mareth. He was to do this by reoccupying the Thelepte airfields, which had been lost in the Kasserine affair, and by advancing to Gafsa where he was to establish a supply base to ease Eighth Army's logistic problems when it emerged north of the Chott-el-Fedjadj. Anderson was to regain certain pieces of important ground lost during von Arnim's offensive, but otherwise he was to concentrate on improving the training of his Army.

Whereas Montgomery and, to a lesser extent, Anderson were given a free hand to plan their operations, Patton was not. He was kept on a very tight rein and given detailed instructions for a strictly controlled offensive which was to be built up by stages, each stage being increased in scope as the training and morale of the Americans improved. He was allotted three divisions for his operations: General Charles Ryder's 34 (US) Infantry Division was to continue to hold the northern half of II (US) Corps sector with the task of demonstrating towards the Fonduk Pass in the Eastern Dorsal. General Terry Allen's 1 (US) Infantry Division was to reoccupy Gafsa. And General Orlando Ward's 1 (US) Armoured Division, concentrated at last, would clear the Thelepte airfields; and, if Allen was successful at Gafsa, advance on Maknassy to demonstrate towards the most southerly pass in the Eastern Dorsal. Alexander made it clear to Patton that he must be ready at all times to meet and fend off the vicious spoiling attacks which the Germans were sure to launch as soon as they felt their flank and rear threatened. There was to be no question, at this stage, of II (US) Corps advancing beyond the relative safety of the mountains of the Eastern Dorsal to cut the Axis supply line along the coast. Patton was to refer any major tactical move to Army Group Headquarters before executing it.

These restrictions irked Patton. He saw the sense of them with one half of his mind, but the true American in him made the other half rebel against such treatment. General Omar Bradley, who had been specially appointed by Eisenhower to act as Patton's deputy commander, was more philosophical and helped to soften many of Patton's more embarrassing outbursts about the British system of command and the command itself. He helped McCreery by filtering and rephrasing Army Group orders, thereby making them more palatable to Patton and to the II (US) Corps staff. During one of Patton's periods of irritability he pointed out the similarity between Patton's task of helping Montgomery with flank operations to Stonewall Jackson's role in the American Civil War. This analogy appealed to Patton and assuaged some of his ire.

Patton took over his corps on 8 March. D-Day for his attack was set for 17 March, three days before Montgomery was due to strike at Mareth. Patton had just eight days in which to impress his personality on his troops. He used shock treatment and achieved his aim. A revitalized II (US) Corps swept forward in heavy rain during the night 16–17 March towards Gafsa with an unmistakable sense of purpose. The first movement of Alexander's symphony had begun. The struggle to pass Eighth Army through the Gabes was a complex series of operations in which Alexander was never quite sure how much he could depend on the American section of his orchestra.

The First Movement

. . . the main object would be to get the Eighth Army north of the Gabes Gap. . . .

Alexander, Despatches (p. 870)

The Mareth offensive gave Alexander his first opportunity to try out his ideas of a two-handed strategy in a major offensive. Unfortunately his two fists were not evenly balanced. His right was experienced, hard-hitting and handled by a commander of acknowledged skill. His left still bore the bruises of Kasserine and was led by a military enthusiast of unproven ability. In such circumstances he was bound to depend upon his right, making use of his left as opportunities presented themselves, and treating any punch landed by the left as a welcome bonus. The story of the Battles of Mareth, Wadi Akarit and El Guettar, seen from Alexander's point of view, resolves around the coordination between Montgomery and Patton. In all, Alexander varied Patton's directive six times to meet Montgomery's needs and to profit by Patton's successes. These changes of directive were milestones on Alexander's road to confidence in Patton's Corps.

Montgomery planned to breach the Mareth Line near the coast, using Leese's XXX Corps to force a passage over the Wadi Zigzaou, while Freyberg's New Zealand Corps outflanked the Mareth defences with a long detour over the Matmata Hills and through the desert beyond to appear in Messe's rear via the Tebaga Gap. Horrocks' X Corps was to be in reserve with two armoured divisions ready to exploit through whichever corps proved to be the most successful.

Patton took Gafsa as planned on 17 March with a well executed operation by Allen's 1 (US) Division. The Axis garrison fell back to the hills to the south-east, taking up a defensive position astride the road to Gabes near El Guettar. Patton ordered Ward to start the Maknassy operation, but Ward was unlucky. Nothing went right. The heavy rain continued, turning tracks into rivers of glutinous yellow mud of a clawing consistency which only those who fought in Tunisia can fully appreciate. Ward

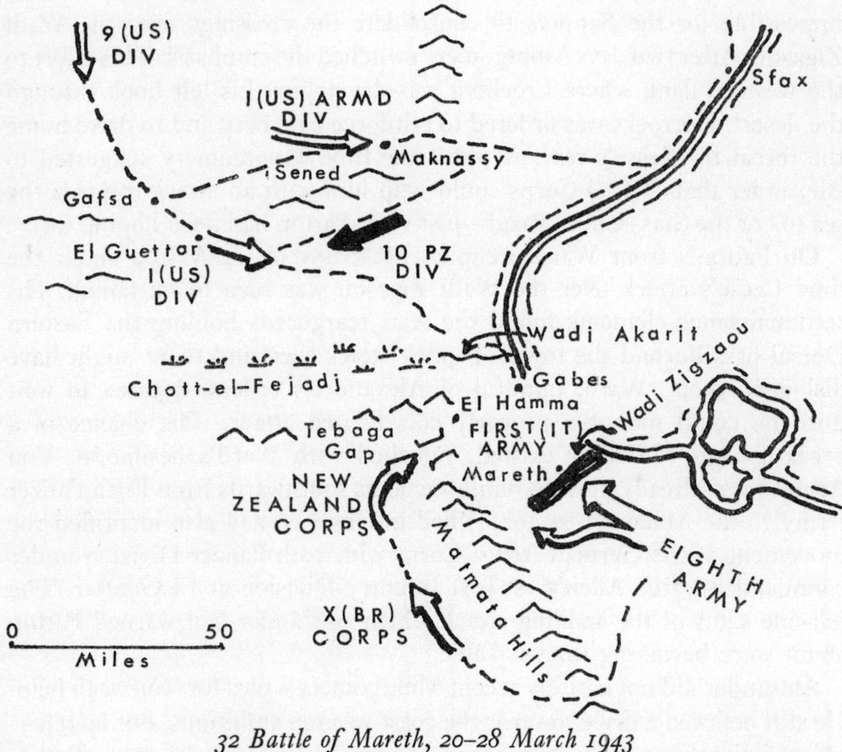

32 Battle of Mareth, 20–28 March 1943

did not take Station de Sened, the first Axis blocking position on the road to Maknassy, until 21 March—the day after Montgomery opened the Battle of Mareth.

Patton's initially encouraging success at Gafsa persuaded Alexander to make his first variation in Patton's directive. Patton was to take Maknassy, seize the pass in the Eastern Dorsal beyond the town, and send a raiding force of light armoured vehicles to destroy Axis aircraft on a group of airfields ten miles east of the pass. Alexander's prohibition of any major move by US troops into the Tunisian plain remained in force. According to Ladislas Farago, Patton's biographer, this continued restriction hurt Patton. While he had accepted the Stonewall analogy, he had hoped that success at Gafsa would bring authority for a Sheridan-like sweep across the Axis rear. Patton had much to learn. The Axis reaction to the fall of Gafsa had already started and was to confirm Alexander's caution.

Eighth Army's attack at Mareth on 20 March began with the accepted Montgomery-style artillery overture. Success did not come easily. Leese's attack slowed, then halted and was finally driven back when rain made it impossible for the Sappers to consolidate the crossings over the Wadi Zigzaou. After two days Montgomery switched the emphasis of his effort to the western flank where Freyberg was developing his left hook through the desert. Horrocks was ordered to reinforce Freyberg and to drive home the threat to Messe's rear. At the same time Montgomery suggested to Alexander that II (US) Corps could help him with an attack towards the sea to cut the Sfax–Gabes Road—just what Patton had been hoping for.

On Patton's front Ward occupied Maknassy on 22 March about the time Leese's attack over the Wadi Zigzaou was seen to be failing. His reconnaissance elements found the Axis rearguards holding the Eastern Dorsal pass beyond the town. A quick attack then and there might have dislodged them. Ward, mindful of Alexander's orders, decided to wait until he could mount a properly coordinated attack. The chance of a breakthrough, if it ever existed, vanished with Ward's hesitation. Von Arnim* was already moving reinforcements southwards from Fifth Panzer Army to the Maknassy sector. Allied intelligence had also identified the movement of the German Africa Corps with 10th Panzer Division under command towards Allen's 1st (US) Infantry Division at El Guettar. The tell-tale signs of the spoiling attack which Alexander had warned Patton about were becoming unmistakable.

Alexander did not entirely accept Montgomery's plea for American help. He still believed a drive towards the coast was too ambitious, but he relented sufficiently to make his second change in Patton's directive. Patton was to prepare a strong armoured force ready for the operation if conditions changed and showed that it would be worth the risks entailed. Meanwhile Patton was to content himself with seizing good defensive ground about Maknassy and El Guettar. He must not be caught off balance by the German counter-attack if it developed.

* Von Arnim took over from Rommel when the latter returned to Rome for consultation on 9 March and was not allowed by Hitler to return to Africa on the grounds of ill health.

The German counter-offensive towards Gafsa did start as predicted. On 23 March, 10 Panzer Division, which had assembled during the night opposite Allen's positions, rolled forward at first light driving all American troops in its path into precipitate retreat. At first everything went the Germans' way. It looked as if another Kasserine was unfolding. Then unexpectedly the German tanks ran into a minefield and a difficult wadi towards the rear of Allen's position. American resistance stiffened as they saw their artillery and tank-destroyers bring the hitherto invincible Germans to a halt. When 10 Panzer Division renewed its attack in the late afternoon the Germans found a new spirit had emerged amongst the troops of the 'Big Red One' as Allen's division was called. The morning's success was all that was needed to restore American confidence. The spirit of Allen's men rebounded in a remarkable way. At the height of the battle the 18 (US) Regimental Combat Team was reporting in the tone of a football commentator: '. . . Troops started to appear from all directions, mostly from tanks . . . our artillery crucified them with high explosive shell and they were falling like flies. . . . Tanks seem to be moving to the rear; those that could move. . . .'

By dusk it was certain that a US Infantry Division had stopped a German Panzer Division. Alexander's policy of keeping new troops to tasks within their capabilities was paying off. The problem in future would be to damp down over-enthusiasm which could easily lead to tragedy. The battle of El Guettar was the first welcome step by the Americans towards balanced battle experience.

While Allen was winning his contest with 10 Panzer Division, Freyberg reached the Tebaga Gap, finding himself opposed by a strong Italo-German force including parts of 21 Panzer Division which Messe had hurriedly despatched to protect his rear. It would be at least two more days before Horrocks' Corps could reinforce him, so there was time for Alexander to take other measures to help Montgomery forward. Two steps which he took were of particular importance. The first stemmed from an idea of Air Marshal Broadhurst, the new Commander of the Desert Air Force.* All available aircraft which could be brought usefully to bear from Tedder's air forces were to concentrate on helping Freyberg and Horrocks through the Tebaga Gap. This was to be the first real attempt by the Allies to emulate the German Blitzkrieg, and was the first time that such a concentration of air power had been tried in a land battle by any of the belligerents. It was also the first time that air forces were to be controlled over a land battle from an aircraft circling overhead and by

* Coningham was now commanding the Allied North-West African Tactical Air Force.

Air Force officers with the leading troops. The whole operation—land and air—was code-named 'Supercharge' as it was to play the same decisive role that its predecessor had done at El Alamein.

The second measure which Alexander took was to make his third change in Patton's directive. Patton had already attracted 10th Panzer Division and stopped it. It was now essential to hold 10th Panzer where it was and, if possible, draw more German reserves away from Montgomery without risking an American disaster. Alexander visited Patton on 25 March and released to him General Manton Eddy's newly arrived 9 (US) Infantry Division. Patton was to abandon his attempts to break through east of Maknassy, where Ward was making disappointing progress, and to concentrate three of his divisions—Allen's, Ward's and Eddy's—for an attack south-eastwards from El Guettar towards Gabes. Plans for this offensive were worked out by the Army Group staff in more detail than would normally be the case, ostensibly to ensure the coordination of Patton's and Montgomery's operations. Alexander was still anxious lest II (US) Corps should blunder into a major tank battle with the Africa Corps in open country before it was ready for such a contest. Patton was delighted with the task, but not with the apron-strings which cut deeper after his success at El Guettar. Writing to George Marshall a fortnight later, he complained: 'All I have is the actual conduct of the operations prescribed [by Alexander].'

Anticipating events, Alexander gave Patton one further instruction. The narrowest part of Messe's withdrawal route back to Northern Tunisia lay between the Holy City of Kairouan in the foothills of the Eastern Dorsal and Sousse on the coast. The Axis still held the Fonduk Pass leading to Kairouan, and so Alexander authorised Patton to give Ryder's 34 (US) Infantry Division the preliminary task of securing the pass as a sally-port from which a force could be launched to cut Messe's withdrawal at the appropriate moment. The operation would be useful in giving Ryder's men battle experience as well as being a wise precautionary move.

'Supercharge' was successully launched on the night 26–27 March. Messe had already decided that he must fall back. 15 and 21 Panzer Divisions fought hard to cover the withdrawal of the rest of Messe's Army through Gabes Gap. The massive air support during 'Supercharge' had an exhilarating effect on the British and an equally demoralising effect on the Axis troops. Only one line of enemy defences now lay between Eighth Army and the Central Tunisian plain—the Wadi Akarit position.

Patton's offensive down the El Guettar–Gabes road started simultaneously with 'Supercharge', but did not go so well. Allen's 1 (US)

17 In Khartoum: Alexander talking to soldiers and airmen while touring his theatre

THEATRE COMMANDER

18 Vast distances: McCreery and Alexander relaxing while flying across the theatre. Distances dividing headquarters were one of the main difficulties in planning the invasion of Sicily

19 Personal observation: Alexander watching the shelling of German positions near Medjez-el-Bab

COMMANDER 18 ARMY GROUP

20 Personal touch: Alexander visiting a forward brigade headquarters in Tunisia

Infantry made some progress, but Eddy's 9 (US) Infantry Division suffered all the problems of a new division in its first night operation—misjudgment of distances, wrong identification of features, loss of direction and underestimation of time needed, all added up to loss of control. Eddy's attack failed with heavy loss. The more experienced Axis troops were too strongly posted on the rocky slopes of the djebels to give way easily. Patton's

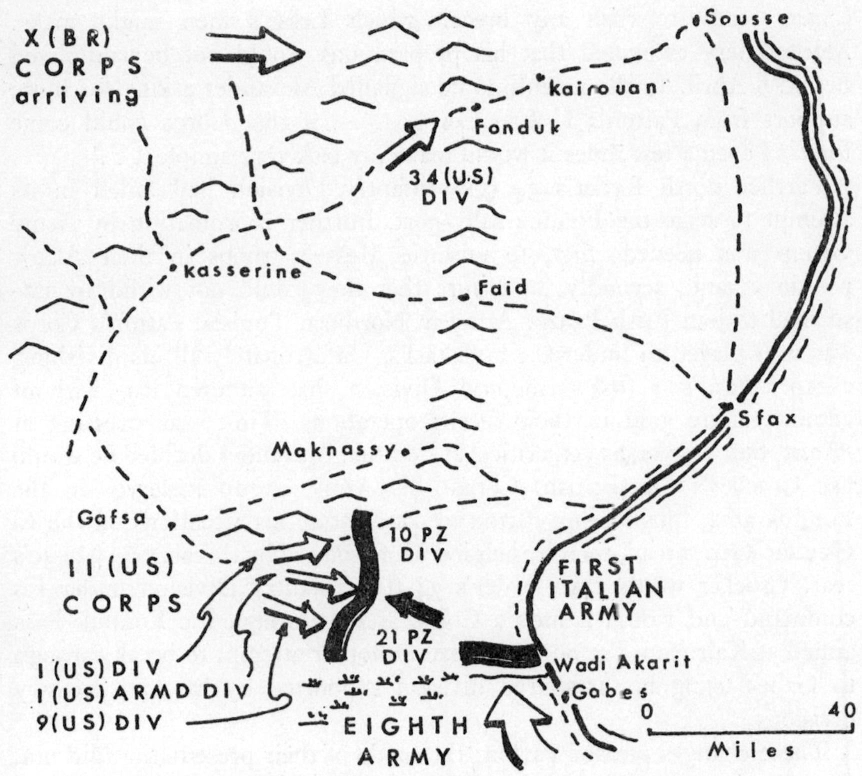

33 Battle of Wadi Akarit and Operations beyond El Guettar, 28 March–7 April 1943

infantry divisions would have to reorganise before they could make another attempt to hustle 10 Panzer Division and its supporting German and Italian troops out of their positions which were growing stronger every day. But before Patton could organise a fresh assault events on Montgomery's front intervened. Alexander changed Patton's directive for the fourth time, giving him his most ambitious task yet.

Horrocks' X (British) Corps led the advance to the Wadi Akarit, hoping to be able to break through before the Axis troops had time to settle down in its defence. Horrocks was out of luck. He found the Axis line too strongly held for a quickly mounted attack by his mobile troops to succeed. Montgomery decided that he would have to stage another properly organised attack to force Messe out of this very strong last ditch position. He ordered Leese's XXX Corps forward to undertake the breaching operation, while Horrocks' X Corps resumed its role as *Corps de Chasse* ready to rush any breach which Lesse's men might make. Montgomery estimated that his preparations would not be completed before 6 April. In the meantime he signalled Alexander asking for more support from Patton's II (US) Corps: '. . . if that Corps could come forward even a few miles it would make my task very simple. . . .'

Farther north Ryder's 34 (US) Infantry Division had failed in its attempt to seize the Fonduk sally-port. Further coordination by Army Group was needed; first, to unsettle Messe's troops in their Akarit positions; and, secondly, to ensure that they could not withdraw unscathed to join Fifth Panzer Army in Northern Tunisia. Patton's Corps was well placed to undertake both tasks. Unfortunately all his divisions, except Ward's 1 (US) Armoured Division, had suffered loss without commensurate gain in their recent operations. Time was pressing at Akarit, but was not, as yet, critical at Fonduk. Alexander decided he would use Crocker's IX (British) Corps—his Army Group Reserve—in the Fonduk area, thus freeing Patton to concentrate his attentions on the El Guettar-Gabes road, thereby helping Montgomery by threatening Messe's rear. Crocker would take Ryder's 34 (US) Infantry Division under his command and would launch a Corps attack through the Fonduk Pass aimed at Kairouan. Patton would make another attempt to break through to Gabes using his armoured division supported by his two infantry divisions.

These changes pleased Patton; the mode of their presentation did not. Once again Army Group Headquarters laid down strict guide lines. Whether these emanated from Alexander or McCreery is not recorded in the official histories, but the US official account says tactfully:

> After some difficulties involved in this set of instructions had been resolved, Patton determined to put the 1st Armoured Divisions' task force under Colonel Benson, whose aggressiveness he admired. . . . (*North West Africa*, p. 573)

Patton reopened his offensive on 30 March, following the course dictated by Army Group. The combined artilleries of Allen's, Ward's and Eddy's divisions were concentrated and used in a British styled 'break-in' battle, and then Benson's tanks attacked in the centre supported by Allen's and Eddy's infantry on either flank. Benson did not get far. Mines blocked his way and the infantry divisions failed to take and hold the high ground overlooking his axis of advance which ran parallel to and just to the north of the Gabes road. For three days Patton did his best to break through with his armour fully engaged, apparently to no avail. Recrimination between the Americans of II (US) Corps and the British of 18 Army Group Headquarters became audible. At the front, the Americans felt that, if only Alexander had not held them back in the early phase of their offensive, the Axis would not have been able to build up so strong a defence. The British held the view, just as strongly, that the Americans' slow progress confirmed their weaknesses in battle training and experience. The US Official History gives the American side of the story:

> It was already painfully apparent that II Corps' progress toward the coast had suffered severely from the cautious restraint and frequent changes in instructions imposed by 18 Army Group. . . . Its restraining influence had permitted the enemy to occupy extremely defensible ground while the Americans were tethered to Gafsa and El Guettar. . . .

But very fairly continues by saying:

> Yet it must be remembered that the object of these operations remained primarily to divert enemy reserves rather than to advance onto the coastal plain against the enemy's principle force. Even if the American armoured column had been in a position to gain access, either by infantry action or its own bludgeoning attack, to the enemy's rear area, General Alexander would then have had to decide whether he thought such an operation was advisable. (*North West Africa*, pp. 572–3)

Amongst the Allied Air Forces tempers became equally ragged. Tedder's policy of winning the air battle first and then concentrating the Allied tactical air effort in support of the land forces' primary thrusts, led to Eighth Army enjoying clear skies and magnificent close air support, whereas Patton's diversionary operations received minimal air cover and support. Patton complained bitterly about the air situation and in his daily situation report of 1 April described Axis aircraft as operating almost at will over II (US) Corps due to lack of Allied air cover. Coningham, who was now in command of the Allied North-West African Tactical Air Force, resented Patton's criticism of his American and British airmen's efforts. In a widely distributed signal he replied to Patton's complaint in a way which the American historians rightly describe as 'sarcastic and supercilious', noting that the same II (US) Corps situation report gave the Corps' casualties for that day as only six. Coningham was, in fact, defending the actions of the US XII Air Support Command against what he considered were unfounded accusations and a complete misappreciation of the use of air power by Patton. The most stinging sentences in the signal were:

> . . . it can only be assumed that II Corps personnel concerned are not battle-worthy in terms of present operations. . . .
> XII Air Support Command have been instructed not to allow their brilliant and conscientious support of II Corps to be affected by the false cry of wolf. (Tedder, p. 410)

It took all Alexander's tact and persuasive powers to smooth over the furrows ploughed in Anglo-American relations by this minor but unfortunate incident. Its occurrence is only recorded here because it illustrates two things: first, the sensitivity not only of international feeling but also of inter-Service susceptibilities at the time; and secondly, the greater importance of persuading the component parts of the Allied orchestra to play the same tune rather than reaching for particular brilliance in the operational theme. Alexander's lightness of touch, which helped him to win a measure of harmony, was a greater asset to the Allied cause, at this juncture, than any Napoleonic inspiration.

Unbeknown to Alexander, Patton's attempt to break through with Benson's armour had gained his strategic purpose. Messe became anxious about his rear and despatched 21 Panzer Division to support 10 Panzer Division in holding Patton at bay. A long argument ensued in the Axis High Command as to whether the Akarit position could be held as the 'final defensive line' in Tunisia as Hitler decreed, or whether the Axis supply position would not, on its own, dictate another withdrawal—this time right back to a closer bridgehead perimeter around the ports and airfields of Tunis and Bizerta. Field Marshal Kesselring, with his proverbial optimism, thought Wadi Akarit could be held; von Arnim and Messe were certain that it could not. Personal animosity was as great, if not greater, in the Axis camp than among the Allies. General Westphal, visiting Tunisia at the time from OKW, remarked that Army Group Africa was always 'squinting over its shoulder'. Von Arnim's tart reply was 'Yes, for supply ships'. Both von Arnim and Messe had mentally given up the Wadi Akarit position and, though they intended to hold it as long as possible, were already making dispositions to extricate the First Italian Army without too great a loss among the slower moving infantry divisions. A sharp blow by Eighth Army was all that would be needed to persuade Messe to fall back, but he knew that the survival of his Army depended upon the security of its western flank—hence his reinforcement of the troops opposing Patton and a general strengthening of all Axis positions along the Eastern Dorsal, including the Fonduk Pass towards which Crocker's IX Corps was beginning to move.

On 1 April Alexander made his fifth change in Patton's directive, ordering him to give up his attempt to break through with his armour since identifications showed that he was opposed by elements of two panzer divisions, and to revert to the process of eroding away the Axis position by limited, well supported infantry attacks. For the next few days Patton's infantry gnawed at the Axis held djebels, suffering uncomfortably heavy losses in the process. On 4 April, unusual movements were observed behind the Axis lines, suggesting another panzer counter-attack of the type which Allen had defeated a fortnight before. Patton took immediate defensive measures and awaited attack during 5 April, while Leese's XXX Corps put the final touches to its plan for the Wadi Akarit assault. No Axis counter-attack came in. Patton's intelligence staff realised that the Axis movements were in preparation for withdrawal and not attack. Patton's whip and spurs came out and II (US) Corps lunged forward as Montgomery opened his attack on Wadi Akarit.

The Battle of Wadi Akarit was one of the shortest but hardest-fought of Montgomery's battles. It lasted for less than 36 hours. The fighting was as brutal as any experienced by Eighth Army and was to make an impression on Montgomery which had a significant effect later on the planning for the invasion of Sicily. Attack and counter-attack swayed the issue all day, and showed the Italians in a much more virile light than hitherto. Patton's II (US) Corps found progress on 6 April just as slow and frustrating. American visions of breaking through to the sea and being able to claim a major share in Eighth Army's victory when it came, shone brightly in the morning but flickered and died by evening. Messe was fighting hard to win time to evacuate his infantry divisions. That evening, 6 April, Alexander issued his sixth and final change in Patton's orders. Appreciating that Montgomery's battle had reached its crisis, he ordered Patton to attack next morning, using his armour regardless of loss. Patton needed no goading. During the night he listened to a noise which American and British troops were to hear so often in the coming months and were to grow to know its welcome significance. A heavy Axis artillery barrage came down as if heralding a night attack. All units stood to. Nothing happened. 10 and 21 Panzer Divisions were disengaging and had pulled back their most exposed tanks and infantry posts under the cover of the barrage. When dawn came II (US) Corps and Eighth Army found themselves opposed only by rearguards. During the day the leading American reconnaissance unit of Benson's armoured column met the most westerly armoured car troop of Eighth Army—Lieutenant J. H. D. Richardson's 5 Troop of B Squadron 12th Lancers. Eighth Army was through the Gabes Gap and 18 Army Group was physically united in a great encircling arc around Hitler's and Mussolini's shrinking bridgehead in Africa. Psychologically, however, the Allies were to suffer further blows to the delicate balance of Anglo-American relations before a real working relationship was established.

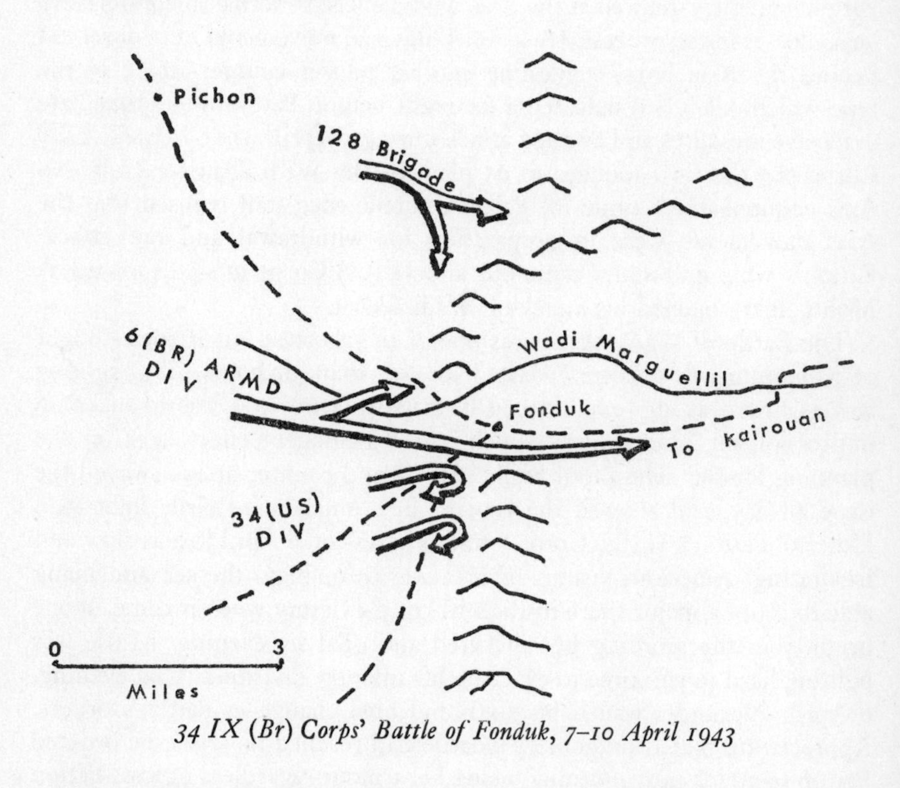

34 IX (Br) Corps' Battle of Fonduk, 7–10 April 1943

Crocker's attack at Fonduk was the initial cause of this fresh wave of Anglo-American recrimination. Crocker's plan was for Ryder's 34 (US) Division to attack the hills on the south side of the pass, while 128 (British) Infantry Brigade cleared the northern side. Keightley's 6 (British) Armoured Division would blast its way through the pass once the high ground on either side had been taken, and would then descend upon Messe's flank as the First Italian Army fell back. Misunderstandings occurred during planning. Ryder felt that he was being committed to a faulty plan because his line of advance could be enfiladed from the hills on the northern side of the pass which would not be taken by 128 Brigade in time to be of much help to the Americans. Crocker seems to have overridden Ryder's objections; and Ryder, for his part, was possibly insufficiently explicit about his fears. Misinterpretation of the common Anglo-American language played its part as well as differences in tactical outlook and method. Unwisely Ryder tried to change his plan at the last moment, turning his attack from a day into a night attack. His troops were already on their way to their start lines from which they were to have attacked at dawn, when Ryder's orders arrived, bringing zero hour forward from 0530 hours to 0300 hours. The air support, which was to have been supplied for the daylight attack, had to be cancelled. Disaster was inevitable. 34 (US) Division failed in the confusion of these last minute changes. Time was slipping by. Messe had withdrawn from Akarit earlier than Alexander had expected. Unless Crocker broke through the Fonduk Pass at once, he would catch none of Messe's troops. Alexander ordered Crocker to commit Keightley's 6 (British) Armoured Division to the unenviable task of breaking through without securing the high ground. Keightley did break through with considerable loss of tanks, but it was already too late to affect the Axis withdrawal in a decisive way. His armour emerged from the hills on 10 April and fought its way to Kairouan which fell next day. Messe's rearguards had withdrawn some hours earlier leaving nothing behind but the sour taste of an unfortunate ending to Alexander's operation of passing Eighth Army through the Gabes Gap.

This incident might have slipped unnoticed into history had it not been for the international press who heard about Crocker's post-mortem conference at which he tried to explain the failings of Ryder's division to a party of visiting American officers. His remarks were meant to be constructive and were accepted as such by his visitors. Malicious tongues soon embroidered the story and allowed it to leak to the press. Once more Alexander had to soothe hurt American feelings. The British Official History cools the smouldering embers of Fonduk by saying: 'It was a pity that injudicious comment on the events of the past three days caused Anglo-American carping which had to be stilled by Eisenhower and Alexander, "Faithful are the wounds of a friend".'

First and Eighth Armies linked hands on 11 April when, by coincidence, the same troop of 12th Lancers met the leading unit of 6 (British) Armoured Division of Crocker's Corps twenty miles south of Kairouan.

The Interlude

> . . . we should be able to co-ordinate to the full the striking power of all three Services in drawing the net round the enemy's position in Tunis.
>
> Alexander, Despatches (p. 870)

Alexander, like all able commanders of modern armies, was building up his dispositions for the next phase of his operations long before the previous phase was over. He knew that his next task was to tighten the ring round the shrunken Axis bridgehead, but the way in which he disposed his troops would depend upon how he saw the final battle being fought.

Ever since Alexander had arrived in Tunisia at the beginning of February he had been discussing various plans for the final battle of Tunis with Anderson whose First Army was best positioned to deliver the *coup de grâce*. It did not take great military insight to discern that Tunis itself with its port and airfields was the key to the Axis' hopes of staying in Africa. It was not quite so easy to decide where to make the final breach in the 120-mile front which was held by the two Axis Armies. The first 40 miles of the Axis defensive perimeter stretching southwards from the northern Tunisian coast offered few attractions for a major Allied offensive. It was too mountainous and led to Bizerta rather than Tunis. The other end of the perimeter was no more attractive. The 40 miles of line running eastwards from the coast at Enfidaville to Bou Arada was also blocked by difficult hill country. Only the central 40 miles offered reasonable prospects. There the Mejerda Valley and the Plain of Bou Arada were open enough for armoured warfare and the routes through them led directly to Tunis. Although the central sector was the obvious point of attack and would be the most heavily defended, Alexander judged that his final offensive must be made there if he was to develop the full power of his Army Group. His strategy and deployment were, thus, based on positioning Anderson's main striking force in the central sector while, at the same time, suggesting to von Arnim by various deceptive measures that Montgomery's Eighth Army would lead the assault in the eastern sector. This was not difficult as Eighth Army had launched all the major offensives so far; and Montgomery still hoped to beat Anderson into Tunis whatever plan Alexander made.

Tightening the noose around von Arnim's forces involved all three Services—sea, land and air. Cunningham and Tedder established the sea and air blockade with Operation 'Flax' which began on 5 April. On that day the Allied Air Forces intercepted 13 German JU52 air transports off Cap Bon and caught 15 more Axis transport aircraft on the ground. The climax of 'Flax' came two and a half weeks later on 22 April when 16 out of 21 of the large ME323 transports, each carrying ten tons of petrol, were shot down before they could reach Tunis. British submarines complemented the efforts of the Allied airmen, gaining comparable successes at

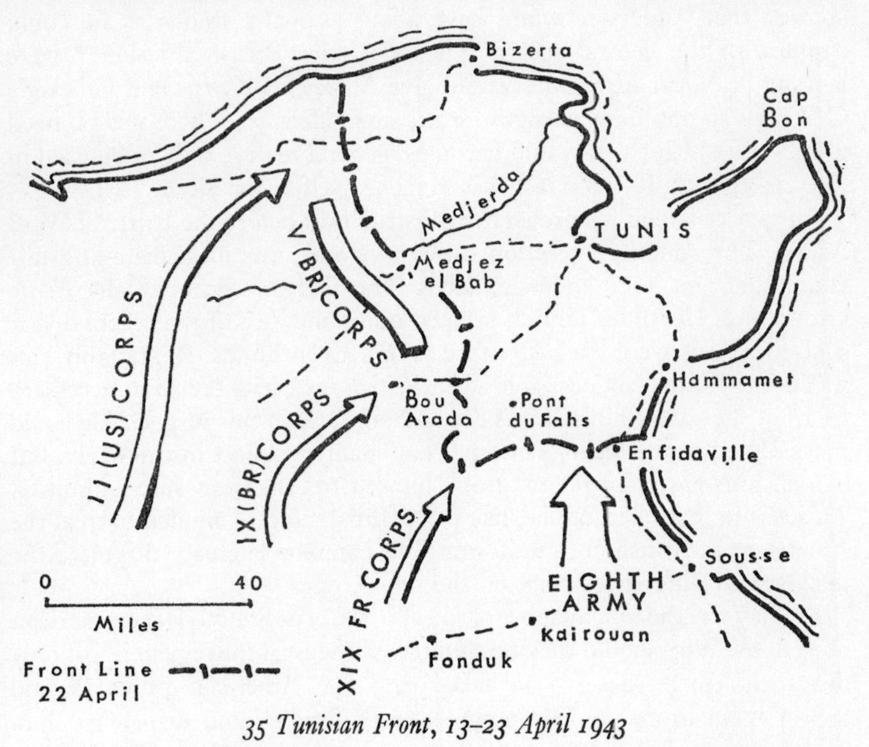

35 Tunisian Front, 13–23 April 1943

sea. By 23 April, when Alexander was ready to tighten the screw of the landward blockade, Axis supplies had been reduced to a trickle as they had been before El Alamein.

Alexander's early thoughts on the deployment of the landward blockade were unfortunate and politically misjudged. As Eighth Army advanced north from Wadi Akarit, Patton's II (US) Corps would be squeezed out of the line. Alexander felt that this was an ideal opportunity to give the American troops the training which they needed for the coming Sicilian campaign. Both the Army Group operational and logistic staffs advised that only one US division could be used in the final offensive, and that this should be deployed in the extreme north to enable Anderson to concentrate Allfrey's V Corps in the Mejerda sector. From the operational point of view the northern sector had already been discarded as unsuitable for major operations and so needed little more than a watching force; and from the logistic stand-point British experience in supplying 46 (British) Infantry Division over the poor northern roads suggested that a force of about one division was the limit for the sector. Similar logistic calculations showed that Anderson would have about as many troops as he could support in the central sector. The two extra British divisions* were landing in North Africa and would give Allfrey's V Corps and Crocker's IX Corps an optimum strength for the final offensive. There was no need to use II (US) Corps. It would become a general reserve only to be used in dire emergency. Its main task was to make itself fit for Sicily.

Alexander issued his preparatory instructions before the battle of Wadi Akarit. The American reaction to his proposals was immediate and unfavourable, but very understandable. The British officers of the Army Group and Alexander himself seemed quite unaware of the reaction that such proposals were likely to cause in American minds. Regrettably this was not to be the last occasion when British insularity led to unnecessary friction. Alexander himself was not without fault in this respect. He could normally sense the feelings of other nationalities almost instinctively, but it took him much longer to attune himself to American susceptibilities. This was perhaps because he, like most British officers, tended to treat the Americans as British in US uniforms. The common language disguised the deep-seated differences between the two Armies.

Bradley was the first member of the II (US) Corps Staff to voice American objections. Why should they be shut out of the final movement? Not only did their troops deserve to take part; the American public would expect them to do so. Patton agreed with Bradley and dispatched him post haste to Alexander's headquarters to protest. There Bradley was given the factors which led to Alexander's operational decisions and the logistic reasoning behind them. None of these satisfied Bradley who flew on back to see Eisenhower in Algiers. The Americans were doing no more than exercise the right, which British commanders have always reserved, of appealing to their own Government over the head of an Allied commander if they considered their troops were being misused—in this case under-used.

* 1st and 4th (British) Infantry Divisions.

Bradley had little difficulty in persuading Eisenhower of the justice of the American case. And Eisenhower, in his turn, found Alexander only too willing to meet the Americans' wishes once their case was put to him. He agreed that, instead of just one US division taking over in the north, the whole of the II (US) Corps of four divisions would be deployed there provided two things could be done. First, the Americans would have to find ways of supplying their troops in that poorly roaded sector; and secondly, the move of II (US) Corps across the rear of Anderson's troops must not disrupt the supply of the First Army. Both provisos offered an organisational challenge of a magnitude dear to every American's heart. Alexander had little doubt that they would find a way of meeting his demands, and so he recast his plan, making Bizerta the American and Tunis the British objectives. Patton would not be commanding II (US) Corps in the final battle. Eisenhower decided that he should hand over to Bradley, so that he could return to his proper job of planning and training the troops for the American part of the invasion of Sicily.

Alexander's relationship with the Americans was still delicate, but his willingness to see their point of view, when it was put to him, prevented any serious loss of confidence on either side. Failure to make American views plain and failure of the British staff to anticipate American disquiet remained a hazard. For the coming offensive the Americans would have a sector of their own in which close inter-Allied coordination would not be needed.

Alexander's relationships with his two British Army commanders, and the feelings of the two Armies about each other, were not entirely harmonious. On the one hand, Alexander was not prepared to trust Anderson's judgment implicitly, nor give him his full confidence; and, on the other, he found Montgomery increasingly demanding. The two Armies reflected their commanders: First Army, orthodox, painstaking and never quite sure of its abilities or those of its commander; and Eighth Army, overbearingly confident and looking down on First Army as just as inexperienced as the Americans. First Army in its turn looked upon Eighth as an overconfident crowd who would meet their match—as they indeed did—when faced with the type of mountain country through which First Army had been struggling all winter. These rivalries were harmless as long as both Army Commanders accepted Alexander's overlordship. Fortunately, as events proved, they were prepared to do so. The two men and their Armies were cast in the wrong roles by the accident of geography and the personality of the Army Group Commander who saw no reason, at this juncture, to move Eighth Army from its coastal axis into the decisive central sector, thereby favouring one section of his orchestra. It was First Army's turn to take the lead.

On 11 April Montgomery asked Alexander in a personal signal to place Keightley's 6 (British) Armoured Division under his command: '... Am going to try and gate-crash position [Enfidaville] this moon period....' Alexander's reply was swift and authoritative: 'Main effort in next phase of operations will be by First Army ... hope you can develop maximum pressure possible against Enfidaville position to fit in with First Army attack....'

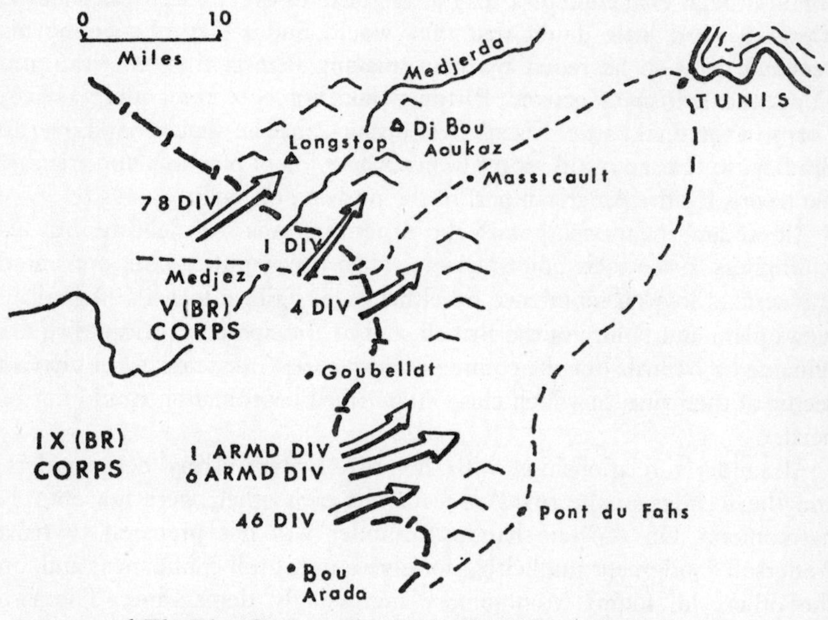

36 The Plan for Operation 'Vulcan' issued on 16 April 1943

Since the end of February, Anderson had been methodically regaining all the important ground lost in von Arnim's offensive. He had secured most of the features needed for an advance on Tunis along the two potential thrust lines which Alexander intended to use. The shorter and more damaging of these two axes comprised the Mejerda Valley and the main road from Medjez-El-Bab through Massicault to Tunis, but this would be strongly held by von Arnim's troops. The other axis lay further south across the Goubellat Plain and thence to Tunis on cross-country routes south of the main Medjez–Tunis Road. Anderson's first ideas called for a concentrated thrust up the main road to Tunis, but in discussions with Alexander this was modified so as to use Alexander's two handed technique. Allfrey's V Corps with 1, 4, and 78 (British) Infantry Divisions would be used to open up the northern axis, while Crocker's IX Corps with 1* and 6 (British) Armoured Divisions and 46 (British) Infantry Division would use the southern approach which was more suitable for tanks. Allfrey's task entailed clearing two long ridges of heavily defended hills which overlooked the Mejerda Valley and the main road. These features were the Longstop Ridge in the north and the Djebel Bou Aoukaz Ridge in the centre between the river and the main road. It was for this reason that his Corps was given three infantry divisions while Crocker kept both Armoured Divisions. Crocker's task was to burst through the rather lower hills surrounding the Goubellat Plain, and, in so doing, to draw von Arnim's three panzer divisions to the southern sector. When Allfrey's Longstop and Bou Aoukaz features had been taken, the time might be ripe to switch Crocker's Corps to the centre for a 'power drive' on Tunis of the Tebaga Gap type. This could only be decided at the time.

Alexander's directive for Operation 'Vulcan', issued on 16 April, gave each principal commander a specific role within the overall plan and a personal prize for which to strive—Bradley to take Bizerta, Anderson Tunis, and Montgomery to prevent von Arnim establishing a final redoubt in the Cap Bon Peninsula. His directive read:

> . . . First Army will:
> (a) Capture Tunis.
> (b) Co-operate with II (US) Corps in the capture of Bizerta.
> (c) Be prepared to co-operate with Eighth Army should the enemy withdraw to Cap Bon Peninsula.
>
> II (US) Corps will:
> (a) Secure suitable positions for the attack on Bizerta, covering the left flank of First Army.
> (b) Advance and capture Bizerta. . . .
>
> Eighth Army will:
> (a) Draw enemy forces off First Army by exerting continuous pressure on the enemy.
> (b) By an advance on the axis Enfidaville-Hammamet-Tunis prevent the enemy withdrawing into the Cap Bon Peninsula.

(*The Mediterranean and the Middle East*, IV, p. 430)

Critics may rightly say, as Montgomery does in his memoirs that the first phase of 'Vulcan' '. . . was more like a partridge drive than an attack. . . .' But herein lies the essential difference between the styles of these

* From Eighth Army.

two great British commanders. The Montgomery, and for that matter, the Napoleonic type of battle, was fought to a clear set-piece plan, based upon concentration of effort at the vital point and upon the commander dictating events—sometimes regardless of loss. Alexander, like Eisenhower was not prepared to stake so much on a single throw, nor were his plans so clear cut. He preferred less rigid methods. He had seen too many battles go wrong to believe that he could dictate events in the grand style. He was convinced that no great battle ever goes to plan. The permutations of chance are too great for such certainty. Alexander preferred to work to an overall pattern in which each subordinate had a clear task and the incentive to do his best. Each man had to feel that his efforts could make or mar the battle. But whatever plan was made must, in Alexander's view, contain within it the flexibility to exploit success and, conversely, to stem failure. This is not the policy of a partridge drive, but follows Alexander's own analogy of the boxing match—wear your opponent down using both hands until an opening for a knock-out blow appears. It is better to win on points than repeat the failures of the Somme with a 'haymaking' right hook before your adversary is weak enough to collapse. Military 'haymakers', which fail, do so with needless loss of life. 'Vulcan', the Battle for Tunis, was to be Alexander's first demonstration of his intuitive military style, born of his extensive battle experience rather than deep military thought. He was to perfect this technique a year later when he launched his 'Diadem' offensive—the Battle for Rome.

The Second and Final Movement

> My next objective was to complete the destruction of the forces still opposing me as quickly as possible in order to obtain the use of the ports of Tunis and Bizerta for the invasion of Sicily.
>
> Alexander, Despatches (p. 878)

The final phase of Alexander's Tunisian campaign began with two operations which did not belong to the main stream of his overall plan. On 19 April Montgomery tried to open up the Axis defences around Enfidaville. His losses were heavy and his gains slight. Eighth Army was operating in mountain country to which it was unaccustomed. However much Montgomery might wish to preempt Anderson by reaching Tunis first, his chances of doing so were dwindling as each day passed. He broke off his offensive on 22 April to regroup and to summon 56 (British) Infantry Division forward from Tripoli to replace 50 (British) Infantry Division which was due to return to the Nile Delta for amphibious training in anticipation of the invasion of Sicily. Plan 'Husky' was beginning to cast its shadow over the Tunisian battlefield. Montgomery, himself, as British Task Forces Commander (designate), became progressively more pre-occupied with 'Husky' problems as the last days of April slipped by.

The other pre-'Vulcan' operation came from the Axis side. A flurry of 'backs-to-wall' orders of the day were issued by all senior commanders from Kesselring downwards: '. . . if every German soldier justified the reliance of the Führer and Fatherland upon him by fighting, in an historic hour, with bravery and unshakable resolution . . . we shall destroy the enemy's hopes and victory will be ours.' General Schmid, acting commander of the Hermann Göring Division, holding the sector due south of the main Medjez-Tunis road, caught the feeling of the hour. He planned and executed a spoiling attack at the junction of Crocker's and Allfrey's Corps. Allied intelligence detected its preparation. In spite of this Allfrey's men were involved in some sharp fighting before Schmid withdrew. He achieved no lasting damage and 'Vulcan' started on time at 3.40 a.m. on 22 April with Crocker attacking in the Goubillat sector. Allfrey followed next day with Evelegh's 78 (British) Division attacking Longstop and Clutterbuck's 1 (British) Infantry Division advancing towards Djebel Bou Aoukaz.

Crocker's attack went slower than was hoped against the stubborn resistance of the Hermann Göring Division. Nevertheless it achieved Alexander's aim of drawing the German armour away from the Medjez-Tunis road. 10 Panzer Division entered the fray on 23 April; 21 Panzer Division followed next day; and elements of 15 Panzer Division were identified about the same time. The German Africa Corps Headquarters took over control of the sector, but could not prevent Crocker's armoured divisions inflicting mortal damage on their German opponents who could no longer replace their tank losses. By 26 April 10 Panzer Division, the strongest of the three, was down to 25 fit tanks.

No one had expected Allfrey's attack to go very fast amongst the jagged rock-strewn features which had to be cleared methodically before real progress towards Tunis could be made. Evelegh's 78 Division mastered 'Longstop' after three days hard fighting and was beginning to make progress along the north side of the Mejerda Valley. Clutterbuck's 1 Division just failed to carry Djebel Bou Aoukaz in the face of determined German counter-attacks mounted personally by von Vaerst, who had succeeded von Arnim as commander of the Fifth Panzer Army, when the latter was promoted to replace Rommel. And Hawkesworth's 4 Division fought its way forward for seven miles down the Medjez–Tunis road. The severity of the fighting in V Corps' sector was reflected in the award of three VCs in the fighting for Djebel Bou Aoukaz, one of which gave Alexander particular pleasure as it was won by L/Cpl Kennedy of the 1st Battalion, Irish Guards.

In the north Bradley's II (US) Corps launched a well prepared and thoroughly thought out offensive towards Bizerta on 23 April. Instead of attempting to crash down the valleys, Bradley sent his infantry along the mountain ridges, taking the high points in methodical succession with hard fought and properly supported operations. American confidence grew with success. Bradley and his divisional commanders were now allowed to fight the battle as they thought best, and this they did with great success.

To the south, between First and Eighth Army, the French XIX Corps followed up a voluntary Axis withdrawal out of the salient caused by Crocker's advance, and came within striking distance of Pont du Fahs (see fig. 35, p. 193). Eighth Army, whose commander had gone sick with tonsilitis and influenza, was not at its best, and continued to regroup for an attack timed for 28–29 April.

As early as 26 April Alexander had begun to sense that Anderson's offensive was beginning to flag. He felt also that the moment was coming when he should give the Germans a dose of their own blitzkrieg medicine. Montgomery claims to have been the author of the idea behind Operation 'Strike' which was to win the battle of Tunis. Alexander, in an unusually outspoken passage, denies this.

> Finally, there is the not unimportant matter of the reinforcing of the First Army. Monty, in his memoirs, gives the impression that this was his initiative and idea—whether he intended to do so I don't know. But, of course, Montgomery had nothing to do with the attack on Tunis. When, to strengthen the blow, I decided to give First Army the two divisions from Eighth Army, I went over to see Montgomery, and found that, like me, he was not satisfied with the progress on the First Army front. I left it to him to suggest the two divisions and he loyally gave me of his best. (*Memoirs*, p. 38)

The idea was to move Crocker's IX Corps in behind V Corps and to attack with it on an extremely narrow front straight down the Tunis road, using three or four armoured and infantry divisions supported by the whole weight of the Allied Tactical Air Forces. Alexander discussed this plan with Anderson and was intending to use Keightley's 6 Armoured

Division, possibly Briggs' 1 Armoured Division, and certainly Evelegh's successful 78 Infantry Division. But before a detailed plan could be worked out, events elsewhere made Alexander change his mind about the divisions to be used.

Montgomery's attack north of Enfidaville on 28–29 April was a costly failure, and showed conclusively that as the British Official History records, '. . . there was no battle to be won in these parts'. Alexander drove to Headquarters Eighth Army on 30 April at Montgomery's request and concluded that the best way that Eighth Army could help the First was to send two of its best divisions across to reinforce IX Corps for 'Strike'. Montgomery nominated Tuker's 4 (Indian) Infantry Division, Erskine's 7 (British) Armoured Division and 201 (Guards) Brigade. Eighth Army and its Commander tended to paint this move as professionals being summoned to help the amateurs of First Army to finish a job which they had bungled. It was nothing of the sort. It was sound strategy on Alexander's part.

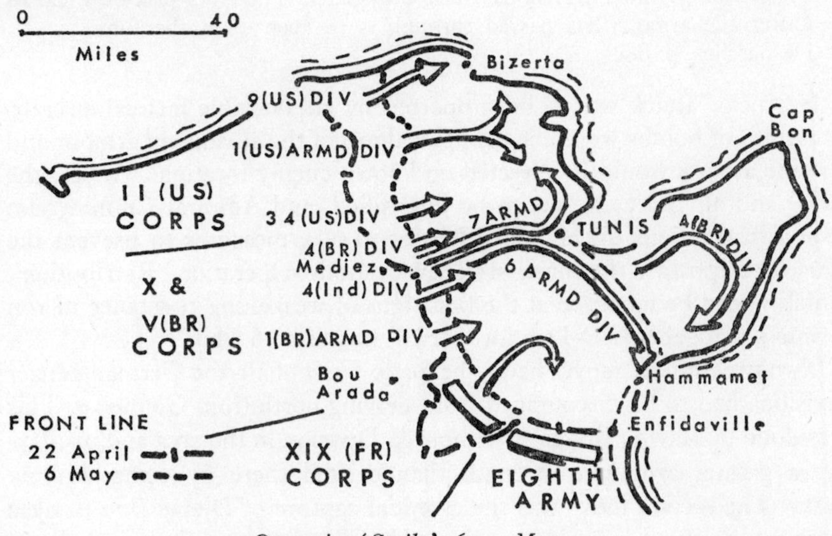

37 Operation 'Strike', 6–11 May 1943

Returning from his visit to Montgomery, Alexander gave Anderson detailed instructions on the use of these Eighth Army formations. Crocker had been wounded and was replaced by Horrocks from X Corps so that use could be made of his experience at Tebaga Gap. IX Corps was to attack astride the Medjez-Tunis road with 4 (Indian) and 4 (British) Divisions north and south of the road. These infantry divisions were to break into the Axis defences on a very narrow front. They would be followed by 7 and 6 Armoured Divisions respectively. These divisions would pass through as soon as the crust was broken. They were to advance on Tunis, ignoring opposition on either flank and without pausing to mop up Axis positions which they overran. Anderson was worried about this policy as he believed mopping up would prove essential if the armoured divisions were to be effectively supported, but Alexander refused to change his orders. The armour was not to pause. To make sure that there was no misunderstanding, Alexander sent Anderson a personal letter on 3 May:

1. The primary object of your attack is the capture of Tunis. Every effort must be made to pass the two armoured divisions through on the same day as the infantry attack starts so that the enemy is not allowed time to build up a strong anti-tank screen.
2. IX Corps must seize a bridgehead through the immediate defences of Tunis as early as possible, before the enemy has time to man these defences.
3. The mopping up of localities, which the enemy continues to hold on the fronts of 78 and 1 Divisions, must come later. The chief task of V Corps after the armour has passed through is to keep open the funnel. . . .

(Despatches, p. 882)

Horrocks' attack was to be supported by all available tactical aircraft. A curtain of bombs would be dropped ahead of the advancing armour and specific attacks would be directed on known enemy locations. At sea, the naval and air blockade was to be intensified, and Admiral Cunningham issued instructions to the Allied Navies to take measures to prevent the Axis attempting a Dunkirk style evacuation—Operation 'Retribution', which would be mounted at the first signs of weakening resistance in von Arnim's bridgehead. D-Day for 'Strike' was to be 6 May.

Two preliminary moves had to be made. First of all, the German panzer divisions had to be discouraged from moving north from Goubellat. This was done by leaving Briggs' 1 Armoured Division in the area and displaying a greater armoured strength than existed there by using dummy tanks. The second move was the essential capture of Djebel Bou Aoukaz from which the Axis could overlook IX Corps' preparations and thrust line. On 5 May, the Irish Guards appropriately attacked and finally cleared Bou Aoukaz on Alexander's behalf. In the valley below, the two 4 Divisions—Indian and British—moved into their assembly areas as soon as darkness fell.

At 0330 'Strike' began with an intense barrage by 650 guns concentrated on a front of 3,000 yards, firing an average of 350 rounds per gun in the first 24 hours. Alexander's own description of the start of the attack reads:

> . . . they (the 4th Divisions) advanced to the attack side by side on a very narrow front. The massed artillery of First Army, backed by dumps of ammunition which we had been nourishing so long for this event, fired concentrations on known enemy localities. At dawn the air forces went in. The weight of attack was too much for the defenders, already weakened physically and morally by the heavy fighting since 22 April. Most of them did their duty. . . . (Despatches, p. 882)

Alexander and the British Army had come a long way since Loos.

The 4 Divisions took their objectives. Keightley's 6 Armoured Division was on the move by 7.30 a.m. and was through the minefields cleared by 4 (British) Division before 11.00 a.m. 7 Armoured Division, following the Indians passed through them at about the same time. By nightfall both armoured divisions were leaguering either side of the main road, some eight miles ahead of the infantry, expecting another hard fight next day. By this time, however, von Arnim had lost effective control of Army Group Africa which had been split in two. 15 Panzer Division came to the support of the defenders of the main Tunis road and stood with them in the path of the British armour, dying in the attempt. Von Arnim's evening report read: '. . . the bulk of 15 Panzer Division must be deemed destroyed. . . . There can be no doubt that on 7 May the road to Tunis will be open to the enemy, and that the fall of Bizerta is only a question of time. . . .'

At first light on 7 May the two British armoured divisions moved forward against failing resistance. The two divisional armoured car regiments were passed through the leading tank regiments in the early afternoon and reached the centre of Tunis almost simultaneously, establishing symbolically both British Armies' share in the victory. Away to the north, Bradley's Americans had been making great strides against determined German resistance until 6 May. The opposition then collapsed and Bradley's reconnaissance units entered Bizerta on the same day that Tunis fell.

Both major Allied objectives had been taken. Alexander always feared that von Arnim might retreat into the fortress like area of Cap Bon and there defy every effort to prize him out while precious months of summer weather were lost. This was not to be. Keightley's 6 Armoured Division swung decisively eastwards followed by 4 (British) Division, and forestalled any such attempt. The German command system had collapsed. Individual formations continued to fight until their ammunition was gone. The Axis bridgehead broke up, first into pockets of resistance, and then into great pools of surrendering soldiers. There was to be no German Dunkirk. Admiral Cunningham had sent his signal initiating 'Retribution': 'Sink, burn and destroy. Let nothing pass.' Alexander's victory was complete. About a quarter of a million men marched into Anglo-American prisoner of war cages.

Alexander chose Tunis as his title. It was his victory. It was not a duet as El Alamein had been. He, and he alone, created the orchestra, which he conducted, from all the discordant elements that he found when he took over in February. Working to a master score and suiting men and units to their parts, he turned the grating notes of Kasserine into a discernible theme. The first movement was, at times, halting as he and the American element of his orchestra sought a mutual understanding. Once this was established, the success of the final movement was never seriously in doubt. His fame does not rest on the strategic or tactical brilliance of 'Vulcan' with 'Strike' as its climax. Set against other great battles in history, it was quite ordinary. He deserved the title of Tunis and the world's applause not as the composer, but as the conductor who made the final movement of the symphony possible in April, and, in so doing, the invasions of Sicily and Italy practicable in 1943. It was his leadership rather than his generalship which was his great contribution to the Allied cause. This is not to say that he was a poor general. He was not. But it was his leadership which the Allies needed most at this particular period of the Second World War.

Harold Macmillan, who was Eisenhower's British political adviser during the Tunisian campaign placed his finger on the reason for Alexander's success in creating a manageable team out of such disparate material:

> I was particularly impressed with Alexander's methods. We stopped at the headquarters of Omar Bradley. . . . He showed us upon the map how the battle was progressing, and there were certain dispositions and movements of troops of which I could see General Alexander did not altogether approve. By a brilliant piece of diplomacy, he suggested to his subordinate commander some moves which he might well make. He did not issue an order. He sold the American general the idea, and made him think that he had thought of it all himself. This system, which he invariably pursued, made Alexander particularly fit to command an Allied army. Later, when he found himself in the Italian campaign controlling the troops of many countries, he developed this method into a remarkable technique. If Montgomery was the Wellington, Alexander was certainly the Marlborough of this war. (*Blast of War*, p. 303)

On 13 May, the last Axis soldiers laid down their arms and Alexander could signal the Prime Minister:

> Sir, it is my duty to report that the Tunisian campaign is over. All enemy resistance has ceased. We are masters of the North African shores. (Despatches, p. 884)

PART III

Triumph of Experience

If I had to pick out his most impressive achievement I would choose the persistence to the final triumph in Italy after the Americans had made it clear more than once that they disliked the idea of any more commitments there.

Sir James Grigg

9

Churchill's Champion

> I have studied the plan you have sent home by your officer, and noted that you have already accomplished the first and second phases of it. I hope the third phase will be accomplished by the end of the month (October 43), or thereabouts, and that we shall meet in Rome.
>
> Churchill to Alexander, 2 Oct 43
> (Churchill, *The Closing Ring*, p. 135)

Alexander's Tunisian victory gave the Western Alliance renewed confidence. It confirmed the verdict of El Alamein, but it could not sweep aside the facts of geography. The Mediterranean and the English Channel still stood between the Allies and their primary target, the mainland of Europe. In May 1943 Europe's moat created doubt and hesitation among the Allied strategists. The greatest optimist would not have suggested that by the beginning of October Churchill would be signalling to Alexander suggesting the fall of Rome by the end of that month. It was one thing to clear the Axis forces from North Africa where they were operating at the end of a long sea and air line of communication; it was quite another to break into Hitler's *Festung Europa* and to seize one of the two enemy capitals. Churchill's Gallipoli campaign was the sole twentieth-century precedent for a major amphibious operation. Its outcome had not been encouraging. Alexander and most of his generation of commanders and staff officers had studied that affair in detail at the Staff College. Alexander himself had walked the battlefields during his sojourn at Constantinople in 1922; and some of his staff had been present at Gallipoli as very junior officers in 1915. Alexander had few illusions about the magnitude of the next military step in pursuit of Churchill's policy of attacking the 'soft underbelly' of Europe; or about the risks involved. The most far-sighted and meticulous planning, and the closest cooperation between the Allies and between their three fighting services, navies, armies and air forces, would be needed to reduce the hazards to manageable proportions. When Alexander was at last able to turn his full attention to 'Husky' planning, he found neither condition was being fulfilled. A deep fissure was opening between British and American strategic thinking; and, at tactical level, there were signs of growing friction amongst the Allied commanders whose reputations were being established as they made history. Ambitions burnt more brightly as success in Tunisia fanned professional and international rivalries, making the planning of 'Husky'—the invasion of Sicily—one of the most disagreeable periods of Alexander's career.

The strategic schism in Allied military planning had been apparent at Casablanca. The arguments are well known. To the Americans, British policy smacked of short-term opportunism and an unhealthy tendency to meddle in the political affairs of Eastern Europe. To the British, the Mediterranean glittered with strategic opportunities which they could not make their less-experienced American cousins understand. Looking back, it is possible to see that there was right on both sides, but, at the time, this basic difference of opinion did not ease Alexander's task as the principal Allied land force commander and Deputy Supreme Commander. Moreover, it tended to polarise the views of the senior British and American commanders in the Mediterranean, making cooperation at the lower levels of command more difficult.

The command structure in the Mediterranean did not help to reduce the effects of strategic differences; nor did the wide separation of key headquarters which were spread from Cairo in the east to Oran in the west. Eisenhower, a convinced internationalist, tried to hold a neutral position, but his neutrality was prejudiced in British eyes because he had been Marshall's chief operational planner and a strong advocate of the direct approach. He was mentally wedded to Marshal's strategy and viewed it with sympathy, although he did more than any other American officer to see the British point of view. His Allied Force Headquarters was organised on American lines and his American Chief of Staff, Walter Bedell Smith, was naturally in closer touch with Washington than London. At Army Group level, the position was reversed. Alexander's headquarters* was organised, as his 18 Army Group Headquarters in Tunisia had been, on British lines with close links to London, in spite of being subordinate to Allied Force Headquarters. Regrettably London often received reports from the field before Algiers or Washington. Churchill tended to depend on direct reports from Alexander and to look upon him as his personal champion in the Mediterranean. As the campaign developed and the

* Renamed HQ 15 Army Group for the invasion of Sicily, and composed of staff officers drawn from Alexander's Tunisian team and from 'Husky' Planning Staff, which had been set up in Algiers after the Casablanca conference. General McCreery left Alexander to become the Commander of X (British) Corps.

divergence in strategic view grew wider, so Alexander's successes and failures in the land battle became crucial factors in the Anglo-American planning. Alexander would have been less than human if he had not identified himself with his patrons' views, recommending courses of action congenial to Churchill and Brooke and, in consequence, though not deliberately, anathema to Roosevelt and Marshall. His greatest successes were won when the British were in the ascendant in the strategic debate and were usually marred when the pendulum swung back in favour of the Americans. This was to happen on three agonising occasions during the Sicilian and Italian Campaigns when great opportunities, brought about by Alexander's victories, were not exploited due to American insistence on transfer of forces from the Mediterranean to North-West Europe.

In his previous appointments in principal command—in Burma, in Egypt and latterly in Tunisia—Alexander had been a salvage master, rescuing, repairing, and bringing into port the wrecks entrusted to him. In each case he had to recreate and re-inspire his force and guide his new subordinates with a steadying hand. After Tunis, he became the leader of professionally manned and commanded Armies. He could leave their day-to-day management to his tried and experienced Army Commanders —Patton and Montgomery in Sicily and Clark and Leese in Italy. His tasks as Army Group Commander became the exercise of professional judgment of what was practical with the resources available under prevailing conditions; how the tasks and resources should be allocated to his subordinates; and the issue of broad directives for the conduct of the offensive campaigns which were about to begin and would last for almost two years. The orchestral analogy used to describe Alexander's Tunisian campaign loses its aptness. It is more appropriate to look upon Alexander as Churchill's champion, standing at the head of the 15th Army Group and challenging Kesselring's Army Group 'C' to contest his advance to the southern gateways of Nazi Germany.

The Allies' strategic objectives in the Sicilian and Italian campaigns changed four times, giving the story of Alexander's contest with Kesselring its natural divisions. At Casablanca, Churchill won reluctant American acceptance of the invasion of Sicily. What was to happen thereafter was left until the 'Trident' Conference in Washington in May. At 'Trident' the Allies defined their objectives more closely when Eisenhower was instructed to plan: 'Such operations in exploitation of Husky as are best calculated to eliminate Italy from the war and to contain the maximum number of German forces.' The price, which the Americans exacted for agreeing to continue operations in the Mediterranean after the conquest of

Sicily, was British acceptance of the transfer of seven experienced divisions from Alexander's command to the United Kingdom in November 1943 in preparation for the cross-Channel assault in the spring of 1944.

Thus Alexander's first objective was the conquest of Sicily, and the second was the elimination of Italy from the war. The third was, as yet, ill defined. It became the diversion of German strength southward into Italy and away from Normandy. Alexander was to find himself playing Patton's role at El Guettar, helping Eisenhower in the place of Montgomery on a far wider stage. Diversion of German effort remained his thankless task up to the last few months of the war. His fourth and last objective became the destruction of Army Group 'C' in the Plains of Lombardy, but this is anticipating the story by almost two years. In May 1943 Alexander's horizon encompassed the Island of Sicily and little more. He knew that his patron was already looking forward to the fall of Mussolini and the triumphal march of Allied troops into Rome. All these dreams would depend upon the fighting spirit displayed by the Italians in the defence of their homeland, and upon Hitler's military intuition. Would he accept Alexander's challenge and reinforce Kesselring, or would he abandon most of Italy?

Planning Husky

> I hear Cunningham and Tedder have told you they disagree completely with our proposed plan for the Eighth Army assault on Sicily. I wish to state emphatically that if we carry out the suggested existing plan it will fail.
>
> Montgomery to Alexander, 25 April 1943
> (Montgomery, *Memoirs*, p. 176)

> What so upset Patton was what he considered to be the hidden purpose of the meeting. . . . It appeared to him that General Alexander had called it to rig 'Husky' in Montgomery's favour, in accordance with Monty's demands. . . . .
>
> (Ladislas Farago, *Patton*, p. 147)

> I think it is as well that you should know of the atmosphere here after the acceptance of the final 'Husky' plan. The Admiral (Hewitt) and the General (Patton) of the Western Task Force are very sore about it. . . .
>
> Cunningham to First Sea Lord, 8 May 1943
> (Cunningham, *Sailor's Odyssey*, p. 538)

> I felt a natural anxiety about American reactions. I wish to place on record that General Patton at once fell in with my new plan, the military advantages of which were as clear to him as to me.
>
> Alexander, Despatches (p. 1013)

These four extracts reflect the unhappy atmosphere which prevailed in Algiers in May while the Allied operational commanders tried to settle their differences over the 'Husky' plan. The tactical dilemma was real, but subsequent events showed that it could have been solved without rancour if Montgomery had been more tactful in his determination not to allow the Allies to make what he considered were fundamental operational errors; or if Alexander had been firmer with him as Cunningham suggested in a signal sent to the First Sea Lord at the time:

> I am afraid Montgomery is a bit of a nuisance; he seems to think that all he he has to do is to say what is to be done and everyone will dance to the tune he is piping. Alexander appears quite unable to keep him in order. (Tedder, p. 432)

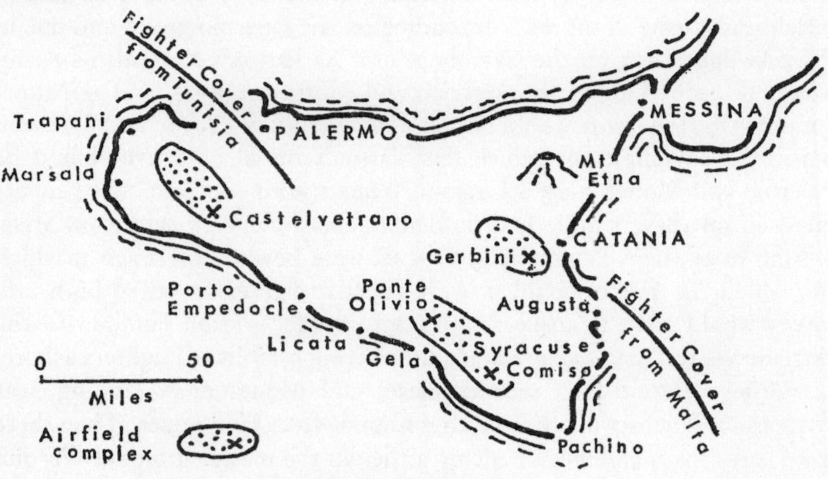

38 The 'Husky' Dilemma

The 'Husky' planning dilemma lay in the difficulty of answering the two questions 'How well will the Italians fight in the defence of their homelands?' and 'How many German reinforcements will Hitler commit to bolster up his ailing Italian ally?' The planning staff, which started work as soon as the Casablanca conference ended, could not possibly give a sound answer to these questions as they did not know when or how the Battle of Tunis would end. They were forced to draw up their plans on certain broad assumptions about relative strengths, but they soon found that the three key considerations were port facilities, the range of Allied fighter aircraft, and the location of Luftwaffe airfields. The general view at the time was that a major force could not be maintained over open beaches for very long. A port or group of ports of adequate capacity had to be captured early in an amphibious operation. The largest port on the Island was Messina, through which the whole invasion force could have been supplied, had it not been located within the strong Axis defences of the Straits of Messina and well beyond the range of Allied fighters based in Tunisia and Malta. The elimination of Messina from the planners' options left three other groups of ports. Palermo, Trapani and Marsala in the west could support half the force; and Catania, Augusta and Syracuse in the east could support the other half. The third group were the minor ports of Porto Empodocle, Licata and Gela on the south coast which were inadequate as a major supply base, though they could be used temporarily to support forces landed near them. It was clear that without any reference to air cover or to enemy-held airfields that there would have to be two beachheads—one in the west depending on the Palermo group and one in the east depending on the Catania group. As Patton's Seventh US Army would be embarking in the Algerian and Moroccan ports, and as Montgomery's Eighth Army would be using the Egyptian, Libyan and Tunisian ports, it was simple to deduce that Patton's initial objective should be Palermo and Montgomery's Catania. When the air problems were superimposed on these simple logistic deductions difficulties started to arise.

First of all, both Palermo and Catania were beyond the range at which the Allied Air Forces could provide effective fighter cover, so both task forces would have to make a two-stage assault; Patton landing on the extreme western end of the island, and, having established fighters ashore, assaulting Palermo in a second phase; and Montgomery landing near Syracuse and subsequently attacking Catania from land or sea. Then there were three main clutches of enemy airfields: the master group at Gerbini in the Plain of Catania and two subsidiary groups—one at Castelvetrano to the south-west of Palermo and the other just inland of the south coast ports at Ponte Olivio and Comiso. The Air Staff insisted that, if they were to give adequate protection to the mass of shipping which would be lying off the beaches, as many of these enemy airfields as possible should be taken early in the operation. The Gerbini group was linked with Catania and was beyond the range of the initial assault. This left Castelvetrano and the Ponte Olivio–Comiso groups. Patton would have to take Castelvetrano anyway in his initial assault to establish fighters on it to cover his main assault on Palermo; but the Ponte Olivio–Comiso group was well outside the beachhead needed by Montgomery in his initial assault, and which did contain enough air strips for his immediate needs. Nevertheless the planners recommended that Eighth Army should extend its frontage to cover this group of airfields and so meet the Air Staff requirement, albeit at the expense of over-extending the land forces.

When Alexander first saw the plan in February he demurred because it committed all the old mistakes of dispersal of effort and 'penny-packetting' which he and Montgomery had set out to stop when they arrived in Egypt six months earlier. Moreover, the two Armies would not be within supporting distance of each other which meant that the Germans might be able to defeat each in detail by concentrating all their efforts against one beachhead before turning on the other. Alexander considered an alternative plan of concentrating both Armies in the south-east corner of the island astride the Pachino Peninsula, but he was persuaded by the planners that the air and logistic factors made this undesirable. When Montgomery saw the plan and his part in it some weeks later he was horrified for much the same reasons as Alexander, but was not so easily persuaded of the validity of the air and logistic factors. He insisted that he needed an extra division for his attack south of Syracuse, and that he could only find this by abandoning the landings on the south coast at Gela and Licata. Tedder immediately objected on the grounds that this would leave too many Axis airfields unsubdued. Cunningham was equally unhappy because he believed that amphibious operations should be carried out on as wide a front as possible to reduce the concentration of shipping to less vulnerable densities.

Alexander's first attempt to bring the land, sea and air together was not very successful. In trying to smooth out the inter-Service differences, he caused international difficulties instead. He accepted the validity of Montgomery's demand for greater strength on the east coast, and decided, reluctantly it is true, to detach one of Patton's US divisions to undertake the Gela–Licata landings under Montgomery's command. This met Tedder's wishes, but Patton rightly objected since it was just as important for him to subdue and then use the Castelvetrano airfields as it was for Montgomery to deal with Ponte Olivio–Comiso.

Patton's objections led Alexander to make another compromise. He decided to delay Patton's assault for several days after Montgomery's initial landing so that Patton's force could be given air cover from Sicilian airfields captured by Eighth Army. This solution enabled Eisenhower to overrule Patton's objections when they were put to him as C-in-C; and planning went ahead on this basis without any of the participants being very happy about the outcome. The British Chiefs of Staff then came to the rescue by providing an extra division for Eighth Army with the necessary shipping, so that the American division could be returned to Patton's command. All seemed to have ended well, but, in fact, the crisis was only just beginning.

Eighth Army had reached Enfidaville in mid-April and Montgomery had found time to fly back to Cairo to study his planners' work in greater detail. He disliked the plan even more than he had done in March in spite of the extra division. The hard fighting which Eighth Army had experienced at Mareth, Wadi Akarit and Enfidaville convinced him that the Italians would fight even better in the defence of Sicily which was part of their homeland. The revised Husky plan was still too optimistic and, in Montgomery's view, still placed too much emphasis on logistics and too little on tactical considerations. It would only work if the Italians collapsed and the Germans did not reinforce the island too heavily. In an unnecessarily blunt signal sent to Army Group, Montgomery demanded the concentration of the whole Eighth Army, including the extra division, on the landing beaches south of Syracuse and to the east of the Pachino Peninsula, ignoring the Air Forces' need to capture Ponte Olivio–Comiso early in the invasion. This signal, which seems to have had a wide distribution among the senior commanders, caused surprise and annoyance in Algiers where it arrived on 24 April. Two of its paragraphs are worth requoting:

> 4. I am prepared to carry the war into Sicily with Eighth Army, but must ask to be allowed to make my own Army plan. . . . The whole united effort of the Eighth Army should be in the area between Syracuse and the Pachino Peninsula.
>
> 9. I must make it clear that the above solution is the only possible way to handle the Eighth Army problem with the resources available. (Montgomery, *Memoirs*, pp. 175–6)

Montgomery had made a personal study of the techniques of high command and devotes a chapter in his Memoirs to explaining the principles which he had evolved before taking command of Eighth Army. Not once does he mention the possibility of there being a senior commander above him or a fellow army commander of equal status with whom he must collaborate. He confines his ideas to handling subordinates and ignores the equally difficult problems of a commander's relationships with his superiors and equals. This omission was not accidental. His actions throughout his career demonstrate the existence of this mental blind-spot.

Alexander has left no similar treatise on the principles of command. He never felt the need to define them. Such things were part of the unwritten code of the British Army, and, in Alexander's case, were wholly intuitive. His wealth of experience in command at regimental level gave him his understanding of subordinates; his personal charm and lightness of touch enabled him to work easily with equals; and his upbringing and family connections put him at ease with the world's greatest personalities. A French General, meeting him for the first time on the beach at Salerno at the height of the battle expressed Alexander's effect upon him in two words: '*Quelle race!*'—what breeding.

The demanding style of Montgomery's signal was deeply resented by the other senior commanders. Tedder and Cunningham were particularly incensed. What should Alexander have done? Sack him in the cause of Allied unity as Eisenhower had decreed should be done if any officer endangered the spirit of cooperation which he, Eisenhower, had been at such pains to build up? Or temporise as Alexander, in fact, did, risking a breach with the Americans as well as the British Navy and Air Force? It is a difficult judgment to make. It was hardly practical to consider dismissing the victor of El Alamein, the British Army's most successful commander, and the British people's military idol. On the other hand, it was dangerous not to put this able Army commander tactfully but firmly in his place. Alexander may well have done this privately, though this is doubtful. He was a man who made bricks with whatever materials were available to him. He was also a man who hated saying 'No' to anyone, especially to someone upon whose energy, judgment and resource he was depending. Among all his many virtues, Alexander did not possess the iron of a ruthless commander. He was a leader *par excellence*, but Montgomery was not a man to be led. Strong men like Brooke could deal with him, but less forceful men like Alexander, Eisenhower and Bradley found it more difficult.

In the series of meetings and conferences which took place to find a new plan, Montgomery gradually asserted his ascendancy, and, in the end, persuaded Eisenhower and Alexander to accept the plan which Alexander himself had suggested in February. All Patton's work preparing for his assault on Palermo was scrapped, and he was directed to take over the Gela–Licata landings with the whole of Seventh US Army. Alexander explains in his despatches that he had to balance the operational against the logistic risks, and how the fortunate arrival in the theatre of the famous American amphibian, the DUKW, enabled him to accept the risks of maintaining Patton's Army across open beaches in the initial phases of the campaign. But it was not the logistic risks which really worried Patton and his staff. This was the kind of challenge which Americans love. The chance to show their flair for beating the most intractable physical problems with organisational and mechanical skill would have delighted them if the operational reward had been commensurate. Unfortunately, it was not. Patton's task was to take the Ponte Olivio–Comiso group of airfields and then to protect Montgomery's flank and rear as he advanced on Messina and, ultimately, across the Straits onto the Italian mainland. The whole idea of playing second fiddle again to Montgomery was

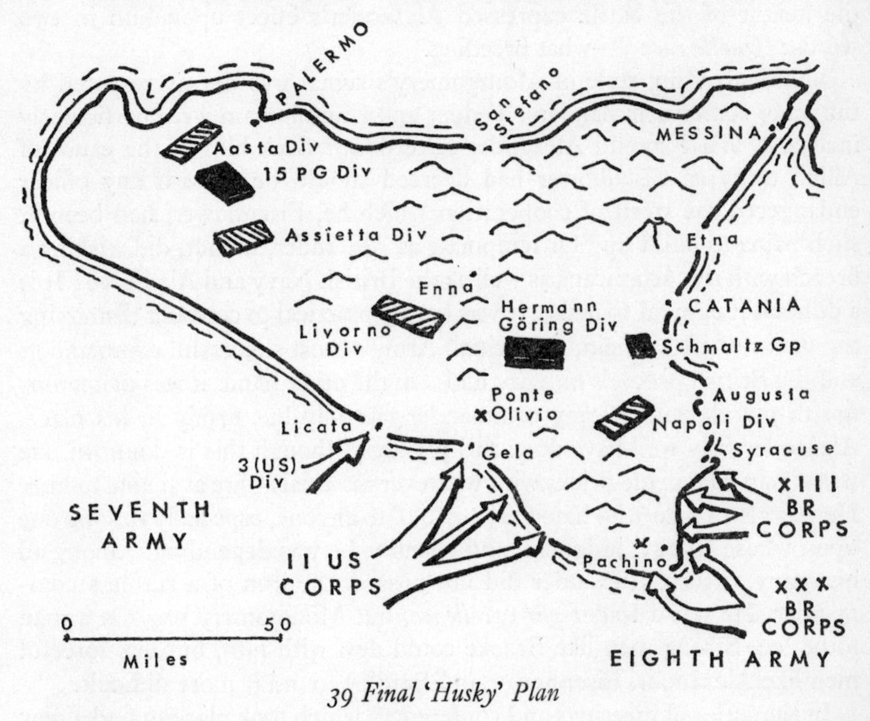

39 Final 'Husky' Plan

repugnant to the Americans. Had it not been for Patton's personal code of obedience to military orders, greater damage might have been done. It is to Patton's credit that he accepted Alexander's change of plan in the spirit in which Alexander himself came to formulate it—for the good of the common war effort. It was nonetheless galling for the Americans to be sacrificed for the common good when Montgomery won everything he wanted. Events were to prove that Montgomery had assessed the German reaction correctly but he had overestimated Italian determination, and both he and Alexander had underestimated their American Allies. Patton was to have the satisfaction of entering Messina ahead of the Eighth Army.

21 The US task force: Alexander visiting Patton's Seventh Army before the invasion of Sicily (*l. to r.*: Alexander, Patton, Admiral Kirk)

THE CONQUEST OF SICILY

22 The Sicilian team (*l. to r.* in foreground): Montgomery, Alexander, Bedell Smith, Patton

23 Changed Circumstances: Alexander and Eisenhower discussing Mussolini's fall

THE INVASION OF ITALY

24 Salerno: Alexander walking along the beach with Clark and McCreery after the crisis

In the final plan Eighth Army was to land with its two Corps abreast: Dempsey's XIII (British) Corps just south of Syracuse and Leese's XXX (British) Corps astride the Pachino Peninsula to ensure the early capture of the Pachino airfield. Patton's Seventh Army was to land with Bradley's II (US) Corps at Gela, and Truscott's 3 (US) Division at Licata. Both Armys' assaults were to be preceded earlier in the night of 9/10 July by landings of airborne troops: 1 (British) Airborne Division using gliders and 82 (US) Airborne Division parachuting.

Conquest of Sicily

> *General Alexander to Prime Minister:* 17 Aug 43
> The following facts are of interest:
> Sicily invaded July 10. Messina entered August 16. Island taken in thirty-eight days. . . . Island is heavily fortified with concrete pill boxes and wire. Axis Garrison: Italian, 9 Divisions; Germans, 4 Divisions; equalling 13 Divisions. . . . Our forces: Seventh Army, 6 Divisions, including airborne division, Eighth Army, 7 Divisions, including airborne and armoured brigades, making Allied total 13 Divisions. . . .
>
> (Churchill, *The Closing Ring*, p. 38)

The conquest of Sicily in 38 days was certainly a feat in which Alexander could take some pride; but neither he, nor Eisenhower, nor any other senior Allied officer in the theatre could take full credit for the speed with which the Axis was driven from the first piece of home territory to be invaded by the Allies. The credit belongs to Churchill and Brooke who appreciated how near Italy was to collapse when they insisted at Casablanca that Sicily should be the next Allied target after Tunisia. It was the fall of Mussolini, reflecting the war-weariness of the Italian people, which ended the Sicilian campaign. Nor would the same result have been achieved six months later. Hitler was still judging strategic issues in a rational way; and, as yet, had not been gripped by his frenzied 'no withdrawal' policy in its more extreme form. His heavy losses at Stalingrad and in Tunisia brought home to him the limits of German manpower resources. He decided wisely not to risk any more troops than absolutely essential in supporting his feckless Italian ally. In consequence, when he heard of Mussolini's fall, he ordered Kesselring to evacuate Sicily as soon as it became militarily desirable to do so.

Although Alexander's generalship did not, of itself, win the Battle for Sicily, the campaign is important in two respects in any assessment of him as a commander. In the first place, it was in Sicily that the American Army found itself, and Alexander found the American Army. Mutual confidence, which had been lacking since the days of Kasserine, was at last established. The second feature of the campaign was less satisfactory. It was Alexander's failure to trap and destroy any sizable body of German troops in the island. There was no Dunkirk at Messina.

The strategic deception plan, organised by Eisenhower's headquarters before the landings, was successful. The German High Command did not appreciate that Sicily was the main Allied target until it was too late. There were only two half-formed German divisions on the island, both of which had been reconstituted since the loss of the original divisions in Tunisia—the Hermann Göring Division and 15 Panzer Grenadier Division.* The main garrison of Sicily was Italian and consisted of four regular mobile divisions backed by three low grade coastal divisions, capable of little more than coast watching. The coastal divisions proved worse than useless, and only a few of the stouter-hearted units of the regular mobile divisions survived as fighting entities after the initial phase of the campaign. The great concentration of Allied shipping, about which Cunningham had been so anxious, went unscathed, thanks to Tedder's handling of the preliminary air operations. The only thing that marred the landings was the weather. Eisenhower had to make the difficult decision the night before as to whether to go ahead as planned or not. The wind moderated in time and both Armies landed successfully in spite of the sea swell and the disasters which overtook the airborne troops of both nations.

The Axis reaction to the landings rubbed salt into the wounds received by the Americans during the planning phase. General Guzzoni, the Italian garrison commander, who was nominally in charge of both German and Italian troops, decided that the American landings looked the more dangerous of the two and ordered the Hermann Göring Division and the Italian Livorno Division to counter-attack Bradley's Gela beachhead. Having been forced to scrap their Palermo plans and accept a risky landing over difficult beaches, Patton's troops were to receive the full brunt of the Axis counter-attack, while Eighth Army advanced upon Syracuse almost unopposed for the first few days. The Napoli Division, covering Montgomery's landing sector, disintegrated leaving only one German battle group of regimental size under the ubiquitous Colonel Schmaltz of 15 Panzer Grenadier Division to oppose Eighth Army as best it could.

* Originally 15 Panzer Division, but reformed as a Panzer Grenadier Division.

Schmaltz reacted in the best traditions of the German Army, slowing down the British advanced guards with determined rearguard actions until he was reinforced by the German 1st Parachute Division flown in on Hitler's orders from Southern France.

For three days the situation at Gela hung in the balance. Bradley's men stood their ground and, supported by American warships off shore, broke the back of the German counter-offensive. On 12 July Guzzoni realised that his forces were outmatched and would disintegrate unless he could withdraw to a more easily defensible line on which he could stand to await reinforcement from the mainland. The line he chose ran across the

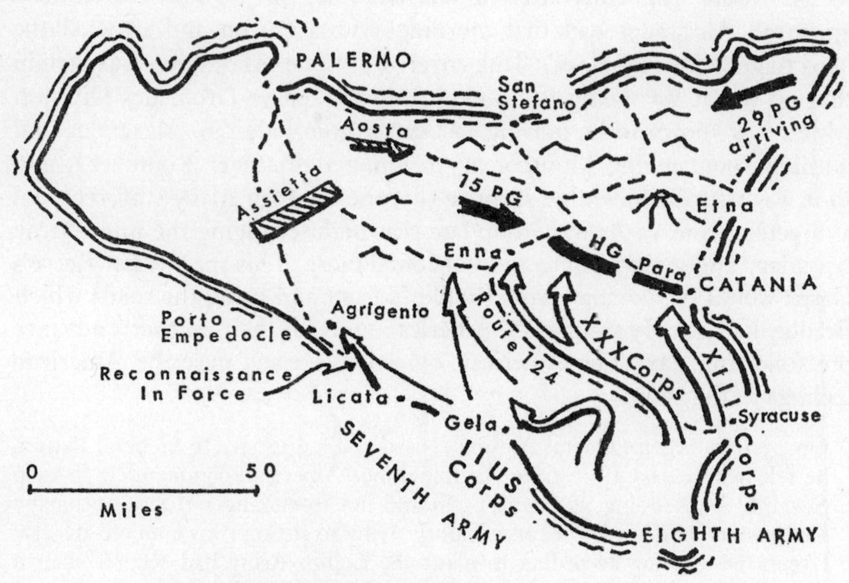

40 First Phase of the Sicilian Campaign, 9–19 July 1943

Messina Peninsula in the north-east corner of the island from Catania on the east coast, past Mount Etna and thence to San Stefano on the north coast. It was a very strong mountain-based position which could be held with relatively few reliable troops. He would have to buy time, withdrawing slowly northwards while the German and Italian troops in the Palermo area escaped eastwards into its security.

Eighth Army, in the meantime, had advanced northwards taking Syracuse and Augusta in its stride, and was well on its way to Catania when it met the leading elements of the German Parachute Division and other German reinforcements which Kesselring had rushed southwards from Italy to cover Catania and the important Gerbini airfields. As more and more German troops arrived, they were thrown in to block Montgomery's advance. In these circumstances it was only natural that the Eighth Army commander should look for ways of outflanking the growing German resistance in the Plain of Catania.

The obvious way round the German opposition was over the mountain roads through Enna to the west of the Catania Plain, but the road from the British sector—Route 124—to Enna had been allotted to Bradley's II (US) Corps for its advance to the north coast, covering Montgomery's flank. Paying little heed to American needs, Montgomery ordered Leese to use Route 124. Only after he had done so, did he seek Alexander's approval. Alexander had that morning visited Patton and stressed the need to keep Montgomery's flank covered until he, Alexander, was certain that no threat was going to develop from 15 Panzer Grenadier Division which was known to be moving eastwards from Palermo. Alexander said nothing about giving Montgomery running rights over Route 124, and so it was with considerable surprise that the Seventh Army staff received a directive from 15 Army Group late that night changing the inter-Army boundary and giving Route 124 to Montgomery. This meant that Leese's Corps would be moving across Bradley's front and using the roads which Bradley had already assigned to American units for their northerly advance the following day. The American official historians describe American feelings at the time:

> On 13 July, when General Alexander issued his directive to General Patton, he felt it necessary to restrain the impetuous American commander, to keep Seventh Army doing its primary job and not to endanger the operation by movements which might expose Eighth Army to strong Axis counter-attacks. Events were going according to plan: the Eighth Army had secured a firm beachhead and was moving on Catania with seeming good speed. The inexperienced American divisions could best be nursed along with assignments which would gradually build up their morale and experience.
>
> In addition to his confidence in the Eighth Army and his distrust of American troops, General Alexander was most concerned about the network of roads which converged in the centre of Sicily. . . . As long as this network remained in enemy hands, General Alexander feared that the Axis might use the area to launch a mighty counter-attack against Montgomery's left flank. . . . Alexander wanted no defeat. He wanted to be certain that the Eighth Army was in a secure position before he let 'Georgie' go and exploit. (*Sicily to the Surrender of Italy*, pp. 210–11)

Patton's patience was wearing thin, but still he obeyed his orders. If Bradley had been allowed to use Route 124 and been able to advance on

Enna in step with Eighth Army, Leese's Corps could have supported and strengthened Dempsey's advance on Catania by heading across the centre of the plain towards Gerbini. As it was, Montgomery soon found his Army over-extended while Patton kicked his heels and looked for other fields to conquer. Patton's mind turned naturally to his old objective of Palermo. He persuaded a reluctant Alexander to allow him to advance on Agrigento and Porto Empedocle on his western flank with a reconnaissance in force. Alexander again stressed the need to avoid becoming embroiled in a battle of secondary importance. Both towns fell with surprising ease and Patton assumed that this would be his signal to clear up Western Sicily. Instead another directive arrived from 15 Army Group on 16 July giving Montgomery Messina as his objective and ordering Patton to continue covering his flank. The American Official History continues the story (p. 235):

> Patton was 'mad as a wet hen' when he got this new directive. What rankled most was not the assignment of Messina to the British . . . but, what he considered a slight to the US Army, the passive mission of guarding Montgomery's rear. The directive also knocked out Patton's hope of gobbling up Palermo.

Alexander had not intended any deliberate slight on the US Army. His Army Group staff were quite unaware of the strength of American feeling. A genuine underestimate of American ability was the root cause of the trouble, but it was contributed to by the two Armies' different attitudes to orders. The British use broadly based directives which they treat as a basis for discussion; the Americans expect decisive command. Patton, at last, did what Montgomery would have done days earlier. He flew back to the Army Group Headquarters, which was still in North Africa, and put his case personally to Alexander, stressing what the Americans wanted to do and why. Alexander took little persuasion. He accepted the force of Patton's arguments when they were put to him, sensing Patton's justifiable frustration. Patton received the go-ahead for his proposed drive on Palermo without further ado.

Once loosed, Patton drove his Seventh Army as a man possessed. He took Palermo in a short five-day campaign, and then received Alexander's permission to turn eastwards to come up on Montgomery's northern flank for a combined assault on the Etna Line and an advance on Messina along the north coast. The American Army had proved itself both in its own eyes and to the world at large. Alexander was never again to make the mistake of underestimating the Americans. From now on he treated them as equals in battle and they responded.

The arrival of both Armies opposite the Etna Line brought the first phase of the campaign to a close. Alexander appreciated that Kesselring could not be forced out of this strong position (which resembled Wellington's Lines of Torres Vedras in the Peninsular War) without a properly coordinated attack using the resources of both Allied Armies. He had cleared three quarters of the island, and had dispersed most of the Italian units; but the Germans, now reinforced and organised as the XIV Panzer Corps of four divisions, had escaped intact and were developing the Etna Line into a formidable sanctuary from which they could riposte if Hitler chose to reinforce them further.

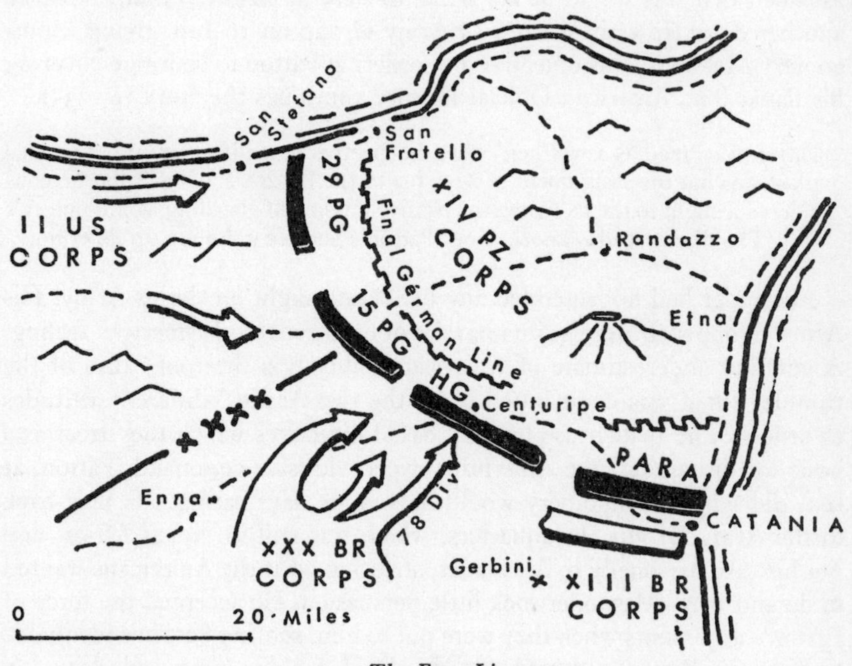

41 The Etna Line

The American historians, dealing with this phase of the campaign, rightly question whether Alexander should have allowed this unsatisfactory situation to arise. He never made a serious attempt to encircle and destroy the Sicilian garrison or to prevent its eventual withdrawal across the Straits of Messina until it was too late.

With hindsight, it is easy to be critical about the apparent lack of imagination shown in Alexander's broad concept of operations. The truth is that it was no more inspired than his conservative handling of the Tunisian battle, but he was being asked for continued success and not for brilliant victories which carried with them the risk of defeat. The Allies, and Churchill in particular, could not afford defeat at this stage in the war. No one had ever mounted an amphibious operation of the scale undertaken by Alexander in 'Husky' against fully developed beach defences. No one had tried to land a modern army and supply it across open beaches. And no one had tried to do these things in the era of air power. The hazards of the landing alone were enough to preclude Alexander from taking any further risks. It is hardly surprising that his principal concern was to land his Army Group successfully; fend off the inevitable Axis counter-attacks; and then use his most experienced Army to drive the Axis garrison from the island. The opening of the Sicilian channel by the physical occupation of Sicily was more important to the Allies than the encirclement of one or two German divisions.

There is another point of view. What would have happened if he had refused to accept Montgomery's second change of plan and had gone ahead with 'Husky' as it stood at the end of April; that is to say with staggered assaults, Montgomery landing on the south-east corner of the Island and providing fighter cover for Patton's attack on Palermo some days later? Guzzoni would probably have directed the bulk of the German garrison to counter-attack Montgomery and in so doing would have opened a clear path for Patton from Palermo to Messina where it is possible that he might have arrived in time to cut off the German withdrawal. This is, of course, conjecture. Whether Patton would have been able to advance quickly enough once the German rearguards started to demolish the difficult mountain roads must remain open to question. Events did, however, show that there was no need to change the landing plan as Montgomery had insisted. The Italian resistance and German reinforcement were on a lower scale than he had feared.

By the time that the Seventh and Eighth Armies were enmeshed in the fighting for the Etna Line there was little scope left for grand manoeuvre. Patton did attempt a series of small amphibious left hooks to ease Bradley's advance along the north coast, but Montgomery made no attempt to do so until almost the last day of the campaign. To be fair to both commanders, there was very little shipping available as most of it had to be used to ferry supplies from Tunisia to the Sicilian ports and beaches.

Alexander timed his main offensive to break the German hold on the island for the beginning of August. Leese's XXX (British) Corps, specially reinforced by 78 (British) Division from Tunisia where it had won fame for its prowess in mountain warfare, was to attack the centre of the Etna Line, while Dempsey's XIII (British) Corps attacked Catania and Bradley's II

(US) Corps continued to force its way across the north of the Island. Before his preparations were completed, events in Italy changed the whole basis of the operation.

On 27 July, the startling news of Mussolini's fall broke in the world press; and, unknown to the Allies at the time, Hitler authorised Kesselring to evacuate Sicily as soon as he considered it expedient to do so. The physical problems presented by a withdrawal across the Straits compelled Kesselring to hold the Etna Line as long as possible so that preparations for an orderly crossing could be made—preparing demolitions, mining roads, establishing ferries across the Straits, and, above all, reinforcing

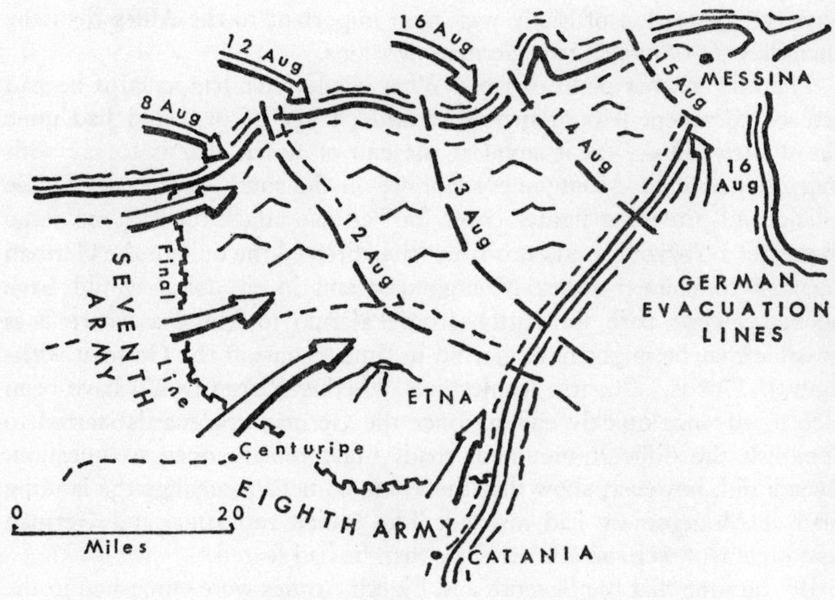

42 German Evacuation of Sicily

the anti-aircraft defences to cover the embarkation and disembarkation points. His plan was to fall back through a series of delaying lines across the Peninsula, each being slightly shorter than the previous one, thus enabling him to thin out his troops for embarkation as he fell back. The countryside was perfect for such an operation: mountain ridges forming excellent rearguard positions, narrow winding roads passing through defiles or over poor stone bridges which could be blocked or demolished, and the natural taper of the Peninsula helped the Germans in every way.

Montgomery's offensive reopened on 29–30 July and led on 3 August to 78 (British) Division's decisive assault on the fortified hill town of Centuripe, the key to the German Line. To the north, Bradley's II (US) Corps had hardly paused since turning eastwards. Leap-frogging divisions through each other, the Americans were making steady but rewarding progress. And to the south Dempsey's men occupied Catania as German resistance weakened on 4 August. The German withdrawal had begun.

Alexander appreciated that the political instability which must have arisen in Rome, might result in the Germans evacuating the Island. His intelligence staff could find no evidence on which to base an estimate of the likely date of a German withdrawal. As far as they could tell, German troops were still crossing into Sicily, suggesting that Hitler proposed to stand and fight despite his ally's discomfiture. Alexander took the precaution of asking Cunningham and Tedder to concert sea and air plans to prevent an evacuation if the Germans tried to stage one, while he renewed the offensive on land using both Armies. In theory, a Tunis-like surrender on a smaller scale should have resulted, but it did not. The Straits were too heavily defended by shore batteries to allow the Allied Navies to intervene; and the Allied Air Forces misappreciated the problem. They assumed that the Germans would not risk ferrying many troops over in daylight and that the Tactical Air Forces would, in any case, be able to deal with the few daylight attempts which might be made. The main air effort to prevent the evacuation would be made by the RAF night bomber force which would keep the embarkation and disembarkation points under attack throughout the hours of darkness. These attacks were expected to disrupt the German evacuation plans to such an extent that Kesselring would be forced to give up.

The German reinforcement of the island stopped and the reverse flow started on 11 August. It was not until 14 August that anyone on the Allied side realised what was happening. As soon as the British Wellington night bombers started counter-evacuation operations, the German schedules were seriously delayed. The German commander of the Straits decided to risk ferrying in daylight. Much to his surprise the German anti-aircraft and naval defences gave him adequate cover. By the time the Allies became aware of their mistake it was too late for the American strategic bombers to be brought in to attack in daylight from above the ceiling of anti-aircraft guns. The German rearguard commander left Sicily unhindered early on 17 August.

On land the two Allied Armies had pressed forward, each hoping to reach Messina first. Patton beat Montgomery by a few hours, but the real winners of the race for Messina were the Germans. Alexander was to remember this failure by the Allied Air Forces six months later when they proposed to win the battle of Cassino for him by air action (see p. 277).

Although there had been no second Tunis at Messina, Alexander was able to signal to Churchill: 'By 10 a.m. this morning August 17, 1943, the last German soldier was flung out of Sicily and the whole island is now in our hands.'

To sum up the Sicilian campaign: Alexander made two major errors of judgment; first, in allowing Montgomery twice to change the 'Husky' plan; and secondly, in acquiescing to Montgomery's theft of Route 124. Both these errors stemmed from one thing: Alexander's style of command. Autosuggestion and leadership by example work when the commander is the most experienced and the acknowledged superior of his principal lieutenants. It tends to fail when one subordinate can claim at least equality of operational judgment and has the force of character to back his arguments. Montgomery had both. He was also the stronger personality and clearer thinker of the two, although he was not necessarily the sounder general. The one-sidedness of Alexander's handling of his Army Group during the Sicilian campaign was compounded by Patton's over-simplified view of military loyalty at the highest levels of command, which prevented him from balancing Montgomery's influence and from presenting the American case to Alexander when he most needed its clear exposition.

On the other hand, Alexander achieved Churchill's purpose as quickly and as economically, in Allied life and resources, as was reasonable to ask. Sicily did not turn out to be a second Gallipoli; and, at the end of the campaign, Eighth Army was poised to carry the war over to the Italian mainland, pausing only long enough for shipping to assemble and load, and for guns and ammunition to be brought up over the demolished Sicilian roads to support his assault across the Straits of Messina into Calabria.

There are two men who were intimately connected with the Sicilian campaign and who, being Americans, could have been the most devastating of Alexander's critics. Bradley was one and Eisenhower was the other. Bradley was Patton's confidant throughout and saw all his difficulties with the British at first hand; Eisenhower saw the same controversies from a different level. Both are numbered among Alexander's staunchest supporters. In his memoirs Bradley sets down his assessment of Alexander when discussing who should be given command of 21st Army Group for the invasion of Normandy:

> To command the British 21st Army Group Eisenhower turned first to his good friend and Tunisian associate, General Alexander . . . he had not only showed the shrewd tactical judgement that was to make him the outstanding general's general of the European war, but he was easily able to comport the nationally-minded and jealous Allied personalities of his command. . . . Had Alexander commanded the 21st Army Group in Europe we could probably have avoided the petulance that later was to becloud our relationship with Montgomery. For in contrast to the rigid self-assurance of Montgomery, Alexander brought to his command the reasonableness, patience, and modesty of a great soldier. . . .
>
> By nature a restrained, self-effacing and punctilious soldier, Alexander was quite content to leave the curtain calls to his subordinate commanders. . . . But while the latter (Montgomery) had emerged as a symbol of Britain's come back in the war, it was Alexander who carried the top rating among Allied professionals who knew both. (*A Soldier's Story*, p. 307)

Eisenhower confirms Bradley's assessment:

> At the time I expressed a preference for Alexander, primarily because I had been so closely associated with him and had developed for him an admiration and friendship which have grown with the years. I regarded Alexander as Britain's outstanding soldier in the field of strategy. He was, moreover, a friendly and companionable type; Americans instinctively liked him.
>
> The Prime Minister finally decided, however, that Alexander should not be spared from the Italian operation. . . . (*Crusade in Europe*, p. 231)

Alexander was to stay in the Mediterranean as Churchill's champion, and, as his champion, he had now to fight the most risky battle of his career—the Battle of Salerno.

Invasion of Italy

> 'Why' Churchill asked, 'crawl up the leg like a harvest bug from the ankle upwards? Let us strike at the knee.'
>
> Churchill to Brooke, July 1943
> (Bryant, *Turn of the Tide*, p. 671)

The conquest of Sicily was the first tentative step towards the 'soft underbelly of Europe'. At Trident the Allies had agreed that the next step would depend upon the degree of resistance offered by the Italian and German troops. Churchill, accompanied by Marshall and Brooke, had visited Algiers a fortnight before the Sicilian invasion began to discuss the various eventualities. Alexander had played a full part in these discussions and so was fully aware of the strategic background against which his future operations would be judged. Churchill and Marshall had polarised the two contending points of view, for and against the immediate invasion of Italy after the conquest of Sicily. They had unconsciously represented the high- and low-risk schools of thought between which Alexander, as their field force commander, had to find a balanced course which he could support. The pressures exerted upon him by the high-risk school were: first, Churchill's political instincts and Brooke's military arguments which demanded concentration on the quickest means of defeating the weaker Axis partner; secondly, intelligence reports which suggested a marked deterioration of Italian morale and the possibility of a German military occupation of Italy if the new Badoglio Government tried to defect to the Allies; and, thirdly, the 'Trident' deadline, which urged the British to achieve an irrefutable success in the Mediterranean by November if they were to soften American insistence on withdrawal of forces for 'Overlord'. The pressures for caution were also three in number: there were Alexander's own personal views on what constituted a balanced strategy and his tendency to mistrust superficially brilliant military solutions which took too little account of the uncertainties of war; then there was the known ability of the Germans to reinforce the Italian theatre almost at will from their strong central reserves; and lastly, there were the inherent difficulties of mounting amphibious operations at short notice which are so often underestimated by continental powers with no experience of the sea.

Alexander had not been forced to side with either school immediately because all were agreed that the decision must await events in Sicily. At Eisenhower's suggestion two separate planning teams had been set up: one from General Mark Clark's Fifth (US) Army Headquarters was to make a low-risk plan for the invasion of Sardinia and Corsica; and the other from two British Corps Headquarters was to plan landings on the Italian mainland. At this stage it was envisaged that McCreery's X (British) Corps might land on the 'Toe' at about the beginning of September and Allfrey's V (British) Corps on the 'Ball' at Crotone a month later.

The influence of Montgomery's views on the likely scale of Axis resistance was obvious in these conservative timings. As events in Sicily unfolded the planning staffs' views swung between extremes of pessimism and optimism. The first swing came with the success of Alexander's landings and the collapse of Italian resistance. Steps were taken to enable Eighth Army to exploit across the Straits of Messina, using Catania as a forward base. Before executive orders could be issued the pendulum had begun to swing back. The arrival of the German reinforcements at Catania had shown that such plans lacked realism. Nevertheless, operations were going sufficiently well for Eisenhower to transfer the Sardinian and Corsican planning to Giraud's French Headquarters and to direct General Clark to look into the possibilities of landing on the 'Heel' near Taranto, or, if events went unexpectedly well, near or directly into the great port of Naples. Eighth Army would be expected to capture Messina and cross onto the Calabrian 'Toe' in one continuous operation.

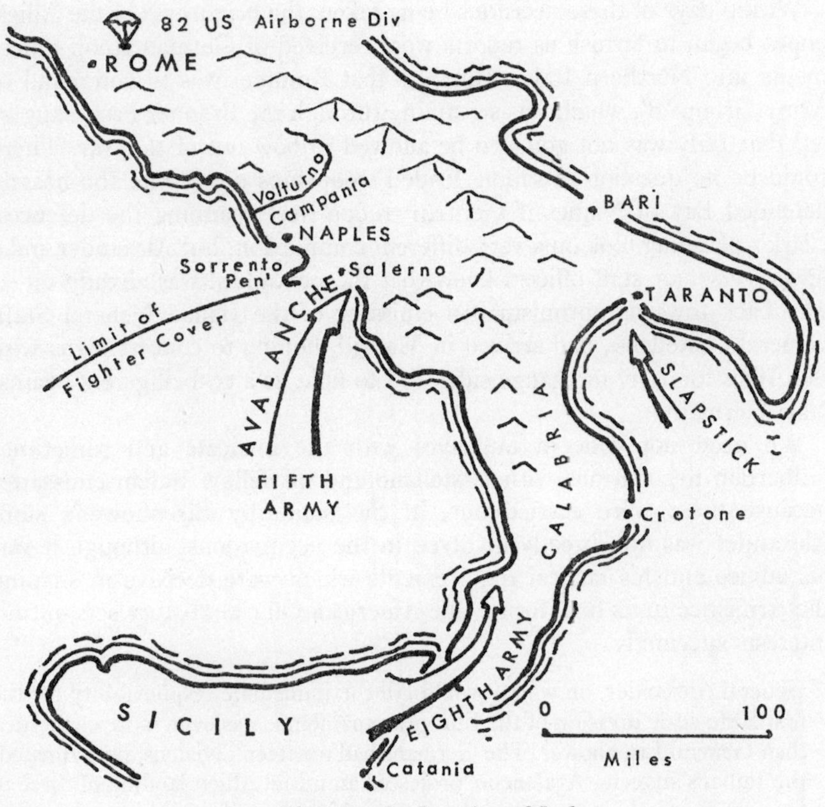

43 Planning the Invasion of Italy

The fall of Mussolini on 25 July caused the next marked swing to optimism. At a meeting of Commanders-in-Chief next day, Eisenhower agreed with Alexander, Tedder and Cunningham that the situation was ripe for high-risk operations. Clark was directed to concentrate on planning an assault on Naples with a target date of 7 September, the earliest that the necessary troops and ships could be assembled, rehearsed and sailed to what might prove to be an opposed landing. Both the troops and shipping had to be found from resources not already engaged in Sicily because no one could tell when the Sicilian operations would end. Much to the surprise of the British, Marshall gave his full support to the Naples plan, code-named 'Avalanche', not because he was any more convinced by British arguments, but because he wanted to clear up the Italian problem once and for all and be able to turn wholeheartedly to concentrating resources for 'Overlord'.

Within days of these decisions being taken, the brightness of the Allies' hopes began to tarnish as reports were received of German troop movements into Northern Italy. Rumours that Rommel was in command of Army Group 'B', which was streaming through the Brenner Pass, suggested that Italy was not going to be allowed to bow out of the war. There could be no question of sailing loaded troopships direct into the heavily defended Bay of Naples if German troops were manning the defences. Clark's planning took on a very different complexion, but Alexander and a few very senior staff officers knew that the pendulum was already on its way back towards optimism. An emissary of the Italian General Staff, General Castellano, had arrived in Madrid, hoping to concert plans with the Allies for Italy to change sides and to fight as a co-belligerent against Nazi Germany.

We need not concern ourselves with the intricate and sometimes Gilbertian negotiations with Castellano and his fellow Italian emissaries because these were carried out, in the main, by Eisenhower's staff. Alexander was not directly involved in the negotiations, although it was his advice and his tactical requirements which were decisive in shaping the Armistice in its final form. The American Official History sets out his interests succinctly:

> General Alexander, on whom would fall the immediate responsibility for the first large-scale invasion of the European mainland, was even more concerned than General Eisenhower. The Germans had nineteen divisions, he estimated, the Italians sixteen. 'Avalanche' projected an initial Allied landing of three to five divisions (shipping being the limiting factor) and a build up over two weeks to a maximum of eight divisions. If the Italian units, fighting on their home soil, supported the Germans, the Allies might face a disaster of the first magnitude, a failure that would have catastrophic repercussions in England and in the United States. Literally everything had to be done, he told Murphy (US political adviser to Eisenhower) to persuade the Italians to help the Allied forces during the landing and immediately afterwards. (*Sicily to the Surrender of Italy*, p. 477)

The degree of risk involved in the 'Avalanche' landing near Naples would be determined by the actions of the Italian Army when Italy's 'volte-face' was made public, and by the use Alexander made of the superb defensive nature of the Italian topography. The latter would help him while he was building up his forces ashore, but would hinder him as soon as he tried to take the offensive. The former would decide when and in what strength offensive action could be taken. If the Italian General Staff planned their coup efficiently, and the Italian Army faced their erstwhile comrades in arms with resolution. Alexander could expect Kesselring to evacuate

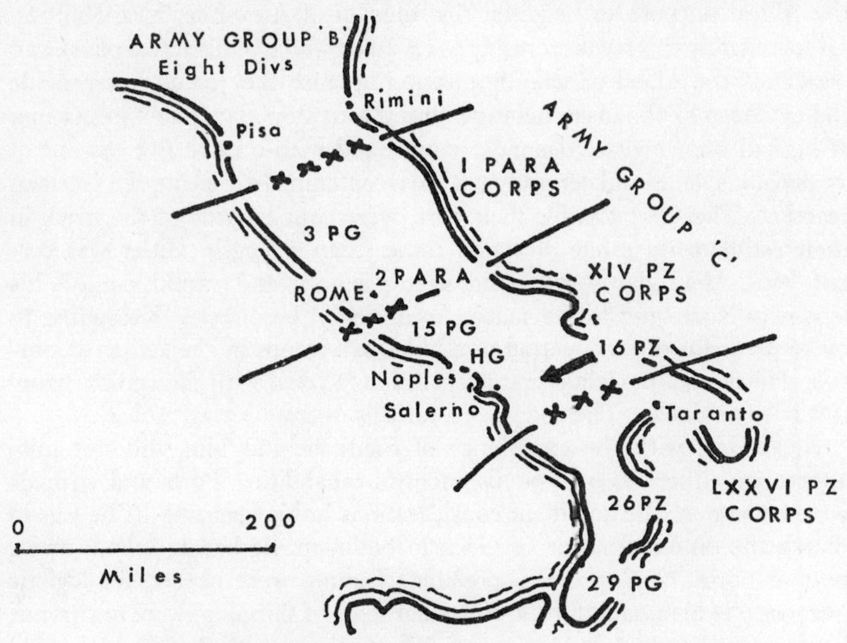

44 German Dispositions prior to 'Avalanche', 9 September 1943

southern and central Italy, and to fall back on Rommel's Army Group 'B' which was holding the North. But, if the delicacy of the manoeuvre proved too much for the Italians and they lapsed, as they might well do, into a helpless apathy, then Alexander would be forced to depend on the defensive nature of whatever beachhead he chose and upon the fire support of the Allied navies and air forces to offset his numerical inferiority to the German forces which Kesselring could concentrate against him. The political stakes were high and delighted Churchill, but the military risks were higher still and had to be carefully judged by Alexander. In the negotiations with Castellano and in Clark's planning everything possible had to be done to reduce these risks. The cards held by Alexander were far weaker than he would have liked.

The poker bidding went on between London, Washington, Algiers, Rome and Alexander's headquarters at Cassibile near Syracuse in Sicily throughout the month of August and the first week of September. The Italians and the Germans both consistently and separately overestimated Alexander's hand. Badoglio, at the head of the Italian Government, was convinced that Alexander could land with 15 divisions north of Rome and so protect the capital and government from German vengeance. It served the Allies' purpose to heighten this illusion of Alexander's capabilities. Unfortunately this meant refusing to reveal anything of his actual plans, and weakened the Allied bargaining position because they could not provide the evidence of the overwhelming strength to stop Badoglio's hesitation. If he had known that Alexander could land with a mere five instead of 15 divisions, he would certainly not have contemplated risking the German reaction. The Germans for their part, were equally wide of the mark in their estimates of range of action rather than strength. Hitler was certain that Alexander would land near Leghorn and would cut off his troops in Rome and to the south. Accordingly, he directed Kesselring to make plans for the evacuation of all German troops in the Italian Peninsula. He also set in train secret preparations to deal with the Italian Army if it tried to defect. The code-word for this operation was 'Achse'.

Alexander, with the experience of Sicily behind him, did not misappreciate either his own or his enemy's capabilities. Ports and airfields were once more the dominant considerations in his planning. If he was to match the potential speed of German build-up, he had to take a major port or ports. Naples and, if possible, Taranto were needed for logistic purposes. If his assault forces, with their mass of shipping, were to survive, he must operate under fighter cover. The farthest north that Tedder could guarantee fighter support, and then only if he had sufficient aircraft carriers to provide dawn and dusk patrols, was the Sorrento Peninsula. Taranto could not be reached until Eighth Army had secured the Crotone airfields in Calabria. And, if Alexander's beachhead was to survive the German counter-attacks, which would be far heavier than those experienced by Bradley at Gela, it must be established where a strong defensive perimeter could be formed. These factors led to Alexander's selection of the Bay of Salerno for the first Allied landing in force on the mainland of Europe. It was a decision which was not accepted unanimously. On this occasion he did not change his plans to meet objections by subordinate commanders.

The two main criticisms came from Clark and Montgomery, his two Army Commanders for the operation. Clark wished to land north of Naples in the Plain of Campania so that his armoured units could be used to best effect and so that he could cut off the German garrison of Naples. Tedder's view on air cover was decisive in overruling this proposal; and Clark himself was to be very glad, later, that he had been ordered to land in a defensible area. Montgomery's doubts were similar to his 'Husky' objections: opposition would be stronger than Intelligence assumed and the two Armies would be too far apart to support each other. He would have preferred Clark to land further south, but to have done so would have allowed the Germans too much time in which to build up the defences of Naples whose port was vital to the Allies for logistic reasons. Montgomery's plea was rejected as well. Events nearly proved him right on this occasion.

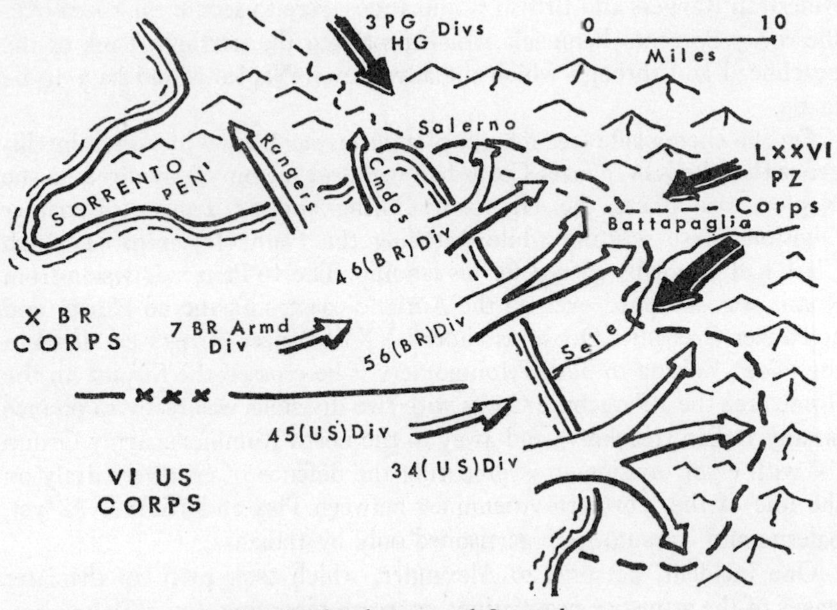

45 Battle of Salerno, 9–16 September 1943

By the time the final phase of negotiations with the Italians was reached, Badoglio's demand for 15 divisions to be landed north of Rome had been watered down to an armoured division at the mouth of the Tiber and an airborne division on the Rome airfields to help the Italians protect their capital from the Germans. Alexander could not accept the landing of the armoured division as a practicable operation of war, but so important was the successful outcome of the negotiations that he accepted the nomination of General Matthew Ridgeway's 82 (US) Airborne Division for the capture of the Rome airfields. Ridgeway's division was to have dropped on the Volturno bridges north of Naples during 'Avalanche' to stop German reinforcements rushing south to attack Clark's beachhead. Alexander had always been sceptical about Clark's use of airborne troops in this way because they could not have been supported by the main body of Fifth Army.

Clark's final plan, which Alexander approved, called for McCreery's X (British) Corps to land with the 46 and 56 (British) Divisions on the northern half of the Salerno beach, while General Dawley's VI (US) Corps with 34 (US) Division leading and 45 (US) Division in the second wave assaulted the southern half. 7 (British) Armoured Division would land in the British sector in time, it was hoped, for the breakout towards Naples. American Rangers and British Commandos were to secure the roads over the rocky Sorrento Peninsula which protected the northern flank of the beachhead and through which the advance on Naples would have to be made.

On the enemy side (see fig. 44, p. 231), it was known by Allied intelligence that the XIV Panzer Corps had withdrawn from Sicily direct to the Naples area where the Hermann Göring and 15 Panzer Grenadier Divisions were refitting while watching the Plain of Campania which Clark had originally chosen for his landing. The 16 Panzer Division from Russia was stationed over on the Adriatic coast; and the 26 Panzer and 29 Panzer Grenadier Divisions under LXXVI Panzer Corps were down in the 'Toe', waiting to block Montgomery if he crossed the Straits. In the Rome area the I Parachute Corps with two divisions was ready to pounce on any Italian treachery; and away to the north Rommel's Army Group 'B' with eight divisions was preparing the defence of Northern Italy on the line of the Northern Apennines between Pisa and Rimini. As yet, Salerno and Taranto were garrisoned only by Italians.

One incident, personal to Alexander, which took place in the later stages of the armistice negotiations, is worth recording. On 2 September, only a week before Salerno's D-Day, the Italian delegation arrived at Alexander's headquarters for what the Allies thought was to be the last session at which signatures would be appended to the final document. Harold Macmillan describes the scene:

> ... they [the Italian delegation] now stated that they had no authority to sign the armistice terms.... The negotiations were of course in the hands of Bedell Smith, representing Eisenhower, but Alexander was the senior officer

on Italian soil. . . . I therefore sent a message to his camp—a little distance from ours—to suggest that the moment had come for a display of firmness. He entered into the spirit of the thing with enthusiasm.

After a little time his cortège arrived, with a number of officers, all in parade order. The guard turned out and presented arms. He himself wore a well pressed tunic, beautifully cut breeches, highly polished boots with gold spurs and a gold peaked cap. . . . There was no shaking hands, no interchange of civilities. He expressed amazement at the behaviour of the Italian delegation. Were they negotiators or spies? Let them make up their minds—and immediately. . . . He carried on this little play-acting with great aplomb and, remounting his car, he and his little procession retired. . . . But the General was as eager as all the rest of us to hear the result. The Italians retired to their tent for consultation. Our tent was behind it. But the only way by which the General could reach us unseen by the Italians and preserving the sense of angry indignation which he had affected was, after leaving the orchard at the far end—to creep round the outside wall till he could climb over to join us. This he did, with schoolboy delight. (Macmillan, pp. 390–1)

All Alexander's demands were met and the armistice documents were signed, but the risks remained. Discounting the two German divisions,* which Kesselring would have to leave in the 'Toe' to block Montgomery's approach, the Germans had three divisions† within easy striking distance of Salerno and two more‡ near Rome. All five divisions could reach Salerno fully supported with tanks and guns before Clark's five divisions could scramble ashore; and, if this was not enough to throw Alexander back into the sea, there was always Rommel's Army Group 'B' in the north which could send divisions southwards quicker than Alexander could ship extra divisions from Sicily and North Africa. Kesselring clearly held the better military hand and would only be beaten if Alexander managed to play three 'wild' cards which he held in his own hand. The first was the disorganisation which would occur in Kesselring's command when the Italians defected. The second was marked Allied superiority in air and naval gunfire support which should help him to offset some of the German numerical superiority ashore. And the third was the advance of Eighth Army to Clark's support if operations went badly awry. Churchill was determined to accept the risks. The British Chiefs of Staff tried to reduce them by sending extra aircraft carriers to strengthen the fighter cover and extra troopships to speed the passage of troops from North Africa to Italy. Alexander judged the operation practicable.

The first week of September ticked anxiously by. No one knew whether

* 26 Panzer and 29 Panzer Grenadier Divisions.

† Herman Göring, 15 Panzer Grenadier and 16 Panzer Divisions.

‡ 2 Parachute and 3 Panzer Grenadier Divisions.

the Italians in Rome could be trusted or not, and to what extent the Germans were privy to affairs at Cassibile. Montgomery crossed the Straits of Messina on 3 September to the accompaniment of a full orchestra of artillery, naval gunfire and air support which proved to be a waste of ammunition as Kesselring had ordered the LXXVI Panzer Corps to withdraw its forward troops and to carry out a methodical retreat up the 'Toe', using demolitions and mines rather than men to slow Eighth Army's advance.

Between 3 and 6 September the Fifth Army assault convoys loaded and sailed for Salerno; and 82 (US) Airborne Division assembled at the Sicilian airfields ready for its drop on Rome. On the Axis side, Kesselring had last-minute doubts about the Salerno area and ordered 16 Panzer Division to move across from the Adriatic coast to reinforce the Italian coastal units south of Naples.

On 8 September, the day before 'Avalanche' D-Day, things began to go wrong. Badoglio's Government tried to have second thoughts. General Maxwell Taylor, who had been smuggled into Rome to arrange the reception of the airborne troops, realised that the Italians were unlikely to be able to keep their side of the bargain. He sent back the codeword recommending the cancellation of the airborne operation. It arrived just in time. The paratroopers were already emplaning. Eisenhower and Badoglio were due to broadcast the announcement of the armistice simultaneously from Algiers and Rome at 6.30 p.m. Eisenhower's broadcast went out on time, but it was not until 7.45 p.m., after an hour and a quarter's suspense, that Badoglio's voice was heard over Radio Roma announcing Italy's change of side. The Italian General Staff had been paralysed by the enormity of their treachery and had made no proper plans for dealing with their German colleagues. The Germans, by contrast, had made their plans several months before and had kept them updated. Without hesitation Kesselring ordered 'Achse'—disarm the Italian Army. So well laid were his plans that not only had 16 Panzer Division disarmed its fellow Italian defenders of Salerno, but it was ready and alert covering the beaches and anchorage of the Bay of Salerno before the darkened hulls of Clark's assault force reached their landing-craft lowering positions. The British and American troops in the ships had heard the armistice announcement over the radio and found it hard to believe that there would be any real opposition ashore. They expected a repeat performance of the Sicily landings—but this was not to be.

The battle of Salerno lasted for nine long, tense days and nights. The Germans outmatched the Allied build-up and soon pinned Fifth Army down on the floor of the great amphitheatre-like plain of the Sele River. XIV Panzer Corps quickly occupied the ringside seats on the circle of hills and mountains surrounding the plain which Alexander had intended should serve as the defensive perimeter of the beachhead. 16 Panzer Division's presence on the beaches had prevented McCreery's and Dawley's men advancing far enough inland to seize these dominant heights. Kesselring ordered LXXVI Panzer Corps to move northwards as fast as it could towards the beachhead, leaving only rearguards to slow Montgomery's advance. He also ordered the Parachute Corps to send troops south from Rome as soon as the capital was secure. When he had sufficient troops assembled, he launched a series of major counter-attacks upon Fifth Army's positions. At one moment the Germans came dangerously close to splitting the Allied beachhead in two. Their tanks and infantry broke through along the Sele River between the British and American Corps sectors and almost reached the landing beaches.

Alexander soon appreciated what was happening as the reports of 16 Panzer Division's resistance began to reach him. The gamble had not come off. Alexander's first 'wild' card had proved worthless. The Italians had failed to play even a minimal part in upsetting the German defence. Cunningham and Tedder sprang to the help of the Army; the former sending the battleships *Valiant* and *Warspite* to strengthen the naval bombarding forces and the latter concentrating all available tactical and strategic air squadrons on the task of destroying the German divisions endangering Clark's beachhead. Alexander himself ordered Montgomery to press his advance northwards regardless of logistic risk; and Patton to despatch units from Seventh Army in Sicily to increase Clark's rate of build-up. Alexander also requested and received authority from the Chiefs of Staff to retain all landing ships in the Mediterranean which were under orders to sail for the Far East. Having taken these measures to help Clark secure his beachhead, he set off himself for Salerno. Two signals from Churchill greeted him; one to himself and the other to Cunningham.

Prime Minister to General Alexander: 14 Sept 43

I hope you are watching above all the Battle of 'Avalanche', which dominates everything. None of the commanders engaged has fought a large-scale battle before. The Battle of Suvla Bay was lost because Ian Hamilton was advised by his CGS to remain at a remote central point where he would know everything. Had he been on the spot he could have saved the show. At this distance and with time-lags I cannot pretend to judge, but I feel it is my duty to set before you this experience of mine from the past.

2. *Nothing* should be denied which will nourish the decisive battle for Naples.

3. Ask for anything you want, and I will make allocation of necessary supplies, with highest priority irrespective of every other consideration.

Prime Minister to Admiral Cunningham: 15 Sep 43

I am very glad you have put in the *Warspite* and *Valiant*, as importance of battle fully justifies exceptional action.

Please give them my best wishes.

Alexander's answer was prompt and, as Churchill says, comforting:

General Alexander (*Salerno*) *to Prime Minister* (*at sea*): 15 Sep 43

I feel sure you will be glad to know that I have already anticipated your wise advice and am now here with Fifth Army. Many thanks for your offer of help. Everything possible being done to make 'Avalanche' a success. Its fate will be decided in the next few days. (Churchill, *The Closing Ring*, pp. 127–8)

The massive weight of shell and bomb which struck the attacking panzer and panzer grenadier divisions in their concentration areas around the beachhead was too much even for their stout hearts. On the Allied side there had been some wavering. At one time Clark himself seriously considered re-embarking Dawley's men and shipping them across to reinforce McCreery. Fortunately McCreery, with Cunningham's help, managed to dissuade him. Alexander's arrival in the beachhead stopped all vacillation. He was in his element: back where he always liked to be, in the midst of a tactical battle. Many officers, who were present at Salerno, believe that it was his appearance in the beachhead which tipped the scales. Physical and moral damage was inflicted on the Germans by the guns of the battleships, the bombs of the air forces, and the efforts of the soldiers on the ground. All of this would have been wasted if the Allied command had lost its nerve. Alexander's unruffled confidence, the obvious soundness of the instructions he gave to meet the crisis which bore no stamp of alarm, and the calming effect of his immaculate appearance, had a decisive effect on men's minds. They felt that he had been in worse situations before and knew what to do. If any individual can ever be said to win a battle, Alexander won Salerno.

By 16 September the crisis was over. The leading elements of Montgomery's Eighth Army made contact with Dawley's Corps, and 7 (British) Armoured Division started to land in McCreery's sector. On the German side Kesselring realised that he must take steps to meet Montgomery's threat from the south. That evening he authorised General von Vietinghoff, who had arrived with his Tenth German Army Staff to take over command of all German troops fighting south of Rome, to abandon the attempt to throw Fifth Army back into the sea, and instead to withdraw northwards establishing a continuous front across the Italian Peninsula from coast to coast. Naples was to be held as long as possible to deny the city to the Allies and to allow the German demolition crews time to block the port and to destroy the harbour facilities. On 17 September von Vietinghoff attacked for the last time at Salerno to cover his withdrawal. The battle of Salerno was over. Alexander had been justified by events in refusing to land further north. His estimates of the risks had proved correct, but only just.

On 19 September he reported to Churchill: 'I can say with full confidence that the whole situation has changed in our favour and that the initiative has passed to us. . . . I am rejoining my main HQ at Syracuse tomorrow.'

Before turning to the last phase of the race against the November deadline, mention must be made of an operation for which Alexander received high praise from Churchill. Intelligence suggested that Taranto was in the hands of the Italian Navy with no German troops within easy striking distance of the port. 1 (British) Airborne Division could not be used for 'Avalanche' due to lack of sufficient transport aircraft. Furthermore, Admiral Cunningham was able to release the British 12th Cruiser Squadron as troop transports since the Italian Fleet was on its way to surrender. A hastily improvised operation was mounted and the British paratroopers landed from the cruisers inside Taranto harbour unopposed on 9 September. The only serious losses were sustained when the minelayer *Abdiel* struck a mine in the harbour and sank while fully loaded with troops. The airborne units held this valuable port until relieved by Allfrey's V (British) Corps a fortnight later. It then became one of Eighth Army's main supply ports.

Stalemate

> The fact of troops and landing-craft being withdrawn from the very battlefield and of units being put under orders for home is in itself injurious. The intense desire to concentrate upon the enemy which carried us from Alamein and sustained us in Tunisia has been impaired. Yet in the Mediterranean alone are we in contact with the enemy and able to bring superior numbers to bear upon him now. It is certainly an odd way of helping the Russians. . . .
>
> Churchill to the British Chiefs of Staff, November 1943
> (Churchill, *The Closing Ring*, p. 293)

As the German containing line unfolded from around the Salerno beachhead and formed a thin but continuous front from coast to coast,

Alexander's hopes rose. He might yet achieve Churchill's political aim of entering Rome and his strategic aim of softening the rigidity of the 'Trident' decisions. Intelligence estimates of German intentions pointed strongly, and, in fact, quite correctly, to a methodical withdrawal by Kesselring's forces into the safety of Rommel's defence line—later to be known as the Gothic line—in the Northern Apennines. So far none of Rommel's divisions had been identified in Southern Italy, and so it seemed fair to assume that Hitler was intent on buying time for the thorough preparation of the Gothic defences.

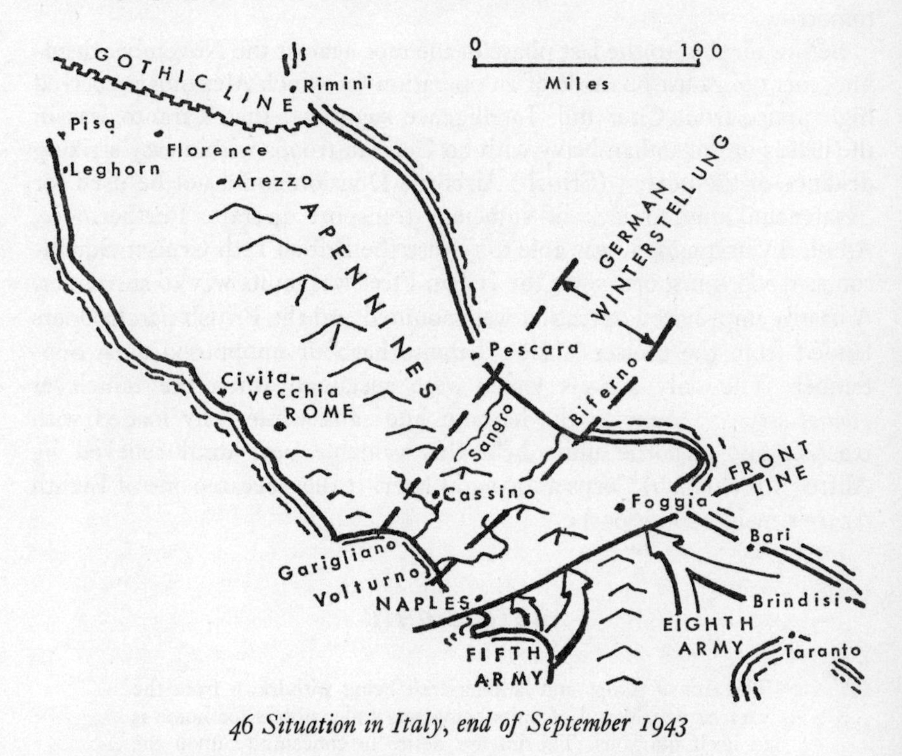

46 Situation in Italy, end of September 1943

Alexander issued his first directive of the Italian campaign on 21 September as the advance from Salerno began. He visualised following up the German withdrawal with light forces and seizing

> certain vital areas which contain groups of all-weather airfields, ports and centres of road communications. On these firm bases the Armies can be regrouped, reorganised and balanced, and from them strong offensive operations can be developed to destroy the German forces in the field. Light mobile forces and patrols will operate ahead of these bases against the enemy con-

tinuously. This advance screen harasses the hostile rear-guards, obtains information of all natures and aids us to keep the initiative. (Despatches, p. 2897)

He defined the advance in four phases: first, the consolidation of the present front based on the line Salerno–Bari which was already accomplished; second, the seizure of the port of Naples and the Foggia airfields which was in train; thirdly, the capture of Rome and its airfields; and lastly, in the distant future, the advance to the Pisa–Florence–Arezzo area preparatory to attacking the Gothic Line. Eighth Army was to advance up the Adriatic side of the Apennines using Taranto, Bari and Brindisi as its base ports; while Fifth Army operated west of the Apennines based on Naples as soon as the port had been cleared. He stressed the need to take full advantage of the Allies' naval and air superiority to land small hard-hitting forces in the German rear to accelerate his withdrawal, but he appreciated that shortage of amphibious shipping, which would also be needed to speed the import of tanks, guns and vehicles into the theatre, would reduce the frequency with which such operations could be mounted.

Alexander's first directive did not withstand the impact of events for very long. The risks which he had accepted willingly to exploit the Italian armistice and so achieve the first half of the Allied strategic aim—the defeat of Italy—now threatened to destroy his ability to undertake the second half of the aim—the containment of the greatest number of German forces (see p. 209). The fundamental weakness of the Allied position was the unfavourable balance of the relative speeds of build-up between the German and Allied forces in Italy. The Italian surrender, which should have corrected this weakness, only masked it for a few weeks. There was a danger, which Alexander fully appreciated, of Kesselring, rather than himself, doing the containing. On 21 September these thoughts were far from everyone's mind, even on the German side where Hitler was anxiously watching events, fearing another Salerno in Kesselring's rear. During the next two and a half months action and reaction between the two opposing commanders, their forces and their strategies, coupled with the advent of autumn weather brought disillusion and frustration to Alexander and new hope to Kesselring. For Alexander there were two distinct stages in this change. Between 21 September and 21 October, when he issued a second directive, he began to realise that there was to be no rush by light forces into Rome. Then between 21 October and 15 December the hard facts of the situation clearly emerged and he was forced to revise his plans again, this time for a long hard campaign whose outcome no one could foretell. The situation at the end of the year confirmed all Marshall's worst fears and held within it the seeds of a stalemate reminiscent of the battles of attrition on the Western Front in 1915–17. Fortunately Alexander had fought in those battles and had no intention of letting another generation suffer as his had done. Moreover, his experiences on the North-West Frontier of India were to stand him in good stead in the mountains of Italy.

The advance from Salerno showed, almost at once, all the disagreeable features which were to become the hallmarks of the Italian campaign. As the Germans fell back they blew up all the bridges and every culvert of any size. Then they mined and booby-trapped the debris. And finally their rearguards covered their own handywork by leaving one or two tanks or self-propelled guns with an artillery observer to engage anyone who tried to tamper with the block. The magnificent view afforded to the artillery observers from their posts on the steep hillsides, and the difficulty of finding and rooting out these small parties amongst the rocks and in the hill-top villages and farms, made advancing against such tactics slow and tedious. A German rearguard battle group of not much more than company strength could hold up a divisional advance for most of a day. When night came the Germans would slip away and repeat the process again a few miles further north. When the Allied advance-guards did deploy to attack, it was no easy matter for their infantry to scale some of the precipitous hillsides; and when they did, they would often find the Germans dug in on the reverse slope with the crest covered by machine guns. There the Germans themselves were immune to all but the most steeply plunging mortar fire, and this could not be corrected because their positions were out of sight behind the crest. Naples is only 30 miles from Salerno, but it did not fall until 1 October; and by then the port was blocked and the dock machinery was in ruins.

On 1 October, as the patrols of the King's Dragoon Guards entered the damaged city, the autumn rains began. 'Sunny Italy' of the tourist brochures disappeared in a slough of glutinous, all-embracing mud that added a further defensive advantage to the Italian countryside which the Germans, with their experience of Russia, knew how to use to the full. The hills gave them observation; the soft ground canalised Allied movement into constricted areas; and the mud held men and vehicles fast in the arcs of fire of the German defenders. Between 5 and 7 October Clark's British and American divisions struggled across the Plain of Campania reaching the river Volturno in succession only to find the Germans dug in on the far side ready to contest their crossing.

On the Eighth Army's front it was not so much the weather which hampered Montgomery's advance beyond the Foggia airfields, as simple lack of supplies. He had rushed his Army forward up the 'Toe' of Italy regardless of the logistic consequences to help Clark at Salerno. In doing so, he had outrun his logistic system and could not undertake full-scale operations until he had reopened and stocked a new base in the 'heel' ports. As Alexander pointed out to Brooke when explaining the delay: 'Men can go hungry, but a truck just won't.'

Both Armies drew level in the middle of October with Clark crossing the Volturno and Montgomery the Biferno Rivers. Both Army Commanders detected a change in German operational policy which was confirmed by Allied Intelligence. This change was to be decisive and finally put an end to any chance Alexander might have had of reaching Rome before Christmas.

In the German High Command the forward school, which believed in holding the Allies as far south as possible, was winning ascendancy. Hitler began to realise that the orthodox school which wished to abandon Italy to save troops for the Eastern Front, had overestimated Allied intentions and resources in the Mediterranean. He could not know to what extent American coolness would reduce Alexander's resources still further, but events spoke for themselves. The Allied landing at Salerno had not been followed by another and possibly more powerful landing north of Rome; nor did German long-range air reconnaissance reveal any potentially dangerous concentrations of Allied shipping; and the German commander on the spot, Field Marshal Kesselring, was confident that, if authorised to do so, he could hold the Allies south of Rome indefinitely. He had already reconnoitred a suitable defensive line (see fig. 46, p. 240) running from the Garigliano River on the west coast, through Cassino and across the Apennines to the Sangro River and the Adriatic. He had recommended that resistance should start on the Volturno–Biferno Line while preparations were being made for the defence of a *Winterstellung* or winter line, based on a belt of defensive localities some 20 miles deep covering the final position, called the Gustav Line, centred upon Cassino. On 1 October Hitler agreed to Kesselring's proposals and allotted him extra engineer troops and men from the Todt organisation to help build the defences of the Gustav Line. From that moment onwards it was clear that Alexander would not achieve Churchill's aim of seizing Rome that winter. Conversely Hitler had made it equally certain that Alexander and not Kesselring would do the containing. Overnight Rome became a military as well as a political symbol. Hitler was to react to threats to Rome in the same way as the French had done at Verdun over a quarter of a century before, throwing division after division into a purposeless, emotional struggle when he should have been conserving his forces for the decisive clash in Normandy.

This turn of events was shrouded in the mists of the future. For the present, Alexander and his Army commanders only saw the frustration of their hopes as German resistance stiffened all along the front. They began to fear that the change of German policy was heralding a counter-offensive which Hitler might attempt to launch before their Armies were fully established and adequately supplied. The onset of the Russian winter might well enable Hitler to free the necessary troops for a major spoiling attack. The rate of Allied build-up had fallen woefully below the level which Alexander had been led to believe would be possible during the planning of 'Avalanche'.

Alexander reviewed the new situation in a memorandum which he presented to Eisenhower at a Commanders-in-Chief conference at Carthage on 24 October. Eisenhower endorsed Alexander's conclusions and transmitted the entire text to Churchill and Roosevelt. The gist of his arguments was contained in his summing up in the last two paragraphs:

> 5. (a) In conclusion, the picture in September looked rosy, provided the initial assault at Salerno was successful. The German divisions in the north were about to be become involved in difficult internal security problems. In the south the rate of build-up was believed to be such that, given no reinforcement by reserve German formations, we should have had twenty divisions opposed to probably his eighteen by the end of December, and our full air force requirements have been on the mainland. It was believed that sufficient craft would be available to turn his sea flanks and maintain forces over the beaches, as might be necessary.
>
> (b) To sum up: Today the situation is that eleven Allied divisions are fighting a frontal battle in country favouring the defence against an immediate strength of nine German divisions, which can be reinforced at any moment. Our build-up has dwindled to a maximum of sixteen to seventeen divisions by the end of January against a present enemy strength of a certain twenty-four divisions, and our resources are not available for amphibious operations of much more than local character. We may be delayed south of Rome sufficiently long to enable the Germans to clear up the situation in Northern Italy and then reinforce their southern front. In this case the initiative might well pass to them. (Churchill, *The Closing Ring*, pp. 219–20)

Churchill added the comment: 'This was indeed a masterly document, which touched all the gravest issues of our strategy.'

Alexander had identified himself so completely with his patron's thinking that, although he could not give him Rome when he most wanted it, he could provide the arguments for Churchill to use in his continuing efforts to revoke the 'Trident' decisions. While these arguments were being used by London and rebutted by Washington, Alexander changed his operational policy to meet the new situation, placing the emphasis not so much on taking Rome as on drawing German forces more deeply into the Battle for Italy. He expressed his thinking at the time in his Despatches (p. 2902):

> . . . If we could keep the enemy 'on his heels' until then (Overlord, D-Day in Spring of 1944), we should be retaining in Italy the divisions already there; we might even (and this, though unexpected, actually happened) draw still more into the theatre, while keeping him sufficiently off balance to be unable to seize the initiative from us. . . .

The phrases 'on-balance' and 'off-balance' often occur in Alexander's and Montgomery's orders and appreciations. The maintenance of balance so that a force can always react to the unforeseen was the touchstone of their policy in the desert and continued to figure prominently in all their thinking. They knew in October 1943 that they were off-balance and vulnerable if Kesselring chose to attack. Clark with little or no experience of defeat could look to the future with greater equanimity. After the Carthage conference Alexander directed his two Army commanders to plan a converging attack upon Rome, stressing that they were to ensure their Armies were properly balanced at all times. Eighth Army was to fight its way up the Adriatic coast as far as Pescara, and then to swing westwards to advance on Rome along Route 5 (see fig. 47 p. 246). Fifth Army was to advance west of the Apennines on Route 6 through Cassino, which, at that time, was little more than a name on the map, to approach Rome from the south-east. Montgomery was to help himself forward with brigade-sized amphibious landings behind the German lines, while Clark was to mount up to a divisional landing if a suitable opportunity could be found to do so. Most of the beaches within supporting distance of Fifth Army's leading troops were either unsuitable for landing-craft or were too heavily defended. Kesselring was highly sensitive to landings on the west coast and so had taken precautions to discourage Clark from attempting any. The beaches in the Anzio area south-west of Rome, however, looked suitable and appeared undefended. They were too far away to be any use until Fifth Army had advanced much nearer to Rome. Frosinone was considered the place that Clark should reach before he attempted a landing at Anzio. The chances of Fifth Army reaching Frosinone within a few weeks did not seem too remote so a special staff was set up to plan a one divisional landing at Anzio—Operation 'Shingle'. It would have to be launched before the landing ships and craft returned to England.

Alexander had reset the scene. Regrettably this second plan was no more stable than the first. Several adverse circumstances conspired to frustrate him. The first was the continued reluctance of the American

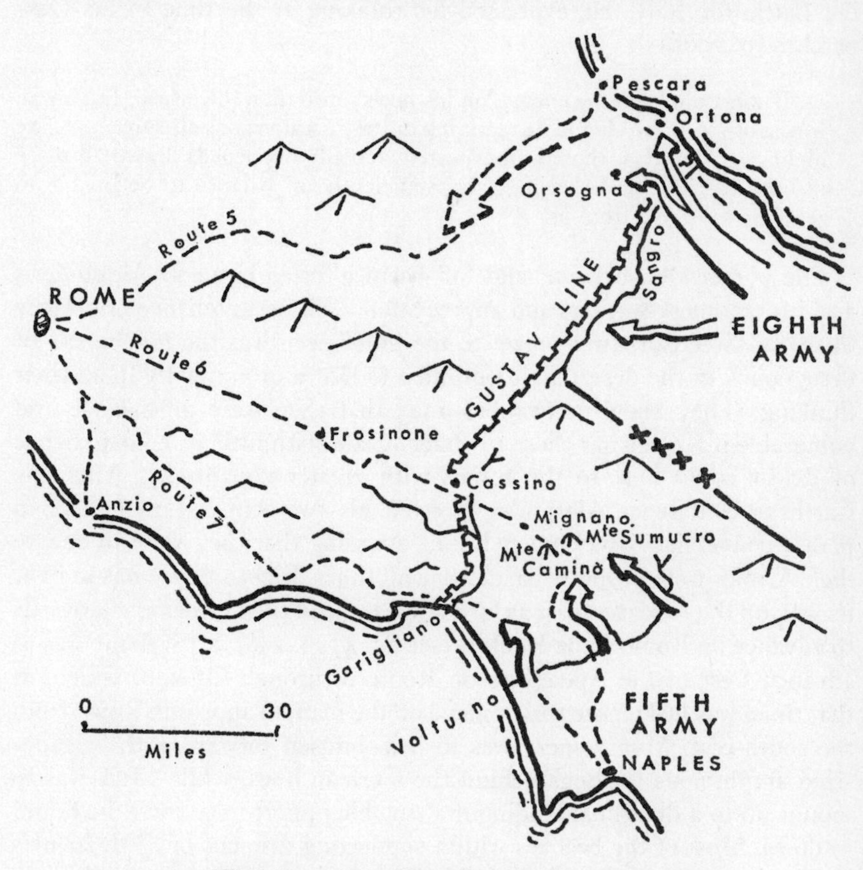

47 Allied Operations, November and December 1943

Chiefs of Staff to vary the 'Trident' decisions in any way, however strong Churchill's arguments might be. In their view Alexander had sufficient resources available for his primary task of containing German forces in Italy. They saw no reason for agreeing to the retention of forces in the Mediterranean specifically to enable him to advance further up the Italian Peninsula. He could do his primary job just as well, if not better, where he was. This attitude resulted in the withdrawal of 7 (British) Armoured Division to England from actual contact with the Germans in front of the *Winterstellung*. The veteran 50 and 51 (British) Divisions, which might have been shipped from Sicily to support Eighth Army, were withdrawn as planned. And the American 82 Airborne Division from Italy and the 1 and 9 (US) Infantry Divisions and 2 (US) Armoured Division from Sicily left the Mediterranean as well. Everyone knew that these moves were scheduled for November; nevertheless, when they actually took place, they caused a far greater loss of Allied momentum than had been expected because German resistance was stiffening at the very moment when Alexander's strength was being weakened.

The second factor compounded the effects of the first. The American Chiefs of Staff decided unilaterally to deploy a major part of their Strategic Bomber Forces to Foggia instead of to the United Kingdom as originally planned. It was a sensible decision, taken in isolation, because it would widen the base of Allied air operations and divide the German air defences. It was not so sensible when set against its effects upon the build-up of Alexander's Army Group. The tonnages of shipping absorbed by the Bomber Groups was so great that it reduced the Army build-up to a trickle. The Americans could rightly claim that one of the original purposes of invading Italy was the seizure and use of these airfields and so they did not view British protests with much sympathy. Alexander had hoped to have some 14 divisions in Italy by mid-October. Now his order of battle was unlikely to reach this figure until the end of December. Some of the reinforcements would be inexperienced Polish and French divisions. A greater strain would, thus, be thrown on those experienced troops left to carry on in Italy.

The third factor stemmed directly from the first two. The troops, particularly in Fifth Army, were beginning to show unmistakable signs of battle-fatigue and exhaustion through lack of reliefs. A vicious circle was beginning. Reduction of Allied resources meant reduced pressure on the Germans, who found they had more time to improve their defences. This respite led them to achieve unexpected successes which improved their morale, whereas the Allied soldiers instinctively felt the lessening of the Theatre's importance and thus had less incentive to drive themselves forwards in the face of worsening weather and firmer German resistance. The British began to feel an exhaustion which they had not experienced since their year of victories began at El Alamein just 12 months before; and the Americans were struck by an aimlessness which was unusual in their temperament. The war suddenly seemed to grow harder again and the success, which both nations had come to enjoy as their right, turned to a sourness of frustration. Unfortunately, at this juncture, Alexander himself fell sick with jaundice.

Events in the field during the latter half of October and November can be summarised briefly by saying that Montgomery fought a series of actions crossing the east coast rivers until he reached the main German positions on the River Sangro in the first week of November. Bad weather, flooding rivers and Kesselring's rapid transfer of reserves from west to east across the Apennines all conspired to make the Battle of the Sangro one of Montgomery's most disappointing operations. He crossed the river in ten days' hard fighting. The weather and the ground slowed his subsequent advance to a crawl, during which the New Zealanders fought the Battles of Orsogna, and the Canadians the Battles of Ortona, both of which proved to lie at the high-water mark of the Allied advance on the Adriatic coast until the following summer. In the west, Clark crossed the Volturno successfully by 15 October and reached the outposts of the *Winterstellung* a fortnight later. The joint Anglo-American attacks on Monte Camino and Monte Samucro, which guarded Route 6 at the Mignano defile, proved just as debilitating as Montgomery's Battle of the Sangro. The hopes of Fifth Army reaching Frosinone before the amphibious shipping had to leave the theatre waned as Fifth Army's exhaustion grew.

Brooke visited Italy on his way to the Cairo–Tehran conferences at which Churchill, Roosevelt, Stalin and Chiang Kai-shek met at the beginning of December. He records his impression of this depressing period of Alexander's Italian campaign:

December 14 (*Monty's HQ Sangro River*)
Monty strikes me as looking tired and definitely wants a rest and a change. I can see that he does not feel that Clark is running Fifth Army right nor that Alex is gripping the show sufficiently. He called me into his caravan just before dinner and asked me how much importance we attached to an early capture of Rome, as he saw little hope of capturing it before March.

To my mind it is quite clear that there is no real plan for the capture of Rome beyond a thrust up the coast by Monty, and no longer any talk of a turn to the left by his forces towards Rome. The mountain roads are considered too difficult for any real chance of success based on such a swinging movement. I must see during the next few days what hopes rest in the plans for the Fifth Army. Frankly I am rather depressed from what I have heard and seen today. . . .

December 15 (*Alex's forward Camp at Vasto*)
. . . My impression of the day is that we are stuck in our offensive here and shall make no real progress till the ground dries, unless we make greater use

of our amphibious power. . . . I have the impression that Monty is tired and that Alex is not fully recovered from his jaundice. The offensive is stagnating badly, and something must be done about it as soon as I get back.

December 16 (Alex's Camp at 5th Army HQ Caserta)

. . . After lunch we motored out to the American Fifth Army HQ Camp, where Alex has a small camp also. We dined with Clark in his Mess. I had a long talk with him about the offensive on his front and do not feel very cheered up as to the prospects of the future from what I heard from him. He seems to be planning nothing but penny-packet attacks and nothing substantial. (Bryant, *Triumph in the West*, pp. 120–2)

Eisenhower visited Clark's headquarters shortly after Brooke's visit. The two Americans discussed the chances of reaching Frosinone before the amphibious shipping had to leave and regretfully concluded that it would be wrong to go on holding out false hopes of a sudden change in the operational situation which was clearly approaching stalemate. On 18 December Clark signalled Alexander:

I feel that I must recommend cancellation of Operation 'Shingle' in January. The limiting date of January 15 makes it impracticable. I will continue planning 'Shingle' in the hope that craft will be made available at a later date, when it will be possible to execute the operation with proper preparation, supported by the main part of the Fifth Army. It is my urgent request that all efforts be made to get the necessary craft for a later time. (Clark, pp. 240–1)

The first autumn offensive of the Italian campaign was over. Rome still lay beyond Alexander's reach. Kesselring's Army Group was settling down into its winter line hopeful, if not confident, that it could hold the Allies indefinitely south of Rome. It was a disappointing time for everyone on the Allied side, and particularly for Alexander who was not fit himself and was to suffer a personal disappointment as well.

Discussions had been going on for some time at the highest levels as to whom should be given command of 'Overlord'. The choice eventually fell on Eisenhower, and so the debate shifted to his replacement in the Mediterranean. Alexander was clearly a candidate. Churchill and Harold Macmillan supported his candidature. Macmillan's minute on the subject read:

Prime Minister

. . . I do not of course know whether General Alexander has the military qualities most suited to the duties of a C.-in-C. in such an organisation. But I feel strongly these points should be weighed:

1

1. General Alexander has commanded with conspicuous success Anglo-American forces in the field. He pulled them out of a hole in Tunisia and his reputation stands high in the forces of both nations.
2. He has now learnt the quite difficult art of managing Americans; both the military and civilians have fallen to his charm.
3. He has—so far as I can judge from the talks I have had with him—the art of simplifying problems instead of making them more complex.
4. He has the simplicity of character and the concentration on the sole purposes of war which are needed in a leader and which do not pass unnoticed by the troops.

If, therefore, your only hesitation is not on professional grounds, but because you fear he may be wasted and unduly immersed in political problems, I hope you will feel that—if you entrust me the job—I ought to be able, with Murphy's support on which I know I can count, to relieve him from any but the more important decisions and thus help to make his task easier. *Harold Macmillan* (pp. 435–6)

But Brooke did not agree, feeling that Macmillan underestimated the politico-military nature of the Supreme Commander's job in the Mediterranean. In the end it was decided that the soundest arrangement would be for General 'Jumbo' Wilson, who was C.-in-C. Middle East and the commander of the Eastern half already, to take over the whole of the Mediterranean as Supreme Commander when Eisenhower left for England. Alexander would remain commanding the Allied Land Forces in Italy. Montgomery was to return to England to take over the 21st Army Group, much to Eisenhower's regret. Brooke sheds a clear light on these decisions:

Ike's suggested solution was to put Wilson in Supreme Command, replace Alex by Monty, and take Alex home to command the land forces for 'Overlord'. This almost fits in with my idea except that I would invert Alex and Monty.

It was very useful being able to have this talk with Ike in which I discovered, as I had expected, that he would sooner have Alex with him for 'Overlord' than Monty. He also knew that he could handle Alex, but was not fond of Monty and certainly did not know how to handle him. . . .

Alexander turned up during the morning and we had a long talk, after which he went for a talk with the PM. As might be expected, Alex is ready to do just what he is told and does not show any great sign of disappointment at the possibility of not being appointed Supreme Commander. . . .

In my talk with Alex about Command I found him, as always, quite charming to deal with, always ready to do what was requested of him, never scheming or pulling strings. A soldier of the very highest principles. (Bryant, *Triumph in the West*, pp. 115–7)

At the end of the year Eisenhower returned to England, Wilson took his place and Leese took Montgomery's place. Alexander and Clark remained to carry on the campaign and to fight it in such a way that they hurt the Germans more than they hurt themselves in spite of having to do all the attacking over the mountains and across the rivers of Italy.

10

Triumph of Generalship

> So Rome fell to the Allied Armies in Italy two days before the Anglo-American invasion was launched against the shores of Normandy. It was but the latest of many captures of Rome in history but it was the first time since Belisarius captured it fourteen centuries ago that the Eternal City had been taken by an invading army from the south.
>
> Alexander, Despatches, p. 2929

Alexander was to stay in Italy while all the rest of the battle-experienced First Team returned to England to command the forces assembling for 'Overlord'. To him went the thankless task of mounting the diversionary operations to help Eisenhower's great enterprise. To him fell the problem of maintaining military enthusiasm among men of many different races, languages and creeds who knew that they were fighting in a secondary theatre. And to him were given all the difficulties of making bricks with the little straw left over after 'Overlord's' demands had been met. No man could have been better chosen for these selfless and unrewarding tasks. He faced a challenge which few of his successful contemporaries would have relished; and which was made no easier by the continued lack of appreciation and support accorded to his theatre by the United States Chiefs of Staff. In his own words his task was to keep Kesselring 'on his heels'. He did not add 'in country ideally suited to defence'. Instead, he assured Brooke, as he had done at Dunkirk and in Burma, 'I will do my best.'

In one respect Alexander's position had improved. He was no longer Deputy Supreme Commander. He was Commander-in-Chief of the Allied Armies in Italy and Military Governor of Allied Occupied Italy. True he was still subordinate to Jumbo Wilson, who had succeeded Eisenhower as Supreme Commander Mediterranean, but the Italian campaign itself was his and his alone. In two other important respects his freedom to operate as he judged best remained circumscribed. His operations were an essential element of Churchill's and Brooke's strategic plans. He was still their champion on the battlefield and could make or mar their chances of reaching a satisfactory outcome in the Anglo-American strategic debate. They were bound to keep in close touch with events in Italy. This did not mean any lack of confidence in Alexander; it stemmed from their need to argue every critical step of his campaign with their American colleagues. They had to ensure that their arguments were reflected in his handling of the Allied Armies in Italy.

The other limitation was the effect of weather. Until the twentieth century warfare in Europe had usually stopped or sunk to a low tempo with the onset of winter. Armies retired into winter-quarters towards the middle of November and did not re-emerge to confront each other again until the spring. Some generals won notable victories by surprising their opponents, either by opening the next year's campaign sooner than expected or by taking the field for a limited period in mid-winter. As a rule little was achieved by the latter. Winter in Europe gave the defender such a marked tactical advantage over the attacker: water-logged ground restricted manoeuvre; swollen rivers and streams provided excellent defence lines; and, although the cold was not particularly intense in Western Europe, living in the open, as the attacker must usually do, tried even the toughest soldiers. By 1944 these ancient truths had been forgotten by the strategic planners in London and Washington, and certainly by the desert-acclimatised commanders in Italy. There was something incongruous about modern armies and air forces being inconvenienced by such a trifle as weather—particularly in the 'sunny Mediterranean'. This illusion had been shattered in October in the mud and slush of the Battles of the Volturno and the Sangro Rivers, but few of the commanders concerned drew the right deductions. Good weather and dry ground always seemed just round the corner. Dry spells did occur, but they never lasted long enough to allow easy deployment off the roads for the soldiers or clear enough skies for the airmen to develop their full potential. In truth, modern armies and air forces are more rather than less susceptible to weather. Winter conditions proved to be Alexander's Achilles' heel from January until April. From May onwards Kesselring found himself praying for an early autumn.

On 21 December, when Alexander accepted Clark's recommendation that 'Shingle' should be cancelled and some other means be found of breaking the stalemate in Italy, both Fifth and Eighth Armies were enmeshed in Kesselring's *Winterstellung*. The ingredients of the deadlock were, very simply, the available roads to Rome and the relative strengths of the two army groups. There were four roads to Rome: Route 16 along the Adriatic coast; Route 6 in the centre of the Peninsula just west of the

Apennine range; and Route 7 on the west coast. The fourth road was the sea route to Anzio. The relative strengths are set out below:

SECTOR	ALLIES			GERMANS		
Route 16		Eighth Army:	5 Divs		LXXVI Pz Corps:	5 Divs
Route 6	Fifth Army	II and IV (US) Corps:	5 Divs	Tenth Army	XIV Pz Corps:	5 Divs
Route 7		X (British) Corps	2 Divs			
		Army Group Reserve:	1 Div		Army Mobile Reserve:	3 Divs
Rome Area					I Para Corps:	2 Divs
Total in Battle Area			13 Divs			15 Divs
Not immediately available		Arriving from elsewhere in Mediterranean:	5 Divs		Fourteenth Army in Po Valley	8 Divs
Grand Total			18 Divs			23 Divs

Kesselring enjoyed numerical superiority in the battle area and would do so as long as Hitler could afford enough troops from elsewhere. His divisions were more experienced than many of the French, Polish and Canadian troops, who were arriving to reinforce Alexander; and his men had the advantage of being able to occupy the well chosen defensive positions of the Gustav Line. Alexander's strength lay in Allied air supremacy and tank and artillery superiority, neither of which could be used to full effect as long as winter lasted, and in Allied naval supremacy.

If logic was everything in war, the American Chiefs of Staff view of the Italian campaign would have been proven by the table of routes and relative strengths. Emotion plays a large part as well. Churchill's sense of history and his susceptibility to the legends of sea power kept the debate open. Alexander knew he would not be allowed to let the front stagnate either by Churchill, who still coveted Rome, or by Brooke, who wished to carry on the process of weakening Nazi Germany using his indirect approach. The fourth road—the sea route to Anzio—using sea power, seemed the only practicable way out of the operational impasse.

> I fully shared General Clark's reluctance to see ourselves forced back on a strategy of frontal assault in the present unfavourable conditions. There was now no hope that Fifth Army could arrive within supporting distance of a landing at Anzio within the proposed time frame; no advantage would be

gained by a landing nearer the present front under the abrupt southern slopes of the Aurunci Mountains (see fig. 52, p. 274); I therefore began to consider the possibility of making the 'Shingle' force much stronger, strong enough to hold its ground by itself for a longer time than we had previously considered. (Despatches, p. 2909)

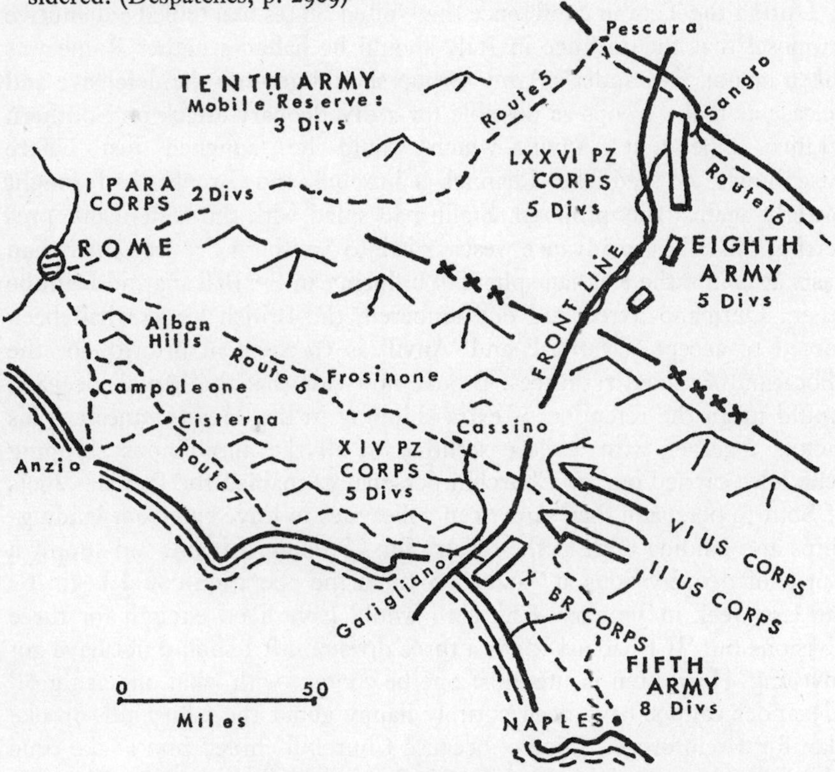

48 Operational Situation in Italy, Christmas Day 1943

It was with such thoughts in his mind that Alexander flew off to Carthage on 23 December to see Churchill and to confer with his fellow Commanders-in-Chief during the handover between Eisenhower and Wilson. As so often happens when major decisions are to be taken, similar thoughts occur to several of the responsible people at the same time. Brooke had discussed the situation with Alexander earlier in December and had concluded that the way to break the Italian stalemate was to give Alexander more shipping so that he could strengthen the Anzio landing. He had called on Churchill at Carthage on his way home on 18 December and had discussed the situation with him at Eisenhower's villa where the Prime Minister was recovering from pneumonia. He did not tell Churchill how depressed he was about the Italian campaign, but he clearly gave the Prime Minister an inkling of how he intended to help Alexander when he reached London. The American Chiefs of Staff had inadvertently given him the opening he needed in his quest for more shipping.

During the Tehran conference the United States had tabled a definitive proposal that the advance in Italy should be halted whether Rome was taken or not. Alexander's Army Group should go onto the defensive and release as many troops as possible for a diversionary attack on Southern France—Operation 'Anvil'—which would be launched just before Eisenhower crossed the Channel. Churchill and Brooke had fought bitterly against this proposal. Stalin had sided with the Americans, preferring the Allies to advance westwards into Southern France rather than eastwards into the Russian sphere of influence in the Balkans and Danube basin. Outmanoeuvred and outnumbered, the British leaders had been forced to accept 'Overlord' and 'Anvil' as co-equal in priority for the allocation of Allied resources. Brooke now saw that the 'Anvil' decision would mean the retention of extra shipping in the Mediterranean. This factor, together with a close scrutiny of all the amphibious shipping schedules carried out by Churchill personally, enabled the British Chiefs of Staff to persuade their American colleagues to leave sufficient landing-ships and landing craft in the theatre for Alexander to land and supply a Corps of two divisions at Anzio, provided the operation could begin by the last week in January. Churchill would have liked enough for three divisions but 'If I had asked for a three division lift I should not have got anything. How often in life must one be content with what one can get!' Alexander cannot have been entirely happy about the Churchill–Brooke plan for a reinforced 'Shingle' because Churchill chided him at the time with lukewarmness: 'Meanwhile I had a long talk with Alexander. He demurred to the suggestion that he was not very keen on the Anzio landing.'

At the Commanders-in-Chief conference, which took place on Christmas day with Churchill present, Alexander accepted the feasibility of a two divisional landing timed for the last week of January. It was a pity that Clark was not present. Churchill acknowledges that this was a mistake because he did not hear, at first hand, the discussions which led to the Anzio decision. He was unaware of Churchill's real intentions when he set about replanning 'Shingle'. Churchill knew exactly what he wanted: 'I had always been a partisan of the "end run" as the Americans call it, or "cat-claw" which was my term. . . . We hoped to land a wild-cat that would tear out the bowels of the Boche. . . .'

Churchill visualised his 'wild cat' springing ashore behind the Germans holding the Gustav Line and ripping up their communications. The whole enterprise appealed to his cavalier instincts. Alexander had to judge the chances more carefully and concluded that the risks were too high for a British Commander-in-Chief to give such a task to an entirely American force. Consequently, he instructed Clark to use Penney's I (British) Division as part of General Lucas'* VI (US) Corps which had been nominated for the operation. Eisenhower appreciated Alexander's dilemma and in one of the last signals which he sent to Alexander before leaving the Mediterranean he said:

> The disadvantages of employing a mixed Corps are of course as obvious to you as to me. I have wondered whether or not you may have been influenced by either of the following factors: that you felt it undesirable, because of the risks involved, to hazard a Corps of two American divisions when you as a British officer have the deciding responsibility or that you may have thought it undesirable from the political view-point for a Corps of two British divisions to be given the opportunity for the direct capture of Rome. In my opinion neither of these factors should be allowed to outweigh the military advantages of launching your assault by any troops you believe best fitted and most available. In giving these views I merely wish to remove any political difficulties that may occur to you in order that you can launch the best military operation that can be laid on in the time available. (Despatches, p. 2909)

In this generous signal Eisenhower put his finger on the three critical aspects of the Anzio operation—the weakness of the force, the psychological issues involved in the capture of Rome, and the short time available. He believed the risks were high and makes it clear in his memoirs that he believed the force to be too weak:

> I argued [at the Christmas Day Conference] that a force of several strong divisions would have to be established in Anzio before any significant results could be achieved. . . . The Prime Minister was nevertheless determined to carry out the proposed operation. . . . (Eisenhower, pp. 233–4)

Eisenhower foresaw also how dangerously charged with emotion the capture of Rome would become. Both sides had made the Italian capital a political and military symbol. It had obvious political significance, but the aim of the Italian campaign had become essentially military. The political aim of eliminating Italy from the war had been achieved. Rome's only military significance was the use that Alexander could make of it as a means of holding and destroying a large part of Kesselring's Army Group. The understandable desire of Alexander's subordinates to be the first to

* General Lucas superseded General Dawley in command of VI (US) Corps at Salerno.

enter Rome from the south since Belisarius, fourteen centuries ago, tended to warp their judgment and, in the end, was to help Kesselring save more of his Army Group in June than he might otherwise have done. This point will become clearer later in this chapter (see p. 288).

On timings, Eisenhower was not alone in his disquiet. Even Churchill disliked the haste with which the operation had to be mounted, but the 'tyranny of Overlord', as he called it, would brook no delay.

Alexander accepted Churchill's direction in spite of Eisenhower's misgivings. Replying to Eisenhower he says, 'the political aspect is of no consequence but I do think the sharing of risks and hazards together is of importance'. There can be little doubt about these risks, which were minimised by Churchill and Brooke in their determination to pursue their Mediterranean strategy. The balance of forces in Italy and the lack of freedom for manoeuvre were such that Alexander was unlikely to succeed unless he surprised Kesselring strategically and tactically, thereby throwing his Army Group 'C' off balance. It can be claimed that Alexander accepted the plan out of loyalty to his patrons. It can be argued equally forcibly that it was an error of judgment to have done so. Brooke found it difficult to stand up to Churchill. Alexander could not resist the combination of Brooke and Churchill even if he had wished to do so. There is, however, no evidence of any such desire on Alexander's part. Before Salerno he had balanced the advantages of exploiting the Italian surrender against the military hazards of the operation and had judged the risks to be worth taking. In his judgment the hazards of 'Shingle' were preferable to unimaginative frontal assaults on the Gustav Line. The use of sea power was the obvious alternative. He would have been castigated by historians had he not tried to use it. Regrettably, his ability to do so was limited by the American Chiefs' of Staff tight hold on the allocation of amphibious shipping, the bulk of which was being built in the United States and used in the Pacific.

It was in these circumstances that the Battle for Rome was conceived. The authors misappreciated Hitler's reactions and the combined effects of the Italian weather and topography. And so there were to be two Battles for Rome: the winter struggles at Anzio and Cassino which Alexander lost; and the summer battle called 'Diadem' which proved to be a triumph for Alexander's generalship. The two battles were complementary: 'Diadem' could not have been won without Anzio and Cassino; and Anzio and Cassino would have been meaningless without 'Diadem'.

The winter and summer battles were complementary in another respect. They throw a different light on Alexander as a commander. After his visit to Italy in December, Brooke realised that he must do something to revitalize the Army Group headquarters staff. On his return to London, he selected General John Harding* to take over as Alexander's Chief of Staff. Harding arrived in January and so inherited the existing plans for the winter Battle for Rome in their fully developed state. There is a marked difference in style between the winter plans which he had to accept and the summer plan which he devised. These differences suggest that Alexander was a man who needed a strong Chief of Staff. From El Alamein to Tunis he was served well by McCreery. During the invasion of Sicily and for the first four months in Italy the Army Group staff were not at their best. Some of the Anglo-American misunderstandings in Sicily and at Salerno could have been avoided by a more imaginative staff. Alexander maintained the momentum of operations more by his own efforts and personality than through the professionalism of his staff. Originality of thought and decisiveness of execution were not of a high order. In the words of one British officer† serving in Fifth Army Headquarters during the Salerno landings 'Army Group Headquarters made no impression'. Harding could not influence the course of events which had been set in train before he arrived, but he showed what could be done by long-range planning and careful calculation when the summer came. Few generals can combine the extrovert characteristics of a great commander with the more introvert thinking of a brilliant chief of staff. History provides many examples of successful partnerships almost as ideal as the Hindenburg–Ludendorff combination. Alexander's pairing with Harding was one of Brooke's happiest inspirations.

Winter Battles for Rome

> Anzio played a vital role in the capture of Rome by giving me the means to employ a double-handed punch—from the beachhead and from Cassino—which caught the Germans in a pincer movement. Without this double-handed punch I do not believe we should ever have been able to break through the German defences at Cassino.
>
> Alexander, Memoirs, p. 124

The time has now come to use Alexander's own analogy to describe his greatest battles. He looked upon them as a boxing match with Kesselring in which he used his left and right hands to feint or punch as the situation

* Now Field Marshal Lord Harding.

† General Sir Charles Richardson.

demanded. Any professional boxing match consists of long periods of sparring for an opening, interspersed with moments of furious activity in which blows are exchanged—some landing with effect and some being parried or missing the target altogether. The winter battles of Anzio and Cassino can be looked upon as the first round and 'Diadem' as the second. In the first round there were three onslaughts: Alexander started the first, and Kesselring the second and the third, although Alexander's reaction to the third was so delayed by weather that it could be considered a separate burst of fighting started by Alexander.

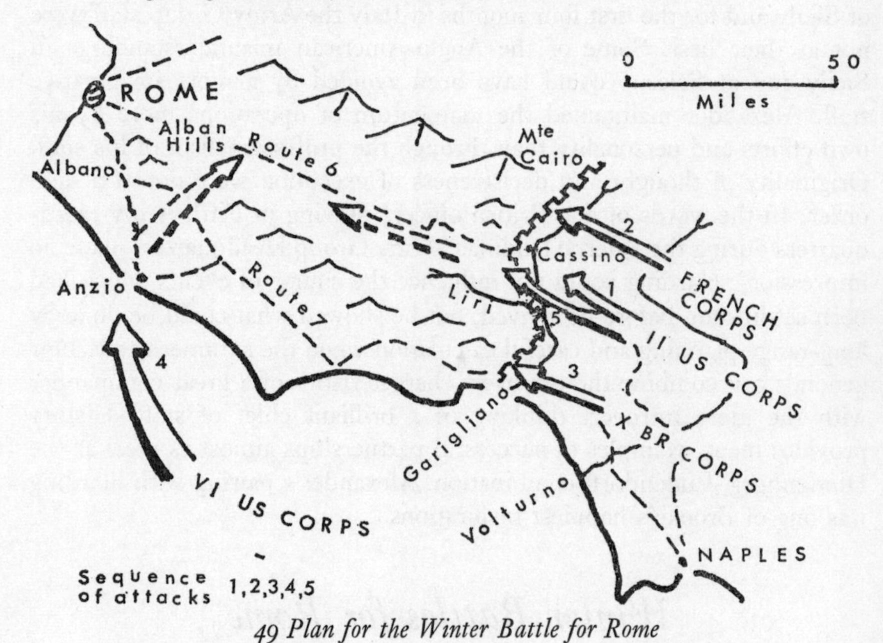

49 Plan for the Winter Battle for Rome

Alexander issued his Operational Instruction for the first round on 12 January, under the optimistic title of 'The Battle for Rome'. The picture painted in the intelligence section of the instruction was of a tired German Army, trying to rest and refit with only two divisions in reserve. It was hoped that the Army Group's renewed offensive would catch Kesselring's troops in the middle of their winter relief programme and lead to the speedy capture of Rome.

Like all good boxers, Alexander knew he should play on his opponent's known weaknesses. Kesselring had two. His frontal defence, based on the Gustav Line, was excellent, but his flanks were wide open to amphibious landings and he knew it. Guarding many hundreds of miles of coast is never easy and is always expensive in terms of dispersion of military effort. In Kesselring's case the costs were compounded by his second weakness—blindness through air inferiority. Alexander had two broad alternatives: feint at Kesselring's flanks to draw his reserves away from the Gustav Line; or feint at the Gustav Line to force him to uncover his flanks. Alexander chose the latter course for 'Shingle'. He planned to land four punches frontally before loosing his left hook to Anzio. Keyes' II (US) Corps was to open the offensive with a renewed advance up Route 6 to reach the main Gustav positions which blocked this road to Rome at the entrance to the Liri Valley near Cassino. The second and third punches were to be subsidiary attacks on Keyes' flanks designed to draw the local German reserves away from Route 6. Juin's French Expeditionary Corps would attack north of Cassino, while McCreery's X (British) Corps would cross the Garigliano astride Route 7 in the south. Keyes would then reopen his offensive with the main attack up Route 6, storming the Gustav defences and advancing on Rome to link up with Lucas' VI (US) Corps.

Keyes' main attack and Lucas' landings were timed for 22 January, a bare ten days after the issue of the Operational Instruction, and just three weeks after Roosevelt had endorsed Churchill's request for the retention of amphibious shipping in the Mediterranean. It is difficult to escape the conclusion that, while the concept was sound, the timings were not. Alexander's usual impeccable military judgment of what was practicable seems to have deserted him in December and January. There are three specific reasons for suggesting this. First of all, Lucas' VI (US) Corps did not leave the front line until 9 January. This meant that there could only be one full scale rehearsal before the landing ships had to begin combat loading if they were to be ready to sail by 20 January. The one rehearsal, which did take place, was not encouraging, but time did not allow any further practice in the complex business of an amphibious landing, made more hazardous by winter weather. Keyes' II (US) Corps was equally hard pressed. It did not reach the Rapido River across the entrance to the Liri Valley, upon which the Gustav defences were based, until five days before it was due to assault one of the strongest sectors of Kesselring's front. Only McCreery and Juin were not unduly hurried. Both succeeded; Keyes and Lucas did not.

The second reason for doubting the soundness of Alexander's judgment at this time was his failure to transmit his intentions clearly to his subordinates. Each level of command from Churchill downwards saw the operation in a different light. Churchill dreamed of 'wild cats'; Brooke looked for the rejuvenation of the campaign without fully weighing the odds as he confesses in his diary later on 25 January: 'News of the Rome landing continues to be good, but I am not happy about our relative strength in Italy. We have not got sufficient margin to be able to guarantee making a success of our attack.' Alexander, at his level, hoped that the Anzio threat would frighten Kesselring into withdrawing from the Gustav Line. He too confesses that he underestimated his opponent:

> Against a less formidable foe an operation such as we had devised would have succeeded; but I think we may well have underestimated the resilience and toughness of the Germans, in expecting them to be frightened by such a threat to their rear. (Memoirs, p. 125)

Clark, at the next level down, was the first man to show real doubts at the time and to act accordingly. His orders to Lucas were: '. . . to seize and secure a beachhead in the vicinity of Anzio . . .' whence he was 'to advance to the Alban Hills'. There was no reference to rapid exploitation across the German lines of communication. Securing a beachhead was his primary concern. Clark's experiences at Salerno were far too recent for him to envisage much more.

And at Corps level, Lucas and his Corps staff were in no doubt about their main task. It was to land, secure a beachhead, stock it and make it defensible before undertaking any Churchillian adventures. The armoured element of the VI (US) Corps order of battle, which would be needed for a thrust across Routes 6 and 7, was assigned to the follow-up convoys, and would not be available for several days. Events were to confirm that Alexander had failed in the important duty of ensuring that his subordinates knew exactly what was expected of them. Too much was left ill-defined and to their initiative and imagination. Faulty staff work in his headquarters added to some of the misunderstandings.

The third reason for criticism is his underestimate of the tasks given to the troops. Anyone looking at the size of the Alban Hills, at their distance from the sea, and at the poor defensive potential of the Anzio beachhead area, must conclude that it was not practicable for two divisions to hold both. Alexander himself confirms this view;

> From the map an operation based on Anzio to secure the Alban Hills, with the object of cutting the German line of communication to Cassino, looks an attractive proposition. But when viewing the objective from the beachhead one appreciates in better perspective the formidability of the task. The Alban Hills are really a massive mountain terrain, much more difficult to gain and maintain than can be apparent from maps. And to have secured the hills and kept open the line of communication to Anzio would not have been an easy task.

> It is of interest to consider what our position would have been if the fresh German divisions had found us stretched from Anzio to the Alban Hills. Could we have maintained our bridgehead intact on such a wide perimeter with the troops at our disposal? We had no more than two divisions. And it would have been disastrous to our ultimate operations if Anzio had been wiped out.
>
> As it was, the comparatively local bridgehead was held with difficulty against extremely serious enemy counter-attacks, but when it was secure it gave us the opportunity to reinforce our positions at Anzio and build up a force of seven divisions. (Memoirs, p. 125)

The first three punches—Keyes' advance to the Rapido, Juin's attack north of Cassino, and McCreery's crossing of the Garigliano—went according to plan. Kesselring did not react immediately to requests for reinforcements that reached him from von Senger's XIV Panzer Corps which was responsible for the defence of the western sector of the Gustav Line from the Apennine watershed to the sea. Kesselring suspected, quite rightly, that Alexander might be attempting to draw his reserves before landing an amphibious force behind the Gustav Line. Admiral Canaris, head of German Intelligence, had reported enough shipping in the Bay of Naples to suggest that a landing was a possibility. On 19 January, Canaris reported that there was no evidence of any amphibious force actually embarking. Von Senger's pleas for help were becoming more pressing as McCreery and Juin made headway on either flank of XIV Panzer Corps' sector. Reluctantly Kesselring accepted that his reading of the battle had been wrong and ordered General Schlemm, commander of XI Parachute Corps* in the Rome area, to counter-attack McCreery's bridgehead over the Garigliano with the reserve mobile divisions. Schlemm's attack opened on 20 January and led to extremely bitter fighting in which McCreery managed to hold most of his bridgehead, inflicting heavy losses on his attackers. On the same day, Keyes launched his attack across the Rapido to open up the Liri Valley, and, in so doing, became the first victim of the baleful influence of Monte Cassino. Walker's 36 (Texas) Division attacked with great verve but with too little preparation and scant appreciation of the tactical significance of the Monastery-capped spur jutting out into the Liri Valley from the great mass of Monte Cairo (see fig. 49, p. 260), which was to provide the awe-inspiring backcloth for the great battles to come. Two out of the three Texan regiments employed were decimated, while von Senger found it quite unnecessary to reinforce

* XI Parachute Corps formed in the Rome area after I Parachute Corps was sent to Russia.

Rodt's 15 Panzer Grenadier Division, which was holding the Liri Valley defences.

In Alexander's headquarters the news of this disaster (which led, after the war, to a Congressional enquiry in which Alexander supported Clark, Keyes and Walker) arrived almost simultaneously with the identification of Kesselring's mobile reserves on McCreery's front. Lucas should be in luck. There could not be many German troops available to oppose him at Anzio. The VI (US) Corps staff took this intelligence with a cynicism born of bitter experience at Salerno and continued to plan for stiff opposition on the beaches and counter-attacks after they had landed.

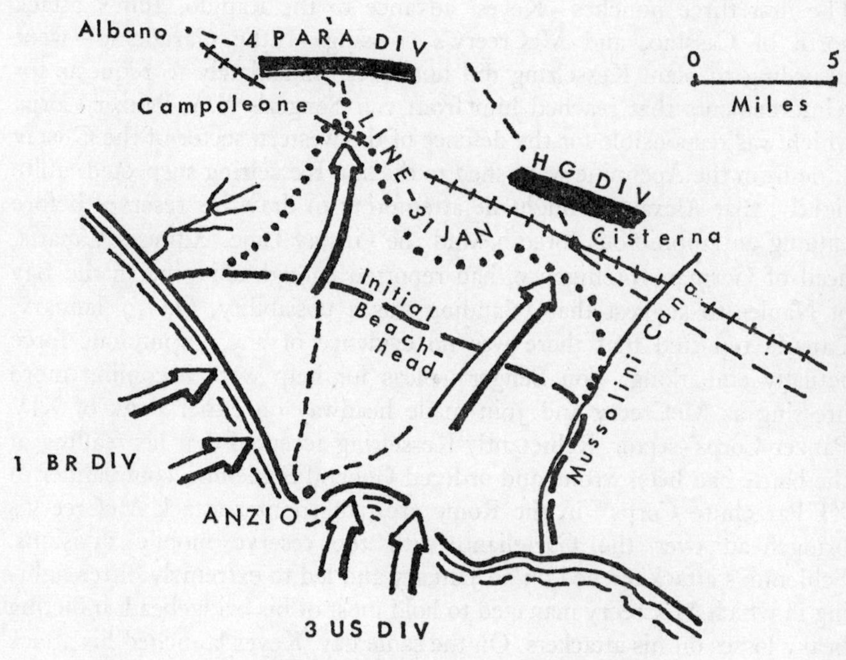

50 Anzio Beachhead, 22–30 January 1944

Kesselring had been caught off balance. Alexander had achieved the strategic and tactical surprise which he needed, but he lost all his advantages within 48 hours because, on the one hand, Lucas was not the right type of man to exploit such an unexpected turn of events; and because, on the other, Kesselring reacted with lightning speed and superb improvisation. The approach of Lucas' amphibious force was not detected by the Luftwaffe. The first reports to reach Kesselring came from a small panzer grenadier detachment which happened to be resting and retraining near Anzio. There was no significant opposition to the Allied landings. Lucas' main difficulties came from the unsuitability of the beaches for unloading heavy equipment. Luckily the small port of Nettuno was taken intact and so by the end of the first day unloading was ahead of schedule.

Kesselring's resilience was typical of the high professional qualities of the best German commanders. He ordered Schlemm to break off his counter-attacks against McCreery, and to hurry troops back to contain the southern side of the Allied beachhead. At the same time, he ordered the anti-aircraft commander of the Rome area, General Phol, to block the roads leading to Rome with anti-aircraft guns sited to deal with tanks, and with an *ad hoc* force from the half formed 4 Parachute Division to contain the northern half of the beachhead. By the time that Lucas felt himself strong enough to break out from his initial beachhead on 25 January, the German containing force was ready and waiting. Penney's 1 (British) Division was stopped short of Campoleone and Truscott's 3 (US) Division was equally roughly handled in front of Cisterna. By 30 January Alexander realised that his opening attack had done no more than increase Kesselring's sensitivity to his open western flank. Lucas was not strong enough to reach the Alban Hills; indeed, there was increasing doubt about his ability to hold the foothold which he had just won. Kesselring had recovered his balance. Alexander had failed to frighten him into dropping his guard on the main front; and so it was now Kesselring's turn to try the process in reverse. He was to find Alexander just as difficult to upset and far more personally involved in the fighting than he, Kesselring, ever needed to be. Kesselring's subordinates were seasoned veterans, whereas Alexander's were, by comparison, enthusiastic military amateurs. For the next two months the security of the beachhead depended more upon Alexander's steadying influence than to any brilliance in tactics or strategy. Both Clark and Lucas came near to recommending evacuation. Kesselring, for his part, found attacking in the Italian winter no easier than Alexander had done.

Alexander's failure to upset Kesselring decisively was offset by the unexpected strategic advantage that he had won for his patrons. Hitler played directly into Churchill's and Brooke's hands by demanding the defence of the Gustav Line at all costs and the immediate elimination of the 'Anzio Abscess' as he contemptuously called Lucas' beachhead. He supplied Kesselring with a stream of reinforcements from all over Europe and authorised the despatch of von Mackensen's Fourteenth Army Headquarters from Northern Italy to handle Lucas' destruction. Alexander heard of these moves through the Allied intelligence organisation. The

Allied Air Forces claimed that they would be able to slow, if not stop, the arrival of these troops, but Alexander could not depend entirely upon their efforts to save Lucas if Kesselring decided to overwhelm his isolated Corps. He concluded that he must punch once more with his right to draw the German reserves away from Anzio. Keyes' II (US) Corps was to attack again up Route 6, this time aiming to take Monte Cassino before advancing up the Liri Valley.

During the last days of January Alexander was constantly on the move, examining the situation for himself on both fronts. He had been at Anzio on D-Day (23 January), but it had been too early for him to influence events other than to congratulate Lucas on his success so far. He visited the beachhead again on 25 January to observe the advances towards Campoleone and Cisterna. While he was there he suggested to Clark that Lucas should mount a coordinated offensive on about 27 January as two more divisions would have arrived in the beachhead by then. Clark demurred, saying that 30 January would be a more practical date. Alexander accepted his reasons and set off back to see how Keyes was progressing on Route 6.

Neither Keyes nor Lucas succeeded in their attacks. Keyes' men fought their way across the flooded Rapido Valley north of Cassino, and then edged their way up the steep rocky ridges, crag by crag, until they were level with but some 1,500 yards away from the Monastery which lay on the far side of a low col—so near but yet, as it proved, so far. There they were held in the bitterest winter weather by the arrival of General Ernst Baade's 90 Panzer Grenadier Division, reinforced by three battalions of parachute troops. The Americans fought on until 11 February, getting no nearer. When the advanced units of 4 (Indian) Division, sent from Eighth Army to relieve them, started to take over the American advanced posts on the 'Snakeshead' Ridge that looks across at the Monastery from the far side of the col in which the Polish cemetery nestles today, the Indians found many of the Americans were too exhausted and frost-bitten to walk and had to be carried out by stretcher. Keyes' men had done their best and could do no more.

Lucas' attacks to expand his beachhead at Anzio started well enough, but fared no better in the end. Penney's 1 (British) Division, supported by the American 1 (US) Armoured Division, drove a deep, narrow salient up the Anzio-Albano road almost to Campoleone. Allied intelligence had suggested that the German troops holding the Campoleone–Cisterna Line were a light screen protecting the preparation of the main German defences further inland. Penney found that there was no screen. He was up against the positions on which von Mackensen intended to contain Lucas' beachhead. Penney's experience was confirmed by Truscott's attack on Cisterna with his 3 (US) Division, reinforced by Ranger battalions. The Hermann Göring Division had returned from the Garigliano and was too strongly posted to be brushed aside. Truscott did not reach Cisterna.

Alexander was back in the beachhead again on 31 January and stayed until 2 February examining the situation closely with Clark, who had

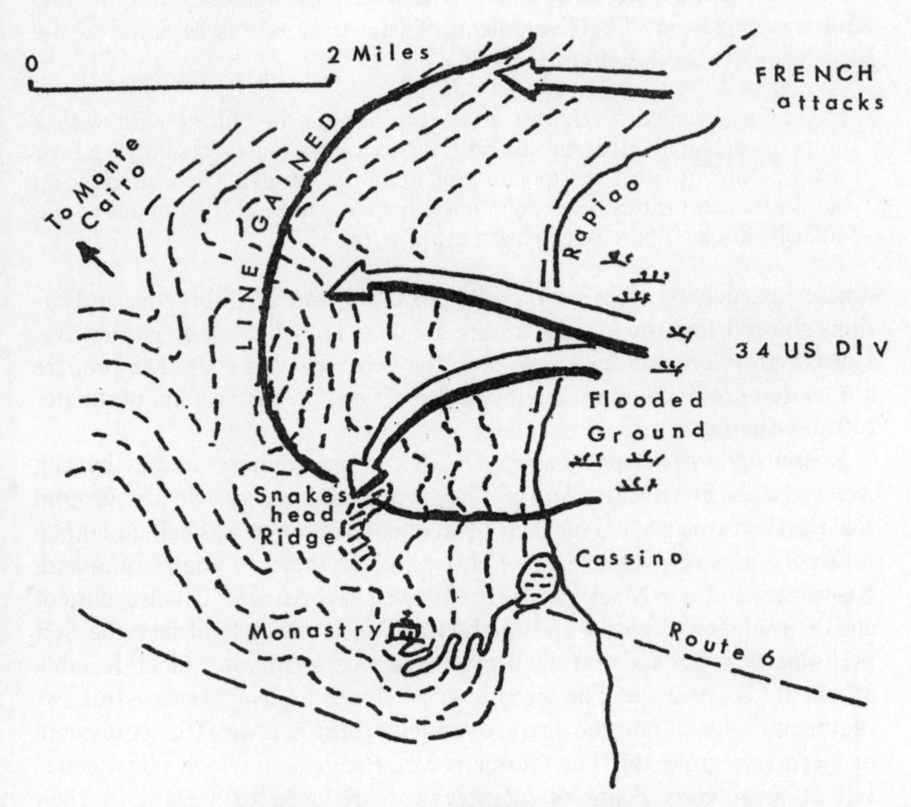

51 First Battle of Cassino, 24 January–11 February 1944

established an advanced Fifth Army Headquarters in Anzio. His talks with commanders and his personal observations as he drove around the beachhead convinced him that something was radically wrong. He sensed that Lucas' operations were halting and ill-coordinated, and reflected Lucas' own pessimistic outlook. He suggested to Clark that it might be advisable to relieve Lucas, but the Fifth Army commander was reluctant to agree. He had relieved Dawley at Salerno. It would have been awkward to do the same thing again at Anzio.

Alexander's personal reconnaissance of the front line convinced him that the beachhead perimeter could not stay where it was. He had not given up the idea of punching with his left again to help Keyes at Cassino, but before he could do so he had to be sure that Lucas would be operating from a secure base. VI (US) Corps was not, as yet, properly balanced and could not mount a major offensive or defend itself against one until this fault was corrected. The Campoleone–Cisterna Line was essential to the security of Lucas' beachhead:

> I therefore ordered a renewed attack on Cisterna in full strength with a properly prepared plan and all possible concentration of artillery and air attacks. Next my plan was to gain ground on the left of 1 Division, clear up our centre and organise our communications so as to be able to mount a solid offensive to cut Route 6. (Despatches, p. 2913)

These instructions were never fulfilled. Clear and unambiguous indications showed that the Germans were about to launch a counter-offensive. Lucas rightly ordered his Corps onto the defensive and started to prepare a final defence line behind his forward positions on the original perimeter of the beachhead.

Kesselring's first riposte started with two preliminary attacks by von Mackensen's Fourteenth Army. They were designed to win the ground that the Germans needed for their main offensive, which was being planned under the personal supervision of Hitler and the German High Command. Kesselring and von Mackensen were allowed surprisingly little freedom of action in choice of sector and method of attack. On 3 February the first preliminary attack successfully drove Penney back from his uncomfortable salient at Campoleone. The second, on 7 February, was less successful. Six regiments were committed against Penney's three brigades (the equivalent of German regiments). The Germans won the ground which they needed but at great cost. Penney's infantry were reduced to a third of their strength while the Germans lost even more heavily and also alerted Alexander to the dangers of the situation. The first burst of in-fighting was over. Kesselring was about to launch the second with a blow which Hitler hoped would teach the Allies a salutory lesson and discourage any cross-Channel operation during the coming summer.

Alexander had few options. He had to guard with his left by reinforcing Lucas as quickly as shipping would allow, and strike with his right by attacking the Gustav Line to relieve German pressure on Anzio. He needed more troops for both purposes. McCreery's X (British) Corps was unlikely to make much headway along Route 7 past the Aurunci Mountains and Leese's Eighth Army was in a *cul de sac* on the Adriatic coast. On Harding's advice, McCreery was ordered to dispatch General Templer's* 56 (British) Division to Anzio, while Leese sent 4 (Indian) Division (already mentioned), 2 (New Zealand) Division and 78 (British) Division to mount a new offensive at Cassino to open up the Liri Valley and Route 6. These Eighth Army divisions were to be formed into an *ad hoc* 'New Zealand' Corps under General Freyberg. The New Zealand Corps offensive was to be opened as quickly as possible to forestall von Mackensen and to compel the diversion of German reserves to the Gustav Line.

Alexander did forestall Kesselring's main offensive. The second burst of in-fighting began on 15 February when the Allied Strategic Air Forces dropped 450 tons of bombs on the Monastery of Monte Cassino in preparation for Freyberg's offensive. The story of the bombing of the Monastery and of Freyberg's subsequent failure to wrest Monte Cassino from Baade's men is well known. Two points are important in the assessment of Alexander in these operations: the decision to bomb the Monastery which was ultimately his; and the reasons for Freyberg's failure.

The bombing of the Monastery acquired far greater significance after the event than it did at the time. The Nazi propagandists seized upon the incident to portray the Allies, and Alexander in particular, as vandals. Nothing could have been further from the truth as far as Alexander was concerned, as his subsequent record shows. Discussing the German destruction of the Italian countryside, towns and villages during their withdrawal later that summer, Harold Macmillan recorded in his diary:

> [Alexander] is very proud of the fact that so far in this campaign he has succeeded in saving Rome, Florence, Pisa, Siena, Assisi, Perugia, Urbino from any except minor damage and that wantonly inflicted by the enemy when retiring. The General has a reputation for his anxiety to spare the lives of his men. He is as careful of the arts. (Macmillan, pp. 450–1)

When it came to balancing lives against art, Alexander had no difficulty in deciding in favour of his men, however priceless the ancient treasures might have been. He saw the problem of Monte Cassino in its simplest terms. The only practicable road to Rome was overlooked by the Monastery Hill; to open that road his men had to take that hill; and they had to be given the best possible chance of doing so with minimum loss of life.

* Later Field Marshal Sir Gerald Templer.

There was no choice to be made. No one could tell whether the Monastery itself was occupied or not. Subsequent evidence suggests that it was not, but the hill on which it stood was strongly held by Baade's troops as earlier American attempts to take Monte Cassino had shown. When Tuker, commanding 4 (Indian) Division, which was to assault Monte Cassino from the 'Snakeshead' Ridge, asked for the neutralisation of the German defences on Monte Cassino, including the Monastery, Alexander could not have refused. He had seen too much of war to hesitate. In his memoirs he reiterates his reasons:

> . . . when soldiers are fighting for a just cause and are prepared to suffer death and mutilation in the process, bricks and mortar, no matter how venerable, cannot be allowed to weigh against human lives. Every good commander must consider the morale and feelings of his fighting men; and, what is equally important, the fighting men must know that their whole existence is in the hands of a man in whom they have complete confidence. Thus the commanding general must make it absolutely clear to his troops that they go into action under the most favourable conditions he has the power to order.
>
> In the context of the Cassino battle, how could a structure which dominated the fighting field be allowed to stand? The Monastery had to be destroyed. Withal, everything was done to save the lives of the monks and their treasures: ample warning was given of the bombing. (Memoirs, p. 121)

The author, who spent some three months in the Cassino sector under the apparently all-seeing eye of the Monastery, can only add 'Amen'. Thank goodness Alexander took the view he did. This is perhaps the appropriate moment at which to make a point which could be reiterated at each critical period in the Italian campaign. Before any major tactical decision was taken, Alexander reconnoitred the ground himself accompanied only by a personal staff officer and the commander of the sector he was visiting. There are many company commanders and gunner observation officers, who recall to this day the surprise they felt on seeing the small trim figure of the Army Group Commander appear at their observation post, unheralded and unannounced. He would scan the hillsides with his glasses; discuss the tactical situation, obviously enjoying every minute of his return to the front line; and then he would disappear as quietly as he had come, leaving an impression of cheerful, sympathetic optimism behind him as he drove away in his open car or jeep—often driving himself if he had an important visitor with him. Somehow he always seemed to be able to match the mood of the men holding the particular post, be they British, American, Indians, Frenchmen, Poles or even Italians of the new co-belligerent units which were formed in increasing numbers as the campaign went on. It never mattered to him who they were: they were soldiers. These visits took him back in memory to Mons, the Aisne, the Somme, Ypres, Cambrai, Latvia, and the North-West Frontier. This was the part of soldiering he liked.

The reasons for Freyberg's failure to take Monte Cassino after the massive air strike lay in two basic misappreciations: first, of the use of air power; and, secondly, of German intentions. The bombing of the Monastery was looked upon as an operation in its own right and not as an integral part of Freyberg's attack. There were two reasons for this—one valid and the other mistaken. The valid reason was that the timing of the bombardment depended on clear skies for the bombers to achieve the pin-point accuracy which was needed for such a relatively small target with Allied troops so close to it. No one could guarantee clear skies in February, and so the bombing programme had to be an entity in itself, superimposed on the land battle. The less valid reason was the airmen's feeling that their new found destructive power would, if used properly in massive concentration, do almost anything that the soldiers on the ground could possibly ask for. They saw little need for close coordination with the soldiers who were to follow up in the wake of their destructive effort. On this occasion a Mediterranean storm raged throughout 13 February. The meteorologists forecast a period of clear weather for 15 February, followed by further periods of rain. It was now or never as far as the airmen were concerned; and so Fifth Army Headquarters authorised the attack. Unfortunately Freyberg's Corps was not ready to take advantage of the bombardment and was unable to follow up as the last bomber flew away from the smoking piles of rubble which had been the Cistine Monastery a few minutes before. When the Royal Sussex Regiment did attack that night from the 'Snakeshead' Ridge, they were rebuffed by Baade's men who were, by then, firmly dug into the ruins. Subsequent attacks by 4 (Indian) Division on Monte Cassino and by the New Zealanders into the town of Cassino below, all failed due to this initial planning error of not ensuring that 4 (Indian) Division was ready to follow up.

The second misappreciation lay in the Allied estimates of when the German counter-offensive at Anzio was likely to start. The Allied airmen were convinced that their attacks on the German troop movements and supply lines would cripple Kesselring's ability to use the reinforcements which Hitler was squandering so lavishly on trying to prove that amphibious operations were no longer practicable. It had been intended to carry on supporting Freyberg's operations at Cassino with further air attacks on subsequent days, but on 16 February von Mackensen opened the Hitler offensive at Anzio. Alexander's and Kesselring's right-hand punches had landed within a day of each other. But, whereas Baade showed every sign of being able to hold Freyberg at Cassino, there were grave doubts about Lucas' ability to hold von Mackensen at Anzio. In consequence, the whole Allied air effort was diverted, with Alexander's agreement, from Cassino to Anzio; and Freyberg was instructed to go on pressing his attacks at Cassino to give Lucas as much help as he could. Freyberg persevered, but the second battle of Cassino died slowly away as the strength of the German defence made itself painfully evident.

The fighting at Anzio between 16 and 20 February was severe. Von Mackensen was wielding ten German divisions against the equivalent of five Anglo-American divisions in the beachhead. At one time the German assault was lapping against Lucas' 'final defence line'. After four days' extreme effort in which the German divisions attacked in succession down the Albano–Anzio road, von Mackensen was forced by the severity of his casualties to halt without achieving Hitler's aim. The Allied infantry, magnificently supported by their own artillery, by the guns of the Allied Fleets and by the Allied Air Forces, had stood their ground. The German soldiers, who had been buoyed up by propaganda stories of the great victory which awaited them, were stunned by their losses. Mud and the difficulties manoeuvring off the roads played their part in the German defeat, but it was the Allies fire power which was decisive. The German Army never again attacked in Italy with such *élan.* They continued to fight with great tenacity throughout the campaign, but their offensive power had been blunted. The second burst of in-fighting had ended with honours even: Kesselring held Cassino and Alexander held Anzio; and Kesselring found attacking in winter in Italy no easier than Alexander had done. Both knew that Hitler would not give up, so each began to spar for the third effort of the winter round.

The end of Kesselring's first attempt also brought the end of Lucas' command of VI (US) Corps. The way in which he was eased out has been criticised on both sides of the Atlantic; the Americans blamed Clark for not standing up for Lucas, and Alexander for not resisting Churchill's wilder ideas; and the British, especially Churchill, blamed Alexander for not insisting upon Lucas' earlier supersession. The painful truth was that the Americans selected the wrong man for the job, and Alexander felt himself in no position to meddle in American domestic business. Alexander's own account of the affair is:

> His [Lucas'] appointment was entirely an American affair, and it would have been quite inappropriate for me to have intervened. However, at last, I brought

> myself to remark to Mark Clark: 'You know, the position is serious. We may be pushed back into the sea. That would be very bad for both of us—and you would certainly be relieved of your command'.
>
> This gentle injunction, I am glad to say, impelled action. (Memoirs, p. 126)

What he did not reveal in his memoirs was the stream of nagging signals and unkind quips which flowed in on him from Churchill:

> I had hoped that we were hurling a wild cat on to the shore, but all we had got was a stranded whale. . . .
> My comment is that senior commanders should not 'urge' but 'order'. . . .
> . . . American commanders expect to receive positive orders, which they will immediately obey. Do not hesitate therefore to give orders just as you would to your own men. The Americans are very good to work with, and quite prepared to take the rough with the smooth. (Churchill, *The Closing Ring*, pp. 431–2)

All this is easier said in Whitehall than done in the field when commanding an Allied force in which personal relationships can make or mar international cooperation. Clark's first step was to appoint Truscott as Lucas' deputy commander to ensure that no failure in leadership occurred at Anzio until a suitable pretext arose for Lucas' supersession. Clark's order reached Truscott just as the Hitler offensive broke over the beachhead. What was happening was transparent to the staff and most of the senior commanders. Lucas' supporters resented his coming replacement, feeling that he had done a good job and had saved the beachhead by his conservatism. Alexander's and Clark's critics saw moral weakness and lack of candour in Lucas' two-phase relief. When the battle was over Lucas left for a nominally higher appointment in the United States and Truscott went on to command VI (US) Corps with the same firmness and balanced tactical judgment that he had displayed at the head of 3 (US) Division. Alexander must have hated every minute of this tortuous affair.

The punching and counter-punching of the last part of the winter round was not as closely connected as either boxer intended or would have liked. Hitler was bitterly disappointed with von Mackensen's failure and ordered an immediate resumption of the offensive, this time on the Cisterna–Anzio axis. Alexander appreciated that a further attack was likely, but was now less anxious about the security of the beachhead. Once a beleaguered force has withstood and thrown back a major assault of the type that the Germans had delivered at Anzio, its morale rises and its defences congeal into a natural impregnability brought about by the hard selective process of battle. Those positions, which are weak, fall and are replaced by others, which are tactically capable of withstanding the storm; and those that are strong enough become stronger as the garrisons gain experience of manning them under attack. Nevertheless, it would not be possible to mount a counter-offensive from the beachhead. The most that could be done, with the shipping available, was to relieve tired units and to replenish depleted stocks of ammunition and supplies. Again Alexander had no alternative but to use his right hand once more. Where the counter-punch would fall depended upon the conclusions of a special appreciation drawn up by Harding and the Army Group staff, and upon the ambitions of the Air Forces and the vagaries of the Italian weather. The last two conspired together to allow Hitler to land his punch first.

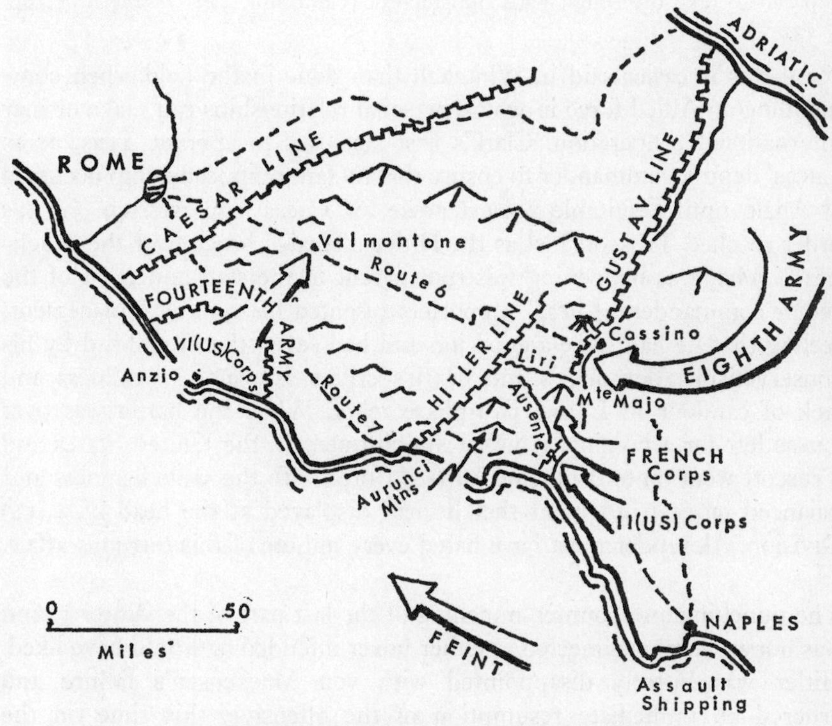

52 Harding's Appreciation, 22 February 1944

While the Anzio fighting was at its height, Harding was working on a far-sighted appreciation of the operational problems of achieving the Chiefs' of Staff aim of drawing the greatest number of German troops into Italy at the crucial moment when Eisenhower set out across the Channel in May or early June. Harding's theme was that it was no use driving the Germans back up the Italian Peninsula. Hitler would not send significantly more troops into Italy unless Alexander managed to trap and destroy a large part of Kesselring's Army Group, thereby uncovering the southern approaches to the Reich and allowing Allied bombers to settle on northern Italian airfields from which they could pound German cities at point-blank range. Before considering ways of trapping Kesselring, Harding isolated certain basic requirements. He must be able to contrive a superiority of at least three to one at whatever point Alexander chose to strike a decisive blow. The weather must be fine and certain so that hard ground and clear skies would enable the Allies to use the full potential of their tank, artillery and air superiority. And the Allied Armies must be given time to rest, refit and retrain before the decisive offensive in support of 'Overlord'. These factors argued conclusively for a pause in operations to build up the numerical superiority needed; to await fine spring weather; and for rest and refit. Such a pause would, however, break the principle of 'keeping the Germans on their heels', so the pause could not be complete. Subsidiary operations would have to go on, but should be planned in such a way as to provide the best possible spring-board for the major offensive. Harding also concluded, and here lay the strategic rub, that 'Anvil' (the spring landing on the south coast of France) should be cancelled and the Mediterranean and Middle East Theatre should be combed for reinforcements to give Alexander the numerical superiority that he would need for success. The 'Anvil' concept should be kept alive in the form of a deception operation to pin German troops on the Riviera coast and in the Rhone Valley.

The tactical factors were the four roads to Rome, the existing deployment of Alexander's troops, and Kesselring's sensitivity to his long, exposed sea flanks. Route 16 on the Adriatic coast led nowhere and so Eighth Army should be brought across the Apennines to increase the striking force on Routes 6 and 7, or the sea. Route 7 would still be constricted by the Aurunci Mountains even in summer, which left Route 6 and the sea route to Anzio as the potential thrust lines. The tactical keys for opening up Route 6 were the two bastions of the Liri Valley—Monte Cassino on the northern side and Monte Majo on the southern. The key to successful operations from Anzio was shipping—to build up sufficient men, guns, tanks and ammunition to blast a breach in von Mackensen's containing perimeter and to sustain Truscott thereafter.

All successful tactical plans, designed for the manoeuvre of some half a million men, have to be very simple in concept. There was only one place for the main striking force to attack and that was up the Liri Valley. There was only one way to encircle the German troops south of Rome and that was a break-out from Anzio. The question to be resolved was which punch should come first? At the beginning of the winter battles, Alexander had attacked at Cassino to draw Kesselring's reserves south. Kesselring had taken the bait in spite of his instincts telling him that it was unwise to do so. If Alexander attacked again at Cassino and showed sufficient shipping in the Naples–Salerno area to suggest another amphibious assault, Kesselring would probably hesitate much longer this time before committing his reserves to underpinning the Gustav defences. Hence Alexander's main striking force might be able to tear a hole in the Gustav Line before Kesselring's reserves could intervene. When they did move south to help extricate the defenders, the moment would have arrived for Truscott to break out from Anzio across the German rear. Under winter conditions such a plan might fail, but in the spring Allied air supremacy and the ability of Clark and Leese to manoeuvre their superior tank and artillery units off the roads should sway the balance.

Alexander approved Harding's appreciation and dispatched it to Wilson and Brooke on 22 February with his own recommendations. The plan which he proposed was for Eighth Army to cross the Apennines and to act as the main striking force at Cassino with a total of four Corps under command—Kirkman's XIII (British) Corps, Anders II (Polish) Corps, Burns I (Canadian) Corps and McCreery's X (British) Corps—a total of some ten divisions. The main Fifth Army effort would be from Anzio, but the rest of Fifth Army would support Eighth Army by attacking up Route 7. Juin's Frenchmen would take over the northern half of Clark's Garigliano sector and would attack up the Ausente Valley to take Monte Majo, thus supporting Eighth Army's southern flank; while Keyes' II (US) Corps would blast its way along the coast astride Route 7 itself. Concurrent with this operational plan there would be a two-tier deception plan. The strategic tier would suggest the 'Anvil' invasion of Southern France, and the tactical tier would simulate a lesser landing at Civitavecchia (just north of Rome), Leghorn or Genoa, ostensibly to help Alexander's advance on Rome. Neither threat would have any real substance, but, as they were what the Germans would expect, it would not be difficult to build up the illusion of reality in their minds. The code-name for the Summer Battle for Rome was 'Diadem'.

Alexander's proposals were not well received in Algiers where Wilson felt it wrong to relax pressure as much as Alexander suggested; nor in Washington where the American Chiefs of Staff objected strongly to the breach in the Tehran agreement to mount 'Anvil'. Churchill was delighted and fought Alexander's battle for him and won. The Americans would not cancel 'Anvil' altogether, insisting that it should be postponed until after 'Diadem' and 'Overlord'. This was an unfortunate compromise which was to hamstring Alexander later.

Once the broad outline of Alexander's 'Diadem' plan had been accepted, the more immediate problems of the campaign had to be settled against its background. Here the ambitions of the Air Forces came into play. Wilson had developed a plan of his own for the Italian theatre in which he had been strongly influenced by his Air advisers. He proposed a two-pronged air-offensive. The first prong was an interdiction programme called Operation 'Strangle', designed to so disrupt the German lines of communication that they would be forced to withdraw through lack of supplies. For this policy to work, Alexander would have to keep up his pressure on the Gustav Line to force the Germans to expend the stocks of ammunition already held south of the interdiction zone quicker than they could be replenished over the broken transportation system. The second prong was to use concentrations of bombers, as had been done during the bombing of the Monastery, to wipe out any major centre of resistance in the German defences which Fifth or Eighth Army could not take by conventional means. Remembering Messina, Salerno and more recently the speed with which German reinforcements reached Anzio, Alexander was less sanguine about the Air Forces abilities to win the land battle on behalf of the soldiers. He was quite prepared to make full use of their help, but he would not base his plans on the fulfilment of the airmen's promises. Replying to Wilson's initial comments on his 'Diadem' plan, Alexander limited himself to hoping 'that the weather will improve in time to give our air forces a chance to carry out their part of your plan. At present it is atrocious and shows no sign of change.'

The weather itself—the third factor in the last cycle of the winter battles—was to play its part to the full. Alexander appreciated that he would need a firm foothold in the Liri Valley if 'Diadem' was to get off to a flying start. He also needed the Campoleone–Cisterna line at Anzio to give himself greater depth to build up Truscott's force. Freyberg's plan to win the foothold at Cassino depended upon the use of the Air Forces as Wilson had suggested in the second prong of his air policy. The town of Cassino was a small pin-point target which was blocking the Allies' advance up Route 6. It offered an apparently ideal opportunity for the Air Forces to show their prowess. General Cannon, the American commander of the Tactical Air Forces, offered 'to wipe out Cassino like an old tooth.' If this novel use of air power would save soldiers' lives, Alexander was prepared to authorise the experiment. No one could guess the outcome, but logic suggested it was the right thing to do. The timing would depend, as usual with air operations, on the weather and the close coordination of Air and Army plans. This time Freyberg had plenty of time to ensure this coordination. All was ready by 24 February for the code-word 'Bradman', signifying the start of the operation—all, that is to say, except the weather over Cassino which stayed foul.

Truscott hardly got as far as considering how he would gain greater depth in his beachhead when von Mackensen reopened the German offensive at Anzio, attacking 3 (US) Division south of Cisterna on 29 February. The bad weather, which prevented the air forces wiping out Cassino for Freyberg, stopped them supporting Truscott as well. 3 (US) Division, now under General Mike O'Daniel's command, gave as good as an account of itself as it had done under Truscott. After three days fighting the German offensive was spent with no material gain. Kesselring knew that he did not possess the strength to achieve a decisive breakthrough in winter and wisely ordered von Mackensen to go over onto the defensive on 1 March. Truscott had won his battle without any relieving attack by Freyberg, who continued waiting for the weather to enable him to seize the bridgehead which Alexander needed in the Liri Valley for 'Diadem'.

The break did not come until 15 March. One thousand tons of bombs and 1,200 artillery shells of all calibres landed on Cassino that day. Little survived in the town itself, but the debris blocked Route 6 just as effectively as its paratrooper garrison had done. The New Zealanders made progress as long as daylight lasted, dealing with the reinforcements from Heydrick's 1st Parachute Division* which re-entered the rubble as soon as the bombing stopped. When darkness came the weather reasserted its dominance. Heavy rain fell throughout the night, turning bomb craters into lakes, and covering the debris with a slippery slime as the water mixed with the layers of dust which had settled after the bombing. Freyberg's men fought on with great skill and epic perseverance for a week. On 20 March, Alexander, who had watched the bombing and had kept in the closest touch with the operation, warned Freyberg that, unless he could make substantial progress in the next few days, the offensive would have to stop so as not to prejudice the 'Diadem' plan. Freyberg's attacks on 21 and 22 March did not produce the hoped-for results. Wilson, who was visiting the front at the time, wished to go on, but Alexander, remembering his experiences in similar conditions in 1917, uttered the

* Baade's 90 Panzer Grenadier Division had been relieved by Heydrick's 1 Parachute Division.

one word 'Passchendaele', and stopped the offensive. The Winter Battles for Rome were over.

Alexander had been accused of obstinately butting his head against the heavily defended spur of Monte Cassino. Churchill accused him of this sin on 20 March in a markedly discourteous signal:

> I wish you would explain to me why this passage by Cassino Monastery Hill, etc., all on a front of two or three miles is the only place which you must keep butting at. About five or six divisions have been worn out going into these jaws. . . . I have the greatest confidence in you and will back you up through thick and thin, but do try to explain to me why no flanking movements can be made. (Churchill, *The Closing Ring*, p. 448)

Juin has some equally caustic comments in his memoirs about the inability of the over-mechanised Anglo-Saxons to find a way round. General Tuker, the commander of 4 (Indian) Division, was just as critical. Neither of these eminent experts in mountain warfare could appreciate that, as long as Route 6 remained blocked at Cassino, the Allied advance could not be sustained. Because of the difficulties of supply, any outflanking force would have been so small that the Germans would have had little difficulty in mopping it up as soon as it emerged from the safety of the mountains in their rear. There was no way past Cassino as long as the winter weather prevented the Allies deploying their great material superiority. Alexander might not have undertaken the Third Battle of Cassino had it not been for the new factor of air power. Theoretically the weight of explosive delivered should have given the New Zealanders the victory, but theory omits such factors as the fanatical resistance of Heydrick's paratroopers and the effect of water on debris—the squelching slime of a bombed town in winter. Some writers tend to equate Cassino with the unimaginative battles of the Somme and Ypres. The losses of the New Zealand Corps show how wrong such comparisons can be:

2 (NZ) Division	1,050
4 (Indian) Division	1,160
78 (British) Division	190
	2,400

This was out of some 50,000 troops employed in the three divisions and their supporting units.

Alexander was no military pedant who stuck to a discredited course in slavish adherence to the principle of concentration of effort at the decisive point. The Winter Battles, particularly the three battles of Cassino, were never allowed to go to extremes.

Diadem—The Summer Battles for Rome

> The Allied armed forces are now assembling for the final battles on seas, on land, and in the air to crush the enemy once and for all. . . . To us in Italy, has been given the honour to strike the first blow.
>
> Extract from Alexander's Order of the Day, 11 May 1944

From 24 March, when Alexander called off Freyberg's battle, until 11 May, D-Day for 'Diadem', preparations for the spring offensive went unobtrusively ahead. Eighth Army crossed the Apennines and took over the Cassino sector; Juin's Frenchmen handed over to Anders' Poles north of Cassino and moved south into Fifth Army's sector on the Garigliano opposite Monte Majo; and Keyes' II (US) Corps relieved McCreery on the lower Garigliano so that the latter could move the remnants of his X (British) Corps, the bulk of which had moved to Anzio during the crisis of the First German counter-offensive, into Anders' old sector to protect Eighth Army's northern flank in the Apennines. These moves had two purposes: first, to bring all the British and British-equipped formations like Anders' Poles under Eighth Army command, and all the American and American equipped forces like Juin's French divisions under Fifth Army command; and secondly, to give each division a spell out of the line to rest and refit within the overall relief programme. While these moves were taking place on the main front, Truscott's divisions were being reinforced and his supplies built up for the decisive role he was to play in the later stages of 'Diadem'. And in rear of both Armies, new divisions—Polish, French, Indian, American and British—were being landed in Italy from the Middle East and elsewhere in the Mediterranean as fast as available shipping would allow in order to give Alexander the measure of superiority which Harding's appreciation prescribed.

However brilliant the plan; however smooth and well thought out the organisation; however ingenious the deception measures; and however well found the logistic support may be, these are all matters which can be attended to by a competent staff. What a staff cannot provide is the inspiration, the determination and the judgment which will turn paper arrangements into a successful military operation. Only the commander can provide these things. The staff can help and sustain him, but no one can replace him in the vital job of command. An army reflects its commander and not his staff. Alexander's task was to inspire the hundreds of

25 Alexander talking to Truscott in the ruins of Anzio

THE BATTLE FOR ROME

26 The Diadem team: Harding, Leese, Lemnitzer, Alexander and Clark

27 The victor of Diadem: Alexander outside Rome on 7 June 1944

THE SUMMER OF TRIUMPH

thousands of men of many different nationalities to give their best willingly in the grim struggle which was about to take place with one of the most professional armies in the world. He had to have the robustness not to falter when things went wrong; and, at the same time, he had to possess that deep-seated instinct which professional soldiers call 'the feel of the battle' with which to anticipate events, making precautionary moves long before there were hard facts upon which to base decisions, and with which to time his blows so that his opponent could never recover from the initial disruption of his plans.

Great military leaders have differing ways of inspiring confidence. Alexander inspired his troops through their commanders, avoiding personal publicity himself. In the multi-racial force which he led, he could not replace subordinates he did not like, because more often than not the particular officer was both formation commander and head of his national contingent with a dual loyalty—to Alexander and to his own national government. He was thus forced to inspire his army group by making each subordinate feel that he and his country were being given the honour and privilege of playing a decisive role in the coming battle. Fortunately this necessity coincided with his personal attributes. He had an inbred quasi-political instinct which told him how to handle this wide cross-section of the human race. In Leese, he had an orthodox, reliable and experienced commander of the Eighth Army, well suited to direct the main striking force which was to batter a breach in the Gustav Line at its strongest point. In Clark, he had a younger, more ambitious and nationally conscious commander of the Fifth Army, who was ever sensitive to the honour of the United States and hence, at times, rather difficult to handle. Anders, commanding the Polish Corps, had a singleness of purpose which was doomed to disappointment: the rebirth of his beloved Poland through the valour of his Corps was all he craved. Juin felt equally strongly about the rebirth of France through the efforts of his French Expeditionary Corps. He had little liking for the British or Americans, and was bent on showing how inept they were compared with his French North Africans. Then there was Burns, at the head of the Canadians, who was as sensitive to national prestige as Clark and just as determined to show that his Canadians were every bit as good as the British and Indian troops. Freyberg, with his New Zealanders, held a very special place in Alexander's esteem. The New Zealanders formed his *Corps de Chasse* throughout the campaign and never let him down. Of the British and American corps commanders, who were not leaders of national contingents, Kirkman and Keyes were experienced professionals with no political axes to grind. They could be trusted to do their jobs efficiently without flamboyance. McCreery remained a close friend and confidant; and Truscott was a man after Alexander's own heart, who possessed the same battle awareness which was so marked in the Commander-in-Chief.

Few occasions in Alexander's career show his facility for suiting men to jobs better than his casting of 'Diadem'. He gave each man the job which he was proud to perform. Where he knew that he would not be able to control a particular commander's rogue energies, he gave him a job which would channel those energies in a direction that would further the overall plan without undue friction. To Leese went the battering-ram role of the main striking force; to Anders the glory of taking Monte Cassino which had defied American, British, New Zealand and Indian troops; to Juin the apparently impossible task of seizing Monte Majo and breaking through the Aurunci Mountains with his experienced mountain troops; to Kirkman and Keyes the uninspiring but nonetheless essential tasks of opening up Routes 6 and 7; to McCreery the selfless task of protecting the extreme northern flank with Freyberg's New Zealanders; to Burns, the honour of rushing the Hitler Line (see fig. 52, p. 274), which blocked the Liri Valley some miles north-west of Cassino as a reserve position behind the Gustav defences; to Truscott, the *coup de grâce*, to be delivered on Alexander's personal orders when he judged the decisive moment had come; and, finally, Clark was to have the honour of entering Rome with his Fifth Army *after* the centre and right wing of Kesselring's Army Group 'C' had been encircled and destroyed. Unfortunately Clark was not certain whether Alexander really intended to allow Fifth Army this honour, even though it was inscribed in black and white in the operational instructions. He believed that the British would, in the end, rob him of the chance to emulate Belisarius. He was wrong, and his mistake cost Alexander the completeness of his victory.

Of the other two qualities needed of the commander—robustness and tactical judgment—little need be added about Alexander. He was too experienced to be ruffled by misfortune. His basic operational policy was founded on the assumption that nothing ever went right in battle. His battle sense was acute, and it was this sixth sense which made him the great commander that he was and won the 'Diadem' offensive for him. In sketching the battle in its broadest outline, it is easiest to follow events in the three phases which Alexander prescribed in his final conference. Phase I was to be the breaching of the Gustav Line with the simultaneous assaults by Anders', Kirkman's, Juin's and Keyes' corps, followed by an advance up the Liri Valley by Kirkman and Burns. In Phase II, Eighth Army would destroy the Hitler Line, while Fifth Army reinforced Truscott who would break out at the appropriate moment. And in Phase III Alexander hoped to crush all Kesselring's troops west of the Apennines between Fifth and Eighth Army before they could occupy the Caesar Line (see fig. 52, p. 274) which constituted the last German defensive position covering Rome.

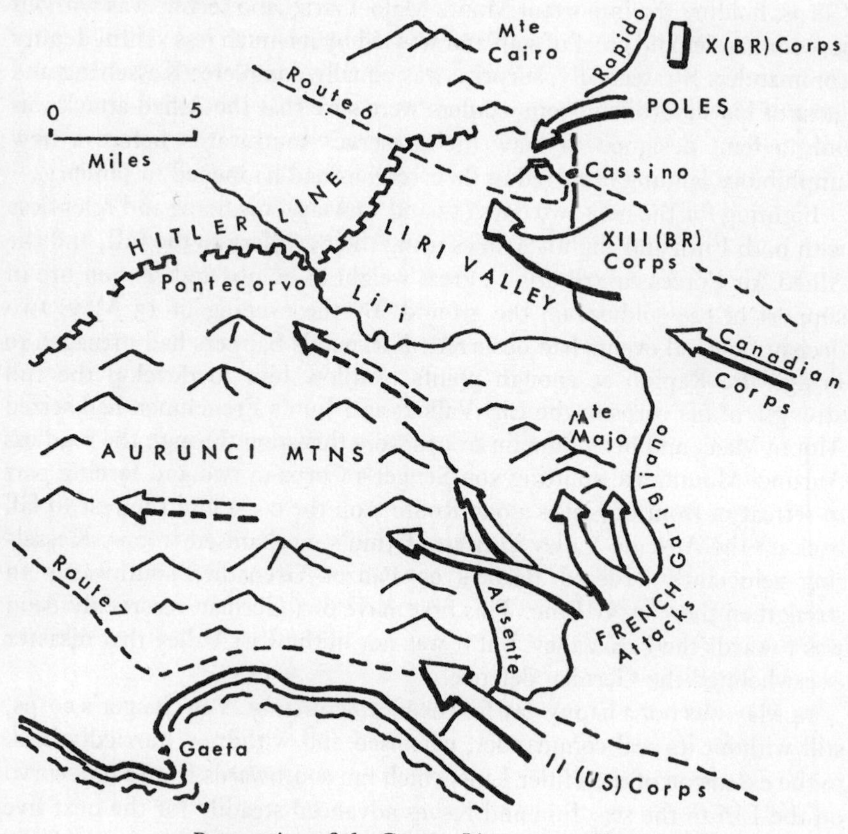

53 Destruction of the Gustav Line, 11–17 May 1944

The offensive opened an hour before midnight on 11 May with the four leading corps attacking the Gustav Line from Cassino to the sea. Next morning it appeared that the Allies had been rebuffed. Anders had failed with heavy losses on Monte Cassino; Kirkman had established barely a toe-hold over the Rapido; Juin had been repulsed on Majo; and Keyes had done no better on the coast. Depressing though the news was,

Alexander had done better than the first reports suggested. The Germans had been surprised tactically and strategically. They had fallen for the deception plan, which suggested an Allied offensive in late May or early June. Their relief programme was incomplete, especially in the Liri Valley where the main weight of Eighth Army was about to pound their defences to pieces; and many of their senior commanders were away at one of Hitler's investitures at Obersalzburg. Von Senger's XIV Panzer Corps, holding the important Monte Majo–Garigliano sector, was without its commander and chief of staff and was led by its much less skilful deputy commander. Strategically, surprise was equally complete; Kesselring and most of his subordinate commanders were sure that the Allied attack was only a feint designed to draw their reserves southwards before a new amphibious landing occurred in their rear, as had happened in January.

Fighting for the next two days (12 and 13 May) was fierce and relentless with both Fifth and Eighth Armies using their artillery to the full, and the Allied Air Forces contributing a great weight of bombs and cannon fire in support of the soldiers on the ground. By the evening of 13 May, two decisive tactical events had occurred: Kirkman's Sappers had managed to bridge the Rapido at enough points to allow him to develop the full strength of his corps in the Liri Valley; and Juin's Frenchmen had seized Monte Majo, and his mountain troops were thrusting through the roadless Aurunci Mountains, splitting von Senger's Corps in two and forcing part to retreat in front of Keyes along Route 7 on the coast and the rest to fall back up the Ausente Valley in front of Juin's mechanised troops. Kesselring reluctantly ordered Baade's 90 Panzer Grenadier southwards to strengthen the Gustav Line. This first move of a German reserve division was towards the Liri Valley, but it was not in the Liri Valley that disaster overwhelmed the German defence.

14 May was not a happy day for the German Army. Von Senger's corps, still without its real commander, collapsed and withdrew hurriedly back to the extension of the Hitler Line which ran southwards from Pontecorvo on the Liri to the sea. Juin and Keyes advanced steadily for the next five days, while Leese developed the Eighth Army operations north of the Liri. By 16 May, Kirkman's Corps had fought its way to within striking distance of Route 6 behind Cassino. Leese ordered Anders to renew his assault on Monte Cassino next day to join hands with Kirkman in encircling Heydrick's Parachute garrison of the town and the Monastery. Kesselring appreciated that the time was coming for the paratroopers to give up 'their' Cassino. He had been forced to divert 90 Panzer Grenadier Division to help XIV Panzer Corps south of the Liri and to check Juin's

triumphant troops. He now ordered 26 Panzer Division forward as well, but it could not arrive in time to affect events at Cassino.

Heydrick's men fought the Poles throughout 17 May and at dusk Kirkman's Corps cut Route 6 behind Monte Cassino. Heydrick chose to slip away over the rock-strewn mountain sides during the night rather than be trapped in Cassino. Next day the Polish standard was broken over the ruins of the Monastery. Two great breaches had been torn in the Gustav Line: one by Juin and the other by Leese before more than one German reserve division had reached the front. 90 Panzer Grenadier Division was in action. Two others were still coast watching north of Rome and the fourth, 26 Panzer Division, which had been waiting to

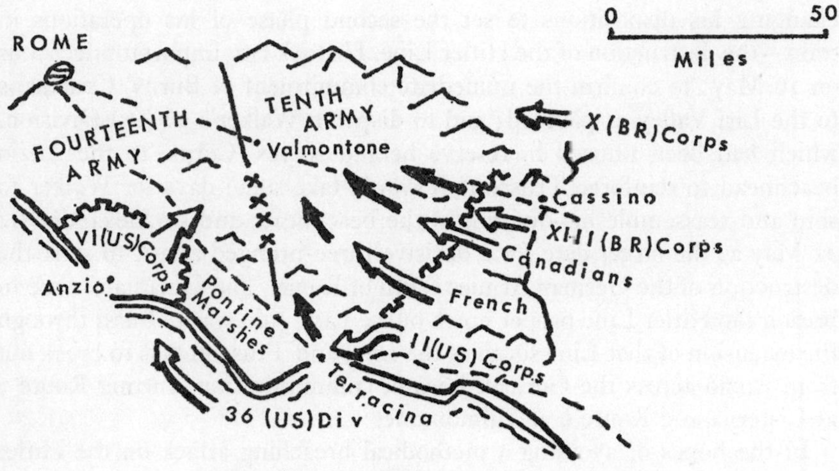

54 Battle for the Hitler Line, 22 May 1944

pounce on Truscott if he tried to break out from von Mackensen's encirclement, was just beginning to move towards the Liri Valley. Kesselring had been out-generalled. He realised, too late, that there was no Allied amphibious force at sea. He had lost the Gustav Line by not committing his reserves in time. He was to lose the Hitler and Caesar Lines through his reserves arriving piecemeal and in an uncoordinated way, having suffered severely from Allied air attacks during their moves.

From Kesselring's point of view, the moment of truth came when his radio intercept units identified Burns' Canadian Corps entering the Liri Valley on Kirkman's southern flank. Kesselring's staff had assumed, as Alexander had intended, that the Canadians were embarking at Salerno to land somewhere north of Rome, possibly at Civitavecchia, which was held by Fries' 29 Panzer Grenadier Division, or near Leghorn, held by Schmaltz's Hermann Göring Division. There was no amphibious force at sea. The battle would be won or lost somewhere between Cassino and Anzio. Kesselring decided that he would try to win it on the Hitler Line. He authorised von Vietinghoff to withdraw into its defences late on 17 May and ordered Fries' 29 Panzer Grenadier Division from Civitavecchia to reinforce von Vietinghoff. In addition, he directed two infantry divisions to move across the Apennines from the quiet Adriatic sector to lend weight to the defence. Only the Hermann Göring Division remained uncommitted in the Leghorn area, because it was under OKW orders to move to France.

Long before the Polish standard broke over Cassino, Alexander was changing his dispositions to set the second phase of his operations in train—the destruction of the Hitler Line. He took two important decisions on 16 May: to confirm the immediate commitment of Burns' Canadians to the Liri Valley as planned; and to dispatch Walker's 36 (US) Division, which had been unused in reserve behind Keyes' Corps, to the Anzio beachhead to reinforce Truscott. It would take some days for Walker to ship and reassemble his division in the beachhead, and so Alexander set 22 May as the target date for a decisive three-pronged attack to start the destruction of the German Armies south of Rome. The Canadians were to breach the Hitler Line proper north of the Liri; Juin was to burst through the extension of that Line south of the Liri; and Truscott was to break out from Anzio across the German lines of communication, cutting Route 7 at Cisterna and Route 6 at Valmontone.

In the hopes of avoiding a methodical breaching attack on the Hitler Line, Leese drove Burns' and Kirkman's Corps forward up the Liri Valley during 18 May, intending to eject the Germans before they could settle down in its defences. Had there been two more hours daylight, he might have succeeded. By dawn on 19 May, German reinforcements had arrived from the Adriatic. Probing attacks by Burns and Kirkman confirmed stiffening German resistance and Kesselring's determination to give no more ground. Alexander sensed the situation immediately and ordered Burns and Juin to launch their main attacks on 22 May, and instructed Clark to loose Truscott a day later, when Kesselring's attention would be focussed on the Hitler Line, and when the Allied Air Forces would be free to switch their main effort to help Truscott's break-out.

The fight for the Hitler Line was short and sharp. Burns' and Juin's men fought throughout 22 May, suffering heavy casualties. At midday it looked as if the Canadian assault had failed. Towards evening German resistance began to crumble under the persistent Canadian attacks, which were supported by the immense weight of Eighth Army's artillery. By dusk there was a clear breach through which the Canadian Armoured Division passed the following morning. The Canadians are rightly proud of their feat of arms that day. It was no easy task to breach in 24 hours a line of defences built with Teutonic thoroughness throughout the winter and liberally supplied with concrete bunkers, turreted anti-tank guns set in concrete, and belts of wire and mines. Juin, to the south, had been equally successful in his struggle with von Lüttwitz's 26 Panzer Division;

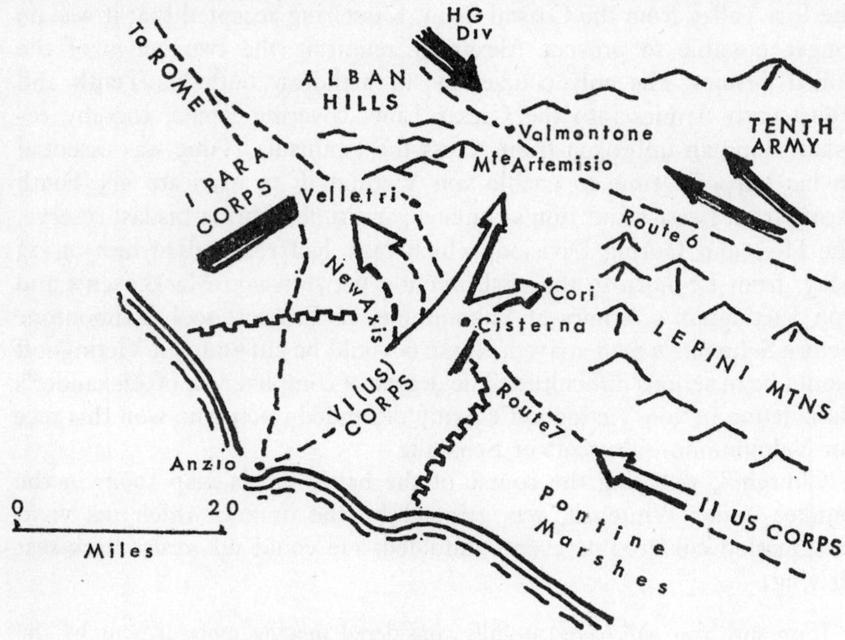

55 Break-out from Anzio, 23–26 May 1644

and Keyes, on the coast, had forestalled Fries' 29 Panzer Grenadier Division at the Terracina defile—the last good defensive position on Route 7 before the Pontine Marshes. The stage could not have been better set for Truscott's break-out. All Kesselring's reserve divisions, except the Hermann Göring Division at Leghorn, were by now embroiled in the struggle to hold the main front.

Truscott's battle with von Mackensen's encircling Fourteenth Army took three days to reach its climax. Supported by almost the entire weight of the Allies' Mediterranean Air Forces, Truscott's Corps acted as a pent-up spring, which had been brought to the highest state of tension in the dreary weeks of waiting since the German counter-offensive died away in February. His men felt an enormous sense of relief when Alexander's orders arrived. The long siege was over, and they would be doing what had been intended of them four months before—tearing up the German communications. On 25 May, the German troops holding the Cisterna sector gave way and Truscott started his thrust towards Valmontone through the breach he had blown in the German defences. Keyes was approaching the beachhead through the Pontine Marshes and Juin was probing forward in step with him in the Lepini Mountains which divide the Liri Valley from the Coastal Plain. Kesselring accepted that it was no longer possible to prevent Alexander reuniting the two wings of the Allied Armies. His only course was to withdraw both his Tenth and Fourteenth Armies into the Caesar Line, covering Rome, thereby re-establishing an unbroken front across the Peninsula. Time was essential to his purpose: time to enable von Vietinghoff to extricate his Tenth Army from Leese's and Juin's clutches; and time to bring his last reserve, the Hermann Göring Division, which OKW had released to him on 23 May, from Leghorn to the vital junction between von Mackensen's and von Vietinghoff's Armies at Valmontone. If Truscott took Valmontone before Schmaltz's men arrived, Route 6 would be cut and von Vietinghoff would be in serious difficulties. The degree of completeness of Alexander's destruction of von Vietinghoff's Army depended upon who won this race for Valmontone—Truscott or Schmaltz.

Churchill, watching the course of the battle in his map room in the bunker under Whitehall, was gripped by the drama, which his vivid imagination coloured as events unfolded. He could not resist back-seat driving:

> I am sure you will have carefully considered moving more armour by the Appian Way [Route 7] up to the northernmost spearhead directed against the Valmontone-Frosinone road [Route 6]. A cop is much more important than Rome, which would anyhow come as its consequence. The cop is the one thing that matters.

Later Churchill ruefully records:

> The Hermann Göring Division and elements of others, delayed though they were by damaging attacks from the air, got to Valmontone first. The single American division sent by General Clark was stopped short of it and the escape route remained open. This was very unfortunate. (Churchill, *Closing the Ring*, p. 536)

Something had gone wrong. Alexander's critics point to the Valmontone débâcle as an excellent example of the weakness of his style of command. He had harnessed Anders' enthusiasm to master Monte Cassino; Leese's loyalty to blast his way up the Liri Valley; and Juin's cynicism to unhinge the Gustav and Hitler Lines. But he had misjudged Clark's motives for a second time. At Anzio he had allowed Clark to let Lucas adopt a plan which was quite contrary to Churchill's strategic intentions. Now he allowed, almost unwittingly it seems, Clark to change direction without any real authority. His instructions to and conversations with Clark during the battle were too indefinite for a man brought up in the American tradition of strict obedience to orders. Instead of putting all his weight on the Valmontone thrust, Clark ordered Truscott to change direction with an attack directed up Route 7—the shortest route to Rome. The Valmontone thrust would be taken over by Keyes' Corps when it reached the beachhead. Schmaltz, though badly mauled by the Allied Air Forces on his way south in daylight, was able to consolidate his positions at Valmontone, and Kesselring was able to hope that he could bring his two Armies into line in the Caesar positions.

Reading the various accounts of this unfortunate incident, it is clear that Clark always intended to advance on Rome at the first possible opportunity to ensure that his Fifth Army, which no one doubts deserved the honour, should be the first to enter the Italian capital. He does not disguise his motives in his memoirs. In the various recorded conversations between Al Gruenther,* Clark's Chief of Staff, and Harding it is clear that Clark had sound military as well as personal reasons for redirecting the main weight of his attack towards Rome, but he did not make his intentions clear or argue his ideas with Alexander. Instead he paid lip service to Alexander's directive in that he could honestly say he was still keeping up pressure on the Valmontone axis while he massed his main effort for the direct thrust to Rome. Alexander seems to have felt constrained to let his American subordinate handle his Fifth Army as he liked. Churchill's strictures at the time of Anzio—'My comment is that senior commanders should not "urge" but "order" . . .'—had not changed Alexander's fundamental style of avoiding unpleasant confrontations with subordinates. Other than seeking an assurance from Gruenther that Clark would maintain his thrust on Valmontone, he made no determined effort to see that his instructions were obeyed. He trusted Clark to carry them out in the spirit, if not quite the letter. Clark, for his part, stretched the spirit too far and paid a price in American lives, because his new thrust struck one of the stronger sections of the Caesar position, held by the

* Later Supreme Allied Commander, Europe, after Eisenhower.

reliable paratroopers of Schlemm's I Parachute Corps, which had not been heavily engaged up to that moment.

In his despatches Alexander loyally says nothing about Clark's failure to follow his instructions. In his memoirs, he says very simply:

> . . . General Clark's Anglo-American forces never reached their objectives, though, according to my information later, there was nothing to prevent their being gained. Instead, Mark Clark switched his point of attack north to the Alban Hills in the direction of Rome.
>
> If he had succeeded in carrying out my plan, the disaster to the enemy would have been much greater; indeed, most of the German forces south of Rome would have been destroyed. True the battle ended in a decisive victory for us, but it was not as complete as it might have been. (Memoirs, p. 127)

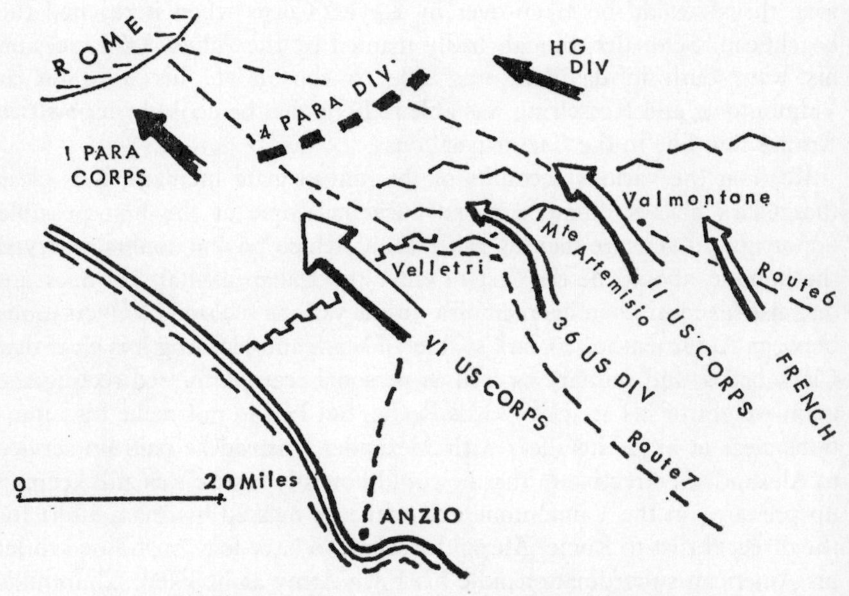

56 Collapse of the Caesar Line, 26 May–4 June 1944

When Truscott's Corps struck north-westwards on its new axis of attack, Schlemm's Corps reacted with the traditional stubbornness of German parachute troops. In the week's fighting that followed, losses were heavy on both sides. From Kesselring's point of view they were well worth while, as they gave von Vietinghoff more time to make good his escape via Route 6 and along the lesser routes through the mountains to the north. Leese and Juin pressed forward as hard as they could, but the country was ideal for the German expertise in rear-guard actions. Progress was disappointingly slow and, at times, positively frustrating as Leese could not deploy the full weight of his Army. The more units he tried to use, the slower his advance became due to the resulting traffic jams on the poor roads.

On 30 May, the first indication of the coming collapse of von Mackensen's Army was spotted almost simultaneously by Kesselring and Truscott. Shortage of troops had compelled von Mackensen to leave Monte Artemesio above Velletri unguarded because it seemed impassable to a force of any size. Kesselring ordered the gap to be closed, but, before von Mackensen could find any troops to fill it, Walker's 36 (US) Division had found and exploited von Mackensen's error with a bold night climb which secured the feature. This was the beginning of the end. Using the magnificent observation afforded by Monte Artemesio, Clark developed the maximum effort of Fifth Army to drive a wedge between Schlemm and Schmaltz. By 2 June Schmaltz's men had reached the end of their endurance and started to withdraw. There was nothing more Kesselring could do to save Rome. That night Fourteenth Army lost cohesion and fell back through Rome, covered by rearguards of 4 Parachute Division. Fifth Army's advanced guards reached the Tiber bridges in Rome as dusk fell on 4 June. Clark entered the city the following day. Alexander made no attempt to share the triumph with him. Instead he concentrated upon his real target, the destruction of Kesselring's Army Group. There were unmistakable signs in signals from Churchill and Brooke that the American Chiefs of Staff were about to help Hitler to rescue Kesselring in his hour of need.

Rome had fallen two days before Eisenhower crossed the Channel with his 'Overlord' forces. Alexander's timing could not have been bettered; and, if his victory was not as complete as he would have liked, there is no doubt that he had accomplished the mission given to him by the Combined Anglo-American Chiefs of Staff before the invasion of Sicily. He had drawn into Italy no less than 23 German divisions and had defeated them with 25 Allied divisions—not a very large margin of numerical superiority in country so ideal for defence. When Rome fell, six out of nine of Kesselring's excellent mobile divisions had been severely mauled and had lost most of their tanks and heavy equipment. Four infantry divisions had ceased to exist. Three more had suffered so heavily that they had to be withdrawn to refit, and a fourth was disbanded to provide reinforcements. Hitler was compelled to send four fresh divisions and three divisions worth of reinforcements into Italy in June, just at the time when he needed every available man in Normandy and on the Russian Front.

Alexander deserved his field marshal's baton which was his reward for 'Diadem'.* The Spring Battle for Rome was a triumph of generalship and the zenith of Alexander's military career. The American Chiefs' of Staff determination to concentrate resources in North-West Europe prevented him ever achieving such decisive results for his patrons again.

* It was not given to him until the autumn.

11

Mirage of Supreme Command

> Despite the disappointments that it brought, I never lost faith in the strategic validity of the Italian campaign, which owed virtually all its inspiration to Winston; nor did I feel any sort of regret when, because I was so close to it, he refused to release me to Ike to become his deputy in North-West Europe. I should have been more than reluctant to have taken farewell of the troops of many nations that fought under my command in the Mediterranean.
>
> Alexander, Memoirs, p. 130

This chapter should have been titled 'Supreme Command'. Alexander was unlucky. Supreme Command came to him in the end, but by then the Mediterranean Theatre had not only failed to win back any American interest, it had lost much of Churchill's enthusiasm and all Brooke's support. Alexander was left with the mirage of the great climax which he and his Army Group deserved.

This chapter could equally well have been called 'Bricks without Straw'. Alexander was not the type of man to bear grudges against people or events. As his resources were drained away to feed Eisenhower's campaign in North-West Europe, he became all the more determined to show that he appreciated the reasoning behind the decisions of his political and military masters by using what was left to him to best advantage. He has been accused on many occasions, particularly by American writers, of unwarranted optimism. There is some truth in this criticism; but what else could he have done? Once a commander loses faith in his mission, his armies lose faith too. Alexander never lost faith. In consequence, his armies kept faith, and carried on their unspectacular task of drawing German troops southward into Italy until in the end they had the satisfaction of forcing German Army Group 'C' to surrender before any other major German formation in the West.

This chapter is the story of the frustrating anti-climax of Alexander's military career. Long before Rome fell, Alexander and Harding had been elaborating their plans for the second phase of their offensive. The capture of Rome was not an end in itself. Rome was but a means of holding and destroying Kesselring's armies which were bound to stand in the defence of Italy's capital city for as long as possible. Once they gave way, they must be hustled through and not be allowed to settle into the Gothic Line defences which had been under construction spasmodically since Rommel started them at the time of the invasion of Sicily. Speed was everything. Alexander would be repeating Leese's attempt to rush the Hitler Line on a much larger scale, using the whole Army Group and aiming this time for Vienna instead of Rome. If Kesselring failed to hold the Gothic Line, he was unlikely to be able to hold the much longer line of the River Po and would be forced to fall back to a line based on the Alps and perhaps

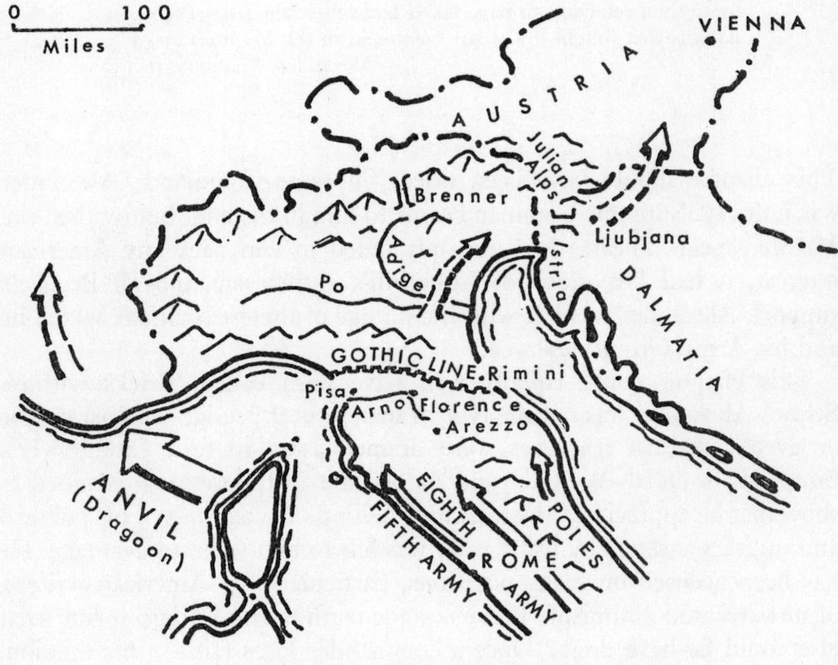

57 Exploitation of 'Diadem', Summer 1944

the Adige River. The combined effects of the Russian summer offensive, Eisenhower's operations in Normandy, and Alexander's own actions in Italy might well make an advance upon the Austrian capital, through the Ljubjana Gap in the Julian Alps, a practical possibility.

Alexander's disappointments, which reduced his hopes of marching on Vienna to unattainable dreams, came in waves which corresponded with the periods of Eisenhower's deepest frustration and Churchill's and

Brooke's consequent alarms that the war might go on beyond the limits of British resources and endurance.

As Rome fell Alexander signalled Churchill setting out his future intentions:

> I have now two highly organised and skilful Armies capable of carrying out large scale attacks and mobile operations in the closest co-operation. Morale is irresistibly high as a result of successes and the whole forms one closely articulated machine capable of carrying out assaults and rapid exploitation in the most difficult terrain. Neither the Apennines nor even the Alps should prove a serious obstacle to their enthusiasm. (Despatches, p. 2931)

He went on to recommend the cancellation of 'Anvil' and the concentration of all Allied resources in the Mediterranean on the exploitation of 'Diadem'. His signal is an accurate description of the feelings in his armies at the beginning of June. Their great victory had given them a cohesion and confidence reminiscent of Eighth Army's heyday in the desert. They were a winning team and knew that they had the measure of the Germans. All the uncertainties and animosities engendered by the winter stalemate at Anzio and Cassino had fallen away like a discarded winter cloak with the return of spring. Even Clark, who was commander designate for 'Anvil', and who never enjoyed his subordination to British command—though he admired and respected Alexander—now backed his Commander-in-Chief in opposing the diversion of troops to the American inspired 'Anvil' landing in Southern France. In his diary he says:

> I have known, of course, that the VI Corps would go [to 'Anvil'] as soon as we had captured Rome. I also knew that most of the French Expeditionary Corps would leave me. I assume that the Combined Chiefs of Staff making these decisions know what they are doing. . . . I am convinced, however, that their decision was made long ago and without realizing the great success the Fifth and Eighth Armies were to have in Italy. The morale of the Fifth is sky-high. Now is the time to exploit our success. Yet, in the middle of this success, I lose two corps headquarters and seven divisions. It just does not make sense. (Clark, pp. 357–8)

The 'Diadem' victory gave Alexander renewed confidence in himself and in his armies. It was *his* victory won without Montgomery or Tedder at his elbow. It repudiated all the rude things said about his generalship by Churchill during the winter battles, and swept away any depression, born of mental and physical fatigue, which the winter had left. He felt himself strong enough to take a leading part in the formulation of Allied strategy which, up till then, he had implemented without question. The plan he was putting to the Chiefs of Staff was his, based on the detailed and meticulous planning carried out by Harding and the Army Group staff. Alexander knew that there was no hope of destroying Kesselring's Army Group south of the Gothic Line by sweeping manoeuvres because the country was far too obstructed by mountains and rivers. Even Brooke found it difficult to understand the problem:

> Alexander turned up early in the morning. . . . I told him that I felt he was missing his chances of smashing up Kesselring before he got back to the Pisa–Rimini [Gothic] Line. . . . I am afraid Alex did not like this much, but it is desirable to make him face the facts confronting him instead of his dreams of an advance on Vienna. (Bryant, *Triumph in the West*, p. 227)

The key to success lay in the rapid breach in the Gothic Line and the entry of the Allied Armies into the wide Po Valley before winter could turn it into a quagmire. Operations to the south of the Gothic could have but one purpose—to bring Alexander's main striking force as quickly as possible through the administrative desert, which he knew from his experiences during the previous autumn that Kesselring would leave behind him. All road bridges would be blown and every railway would be rooted up by the retreating German rearguards. Alexander's pursuit would have to be carried out by light forces heavily supported by sappers to reopen the routes northwards. So daunting would the logistic problems be that concentration of effort would be needed to ensure that the main striking force was brought forward opposite the most suitable sector for an assault on the Gothic Line with as little delay as possible once the Germans fell back into its defences. The correct selection of the sector for breaching was crucial to the success of the operation. There could be no two-handed punch; speed was all important and available engineer effort dictated one thrust line only.

Harding and his staff carried out an exhaustive examination of the Gothic defences and the approaches to potential breaches. There appeared to be three practicable axes of advance. The first was up the Ligurian coast from Pisa northwards. This approach would bring Alexander, like Napoleon in 1796, into the Plain of Lombardy via the passes in the lower reaches of the Ligurian Alps above Genoa. It was a narrow route, obstructed throughout by the spurs of the Apennines as they tumbled down to the narrow and sometimes non-existent coastal strip. It led, moreover, to no significant strategic objective other than a difficult entry into Southern France over land instead of by sea. The second possibility was the similar approach up the east coast from Rimini northwards into the Plain of Romagna and the Po Valley. This was topographically slightly easier in that the coastal strip was wider and the Apennine spurs were lower. Furthermore it did lead directly towards Venice, Trieste, Ljubjana and Vienna. The third approach, which Alexander decided to use, ran through the centre of the German defences and was based on the network of roads which fan outwards from Florence over the Apennines to the old cities of the Po Valley—Bologna, Imola, Faenza and Forli. This was potentially the strongest sector of the Gothic Line, but it should not be difficult to persuade Kesselring with a suitable deception plan that the

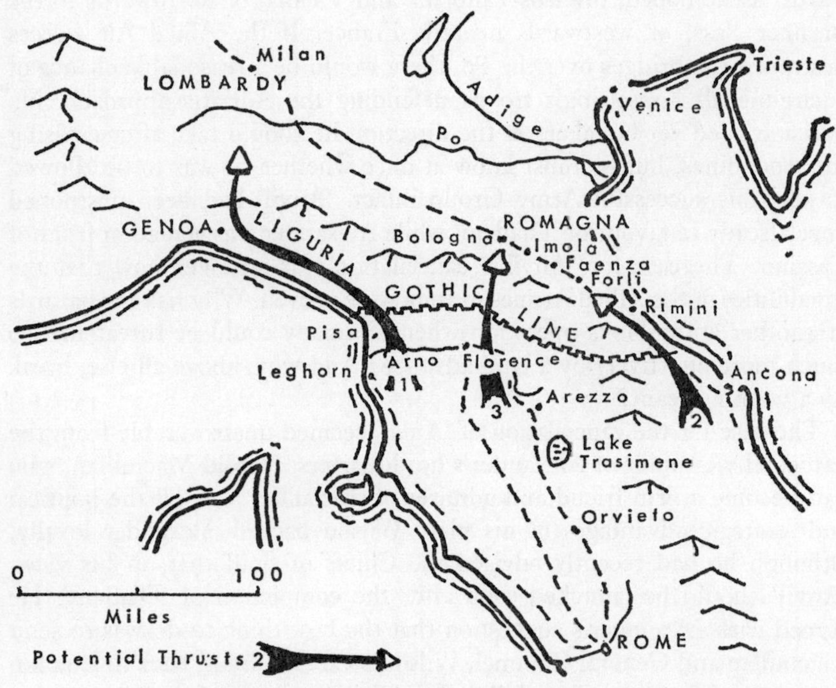

58 Plans for the destruction of the Gothic Line

main Allied effort would come along the east coast axis. He would probably depend upon the natural strength of the Apennine passes in his centre and concentrate most of his troops for the defence of the weaker eastern sector. Three further considerations favoured an assault in the centre. The Allies would be attacking with, as opposed to across, the grain of the country. That is to say they would be advancing up the spurs, up the valleys and along the rivers instead of across them as they would be doing on the coast. Provided Juin's French North African troops were available, they and the Indian divisions, which were equally at home in mountain country, could be used to clear the high ridges, while the more heavily armed and equipped British and American formations smashed their way up the valleys, using their mass of tanks and artillery and air power. The second factor was the logistic problem. It would be easier to concentrate the main striking force in the Florence area, which was a nodal point in road and rail communications, than it would be on the Adriatic coast. And finally, from the strategic point of view, arriving in the Po Valley near Bologna would give Alexander more scope for exploitation. He could press eastwards, as he hoped, towards Ljubjana and Vienna, or northwards to the Brenner Pass, or westwards towards France. If the Allied Air Forces destroyed the bridges over the Po, there would be a reasonable chance of encircling all Kesselring's troops defending the Adriatic approach. No decision need yet be taken on the direction he should take after crossing the Apennines, but he must know at once whether he was to be allowed to keep his successful Army Group intact. 'Anvil' had been postponed once already in favour of 'Diadem' while Alexander was stalled in front of Cassino. The case for 'Anvil's' cancellation was stronger now that the capabilities of the Allied Armies in Italy were proven. Why risk the hazards of another amphibious operation when Germany could be threatened so much more effectively by a land advance? And why, above all else, break up a winning team?

The case for the cancellation of 'Anvil' seemed unanswerable from the parochial viewpoint of Alexander's headquarters. Harold Macmillan, who had become a firm friend and admirer of Alexander, saw all the political and strategic advantages of his plan. Wilson backed Alexander loyally, although he had recently advised the Chiefs of Staff that, in his view, 'Anvil' should be launched soon after the completion of 'Diadem'. He agreed with Alexander's suggestion that the best thing to do was to send Macmillan and General Gammel, Wilson's Chief of Staff, back to London to present the case to Churchill and the British Chiefs of Staff.

Macmillan found that there was no need to argue with Churchill. Alexander's plan rekindled all his old enthusiasm for the Mediterranean. Macmillan records:

> I did not feel that anyone who had not been in close contact with General Alexander could sufficiently realise the growth in his authority and confidence in himself. The fact that his plan was put forward so firmly and with such a certainty of success meant more from him than from any other commander. He is not a man given to overstatement or boastful phrases.
> . . . He (Churchill) asked me to put forward the plan as I understood it. . . . It

was clear that the Chief of Air Staff was very much attracted. . . . The CIGS seemed more uncertain. . . . (Macmillan, pp. 504, 506)

Brooke could see all the difficulties which he would have to face with his American colleagues if Churchill fell hopelessly in love with Alexander's plan. It could be dressed up in the very attractive wrappings which Alexander had set out in his original signal. This had suggested that Kesselring could not hope to hold the Gothic Line unless Hitler reinforced him with some ten divisions at the expense of the Eastern or Western Fronts. If he did not provide these reinforcements, Alexander would arrive in Hitler's backyard. Whichever way the Germans chose to react, Eisenhower would benefit more by Kesselring's discomfiture than by launching another amphibious operation. Brooke knew that the Central European slant of Alexander's arguments, attractive though it was to Churchill, would be offensive to the anti-imperial sentiments of the Americans. Moreover, Brooke had his own doubts about the military viability of Alexander's plans:

June 23rd. We had a long evening of it listening to Winston's strategic arguments. In the main he was for supporting Alexander's advance on Vienna. I pointed out that, even on Alex's optimistic reckoning, the advance beyond the Pisa–Rimini line would not start till after September; namely we should embark on a campaign through the Alps in winter. It was hard to make him realise that, if we took the season of the year and the topography of the country in league against us, we should have three enemies instead of one. (Bryant, *Triumph in the West*, p. 223)

In spite of their doubts Brooke and the British Chiefs of Staff backed Alexander's plan as a better way of weakening German resistance to Eisenhower than the 'Anvil' landings. They knew that the Americans would be hard to convince, but they did not anticipate the bitterness with which their proposals were greeted in Washington. The exchange between the two capitals was perhaps the most acrimonious of any of the Anglo-American strategic arguments. In the end Brooke advised Churchill to give way in the interests of Allied unity. It was not until the last paragraph of Roosevelt's final signal that the fundamental reason for American antagonism to Alexander's plan emerged: 'Finally for purely political considerations over here (the Presidential Elections were due in November) I would never survive even a slight set-back in "Overlord" if it were known that fairly large forces had been diverted to the Balkans.'

In fairness it must be added that Marshall disliked Alexander's plan for military as well as political reasons. He was convinced that Kesselring would withdraw to the Alps, leaving Alexander punching air while Hitler dispatched Kesselring's best divisions to oppose Eisenhower. Marshall was proved wrong by events as Hitler did send the necessary reinforcements to enable Kesselring to hold the Gothic Line, but it was Alexander himself who inadvertently weakened his own case through lack of the deeper political insight needed for high level negotiations of this type. Brooke expresses this in his diary for 30 June: 'It is very unfortunate that Alex and Winston ever started their scheme about going to Vienna. This has made our task with the Americans an impossible one. . . .' A few days later Brooke makes another interesting entry:

> After finishing office work drove Alexander down to Virginia Water which gave us a good chance to talk. He is the most delightful person and most attractive, but I am afraid entirely innocent of any understanding of political methods. . . . (Bryant, *Triumph in the West*, p. 231)

In high-level strategy political motives play an essential part. Successful strategists must be able to sense national and personal prejudices. Logic alone is not enough. It is the ability to deploy those arguments which play on favourable instincts while suppressing those that touch raw nerves, which leads to success at these levels. Building a case by omission is almost as important as the soundness of the basic proposals. Such methods are alien to men of Alexander's stamp. Raising Churchill's enthusiasm for his plan on the grounds of an advance to Vienna was one thing; using the same arguments to the Americans was another. A subtler man would have highlighted the opportunities of destroying Kesselring between the Apennines and the bridgeless Po as the overt reason for cancelling 'Anvil', while using the Vienna argument covertly in discussions with Churchill. Proposals for an advance eastwards could have come later when conditions were more propitious—as they indeed became.

The debate on 'Anvil' did not end until 2 July. Meanwhile, both Fifth and Eighth Armies advanced north of Rome as quickly as German demolitions and Allied logistic problems would allow. Fifth Army made the better progress because the country on its front was more open and the German Fourteenth Army retreating before it was in greater disarray than the von Vietinghoff Tenth Army which was falling back through the foot-hills of the Apennines in front of Eighth Army. Kesselring had sacked von Mackensen after his failure to hold the Caesar Line and had replaced him with General Lemelsen. Towards the end of June German resistance began to increase as reinforcements arrived from Germany. Kesselring's first real attempt to slow Alexander's advance was on a line running east and west through Lake Trasimene. Warning orders had already reached Alexander's troops for the withdrawal of the divisions for 'Anvil'. These had a very unsettling effect at all levels of command, causing an unmistakable lack of enthusiasm and reluctance to take risks in pressing the northward advance. In his orders to his army commanders Alexander had said: 'The Commander-in-Chief authorises Army Commanders to take extreme risks to secure the vital areas mentioned in paragraph 2 above (Florence–Arezzo) before the enemy can reorganise or be reinforced.' But by the end of June he was forced to report:

> The ghost of 'Anvil' hangs heavily over the battle front. For example the Americans have been ordered to send back 517 Regimental Combat Team and 117 Cavalry Reconnaissance Squadron which are actually in contact with the enemy. . . . The French do not appear to be putting their hearts into the present operations and the reason is undoubtedly because they have their eyes turned in another direction (France). . . . Eighth Army are not directly concerned with 'Anvil' but as long as there is doubt and uncertainty about the future so long will there be moral weakening. Armies have a very delicate sense and they are beginning to look over their shoulders. You will no doubt remember the biblical quotation 'If the trumpet give an uncertain sound who shall prepare himself for battle?' (Despatches, p. 2934)

After ten days' sharp fighting on the Trasimene Line, Kesselring fell back through a series of delaying positions to his next line covering the important road and rail junction of Arezzo. On the same day the Chiefs of Staff directive reached Wilson ordering 'Anvil' under a new code-name 'Dragoon', which enabled Churchill to mouth a number of quips about being 'dragooned by the Americans'. Alexander was instructed to release Truscott's and Juin's Corps which had played such decisive roles in 'Diadem', but he was told that his task remained the destruction of the German forces in Italy! This was the hardest cut of all. He was being asked to do the same job shorn of seven of his best divisions, including the French mountain troops on whom he was depending for his plan to burst through the centre of the Gothic Line.

Alexander may have been ill-advised in the way he deployed his arguments against 'Anvil', but he did not blind himself to the possibility of the failure of his case. While the arguments went on, Harding was elaborating alternative plans, but these plans could not prevent a loss of momentum in the Allied advance. Hitler had done what Alexander had predicted. Kesselring received the equivalent of seven new divisions almost simultaneously with Alexander's loss of an identical number. Arezzo did not fall until 15 July, and neither Army managed to close up to the River

Arno between Pisa and Florence until the first week of August. On 15 August, the date Alexander had estimated for his entry into Bologna, 'Dragoon' was launched against negligible resistance on the Riviera coast. It was little consolation to Alexander that Marshall's fears had been reversed. 'Dragoon' hit air while Alexander's men found themselves faced once more with a superior number of German divisions. The score was 20 Allied attacking 22 German divisions. He made no protest, but he did make a sudden and radical change in his plans to breach the Gothic Line.

At an impromptu conference with Leese and Harding, which took place in the shade of an aircraft's wing on Orvieto airfield, Alexander accepted a proposal put forward by Leese, who pointed out that the whole basis of the original plan had been destroyed by the withdrawal of Juin's mountain troops. Eighth Army had become the predominant force and would have to provide the bulk of the assault troops as Fifth Army had been reduced to a mere handful of five divisions, Eighth Army was quite unsuited to operations in the central sector and would prefer to attack on the Adriatic coast where its superiority in guns and tanks could be used to better effect. Leese saw another advantage in this change of plan. He would not have to coordinate his operations so closely with Clark—a thing that he found far from easy. The penalty, which would have to be paid for such a major change of plan, would be loss of time. Eighth Army could not be moved over the Apennines overnight. It would take a fortnight to three weeks to redeploy across the narrow passes of the central Apennine Range east of Arezzo. In addition, the cover plan would have to be reversed at this late stage. Kesselring would have to be persuaded that the real attack was coming in the centre. It would not be easy to disguise the purpose of the heavy traffic of Eighth Army's redeployment eastwards.

Alexander decided that the loss of three weeks valuable summer weather must be accepted. It was no use forcing a subordinate to undertake a battle plan in which he had no confidence. Furthermore, it would allow Alexander to revert to his two-handed strategy. Eighth Army would cross the Apennines in the greatest secrecy, while Fifth Army created a show of force in the centre. Eighth Army would then attack the Gothic defences on the east coast, and as soon as most of Kesselring's reserves had been drawn into the fight, Clark, reinforced by British and Commonwealth units from Eighth Army, would try to breach the centre. Thereafter Alexander would make progress by forcing Kesselring to shuttle his reserves to and fro between the two Army sectors under the watchful and destructive presence of the Allied air forces. If Plan 'Olive', as Leese's new plan was called, could be implemented by the last week of August, there would be just one month in which to destroy the Gothic Line before the weather was due to break in September. One month was all too short a time in which to breach such a position, which had been prepared and strengthened for so many months in ideal defensive country. Again Alexander could be accused of over-optimism; but again the rebuttal must be, what else could he do? He could not sit down and do nothing; or use a plan which his principal Army Commander felt he could not implement. The unexpected might easily happen. A sudden German national collapse was already being considered a possibility. Churchill, in a message to General Smuts after the 'Dragoon' landings makes a point

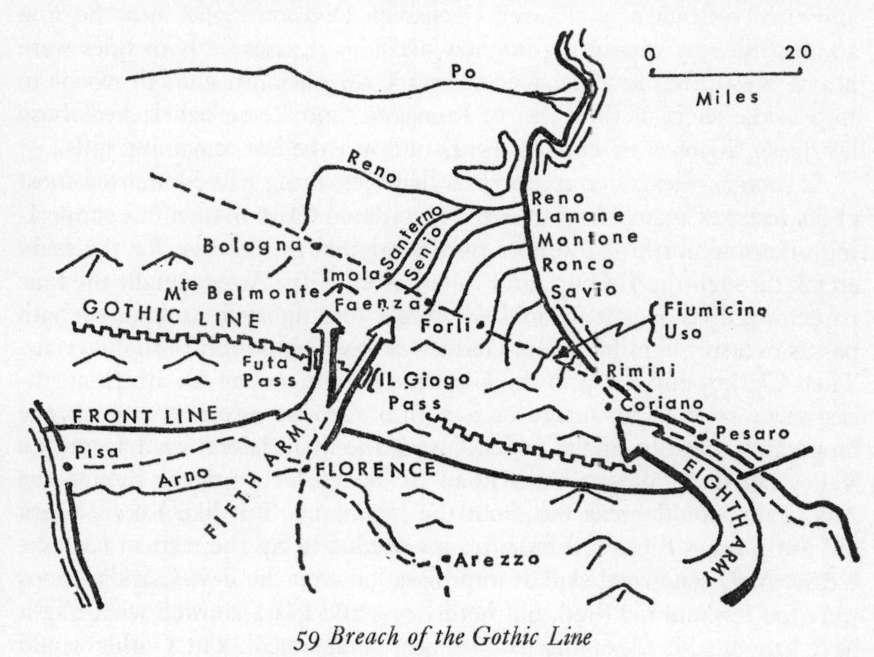

59 Breach of the Gothic Line

which illustrates how impossible it would have been for Alexander not to have attempted the breach of the Gothic Line with numerical inferiority so late in the season.

> ... I hope to turn and break the Gothic Line, break into the Po Valley, and ultimately advance by Trieste and the Ljubjana Gap to Vienna. *Even if the war came to an end at an early date I have told Alexander to be ready for a dash with armoured cars.* (Churchill, *Triumph and Tragedy*, p. 91)

The transfer of Eighth Army to the Adriatic coast was a model of staff work. It was accomplished over poor mountain roads in complete secrecy.

Eighth Army rolled forward over its start line in the 'Olive' offensive on 25 August. It was some days before Kesselring appreciated that a major offensive had opened on the Adriatic coast. The Gothic defences were overrun almost unmanned and it was not until Leese was well over half way through the remaining mountain ridges which blocked his way to Rimini that Kesselring managed to concentrate enough of his mobile divisions on the Coriano Ridge to check him. The First and Second Battles of Coriano were as hard fought as any in the Italian campaign. Many of the Eighth Army's old opponents appeared in the fray: von Lüttwitz's 26 Panzer Division, then Fries' 29 Panzer Grenadier Division and finally Baade's 90 Panzer Grenadier Division came into the line accompanied by supporting infantry divisions. Losses on both sides were heavy. Kesselring had managed to scrape together just enough troops to stop Leese short of the Plain of Romagna; and Leese had lacked those few fresh troops with which to break out over the last remaining hills.

As soon as Alexander appreciated that Kesselring had committed most of his reserves against Eighth Army he ordered Clark to open his supporting offensive north of Florence on the original axis chosen for the main attack through the Il Giogo and Futa Passes. Fifth Army caught the lone parachute division left to hold the sector unsupported, and seized both passes in heavy fighting before German reserves could return to intervene. Then Clark found a gap in the German line and swung his attack north-eastwards to take advantage of it with a surprise advance through the mountains towards Imola, which lies on the main lateral road in the Po Valley between Bologna and Rimini. It looked for a time as though the Americans would break out from the mountains, but like Leese, Clark did not possess those few fresh troops needed to tip the tactical balance. Kesselring's renowned skill at improvisation won the day. Clark's troops were too few and too tired, but both Leese and Clark showed what might have happened if Alexander had not been 'dragooned'. The Gothic would have been attacked six weeks earlier with two extra corps and before Kesselring had absorbed his reinforcements. The result cannot be in doubt.

The margin by which Alexander failed to break through the Northern Apennines with his very reduced forces was slender indeed. Had the fine balance between success and failure been swayed in his favour, he would have been applauded for his great flexibility of mind and quickness in seizing upon Leese's suggestion of switching Eighth Army across to the Adriatic. All that is remembered about the Gothic battles is the heavy losses suffered by both Allied Armies for so little reward. Leese took

Rimini on 21 September and emerged in the Plain of the Romagna as the autumn rains broke, turning what had been excellent tank going, which his armoured formations had been looking forward to for so long, into a lush green agricultural paradise and a military nightmare. The plain, from which clouds of dust were to billow up under the tank tracks next spring, was soft and waterlogged. It was criss-crossed with irrigation ditches, now full of water, and traversed by a series of rivers flowing down from the Apennines in a generally north-easterly direction to empty their flood waters into the River Reno and the Adriatic. In summer these ditches and rivers were fordable and the meadows were hard, but as soon as the rains broke the Po Valley lost all its charm for an attacking army. Alexander had reached it too late.

In North-West Europe Montgomery was suffering a similar reverse, for quite different reasons, at Arnhem. The consequences reverberated throughout the Allied command structure and spread to the Italian Theatre, upsetting Alexander's plans for a second time. Brooke and Montgomery were convinced that Eisenhower's handling of the advance into Germany was fundamentally faulty. Both believed that concentration of effort should be the key-note of Allied plans to force Germany to her knees as quickly as possible. Brooke knew from his central position in Whitehall how essential it was to bring the war to an end quickly before Britain's life blood drained away. Montgomery was more interested in military efficiency and believed that Eisenhower, who lacked battle experience, but who was a master of high politico-military direction, was unsuited to command land operations in person. Montgomery argued that Eisenhower should be given an Army Deputy who would control the land battle as Alexander had done for him in Tunisia and Sicily. Thus the idea was generated of bringing Alexander back from Italy to assume command of the three Allied Army Groups advancing on Germany commanded by Montgomery, Bradley and Devers.

These pressures were, as yet, unknown to Alexander who had his eyes fixed on Vienna in spite of the 'Anvil' rebuff. 'Dragoon' had altered the strategic situation in one welcome but unexpected way as far as he was concerned. There was no longer any point in considering an advance westwards when he reached the Po Valley. The American Chiefs of Staff accepted that the only direction worth contemplating was north-eastwards via Venice and Trieste to the lowest point in the great Alpine curtain—the Ljubjana Gap in the Julian Alps. Alexander's task remained the prevention of German withdrawals from Italy to help other hard-pressed

German fronts. He could not succeed in this task unless he threatened an objective vital to Germany. There was also the question of time. If the war was to be ended quickly, then pressure must be maintained throughout the winter. Alexander's problem was to decide how this could best be done on the Italian front. Battering away at the last few ridges which stopped Fifth Army from entering the Po Valley, or fighting over the series of river lines facing Eighth Army had just as few attractions as frontal assaults on the Gustav Line had during the previous winter. Some other solution had to be found. The sea again presented possibilities.

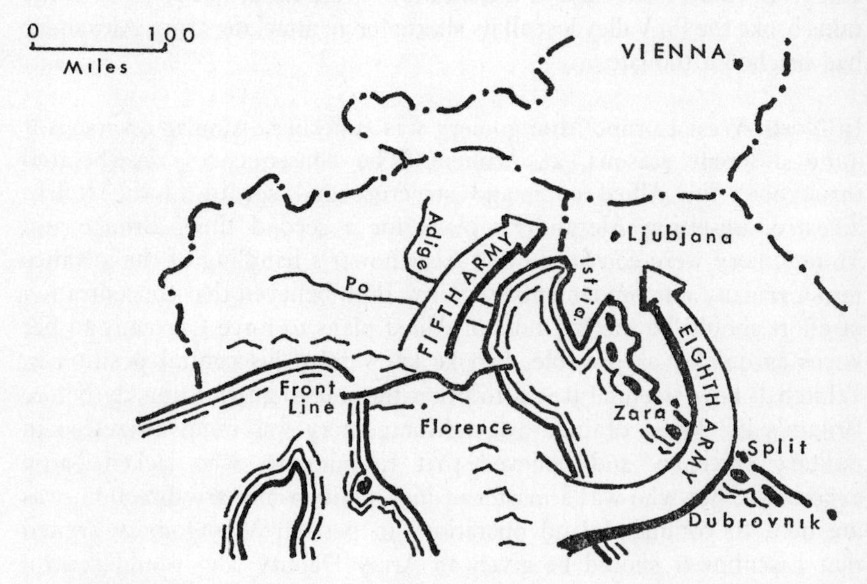

60 Alexander's Plan for his advance on Ljubjana via Venetia and Dalmatia

In retrospect the plans, which flowed from Alexander's headquarters, had an air of unreality about them; but, at the time, they seemed far from unreal. With Leese already in the Po Valley and Clark just a few ridges off, Alexander believed he could reach the Adige by winter if he pressed on resolutely during the autumn, using his two-handed strategy to wear Kesselring down. Once on the Adige, the front would be narrow enough to be held by Fifth Army alone. Eighth Army could be shipped across the Adriatic to join up with Tito's partisans for an advance northwards up the Dalmatian coast from Dubrovnik, Split and Zara to take the Istrian Peninsula and the Ljubjana Gap in a wide enveloping movement timed to coincide with an advance by Fifth Army over the Adige. Alexander acknowledged that this operation would not be practical unless three things happened: the Germans fell back to the Adige; the Italian Theatre was not ordered to give up any more troops; and the Chiefs of Staff provided the necessary shipping for Eighth Army. The first prerequisite was less far-fetched than it may seem, because it was known from Intelligence sources that Kesselring had been pressing Hitler to allow him to put a plan called 'Autumn Mist' into effect for some time with the aim of shortening the German line in Italy, thus creating stronger reserves. Hitler refused, otherwise Kesselring would have withdrawn to what the Germans called the Venetian Line, which was based on the Adige. The other two prerequisites were the subject of renewed Allied debate in which Alexander was to see the relentless erosion of his plans by events as well as high level decisions.

In order to encourage Kesselring to put 'Autumn Mist' into effect, Alexander decided to reopen his offensive. Eighth Army, now under command of McCreery,* struck first with a series of operations which lasted throughout the autumn and can be called the Battles of the Rivers. Eighth Army crossed the River Uso at the end of September and in the succeeding weeks forced its way over the Fiumicino, the Savio, the Ronco, the Lamone, and finally came to rest for the winter on the Senio (see fig. 59, p. 303). Each crossing was an epic of endurance for the men who took part: there was always one more river, one more irrigation ditch, one more flooded field to cross at the end of each operation. The days became interminable and the nights all too short. Fifth Army joined the battle again early in October with a successful advance towards Bologna. The Americans reached Monte Belmonte, a few kilometres short of the Bologna–Rimini Road by the last week of October. The last remaining ridges were held by some of the best troops in the German Army—Baade's 90 Panzer Grenadier and Heydrick's 1st Parachute Divisions who were no more prepared to give way than they had been at Cassino nine months before. The men of Fifth Army remember the ridge after ridge, the steep slippery slopes, the drizzling mist around them and the mud under foot, which were the mountain counterparts of Eighth Army's rivers, ditches and quagmires.

Alexander spent much of his time moving about the front watching conditions and the state of men's morale more than most generals have ever managed to do while still controlling policy at the highest level. He was able to do this because he had full confidence in his Chief of Staff and could leave him to deal with the day to day affairs. His Army Group

* General Leese went to Burma to command Fourteenth Army.

remained a happy team in spite of the foulness of conditions and the disappointments which he and they had suffered in the last few months. He knew that this would cease to be so if he drove his Armies too hard and continued operations too long without any real reward. He set 15 November as the date by which all operations should stop if the Germans had not put 'Autumn Mist' into effect by then. Wherever the Armies stood on that date would become the Allied front line for the winter and the start line for the next spring offensive. Divisions would be withdrawn to rest, refit and retrain in succession. Eighth Army would place an emphasis on amphibious operations, while Fifth Army would master mountain and river-crossing techniques so that both Armies would be ready as soon as the Chiefs of Staff agreed to the 'Dalmatian' operation. As the weeks went by the chances of Kesselring implementing 'Autumn Mist' dwindled. Unless Alexander made one more concerted effort, Fifth Army would be forced to winter on the bleak Apennine hill sides instead of in the relative comfort of the towns of the Po Valley. He extended the date for ending operations, but, by the turn of the year and the onset of winter, Fifth Army was still in the hills. Alexander stopped all offensive operations on 30 December and both Armies went over onto the defensive six weeks later than he had intended.

While Eighth Army's Battle of the Rivers and Fifth Army's advance on Bologna were in progress, the strategic debate on the best way to end the war quickly went on in London, Washington and Caserta. Brooke finally abandoned supporting Alexander's projects and joined the American school of thought on Mediterranean strategy. He could not see how Alexander could accomplish anything significant in time to effect the main issues in the West. Brooke preferred to expend his energies on trying to persuade the Americans to abandon Eisenhower's policy of an advance on a broad front which he had come to realise was an article of military faith as far as the Americans were concerned. In his struggle to win a change of policy and so speed the end of the war, Brooke saw no point in irritating his American colleagues by pressing the Mediterranean's case as well. Churchill, on the other hand, remained open to Alexander's suggestions. The Dalmatian idea fired his enthusiasm yet again; and the thought of leaving his favourite general without a decisive part to play in the final phase of the war worried him. Unbeknown to Brooke he had dispatched a personal signal to Roosevelt begging him to send Alexander three new American divisions direct from the United States to strengthen Fifth Army and so make the Dalmatian plan a practical proposition. This approach met with the rebuff it deserved. The United States Chiefs of

Staff advised the President that they saw no reason to alter the agreed policy. It was up to the Supreme Commander, Mediterranean, to decide whether he had sufficient resources in his theatre to carry out the Dalmatian operation or not. Wilson decided that he did not. He was short of both men and ammunition. 'Overlord' had enjoyed priority in the allocation of resources for so long that the Italian Theatre's reinforcement camps were almost empty and few new drafts of men were expected from the United Kingdom or from the United States. Wilson had been forced to authorise the disbandment of one British division and several battalions to keep the rest of Alexander's units up to minimum battle strength. All theatres were short of artillery ammunition because consumption exceeded production. Allied commanders preferred to use shell rather than lives. Before Alexander had authorised the last attempt to extricate Fifth Army from the mountains before winter, Clark had reported having barely enough artillery ammunition for ten days intense action and McCreery fifteen days. Wilson advised the Chiefs of Staff on 22 November that he would have to confine Mediterranean operations to Italy. The Dalmatian operation was impracticable with the resources available. Only by husbanding men and ammunition for the next three months could he hope to give Alexander the support he needed for operations in the Po Valley in the Spring.

This was the last major decision taken by Wilson in the Mediterranean. Three weeks later Alexander was appointed Supreme Commander in his place. The illness and subsequent death of Field Marshal Sir John Dill in Washington caused the reshuffle of the command pack. Wilson replaced Dill. Churchill would have liked Alexander to have undertaken both Supreme Command and command of the Allied Armies in Italy, but Brooke pointed out that this was the organisation which the British had been objecting to for so long in North-West Europe. Eisenhower had been trying to act as Supreme and Land Force Commander with unfortunate results. Churchill would undermine the whole case for placing an Army Deputy under Eisenhower for the final phases of the war against Germany. Brooke did not win the ensuing argument very easily. Much to his annoyance, Churchill went behind his back and signalled Alexander direct, asking for his views. Brooke makes a revealing entry in his diary of 17 November during this argument:

> . . . Winston was still confused about the system of Command in Italy and the Mediterranean. Having tried hard to warp the whole organisation while Wilson was Supreme Commander and Alex commanding the Group of Armies so as to try and put Wilson in the shade for the benefit of Alexander, now he

places Alexander as Supreme Commander he is frightened lest his powers should be restricted in the manner he has endeavoured to reduce those of Wilson! We had to meet at 4 p.m. and, after laborious explanations, I at last got him to accept matters as they are. (Bryant, *Triumph in the West*, p. 333)

Brooke won the contest with the Prime Minister in the end. On 12 December, Alexander became Supreme Commander; Clark succeeded him, reverting to the title of Commander 15 Army Group; and Truscott was brought back from France to command Fifth Army, much to Alexander's delight.

Promotion to Supreme Command had come to Alexander too late. 'Dragoon' had killed his chances of winning a victory of first magnitude; Dalmatia was closed to him; and the Greek situation was about to weaken still further his abilities to achieve anything worthwhile. It was like being promoted chairman of a company about to go into liquidation. In some ways it was worse because Alexander soon found out on a visit which he paid to London before assuming Supreme Command that his transfer to North-West Europe as Eisenhower's Deputy was still a live issue. This possibility would have distracted any lesser man. Fortunately the counter-distraction of the Greek Civil War soon engulfed him in its affairs.

Harold Macmillan sets the stage for the Greek interlude with his description of Alexander's arrival in Athens on 11 December, the day before he officially assumed Supreme Command.

I watched with interest how quickly the Field Marshal made himself aware of the rather disagreeable facts. Actually, the position could hardly have been worse. We had been taken by surprise, hoping up to the last that things would be settled, and we had underestimated the military skill, determination and power of the insurgents. (Macmillan, p. 607)

Wilson had been directing the re-establishment of the exiled Greek Government in Athens since the Germans started to withdraw from Greece in September. The original Allied landing force under General Scobie had consisted of two under-strength British brigades and the Greek Mountain Brigade, which had recently acquitted itself well in the battle for Rimini under Leese's command. The exiled Greek Government was not received with any great enthusiasm on its return. As the political situation deteriorated, Scobie's force was reinforced with two more brigades. His troops were initially deployed more to help the distribution of relief supplies, and the maintenance of local order until the Greek Police could be re-established, than to uphold the Papandreou Government in office against the will of the Communist EAM organisation, backed as it was by the only real power in Greece—the ELAS divisions. These Communist units had been formed from the Communist-controlled guerilla bands which had been fighting the Germans throughout the occupation and, at the same time, liquidating all other guerilla forces. At the beginning of December the Communists gave up their pretence of trying to cooperate with Papandreou in the formation of a truly representative Greek Government and set about seizing power by force, using the ELAS divisions. They occupied most of the Greek capital, pinning Scobie's small Athens garrison and the Papandreou Government into a confined area around the British Embassy, cut off from the Port of Pireas and the airfield through which reinforcements and supplies must come.

At Churchill's request Alexander flew with Macmillan to Athens on 11 December to take control of the situation and to re-establish the British position and, if possible, that of the Greek Government. They had an exciting ride from the airfield to the British Embassy in armoured cars which came under rebel small-arms fire as they sped through the city streets. The situation Alexander found took him back 25 years to his days with Talents in Riga. Many elements of the situation were remarkably similar. The Communist forces were ill-equipped, ill-trained and ill-assorted by regular standards. There were the same extreme right-wing elements, a mass of 'middle-roaders' and 'fence-sitters', and a band of convinced but inept liberals, as there had been in the Baltic Provinces. The only element missing was von der Goltz's German Frei Corps whose place was unfortunately taken by the British occupation forces. They, like von der Goltz's men, were the only properly equipped and professionally commanded force in the country, although their motives could hardly have been more different. The last thing Scobie's men wanted to do was to get embroiled in Greek politics or to settle in Greece. Their task was to hold the ring until the Greeks could settle their own domestic differences. Scobie's aim was to leave a stable peaceful country governed by and protected by Greeks in a way that suited the majority of the Greeks.

Macmillan sets out Alexander's short appreciation of the situation which he gave verbally to Sir Harold Leeper, the British Ambassador:

> You are in a grave situation. Your seaport is cut off, your airport can only be reached by tank or armoured car, you are outnumbered, your dumps are surrounded and you have three days ammunition. I can put that right in time, but it may take a fortnight. It will need two fighting divisions to come from Italy. The heavy stuff will have to be landed on the open beaches of Phaleron and December is not the best month for that. (Macmillan, p. 605)

Alexander knew from his Riga experiences that nothing could be achieved politically until the military situation was defused. This could best be done by firm measures. He ordered two divisions to be flown in from Italy, using every available transport aircraft. Scobie could not deal with the politico-military situation and, at the same time, command a major tactical battle involving a corps of British troops, so Alexander ordered General Hawkesworth to fly with his X (British) Corps headquarters on light scales to Athens to direct operations against the ELAS divisions.

Alexander had judged the position exactly. Hawkesworth re-established the military situation, teaching the ELAS divisions that they could not resist regular troops in a pitched battle. The ELAS men soon lost heart and fell back from Athens, but the political situation remained unstable. Alexander, working closely with Macmillan and Leeper, persuaded Churchill to bring pressure to bear on the exiled Greek King in London to appoint Archbishop Damiskinos as Regent to give all Greeks an acceptable focus for their national loyalties. The culmination of these political negotiations and of Hawkesworth's military successes was the arrival of Churchill himself in Athens on Christmas day, accompanied by Anthony Eden and Alexander, for plenary political discussions at the highest level with both the Communist and anti-Communist leaders in an effort to bring the civil war to an end. Alexander had temporarily defused the bomb and hoped to be able to move his two divisions back to Italy in time for his Spring offensive.

While the Greek crisis was diverting Alexander's attention, two events were taking place which were to pile further indignities on the Italian front and disrupt Alexander's operational plans for a third time. Eisenhower had been surprised and caught off balance by von Rundstedt's Ardennes offensive. Hitler's last gamble in the West did not succeed, but it shook the fabric of the Allied High Command more than anyone would have liked to confess at the time. The strategic planners began to look round for battle-experienced reinforcements with which to build up Eisenhower's forces for a major effort to overthrow Nazi Germany in the early spring of 1945. Staff calculations showed that if the Allies wished to build up a decisive level of superiority to deliver a *coup de grâce*, either Alexander or Eisenhower would have to provide reinforcements for the other. A choice would have to be made between them. Even Churchill agreed that it was Alexander who would have to make the sacrifice and send troops to Eisenhower.

28 The Gothic line: Leese, Harding and Alexander conferring near one of the Panther turrets in the Gothic Defences

MILITARY ANTI-CLIMAX

29 Arrival in Athens: Alexander getting out of the armoured vehicle which carried him from the airfield to the British Embassy

30 Looking for peace: the Christmas meeting in Athens (*l. to r.:* Churchill Archbishop Damaskinos, Alexander, Macmillan and Scobie)

31 Victory: Montgomery, Churchill, Alexander and Eden on the reviewing stand at the British Victory Parade in Berlin, 22 July 1945

The second factor was the opening of the great Russian winter offensive of 1944–45 which brought Malinovsky and Tolbukin into Budapest on 13 February barely 150 miles from Vienna. Even if Alexander had been allowed to retain all his forces, he could not have forestalled the Russians in the Austrian capital as long as Kesselring obeyed Hitler's orders to fight it out south of the Po. It came as no surprise to Alexander when he flew to Malta for the pre-Yalta meeting of the British and American Chiefs of Staff to be told by Brooke that he was to lose three more divisions immediately and two more later when the Greek situation allowed their withdrawal. The Canadian Government had been hoping for some time to concentrate all Canadian forces under the 1st Canadian Army in Montgomery's 21st Army Group, and so Alexander agreed that the three divisions of Burns' 1st Canadian Corps were the obvious candidates for transfer. The move of the Canadian Corps out of Italy was set in train at once, reducing Alexander's forces to their lowest ebb. For his spring offensive, the plans for which he had submitted to the Chiefs of Staff in January, he would have 17 divisions with which to defeat 19 German divisions under Kesselring. There was, however, one meagre consolation. He knew, at last, where he stood. The task given him in Malta remained substantially the same as it had been ever since Salerno:

> Within the limits of the forces remaining available to you . . . you should do your utmost, by means of such limited offensive action as may be possible and by the skilful use of cover and deception plans, to contain the German forces now in Italy and prevent their withdrawal to other fronts. (*Grand Strategy*, vi, p. 95)

Alexander thought he knew where he stood in another context. The Rundstedt offensive had reraised the question of a land force deputy for Eisenhower. The proposal was talked out again and died away because such a move could only upset the delicate balance of the Anglo-US chain of command around the world. Had it not been for Montgomery's habit of continually harping on the unsoundness of the chain of command, this intractable problem would never have been resurrected. Unfortunately it was not to be the last time that the Commander of the 21st Army Group would become restive on the subject. For the moment the question was dormant. George Marshall was adamant that there would be no British land force deputy under Eisenhower, so Alexander felt himself entirely free to plan his last great battle which he would be fighting with fewer troops than he had had under his command at any time since Wadi Akarit/El Guettar.

The issue of Alexander's move to France as Eisenhower's deputy was not settled finally until the beginning of March when Churchill wrote to Alexander to tell him that he was to stay in the Mediterranean. Arthur Bryant records on Brooke's behalf:

> . . . as Montgomery had now declared himself in perfect accord with SHAEF (Eisenhower's headquarters), it seemed better to leave him in the Mediterranean where the Greek situation, the delicate relations with Tito and the Yugoslav partisans and the possibility of a new offensive in Italy all made his presence as Supreme Commander essential. 'I know' he (Churchill) wrote 'that you will adhere to your becoming attitude of serving wherever you are ordered and discharging whatever duties are assigned to you.' To which Alexander replied 'You already know that my only wish is to serve where I am most useful and feeling that way, I am well content.' (Bryant, *Triumph in the West*, p. 426)

The last battle in Italy, which was fought from 9 April to 2 May, was a masterpiece, reflecting all Alexander's long and varied military experience. His subordinates were, like Napoleon's Marshals, men who had come a long way with him through varying periods of success and failure, triumph and defeat, and all the many stresses and strains of war which go to build up and strengthen a great military team. Clark, whom he had grown to like and trust, and who had in return mirrored these feelings, handled the details of the battle for him. McCreery, his old Chief of Staff from El Alamein to Tunis and the commander of X (British) Corps throughout the major part of the Italian campaign, commanded his right hand—the Eighth Army. And Truscott, who had won his spurs as a Corps Commander at Anzio, commanded his left—the Fifth Army. Within Eighth Army, John Harding, his most recent Chief of Staff and co-author of 'Diadem', commanded XIII (British) Corps—the main breaching force, which was to tear apart the German defences on the Senio and so create the situation which led to the destruction of the German armies in Italy.

Alexander has described his last great set-piece battle succintly in his despatches:

> Indeed the last battle in Italy was as hard fought as the first. I was not faced with a broken and disintegrating army, nor was the outcome influenced in any degree by demoralization or lack of supplies on the German side. It was a straightforward military operation which, by first enveloping the enemy's left wing in a classic outflanking manoeuvre and then breaking through with a sudden blow his weakened centre, drove him against the Po and annihilated him there. (Despatches, p. 2959)

It was not only a classic battle; it was a classic 'Alexander' battle based on the two-handed punch. Thorough planning and careful training and rehearsal, spread over three months while reserves of men and ammunition were built up, ensured that the troops were launched with an optimum chance of success. Artillery fire plans and air bombardment programmes were based on extensive experience and incorporated many novel features. No man advanced to the attack without his opponent having suffered his full share of the Allies' material superiority. The deception and cover plans, mentioned by the Chiefs of Staff, were as simple and yet as effective as ever in confusing von Vietinghoff, who had recently taken over from

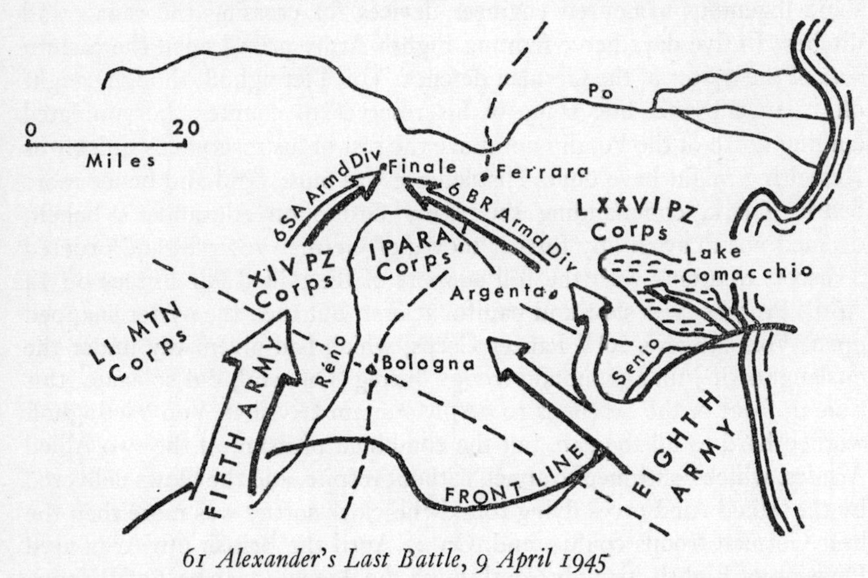

61 Alexander's Last Battle, 9 April 1945

Kesselring on the latter's promotion to Supreme Command in the West. His mobile divisions were caught moving eastwards to repel a non-existent landing on the Venetian coast when the storm broke south of the Po on 9 April.

Alexander's last battle was perhaps the most intricate and complex of all, but he had a correspondingly experienced team. In essence the deception plan suggested an amphibious landing on the Venetian coast north of the Po, which would be launched in conjunction with an assault by Eighth Army from the south towards the Po at Ferrara. Fifth Army was depicted as being too weak to launch more than a holding attack against the deep and powerful German defences covering Bologna. The actual plan was for McCreery's Eighth Army to attack first across the Senio in a north-westerly direction just north of the main Rimini–Bologna road. As soon as the German reserves were fully committed to stopping Eighth Army, Truscott would open Fifth Army's attack well west of Bologna in the power-drive style which he had used at Anzio. If all went well, the two Allied Armies would join hands on the Po due north of Bologna, encircling a substantial proportion of von Vietinghoff's best troops who were holding the southern and eastern approaches to the city.

Alexander's final offensive ran as near to the original concept as any major battle is ever likely to do. Eighth Army breached the Senio defences, using a closely coordinated air and artillery support plan, together with some ingenious armoured engineer devices for crossing the canals and ditches. In five days fierce fighting Eighth Army prized open the eastern side of the oyster of the German defence. Von Vietinghoff, though caught off balance by sending some of his reserves to counter the simulated landing north of the Po, did not move the rest of his reserves as quickly as Kesselring might have done. His defence was more rigid and hence more brittle. Clark, commanding the Army Group on Alexander's behalf, decided not to await any further moves of German reserves and ordered Truscott to attack with the full support of the Allied Air Forces on 14 April. Progress was slow and painful at first, but then the oyster snapped open. Von Senger's XIV Panzer Corps, which had given way under the onslaughts of Juin's mountain troops during 'Diadem', did so again, this time in front of the excellent 10 (US) Mountain Division. Von Vietinghoff worked hard to fill the gap, but the combined pressure of the two Allied Armies, which continued to attack without respite, and the blows delivered by the Allied Air Forces flying round-the-clock sorties was more than the best German troops could stand. On 22 April the British 6th Armoured Division of Eighth Army broke through the Argenta Gap east of Bologna and the South African 6th Armoured Division under Fifth Army command thrust through the breach in von Senger's line west of Bologna. Next day the two 6th Armoured Divisions joined hands at the town on the banks of the Po appropriately called Finale. Relatively few German troops escaped north-westwards. General Heydrich, the hero of Cassino, now commanding I Parachute Corps, swam the Po to escape. Von Vietinghoff's last-minute attempt to withdraw across the Po, in spite of Hitler's orders to stand and fight, was a disastrous failure. Most of Army Group 'C' died or were captured south of the river. This time Alexander's victory was complete.

For some weeks before the final battle Alexander had known that General Wolff, senior SS officer in Italy, had been trying to make contact with the Allies to negotiate the surrender of all German troops in Italy.

Negotiations were well advanced when Kesselring, who might have agreed to Wolff's proposals, was transferred to the West, leaving von Vietinghoff—a much less politically minded officer of the old school—in command of Army Group 'C'. Negotiations came to an abrupt end until von Vietinghoff himself was rebuffed by Hitler when he recommended withdrawing to the Adige. Appreciating all was lost, he authorised Wolff to reopen negotiations. General Sir William Morgan, Alexander's Army Group Chief of Staff, received the German plenipotentiaries on 28 April and agreed to a cease-fire timed for 2 May. After a number of last-minute difficulties caused by inadequate communications and by confusion in the German High Command, Army Group 'C' laid down its arms at 6 p.m. on 2 May 1945—just 32 months after Alexander had arrived in Cairo to take up Kesselring's challenge to British power in the Middle East.

When the time for the cease-fire came, Freyberg's New Zealanders had reached Trieste and other Allied formations had fanned out into all the corners of Northern Italy. Trieste was to become a thorn in Alexander's side for many weeks to come as he tried to prevent the Yugoslavs taking over Venetia Giulia. He had no desire to use force against his old ally, Marshal Tito. This was, however, part of the political problem of winning the peace which does not belong to this story.

There is one last phase of Alexander's military career which must be recorded. Brooke decided to retire as soon as possible after the war was over. He recommended Alexander as his successor as CIGS, the professional head of the British Army. It was as CIGS (designate) that Alexander went to Potsdam with Churchill:

> During that period in Berlin I used to go to the Prime Minister's villa in the evening to discuss the events of the day. It was on one of these occasions that Winston Churchill said to me: 'Let's take a stroll in the garden—there is something very important I want to talk to you about.' I was, of course, interested and intrigued. My former confidential talks with the Prime Minister had always been about military operations, and I wondered what new military adventure might be in contemplation. He said bluntly: 'Canada has asked for you to be its next Governor General. I know that Brookie wants you to succeed him as CIGS, but this is a much more important post, and I hope you will accept it. (Alexander, Memoirs, p. 159)

Thus it came about that Alexander started a new career for which he was ideally suited. He had served his Sovereign as a soldier for 35 years. Now he was to serve as his Sovereign's representative in a country which had sent so many fine men to fight under his command in Italy. It could not have been a happier choice.

12

Alexander as a Commander

> If Montgomery was the Wellington, Alexander was certainly the Marlborough of this war.
>
> Macmillan, *The Blast of War*, p. 304

An invaluable description of Alexander has been left by one of his contemporaries, Sir James Grigg, who was Permanent Under Secretary at the War Office throughout the war and who had known Alexander personally since he travelled out to India with him in 1934. Two extracts in addition to the paragraph quoted in Chapter 2 (see p. 29) build up the picture of Alexander as his own generation saw him:

> If I had to pick out his most impressive achievement I would choose the persistence to the final triumph in Italy after the Americans had made it clear more than once that they disliked the idea of any major commitment there. . . .
>
> But what was Alexander's essentially personal contribution to all this. I doubt if anybody will ever know. He believed in trusting his subordinates as much as Montgomery did; he gave them credit in full measure; it may be that he did not impress his own stamp on the plans and operations in the same decisive way as Montgomery and that he accordingly appeared to be reflecting the views of his staff rather than emitting his own ideas; he certainly had not Montgomery's flair for deliberate and planned publicity.
>
> But it is the man at the top who is blamed or superseded when things go wrong, and it is he, therefore, who is entitled to the credit when things go right. And what a balance of right over wrong Alexander has! How often has he been sent for to cope with militarily impossible situations! How often has he warded off disaster! But more than this, how many of our most sparkling triumphs have been won under his command! It is idle to go on comparing him with Montgomery. We are fortunate to have had two such commanders during this most testing of all wars. (Grigg, pp. 426–9)

But, how should we, who belong to another generation, judge him? What yard-sticks should we use in assessing his merits and his weaknesses as a military commander against the full spectrum of the history of war? What is a commander and what attributes make him great? Should he be judged by the victories he has won? Surely not: many commanders have won their nation's gratitude and affection by staving off defeat against apparently impossible odds. Should he be judged by the originality and brilliance of his concepts and manoeuvres? No: manoeuvres only become brilliant in retrospect and depend, more often than not, upon the ineptitude of the opposing commander. Or should he be judged more simply on the effect that he has on the soldiers under his command? This is, perhaps, coming nearer to the mark. Armies are nothing more than a large gathering of men, brought together and organised for the purpose of applying force on behalf of their nation or cause. They are disciplined; they are equipped; and they are trained; but each remains an individual with his own motives, desires, fears, strengths, weaknesses, abilities, loyalties, varying degrees of determination and all the other characteristics which make soldiers men, and not military automata. A commander is a man who can inspire men at every level to work together in the common cause, knowing that, in so doing, each individual may lose the thing most precious to him —his life.

There are two sides to a commander's character—his personal attributes and his military abilities. He must win men's trust in both respects. The soldier's remark when Wellington rode up during a crisis in one of the Peninsular battles, 'Here comes the long-nosed bastard who beats the French', sums up what is needed. Wellington was respected as a man for his strength of character and as a soldier for his military efficiency. But there are many variations of personal and military characteristics which are equally effective. When the two are brought together the permutations are infinite. There is no scientific formula or computer matrix by which command ability can be judged. Commanders are selected to grapple with the problems of the day; their selection is relative and particular to the generation concerned. As Sir James Grigg points out, the United Kingdom was lucky to find two men in the same generation—Alexander and Montgomery—who were so different in personality and style of command, and yet who so closely matched the needs of the hour. A Marlborough could well have failed in Alexander's shoes, or a Wellington in Montgomery's. Each is a creature of his own time and the tasks which are laid upon him. Events shape the man as much as the man shapes events. The real question that we have to ask is how nearly did Alexander match up to the requirements of his own age?

Alexander's selection from among the many able and experienced soldiers, who were commissioned between the Boer and First World Wars, owed much to his close reflection of the best traditions of the British Army. The cynic would suggest that he reflected all that the British Army would have liked others to have seen it to be—a humane body of men of unmistakable integrity and singleness of purpose; able to achieve the highest professional standards in the application of force with the greatest economy of life and human suffering; the whole being based upon the unbroken tradition of centuries of military experience in the service of Great Britain. Alexander's personal integrity, his enthusiasm for the British Army's way of soldiering, his humanity, and his wide battle experience in so many parts of the world, matched the British Army's image of itself and would have made him an attractive candidate for high command whenever he had lived. His own age fell into four distinct periods: the desperate contest of the First World War; the restless period between the wars; the disastrous opening phases of the Second World War; and finally, its triumphant last two years.

Few soldiers are professionally fortunate enough to join the Army just before a major war in which they can prove themselves and gain essential practical experience early in their careers. Alexander was lucky in this respect. He was doubly fortunate in that he enjoyed active service. Men do best at the things they like most. But the First World War was not a gentleman's war of the type that pleased the British Army. Boyish enthusiasm was not enough. To achieve and survive—a difficult thing to do in that war—he had to have an acute tactical sense. Not only did Alexander survive most of the major battles of 1914–18, he learned quickly from them and came to terms with the radical changes in warfare, enabling him to gain a reputation for constructive commonsense. He tried novel ideas, but the most lasting lesson which he learned was the need for careful planning, training and rehearsal. There could be no certainty in war, and so every plan had to be simple and methodical, and possess within it sufficient reserves of men, material and, above all, time. The greatest reserve of all, to his mind, was the wholehearted support of his men, for they could make or mar anything he undertook. The trust in his fairness and firmness was the foundation of their confidence in him and of his success as a regimental officer in the Irish Guards. When Kipling wrote the eulogy to him at the end of his regimental history (see p. 52), Alexander was still an unknown junior officer. No other commanding officer in the Irish Guards received such a mark of respect in a regiment with so many fine commanding officers. He was chosen from among his contemporaries through the ruthless selection of war, because he matched the needs of the regiment most closely.

The restless years between the wars called for different attributes. Only men with an honest liking for military service were prepared to stay in the Army at a time of such severe financial retrenchment. The twenties and thirties were years of exhaustion and disillusion in which it was hard to maintain traditional standards. For Alexander, they were years of consolidation and broadening of horizons. He and contemporaries like Brooke, Dill and Montgomery soldiered on, convinced that their country's refusal to pay even a modest defence insurance premium must lead to further demands on their professional services. The philosophy of military deterrence had not been formulated in those pre-nuclear days in the same finite form as it has today. The real professional soldiers sought and found active service around the world, doing the things their forbears had done—fighting small wars humanely and with success, providing stability in which developing people could live and trade in peace. The ability to lead men of any nation was, and still is, prized by British professional soldiers. Those who were good at it rose in the Service. Alexander showed he had a flair for such leadership. The Baltic Landeswehr which had no reason to like an interloping British officer, recognised him as a fine soldier and served him loyally in spite of the political turmoil of their native land. Later, on the North-West Frontier of India, he confirmed this flair in the Mohmand campaigns. His Baltic, Turkish and Indian experiences laid the foundations of his successful handling of his polyglot Allied Armies in Italy at the zenith of his career.

The disastrous opening phases of British wars always provide the Army with its own harsh mode of weeding out men who have risen beyond their real capabilities in peace. To be a big man in the days of disaster needs personal courage, a stout heart and a professionalism which will leaven the very unprofessional mass of a quickly raised national army. Alexander's 1st Division fought professionally in 1940, never losing cohesion and working methodically back to Dunkirk, covering chaos and confusion in its rear. Alexander had mastered fear in his early career, and knew the effects of fatigue and loss of sleep on men's judgment. He had experienced the exaggeration of difficulties and the illusions of disaster which well up in tired men's minds long before disaster has actually struck, causing the horrors of uncontrollable panic and all its subsequent disgrace. He knew from his experience in March 1918 that example is one of the surest ways of arresting panic. One good formation, acting with exaggerated steadiness, can shame others into copying its example. His 1st Division was never hustled; was rarely unrested; and reached Dunkirk, bewildered it is true, but still a fighting force. It was then that war's own selection system did its work. The turning point in Alexander's career came when Montgomery, one of the shrewdest judges of soldiers, advised Gort and Brooke to leave Alexander in command of the rearguard at Dunkirk. He became known to his country, to its politicians and to its Army as a man who could be trusted. Churchill began to build legends around his name in his quest for leaders. Brooke noted Alexander's performance. He had certainly matched the needs of Britain's darkest hour.

It is idle to speculate what would have happened if Alexander had not been sent to Burma and had remained as Eisenhower's Deputy for 'Torch'. El Alamein might never have been fought; and certainly not by Alexander and Montgomery. Burma itself might have destroyed Alexander's reputation; and, of course, he could easily have been captured when the Japanese surrounded Rangoon. Neither of these things happened. Alexander provided, as he had always done in battle since the Retreat from Mons, that essential steadying influence which brings order out of chaos. His strategy and tactics were always sound though rarely remarkable. He was undoubtedly over-optimistic about what he could achieve. Field Marshal Slim complained that Alexander was out-generalled. This is probably true, but Alexander's success lay in turning a potentially disastrous rout into a withdrawal. Only a very lucky commander, or enormous incompetence on the part of the Japanese, could have altered the final issue once the Allied Air Forces had been driven out of Burma.

The years of victory which followed Burma were the consummation of Alexander's years of service in which he had built up unrivalled experience of men, conditions and hazards of war. The reason for his selection to succeed Auchinleck in the Middle East was a combination of Churchill's romanticism and Brooke's search for new blood to revitalise Britain's flagging fortunes in the Middle East. They needed a man who would stop the rot—a man who would not be panicked into a premature withdrawal to the Nile and thence to Khartoum or Palestine. It is easy to see in retrospect that Auchinleck had already turned the tide of defeat before Alexander arrived. No one will ever know whether or not Auchinleck could have accomplished what Alexander did, if he had been given the same support by Churchill and Brooke. All that is certain is that Alexander did once more meet the needs of the hour. He provided the stabilizing influence and set the stage for his great subordinate's victory at El Alamein.

It is often suggested that Alexander was little more than the catalyst which enabled the El Alamein reaction to occur. Churchill and Brooke provided the ingredients; Montgomery, the heat; and Alexander, the inert catalytic function without which certain chemical reactions cannot take place although the catalyst itself plays no active part in the process. Such an analogy reveals a misunderstanding of the roles of theatre and army commanders. Montgomery could not, and would not have accepted, the dual role. Auchinleck had failed because he had tried to do both, and Eisenhower ran into similar difficulties in Algiers and in North-West Europe. The casting of Alexander and Montgomery in their respective roles was near-perfect. Montgomery—extrovert, extreme and abrasive—was just what the Eighth Army needed to set it on the path to victory. Alexander—introvert, balanced and charming—was equally well chosen to chair the Middle East Commanders-in-Chief Committee, to draw together the military and political leaders in Cairo, and to handle the problems of the great mixture of the human race which made up the sprawling British Middle East Base. The differences in the two men's characters complemented each other, while their ideas ran in parallel. Both agreed that the secret of success lay in fighting divisions as divisions and not breaking them up into *ad hoc* forces to suit the needs of the moment as had happened so often in the desert; in always maintaining balanced dispositions from which success could be exploited or disaster checked; and in insisting upon the most thorough preparation, training and rehearsal for all major operations. Alexander provided the resources and dealt with the politico-military problems in Cairo while Montgomery breathed new life into the Army in the desert. In the one-over-one situation, which existed due to force of circumstances, Alexander's most difficult task was to provide his demanding subordinate with unstinting moral and material support without infringing Montgomery's prerogatives as Eighth Army Commander. A theatre commander in the British system of command is responsible for everything that happens in his theatre, but if he interferes too much with his principal subordinates, they will not give their best. It needs nice judgment to know how tight to hold the reins.

In August 1942, when Alexander reached the Middle East, he knew that he could count on the support of Churchill and Brooke, but he knew equally well that he still had to prove himself in offensive operations. Stemming defeat and bringing order out of chaos, would not be enough. His country needed victory out of defeat. Whoever gave her that would win her trust. The victory at El Alamein made Montgomery the popular hero. It made Alexander Britain's nominee for Anglo-American command.

The Battles of Tunisia and the victory of Tunis were a repetition of the El Alamein campaign fought in a larger arena with a mixed Allied force instead of a homogeneous national army. Such forces are never easy to handle and tend to fall apart if things go wrong. Alexander never allowed this to happen, creating instead the cohesion and military confidence needed for the first major Allied victory in the West.

After the Fall of Tunis we must judge Alexander as the commander of successful armies which knew their business and no longer needed nursing. It is the degree of efficiency with which he managed to weld together and direct the efforts of the large Anglo-American forces available to him under Eisenhower's overall command which we must assess. The planning, invasion and conquest of Sicily can and should be criticised. Much of the difficulty stemmed from the wide dispersion of headquarters, but the vacillation in the 'Husky' planning, though understandable, does not reflect great credit upon him. The altercation between Patton, on the one hand, and Montgomery, on the other, need never have happened if he had not underestimated the worth of the American forces. The principle of two landings could have been retained. The actual invasion proved Montgomery's estimate of the Axis forces' capabilities to have been as wrong as Alexander's estimate of the Americans.

The troubled period during 'Husky' planning highlighted the main weakness in Alexander's style of command. It was apt to be misunderstood by the Americans, who are more used to direct orders than orders disguised as suggestions. It also highlighted his dependence on a good Chief of Staff. McCreery's departure to command X (British) Corps after the fall of Tunis left a void which was not filled properly until Harding arrived in January 1944. Men who watched the work of the 'Husky' planners and the 15 Army Group staff from Sicily to the Anzio landings confirm the ineffectiveness of Alexander's headquarters during this period. He was seen and listened to personally as much as ever, but his command organisation lacked bite. The conclusion is unavoidable. Alexander needed a strong Chief of Staff to do the hard and sometimes unpleasant work which falls to executives. He was too great a gentleman to hurt other men's feelings if he could avoid doing so. Moreover, he did not possess marked originality of thought. McCreery and Harding complemented these failings. Both were men who did not shrink from the harsher actions of command and both could embroider Alexander's straightforward ideas and concepts with those flashes of brilliance which distinguish ordinary from remarkable plans.

The strategic policies forced upon the reluctant Americans by the Churchill–Brooke combination, which led to the long frustrating Italian Campaign, have been severely criticised by British as well as American historians. Alexander was not responsible for these policies, but there is little doubt that he agreed with them. His part was crucial in two respects: he was responsible for the estimates of what could or could not be done at each phase of the campaign; and he was the man who had to make those estimates good through the action of his armies. In the first, he was prone to overestimate the possibilities and underestimate the difficulties. He knew what Churchill wanted. Whether consciously or subconsciously—there is little evidence to show which—he provided the arguments which his patron wanted, and, in so doing, gave his armies tasks which they could only carry out if all went well. He made ample provision for failure; he was never caught off balance; and he always stopped a lost battle before it went too far, but regrettably the facts cannot be avoided. His strategic estimates were only proved correct on two occasions—before 'Diadem' and before the battle of the Po. In all his other operations during the Italian Campaign the achievements of his Army Group fell short of his expectations. The Americans can rightly claim that it was his rose-tinted views which led Churchill so often into head-on collisions with Roosevelt and Marshall.

These criticisms do not mean that Alexander failed in Italy. He did not. He succeeded in a most remarkable way to carry out the strategic aims set for him by the Combined Chiefs of Staff. He drew German strength southwards throughout the later months of 1943 and early 1944, and created his decisive diversion with 'Diadem' at the exact moment when Eisenhower needed his help most. He was successful enough to encourage Churchill to back his demands for retention of troops in Italy, but only once sufficiently successful to persuade the Americans to change their attitude to the Italian campaign. The postponement of 'Anvil' was Alexander's greatest debating success; and 'Anvil's' subsequent launching instead of cancellation was his worst failure. No one can deny that he was a good loser. He was the right man to command a diversionary campaign. Most men, faced with the disappointments which he suffered, would have resigned or allowed the campaign to drift into a listless stalemate. Alexander continued to do his best without recrimination.

Alexander's greatest triumphs in Italy were his two Spring Battles—'Diadem' and the Po. In both he showed his grasp of the principles of war and the basic simplicity of his theory of the two-handed punching which gave him his successes. His timing was perfect and his inspiration of his subordinates all that any critic could ask. His greatest operational disappointment was the American rejection of his plans to exploit 'Diadem' and the consequent dismemberment of his successful 'Diadem' team. Who can tell what would have happened if he had been allowed to pursue his plans for an advance on Vienna with his victorious Army Group intact. Harold Macmillan had no doubts about the outcome. When discussing the fateful decision not to cancel 'Anvil', he says:

> Thus were sown the seeds of the partition of Europe, and the tragic divisions which were destined to dominate all political and strategic thinking for a generation . . . through all these years I have looked back on this decision of June 1944 as one of the sad turning points of history. . . .
> . . . If only General Alexander had been allowed to follow his strategic plan in the Summer of 1944, how different might the story have been! (Macmillan, pp. 511, 537)

The British have always favoured the indirect approach when opposing continental powers. The Americans take the diametrically opposite point of view expressed by Roosevelt in his signals to Churchill, during the 'Anvil' controversy. Two extracts make the point:

> I agree with you that our overall strategic concept should be to engage the enemy on the largest scale with the greatest violence and continuity, but I am convinced that it must be based on a main effort together with closely co-ordinated supporting efforts directed at the heart of Germany. . . .
> . . . I always think of my early geometry: 'A straight line is the shortest distance between two points.' (Grand Strategy, v, pp. 355, 357)

Alexander's desire to beat the Russians into Vienna was too eccentric for Roosevelt's geometry!

Although British and American strategic thinking was divided on the Mediterranean issues, both nations can pay tribute to Alexander for the care which he took to avoid squandering their manhood. His task was essentially one of attrition which, in war, so often leads to profitless loss of life. Alexander drew his opponent, as he was required to do, without repeating casualty lists of the dimensions which have so marred the reputations of British generals of the First World War. He fought his offensive campaign in naturally defensive country and lost fewer men than the German defenders. The relative losses on the two sides during the Italian campaign speak for themselves:

The attacking Allied forces	312,000
The defending Axis forces	536,000

In conclusion, what is the picture that we see hanging in the gallery of great military commanders which is entitled

Field Marshal the Earl Alexander of Tunis,
KG, PC, GCB, OM, GCMG, CSI, DSO, MC.

A trim, impeccably dressed Field Marshal stands against a background of wider and deeper battle experience than any other soldier—British or American—of his generation.

As a man, he possessed a charm of manner, a degree of moral integrity and a quiet, self-effacing style unusual in great military commanders. He was a natural gentleman, sensitive to other men's feelings and selfless to a fault. This sensitivity enabled him to identify himself with all types of men and so lead by example. His greatest personal satisfaction came from the service of others; and, conversely, men of many nations enjoyed service under his command. It was this ability to inspire others to do their best and to work together for the good of the Allied cause that made him the Marlborough of the Second World War.

As a soldier, he was first and foremost a professional who believed in and insisted upon the highest standards. The driving force of the military side of his character was his determination to do his duty at all times. He was a sound but uninspired strategist and an intuitive tactician whose military instincts were enhanced by a wealth of operational experience and love of soldiering. He possessed a fine judgment of what was practical in war and never allowed unsuccessful operations to be pressed to extremes. His shortcomings in decisiveness, caused by dislike of hurting others, and in his strategic originality, were more than offset by his genius for leadership which won him the loyalty and respect of all the many different national contingents of the Western Alliance which fought under his command.

He was a great military servant of his Sovereign and country. His character is best summed up in the words he used when leaving for Burma:

'I will do my duty.'

Bibliography

This assessment of Alexander of Tunis as a military commander is based on four groups of sources:

1. *The Official Reports and Despatches of Commanders*

Documents on British Foreign Policy, 1919-1939
Despatches of the Viscount Gort on Operations of the British Expeditionary Force to France covering the periods: 3 September 1939–31 January 1940; 1 February–31 May 1940; with Appendix I reporting the actions of 1 Corps under General Alexander, 31 May–2/3 June 1940.
Despatches of General Sir Archibald Wavell on Operations in Burma, 15 December 1941–20 May 1942
Report by General the Honourable Sir Harold Alexander on Operations in Burma, 5 March–20 May 1942
The Despatches of Field Marshal The Earl Alexander of Tunis on:
The African Campaign from El Alamein to Tunis, 19 August 1942–13 May 1943
The Conquest of Sicily, 10 July–17 August 1943
The Allied Armies in Italy, 3 September 1943–12 December 1944
The Report of the Supreme Allied Commander Mediterranean to the Combined Chiefs of Staff on:
The Italian Campaign, 12 December 1944–2 May 1945
Greece, 12 December 1944–9 May 1945

2. *The Official British, Commonwealth and United States Histories so far published*

BRITISH

Military Operations in France and Belgium, 1914–1918
The War in France and Flanders, 1939–40
The Defence of the United Kingdom
The War against Japan, Vol. II
The Mediterranean and Middle East, Vols III and IV
Grand Strategy, Vols V and VI
The War at Sea, Vol. III
The Strategic Air Offensive, Vols I–IV
The Royal Air Force, 1939–45, Vols I–III

COMMONWEALTH

Operations on the North-West Frontier of India, 1920–35, Part III
The Indian Armed Forces in the Second World War:
The Retreat from Burma, 1941–42
The North African Campaign, 1940–43
The Italian Campaign, 1943–45
The Official History of New Zealand in the Second World War:
Alam Halfa and Alamein
Bardia to Enfidaville
The Campaign in Italy
The Official History of the Canadian Army in the Second World War:
The Canadians in Italy

UNITED STATES

The US Army in World War II:
Stilwell's Mission to China
Stilwell's Command Problems
Strategic Planning for Coalition Warfare
Northwest Africa : Seizing the Initiative in the West
Mediterranean Theatre of Operations (Sicily to the Surrender of Italy)
The History of the Fifth Army, 1948
The US Army Air Force in World War II, Vols I and II
The History of United States Naval Operations in World War II, Vol IX

3. *Memoirs and Biographies of Senior Commanders*

Alexander, Field Marshal the Earl, *The Battle of Tunis*, Basil Hicks Lecture 1957
Anders, General, *An Army in Exile*, 1949
Badoglio, Marshal, *Italy in the Second World War*, 1948
Barnett, Corelli, *The Desert Generals*, 1960
Bradley, General Omar, *A Soldier's Story*, 1952

Bryant, Arthur, Lord Alanbrooke's Diaries: *The Turn of the Tide*, 1956; *Triumph in the West*, 1959
Butcher, Harry C., *Three Years with Eisenhower*, 1946
Churchill, Sir Winston, *The Second World War*, Vols II–VI, 1949
Clark, General Mark, *Calculated Risk*, 1950
Cunningham, Admiral of the Fleet, *A Sailor's Odyssey*, 1951
Eden, Antony, *The Reckoning*, 1965
Eisenhower, General, *Crusade in Europe*, 1948
Evans, Geoffrey, *Slim as Military Commander*, 1968
Farago, Ladislas, *Patton*, 1963
Gough, General, *Soldiering On*, 1954
Grigg, Sir James, *Prejudice and Judgement*, 1948
Guingand, General de, *Operation Victory*, 1947
Hillson, Norman, *Alexander of Tunis*, 1952
Ismay, General Lord, *The Memoirs of*, 1953
Kesselring, Field Marshal, *The Memoirs of*, 1953
Liddell-Hart, Sir Basil, *The Rommel Papers*, 1953
Macmillan, Harold, *The Blast of War*, 1967
Montgomery of Alamein, Field Marshal the Viscount, *The Memoirs of*, 1958; *The Path of Leadership*, 1961; *El Alamein to the Sangro*, 1948
Mumery, R. J., *The Private Papers of Hore Belisha*, 1960
North, John, *Memoirs of Field Marshal Earl Alexander of Tunis*, 1962
Senger und Etterlin, General von, *Neither Fear nor Hope*, 1963
Slim, Field Marshal Sir William, *Defeat into Victory*, 1956
Smyth, General Sir John, *Before the Dawn*, 1957
Stilwell, General Joseph W., *The Stilwell Papers*, 1949
Talents, Sir Stephen, *Man and Boy*, 1943
Tedder, Marshal of the Royal Air Force, Lord, *With Prejudice*, 1966

4. *Other Works Including Regimental Histories*

Barclay, C. N., *The History of the Duke of Wellington's Regiment*, 1953
Bennett, Geoffrey, *Cowan's War*, 1964
Benoist-Mechin, *The Sixty Days that Shook the West*, 1963; *Histoire de l'Armée Allemande*, 1966
Bihlmans, A, *Latvia in the Making*, 1928
Böhmler, Colonel R., *Monte Cassino*, 1964
Buckley, Christopher, *Road to Rome*, 1945
Carver, General Sir Michael, *El Alamein*, 1962
Collier, Richard, *The Sands of Dunkirk*, 1961
Daniell, D. S., *The Royal Hampshire Regiment*, Vol III, 1955
Dean, C. G. T., *The Loyal Regiment–1919–53*, 1955
Divine, David, *The Nine Days of Dunkirk*, 1959
Durante, Walter, *I Write as I Please*, 1935

Eldridge, Fred, *Wrath in Burma*, 1946
Elliott, General J. G., *The Frontier, 1839–1947*, 1968
Farrar-Hockley, General, *The Death of an Army*, 1967; *The Somme, 1964*
Forbes, Patrick, *The Grenadier Guards in the War, 1939–45*, Vol I, 1949
Harding, Field Marshal, Lord, *Mediterranean Strategy 1939–45*, 1955
Howard, Michael and John Sparrow, *The Coldstream Guards, 1920–46*, 1951
Hunt, Sir David, *A Don at War*, 1966
Jackson, General W. G. F., *The Battle for Italy*, 1967; *The Battle for Rome*, 1969
Kipling, Rudyard, *The Irish Guards in the Great War*, Vols I and II, 1923
Kippinberger, General, *Infantry Brigadier*, 1949
Linklater, Eric, *The Campaign in Italy*, 1945
Loffler, G., *Die Baltische Landeswehr*, 1929
Mackenzie, Compton, *Eastern Epic*, 1951
Majdalany, Fred, *The Battle of El Alamein*, 1965; *The Monastery*, 1945; *Cassino; Portrait of a Battle*, 1957
Masters, J. W. A., *2nd Battalion The Sherwood Foresters, 1939–45*, 1946
Miles, W., *The History of the Gordon Highlanders*, Vol V, 1962
Moorhead, Alan, *The Desert War*, 1965; *African Trilogy*, 1966
O'Ballance, Edgar, *The Greek Civil War*, 1966
Pond, Hugh, *Sicily*, 1962; *Salerno*, 1961
Sherwood, Robert, *The White House Papers of Harry L. Hopkins*, 1949
Spears, General Sir Edward, *Liaison, 1914*, 1930; *Assignment to Catasrophe*, 1954 Vol I: *Prelude to Dunkirk*, Vol II: *The Fall of France*
Starr, Colonel C. G., Salerno to the Alps; *A History of Fifth Army*, 1948
Terraine, John, *Mons*, 1960
Ullman, *Britain and the Russian Civil War*, 1969
Wagg, A., *A Million Died*, 1943
Waite, Robert, *The Vanguard of Nazism*, 1952
Warlimont, General Walter, *Inside Hitler's Headquarters*, 1964
Woodhouse, C. M., *Apple of Discord*, 1948
Woolcombe, *The First Tank Battle*, 1967

Index